Swedish Marxist Noir

Swedish Marxist Noir

*The Dark Wave of Crime
Writers and the Influence
of Raymond Chandler*

PER HELLGREN

McFarland & Company, Inc., Publishers
Jefferson, North Carolina

ISBN (print) 978-1-4766-7371-4
ISBN (ebook) 978-1-4766-3415-9

LIBRARY OF CONGRESS CATALOGUING DATA ARE AVAILABLE

BRITISH LIBRARY CATALOGUING DATA ARE AVAILABLE

© 2019 Per Hellgren. All rights reserved

No part of this book may be reproduced or transmitted in any form or by any means, electronic or mechanical, including photocopying or recording, or by any information storage and retrieval system, without permission in writing from the publisher.

Front cover photograph by Iakov Kalinin (iStock)

Manufactured in the United States of America

McFarland & Company, Inc., Publishers
Box 611, Jefferson, North Carolina 28640
www.mcfarlandpub.com

For Maria

Table of Contents

Acknowledgments	ix
Preface	1
Introduction: Marxist Noir at the Gates	3
1. A World Gone Wrong: Raymond Chandler	29
2. The Accord: Per Wahlöö and Sjöwall-Wahlöö	46
3. The Fall from Grace: Henning Mankell	79
4. The Collapsed Dream: Stieg Larsson	94
5. Excavating the Swedish Underbelly: Roslund & Hellström	128
6. A Brave New Sweden: Jens Lapidus	150
7. Sleuths of the Post-Political Condition: Arne Dahl	164
8. The Age of the Manhunter: Lars Kepler	190
Conclusion: The Dialectics of Crime Fiction	206
Chapter Notes	221
Works Cited	238
Index	247

Acknowledgments

This work has—as writing a book usually does—taken several years of my life to finish. During this period, the past three or four years, some people have been of crucial importance.

The first seed for the idea of actually writing about a transatlantic pollination between Raymond Chandler and Per Wahlöö came when I was in the apartment of Sylvia Wahlöö, the writer Per Wahlöö's second wife, in Stockholm in January 2015. Sylvia and Per were married from the end of the 1950s until the early 1960s. Sylvia and I were looking at photos for my book about Per Wahlöö that would be published in the autumn of 2015. Later that day she showed me her bookcase where she had saved her and Per's readings from the old days. One glance at it revealed that he had a surprising number of Chandler's books in old rugged English paperback originals, and she told me they had read Chandler a lot in the 1950s.

Later this fact got me thinking about the connection between Chandler and Swedish crime fiction, and soon my theory of Swedish Marxist Noir started to unfold, bit by bit. Thanks, Sylvia, for showing me your bookcase and for telling me all the wonderful stories about you and Per.

I also owe debts to the wonderful, indefatigable staff at Eskilstuna City Library, Sweden, especially crime fiction librarian Synnöve Hansen (who is actually the only one in Sweden), for helping me to dig out the dusty crime fiction past and some of the scholarly research performed through the years.

I need to reserve a special word of appreciation for Alan Wald, whose concept of Marxist Noir has been of great importance for this study, and I would like to thank him for his thoughts and for answering my questions and helping me to find one of his most defining texts on the subject. Even though I've never met him in person, I wish he had been my teacher in high school or at the university.

Göran Therborn is another scholar who has been important for this study because of his critical thinking, to which I frequently refer in this book, and I would like to thank him for answering my letters.

My old comrade Carl Claeson has also been important for my thinking and for the development of a theory of Marxist Noir. Many critical thoughts have originated from our discussions, not the least of which from his healthy skepticism towards anything carrying the prefix "post" in times when questions of identity seem to be more prevalent than class issues.

I am grateful to the anonymous peer reviewers who have made a range of valuable comments that have been implemented in the finished book.

Being a Swedish writer writing in English has been one of the toughest roads to travel to get this book into press. For all your exhaustive reading (and red pen) I am forever in your debt, my friend Tony Burden, as you have given me an English lesson I will surely never forget. Thanks!

Finally, for putting up with piles of books, heaps of papers, enormous amounts of domestic absent-mindedness over several years, and for listening to my readings aloud of Sjöwall-Wahlöö, Henning Mankell, Roslund & Hellström, Lars Kepler, and Jens Lapidus, I have to acknowledge Maria, my wife. I will never stop reading for you. This book would never have been written without your endless love and devotion.

Preface

This book explores and develops a theory of Swedish Marxist Noir. In order to expose the dialectics of crime fiction, from *then* (the American 1930s) to *now* (the Swedish post–1990s), we must examine, through a Marxist reading of several central works of crime fiction, the Marxist connection between the writings of Raymond Chandler and the Swedish wave of crime fiction since the 1960s. This dialectic, thus, consists of a long-term evolution of ideas from Chandler, via the founders of Swedish social crime fiction, Sjöwall-Wahlöö, to modern bestsellers such as Henning Mankell, Stieg Larsson, Roslund & Hellström, Jens Lapidus, Arne Dahl and others.

Marxist theories have had a profound influence on the crime genre ever since the American 1930s, and there is a strong link between the Swedish writers and the work of Chandler, both in terms of direct influence and philosophy: their view on society and the ambition to write about a modern world gone wrong. Consequently, a Marxist view on existence makes all these writers part of the same tradition, despite the eighty years that have passed since Chandler initiated his Marlowe novels.

Introduction
Marxist Noir at the Gates

Something happened around 1990. A great historical motion, a dark wave, moved across the entire Western world, and not just in Sweden and the small town where I was living at the time. This change, called "the modern rupture with the past" by some scholars, took place at various moments in history, such as in 1973, during the Oil Crisis, in 1968 with the first signs of the decline of the Soviet Union with the invasion of Czechoslovakia, in the "British winter of discontent" of 1978–79, in the fall of 1989 with the tearing down of the Berlin wall, and in 1991 with the definitive fall of the Soviet empire. In other words, during this period, from the 1960s to the 1990s, there were many historical turning points.

When I graduated from high school in the beginning of the 1990s, a crisis had been going on for a couple of years in Sweden. A rightwing government was in place and a xenophobic populist party had been voted into parliament for the first time. Something had happened. It was a time of mass unemployment, and the "happy" 1980s, with their economic boom of prosperity, were definitely over, replaced by something that resembled a permanent crisis. Unemployment has been high ever since, as some people never got a job after that; public expenses for the welfare state decreased; and privatization triumphed in the 1990s at the same time as neo-liberal market-managing systems plowed their way into welfare sectors such as health care. Everybody I knew experienced a deterioration in society, and so did I. This feeling is still prevalent in contemporary Sweden with increased xenophobia, racism, inequality, and segregation. An idea of what actually happened in my youth has only recently surfaced in my mind: it was the emergence of the post-industrial society, or what the Marxist sociologist Göran Therborn calls a historical turn from socialization to privatization.[1] He explains this change with the confluence of three systemic processes, under the conditions of contingent events:

1. The development program of the communist states was beginning to exhaust itself. How these nations could generate new technology and more productivity was a question that never got answered. The stagnation started with the Soviet invasion of Czechoslovakia in 1968 that froze new communist initiatives.
2. The post-colonial states became failures in social planning and economic development.
3. New sources of capital generation and management technologies challenged capacity in the core capitalist countries. The explosions of the financial markets generated much more private capital at the same time as heavy social commitments made it difficult to make increased investments in infrastructure.[2]

Some of the greatest crime fiction writers in Sweden have spent their entire careers explaining these processes, this historical turn, for all those people who read crime fiction when relaxing on their vacations or when they go to bed at night, reaching for a paperback to get a lesson in contemporary social theory. Of course, most of the readers do not see the political dimensions and the philosophical potential, nor all the didactic meaning, of crime fiction. For most people it is just entertainment, a short thrill before going back to the grey striving of life. But still, this is one of the most important, and mostly self-imposed, duties that Swedish crime fiction has had since the 1970s: to open the eyes of a slumbering population to the crimes committed around them, in the open, by politicians, bureaucrats, drug lords, lobbyists, and CEOs of transnational corporations—i.e., the *System* known as *Capitalism*.

Most of the writers in this study have a Marxist or a leftist past. Giants such as Henning Mankell and Stieg Larsson were members of Communist parties in the 1970s, as were their political genre predecessors Sjöwall-Wahlöö in the 1960s and 70s. These Marxists set the tone for the Swedish crime novel up until today. Still, a writer such as Arne Dahl never really falls back on a theoretical tradition, but argues from the perspective of the empirical issues of the day, the political and social processes that are changing Europe, for example, leaving the one-dimensionality of the Cold War behind and exploring a new more complex postmodern, post-political, condition instead. As Therborn has suggested, Marxism is not just any old theoretical corpus. In social significance, as a distinctive cognitive perspective on the modern world, it is only surpassed by the great world religions.[3] Sjöwall-Wahlöö gave readers a general lecture in Marxism-Leninism during the 1970s, thus creating the *grundrisse* for Swedish Marxist Noir, later elegantly administered by the pen of Henning Mankell and other radical writers to explain the crisis of the post-industrial world.

But my study will start in another age, another place, and with entirely different people in the forefront: the American 1930s and the hardboiled prose of Raymond Chandler. In my opinion, this is the true source of the modern literary critique against Big-Business capitalism, both as written by a blatantly liberal writer such as Chandler, or by a more Marxist oriented author such as Dashiell Hammett.[4] Los Angeles of the 1930s was an interesting milieu where Marxism thrived, in philosophy, art, movies, sociology, and literature. This fact shows that the connection between Marxism and the modern crime fiction novel is inevitable. However, the emphasis of this study will be on the post–1990s Swedish crime fiction up until today, naturally not without first taking a thorough look at Sjöwall-Wahlöö.

In order to achieve this, I have to put forward a number of questions to the source material for my study. The first main question, which I will be trying to answer as we go along, is: Which political ideas and philosophies were some of the possible reasons for crime writers to write as they did, or still do?

* * *

On a more personal level I could ask myself: what on earth has made me curious enough to write an entire book on the subject of Swedish Marxist Noir? Well, in Sweden Marxism is still obsolete, vaguely connected to an old dusty Eastern world of crudities in the Soviet Union, communism, and the oppression of the masses during almost the entire twentieth century. The average citizen doesn't really understand what Marxist philosophy is, although this citizen almost certainly reads crime fiction with, more or less, some Marxist, or at least social critical, content.

Marxism had its great renaissance in Sweden during the second half of the 1960s and on into the 1970s, when students and intellectuals tried to foment a revolution, as in big European cities such as Paris and Rome in the spring of 1968. Huge masses of enraged people demonstrated in the streets against the Vietnam War and colonial oppression in Africa and Asia; well-known writers went to Chinese villages and Eastern European countries behind the Iron Curtain to look for the perfect socialist society. The dream of Utopia was very much alive. Many read the great Marxist classics that had been quickly translated by a growing number of enthusiastic leftwing publishers. A prevailing thought that something other than capitalism was actually possible reigned in society. This movement, primarily known as "New Left," had come quite late to Sweden, in the mid–1960s, and had its background in a deeper ideological crisis within the European communist movement and social democracy, mainly because of three historical processes in the 1950s and 60s. First, when the Soviet leader Nikita Khrushchev initiated a de-Stalinization in a speech at the twentieth party congress in 1956; second, the revolt in Hungary the same year when Russian tanks rushed in to support the regime against a popular uprising; and third, the conflict between Russia and China.⁵

According to the Swedish historian Kjell Östberg, the Swedish "1968" was a process that stretched over several decades in three distinct phases. From the close of the 1950s to 1965, the period was dominated by liberal ideas and old social movements that often served as "early risers." Between 1965 and 1970 the Marxist and leftist ideas were predominant, driven by the Vietnam movement, student revolts and the emergence of new social movements. The period during the 1970s to about 1980 was more varied and initially the radicalization process was intensified, stretching from a reconnection to more orthodox Marxist ideas, such as the revolutionary theories of Lenin, Trotsky, Mao and Stalin, to feminism and the eco-humanist ideas of the environmental movement following the troublesome success of Rachel Carson's book *Silent Spring*.⁶

This was the age when the modern Swedish crime novel was born: politically (leftist) conscious, inspired by American hardboiled crime fiction, international, cinematic, funny, groundbreaking, anchored in reality and, above all, astoundingly exciting. This was a time when Marxism had a huge influence on cultural phenomena such as movies, literature, theatre, and different sorts of art. It became the most important philosophy used to explain the new complex society, its influence on humans and, most of all, how humans in this society of Western capitalism were exploited by a faceless system.

Before Marxism became trendy in Sweden it had a long European tradition (both academic and political) in countries such as France and Germany, where it was initially expressed by names such as Friedrich Engels and Karl Kautsky in the 1880s. Ever since then the Marxist tradition has survived in different shapes in these countries, even after the fall of the Soviet empire. This long critical tradition has never really had its firm place in Sweden, neither in politics nor in the academic circles where Marxism is marginal today. In the Academy Marxist theory has, to a large extent since the 1980s (when Marxism had its huge crisis) often been hidden under obscure (and harmless) names such as *sociology, cultural studies, structuralism, discourse analysis* or *critical theory*. The cause of this name changing over the years is probably to earn scholars their research grants from investors with an obvious capitalist agenda (in Sweden, banks are some of the biggest funders of historical and cultural research). Still, once it had broken through in the 1960s, Marxism—both as theory and practice—has survived in one incredibly widespread literary tradition: crime fiction.

What does this tradition look like, from the first Chandler-inspired attempts at Marxist Noir by Per Wahlöö in the 1960s, to today's sophisticated and utterly complex swirling crime novels by authors such as Arne Dahl and Stieg Larsson? That is the second general question I will explore in this book.

A few years ago I wrote the first biographical account of Per Wahlöö, arguably the founder of modern crime fiction in Sweden. For four years I studied everything he had ever done—from thousands of journalistic articles, written in the 1940s, 50s and 60s, to his political novels in the 1960s—and there, in this vast array of material, I encountered Marxist philosophy as well as American hardboiled crime fiction. Both of these literary traditions interested Per Wahlöö and made me want to write a book about the Swedish Marxist tradition in crime novels as he initiated it. One of my fundamental hypotheses is that Wahlöö constitutes a *bridge* between American, socially concerned crime fiction and a similar Swedish genre during the 1950s that later developed into the style still dominating Swedish crime writing today.

The Nature of This Study

The intention of this book is twofold: a thorough introduction for English-speaking readers to some of Sweden's most popular crime writers (who have also been published in the English language), and a theoretical study of Marxist ideas in some of the most read novels of our time. My approach is to carry out *a Marxist reading* of the fiction of these writers in the contexts of the political ideas and the social and cultural history of the societies where they have been produced. As I have already emphasized, my perspective will be a Marxist one, where I stress the Marxist theories surrounding the works, *not* a historical materialistic approach, which is generally what is meant by a Marxist perspective in historical research. My method is an interpretative one, in which I perform a Marxist *reading* of the proposed works. In Sweden, and elsewhere in international crime fiction research, there is a lack of knowledge concerning the Marxist ideas stretching from Raymond Chandler to the modern crime fiction in Sweden that has reached an increasing popularity around the world today. This book is an attempt to fill this gap.

I will show the traces of some feasible ideas—mostly concerning social theory, philosophy, and economic theory of the twentieth century—running from the age of Karl Marx, via the end of the American 1930s, to the Swedish 2010s, and investigate how they have influenced the international bestselling phenomenon known by a number of marketing brands: from the German "Schwedenkrimi," to the French "polar polaire," to the more established names of Swedish crime fiction, Scandinavian Noir, Scandicrime, or Nordic Noir.[7] Crime fiction scholar Andrew Pepper, for example, uses the term "Swedish noir" for writers such as Sjöwall-Wahlöö, Stieg Larsson, and Henning Mankell.[8]

The Concept of Nordic Noir

The concepts surrounding the Nordic crime fiction tradition deserve a short exposition, and I am going to focus on *Nordic Noir* below since it is probably the most recent and frequently used term in the crime fiction business right now.

The term Nordic Noir is very new and did not come into common use until the 2010s.[9] However, *the concept* of Nordic Noir is a bit older than that, but still quite new, probably deriving from the late 1990s when somber, violent and grim crime fiction stories, mostly from Sweden, started to spread across the world. Nonetheless, it is not only a literary phenomenon. It consists of everything from books to TV series and films. The visual style is dark and gloomy, framed by a decaying society, the post-welfare state, drenched in crime, permeated by capitalism and immoral white-collar crooks, mirroring a hurting pensive nostalgia, the phantom pains of better days in the past.[10] The literary language is marked by a "no-nonsense efficiency of the prose," as Barry Forshaw expresses it.[11] The Scandinavian setting is essential, with its long, dark winters and light summers, exquisite lakes and massive forests, its deserted summer cottages, white winter landscapes, and cold weather. Bear in mind that Nordic Noir is also a successful brand, probably created by critics in close collaboration with eager publishers that want to package a hugely disparate collection of authors as one and the same product in the wake of Stieg Larsson's global success. These authors range from outspoken Marxists, such as Larsson and Henning Mankell, to female writers with an apparent business-like approach to their handicraft, such as Camilla Läckberg, Mari Ljungstedt, and Camilla Grebe.

In the late 1990s the Swedish Beck series started with made-for-TV movies based on the characters created by Sjöwall-Wahlöö. These films were not based on any of the novels about Martin Beck. At the same time, around 1997, Henning Mankell had his big breakthrough on the international markets. Barry Forshaw has called the Nordic Noir boom "the slow explosion," meaning that Sjöwall-Wahlöö, and even Henning Mankell, were isolated events from the beginning, slowly becoming what we nowadays see as a "scandi-crime" wave, with Stieg Larsson as the prime engine.[12]

So, how do we define Nordic Noir? Well, Forshaw employs the widest possible definition in his book *Nordic Noir* (2013), where he includes novels, TV series and films from all the Nordic countries: Sweden, Norway, Finland, Iceland, and Denmark.[13] Sometimes it's not even crime fiction, but political thriller TV series such as the Danish *Borgen*.[14] Obviously, according to Forshaw, there doesn't have to be much *Noir* in the fiction at all to be termed Nordic Noir, just Nordic crime fiction in its entirety.

Bearing this in mind, I would like to emphasize that Nordic Noir is far more than the writers included in this study, since my aim is to analyze just a small part of this phenomenon, the Marxist Noir. So I am going to mention only some of the works and authors of Nordic Noir to delimit the phenomenon. Of course, Sjöwall-Wahlöö, Henning Mankell, Stieg Larsson and other authors are all part of Nordic Noir. Some of Sweden's most famous names outside the immediate Marxist circle are Leif GW Persson, Liza Marklund, Håkan Nesser, Åke Edwardson, and Anna Jansson.

In Norway the phenomenon goes from the new crime king Jo Nesbø, who showed up in the 1990s, all the way to the boosted film version of his *The Snowman* (Tomas Alfredson, 2017). Other Norwegians are Karin Fossum, Anne Holt, and Thomas Enger. In recent years, Norwegian television has produced several TV series with a strong Nordic Noir feeling: *Mammon* (two seasons, 2014–16) and *Monster* (2017).

However, perhaps the Danes are most appreciated for their televised crime fiction due to series such as *The Killing* (three seasons, 2007–2012) and the semi-Swedish *The Bridge* (four seasons, 2011–2018). Denmark's biggest crime author is Jussi Adler-Olsen, but there are other names as well: Leif Davidsen, Sara Blaedel, the writing duo Lene Kaaberbøl and Agnete Friis, and Mikkel Birkegaard. Less known in the rest of the world are the Finnish crime writers who make an explicit critique of neoliberalism: Matti Joensuu, Hannu Vuorio, Seppo Jokinen, and Leena Lehtolainen.[15] Even Iceland has its own crime fiction king in Arnaldur Indriðason, but Scandicrime is a growing phenomenon on this small island in the North Atlantic with authors such as Yrsa Sigurdardóttir, Arni Thorarinsson, and Ragnar Jónasson.[16]

Many of the Nordic Noir writers have been launched in close collaboration with the adaptations of their novels into TV series or films. In Sweden Stieg Larsson is probably the most famous author of them all; his Millennium trilogy was turned into three feature films and a TV series (six episodes) in Sweden in 2009, and in 2011 a Hollywood production starring Daniel Craig and Rooney Mara was launched all over the world. Mankell's Wallander series has been made into numerous films (Swedish and British), and Sjöwall-Wahlöö's novels have been converted into films in different countries through the years.[17]

Nordic Noir is a disparate and huge field of research to which I only wish to make a small contribution. Therefore, in what follows I stake out more precise demarcation lines for this study.

Fields: Research Note

The research this book covers is threefold: *First* of all, the vast field of research concerning Raymond Chandler and the American noir genre, which is not a field that I claim to revivify at all since it is only a basis for my arguments proposing a Swedish Marxist Noir. *Second*, research on how Chandler and other American noir writers have influenced Swedish crime fiction. This is a field to which I wish to make a new contribution. As a *third* field, I have used the research about Swedish or Scandinavian crime fiction in general. This book is a substantial contribution to this third field in particular, especially concerning the concept of Swedish Marxist Noir that I am introducing here.

The combination of Marxism and crime fiction could be a field of its own, but the literary examples are far too few. Most notably, however, is Ernest Mandel's book *Delightful Murder* (1984), which contains thorough analysis of the great genre tendencies. Despite the fact that it is quite an old critical work, published over thirty years ago, I have found it very useful in a variety of ways while working on this project. For example, I consider Mandel's theories on the connection between bourgeois society and organized crime to be especially important for my study. However, my study contradicts the arguments of Mandel on one distinct point. This concerns his view on crime fiction as a genre that only *confirms* the bourgeois rationality in society, instead of going against it.[18] On the other hand, Mandel never studied Swedish crime fiction authors with an outspoken or subversive radical leftist agenda, as I have done. Standpoints similar to Mandel's were made even earlier by Stephen Knight in his socio-politically oriented study of the genre, *Form and Ideology in Detective Fiction* (1980). Knight states the following about popular culture: "Cultural productions appear to deal with real problems but are in fact both conceived and resolvable in terms of the ideology of the culture group dominant in the society."[19] Hence, the Marxist critical stance on crime fiction in the early days of ideological genre research, as Karl Berglund argues, seems to have been the notion that crime stories reflect the moral of the majority and the norms of the major groups of readers rather than making claims to be social critique.[20] In other words, Horkheimer and Adorno's theory of the culture industry, in which popular culture is seen as a secret code for reactionary ideology, seems to be the prevalent notion amongst leftist scholars even until the 1980s. Another notion coming from Marxist scholars during the 1980s was the crime novel as being "exemplary of the individualizing tendencies of bourgeois culture," as Pepper describes it.[21] This has, of course, changed a lot since then.[22]

An interesting and bold account on the crime genre is Josef Hoffman's *Philosophies of Crime Fiction* (2013). Hoffman mentions some Marxist theorists and their theories of crime fiction: Ernst Bloch, Walter Benjamin, Siegfried Kracauer, Slavoj Žižek, and Fredric Jameson. Still, the Marxist issues are not foregrounded in Hoffman's study, and it mostly concerns classic crime authors, absolutely no Swedish ones. Instead he emphasizes philosophers such as Ludwig Wittgenstein and Albert Camus and the mutual influence between philosophy and crime stories. Hoffman touches upon Marxism, in his brief study of Dashiell Hammett, where he argues that Hammett is more of a pragmatist than a Marxist in his crime novels: "Hammett's literary depiction of American society and the violence, greed and dishonesty of its people could also have been influenced by his reading of Shakespeare."[23]

Andrew Pepper's compelling book *Unwilling Executioner: Crime Fiction and the State* (2016) probably comes closest to this study since it contains a thorough Marxist approach to the crime fiction genre and its ties to the consolidation of the modern state. Although Pepper's study lacks more recent Swedish authors, as context and focus for understanding the phenomenon of a radical Swedish Marxist Noir, he goes deeper into the radicalism of Sjöwall-Wahlöö than any other non–Swedish scholar I have read. Pepper views different national crime fiction traditions (i.e., British, American, French and even Swedish) as transnational and transatlantic, and he argues that political crime fiction "has a much longer historical lineage and much broader geographical trajectory than we sometimes seem to want to admit."[24] To some extent this view is also my own approach.

The Marxist literature otherwise used in this study is more thoroughly described in the section below titled "A Marxist Perspective."

As I have noted, the first of the three fields mentioned above (literature on Chandler) is a huge one that I am only going to touch on briefly. The second field is not really a field but only a collection of references to how different researchers have connected Chandler with Swedish crime writers. The third is really a field, and an international one as well. English, American, and Scandinavian scholars have all made many fine contributions to the research on Swedish crime fiction through the years, especially during the post-millennium era. Unfortunately, not all of the research I am referring to is accessible in English, because some of it has not been translated.

The combination of, and tight bonds between, Marxism and crime fiction is an undeveloped area. Research has been carried out on Dashiell Hammett's communist affiliation and on communist authors in the U.S., etc. But thorough research on the Marxist and leftwing concerns of Swedish crime writers since the 1960s, and particularly since the 1990s and 2000s, when giants such as Henning Mankell and Stieg Larsson hit the American market, has been lacking up to now. Closest to filling the gap is the Swedish film scholar Michael Tapper with his book *Swedish Cops* (2014), where he takes a close look at the genre and how it developed in Sweden between 1965 and 2010. This impressive work is an English version of his even more monstrous (well over 800 pages) and very comprehensive dissertation, *The Cop in the Twilight Land* (2011). According to Tapper, crime fiction of the 1960s and 70s was thoroughly inspired by Marxist-Leninist ideas, and the genre (novels, films and television) has since then changed and contributed to a more neoliberal focus (fewer social concerns in the plot, more focus on evil perpetrators instead of the criminal as victim), something that has been seen in contemporary politics and in public notions of crime and punishment. The Swedish crime fiction boom has evolved in dialogue with the surrounding world, Tapper argues. An even more extensive treatment of the genre, though not as detailed as Tapper's, has been carried out by literary scholar Kerstin Bergman in *Swedish Crime Fiction* (2014), which takes the end of the nineteenth century as its starting-point, when the Swedish crime novel was born. Her book is more of a fundamental historic description of the genre; however, she too embraces the theory that Sjöwall-Wahlöö is the genre's new groundbreaking paradigm in the mid–1960s. A more recent contribution to the research on the sociological phenomenon of Swedish crime fiction is Karl Berglund's dissertation *Death and Everyday Life: A Quantitative Analysis of Swedish Crime Fiction from the Early 21st Century* (2017). One of his most spectacular conclusions is that the majority of Swedish crime novels released in the late 1990s and the first decade of the 2000s *are not* as socially critical as the novels published during the formation of the genre by Sjöwall-Wahlöö in the 1960s. Instead, Berglund argues, the alleged realism and social criticism seems to be a consciously constructed *story* about the genre, spread by the crime fiction industry.[25]

Regarding research about individual writers, the list of literature can be comprehensive. The most discussed Swedish writer is by far Stieg Larsson. I am only going to mention some of those books here. They are all available in the English language, although my references will be from the Swedish editions. Jan-Erik Pettersson's book *Stieg: From Activist to Author* (2010, in English; published by Quercus in 2012) is a personal tale of the hard-working man Stieg Larsson as well as of the times he lived in, and Pettersson also makes excellent references to the crime fiction genre in general and the political scene during Larsson's lifetime. Two other books written by people close to Stieg Larsson include journalist colleague Kurdo Baksi's *Stieg Larsson, My Friend* (2010) regarding the work in the anti-fascist press during the 1990s, and of course the controversial memoir *Stieg & Me: Memories of My Life with Stieg Larsson* (2011), written by Larsson's fiancée since the 1970s, Eva Gabrielsson. These three books are important, even though they are not a part of the international scholarly research on Stieg Larsson.

An interesting volume of texts written by researchers and scholars about Larsson is the substantial anthology *Secrets of the Tattooed Girl* (2011). The discerning biography *The Man Who Left Too Soon* (2010) by the British crime fiction critic Barry Forshaw takes us through the life of Larsson and his three Millennium novels. The international research on Stieg Larsson has basically exploded since 2008, when the Millennium series was released in the U.S.

and Great Britain and subsequently gained massive success all over the world, selling over 90 million books so far, including the David Lagercrantz sequels.[26] At the same time, both the Swedish and American blockbuster film versions hit cinemas around the world. As I am writing this, the Swedish author David Lagercrantz has also penned new sequels to the Millennium trilogy, which have been released all over the world. Several anthologies with scholars writing about Larsson and his books have appeared on the market, but none of them have explored the *leftist* Larsson as I am about to do in this book. Eric Bronson's (ed.) *The Girl with the Dragon Tattoo and Philosophy* (2012) would have been a terrific place to take a look at Larsson's relationship to Trotsky or Marx, but it does not. Likewise, the anthology *Stieg Larsson's Millennium Trilogy: Interdisciplinary Approaches to Nordic Noir on Page and Screen*, edited by Steven Peacock (2013) would have been a great place for further Marxist analysis. Instead, all these writers are concerned with the "phenomenon" Larsson, mostly as a market actor serving capitalist and consumerist urges.

The feminist approach to Larsson lies closest to my analysis: the view that his novels are vehicles for critiquing the welfare state and the commodification of the body in a globalized economy. There are several scholarly anthologies on the subject, but I am only going to mention one: *Rape in Stieg Larsson's Millennium Trilogy and Beyond* (2013).[27] All of the writers in this book agree that Larsson is a feminist and a social critical writer. However, his Trotskyite roots never get foregrounded, and the closest we get to a Marxist analysis of his work is Katarina Gregersdotter's exploration of the relationship between Larsson, Roslund & Hellström and Marx's commodification theory.[28] But the overall concern of the *Rape* anthology is to explore "the ways rape is used to voice social and political criticism and to explore questions of victimization and agency."[29] Furthermore, the authors of this anthology attempt to argue for the subversive potential of crime fiction, which is a basis for discussion that I indeed share with them.[30]

Maj Sjöwall and Per Wahlöö were the first modern Swedish crime writers to succeed in the American market in the beginning of the 1970s,[31] and the research on this writing duo is substantial, yet the number of books written about them is surprisingly small. One of the first is the Danish *Novel of a Crime* (1976) by Ejgil Søholm, unfortunately only available in Danish. In 1993 the American critic Kenneth Van Dover released his short and well composed study of Sjöwall-Wahlöö's entire corpus, *Polemical Pulps*, and there was no similarly extensive research on Sjöwall-Wahlöö before Tapper's dissertation. My own biography of Per Wahlöö, *Per Wahlöö: Paving the Way for Swedish Crime Fiction* (2015), so far only available in Swedish, describes Wahlöö's career as a journalist and writer from the late 1940s until the end of the 1960s.

Regarding research on Raymond Chandler, I will only mention a small slice from this monumental field of research. Frank MacShane's 1976 biography

The Life of Raymond Chandler is important, of course, as it is based on the letters Chandler wrote through the years. These letters reveal Chandler's views on different topics that are important for my discussion, for example his notions of communists, of Dashiell Hammett, and his political views that eventually shape his writing. MacShane has also edited the voluminous *Selected Letters of Raymond Chandler* (1981) in one large collection for those who want to know even more. Several American researchers have also used Chandler in a broader discourse, for example Sean McCann who, in his bold account of the hardboiled genre, *Gumshoe America* (2000), emphasizes the New Deal liberal era and its impact on hardboiled writers such as James M. Cain, Chester Himes, and Raymond Chandler. More focus on the city of Los Angeles and its history, along with noir writers such as Chandler, has been given by Mike Davis in his revolutionary exegesis *City of Quartz* (1990), printed in several editions through the years. In literary critic David Fine's ambitious *Imagining Los Angeles* (2004), Fine investigates the literary image of Los Angeles since the 1880s and how Chandler and others use the city in their novels. Several writers use Los Angeles as a poetic landscape that shapes the stories with the help of both history and topography. L.A. is the end of the trail to the American West, which symbolizes death (James M. Cain), or a strain of social enclaves where the rich live isolated from the poor (Chandler). Both Davis and Fine emphasize the social, architectural, political, and philosophical milieu and its importance for the literature. Davis, in particular, employs a Marxist perspective on the genre. A closely related study, partially with the same perspective, is Fredric Jameson's groundbreaking *Raymond Chandler: Detections of Totality* (2016). Jameson's study consists of three essays, originally published at different moments through the years, from the 1970s and onwards. Jameson reconstructs both the context in which Chandler wrote his books and the social world it projects. Similar to Davis, Jameson sees Chandler's Los Angeles as a forecast of the United States as a whole, which has been an important theory in Marxist studies ever since Horkheimer and Adorno wrote their book *Dialectic of Enlightenment*.[32]

More than twenty years after MacShane's account of Chandler, new source material was revealed in Tom Hiney's *Raymond Chandler: A Biography* (1997), where Hiney, a British journalist, focuses on Chandler's spectacular private life, rather than his fiction. Tom Williams' biography *A Mysterious Something in the Light: The Life of Raymond Chandler* (2012), which is the third biography, likewise mostly centered upon the personal life of Chandler, rather than his writings. In contrast, the writing is the prime focus of Anthony Fowles' literary study *Raymond Chandler* (2014), where Fowles refuses to treat Chandler simply as a genre writer, but instead approaches him as a high-class literary writer working in a long European and American tradition.

Few scholars make even brief connections between Chandler and Swedish crime fiction. The author that makes the most vigorous connection is Mattias Hagberg (2014), who, in an essay, makes interesting parallels between Chandler's novel *The Big Sleep* and the Swedish writers of novels and movies that tell dystopian stories of a Nordic country where cops know more about the downfall of society than the politicians. Examples that Hagberg foregrounds are Henning Mankell's novels about Kurt Wallander, Stieg Larsson's Millennium trilogy and Swedish and Danish television series such as *The Bridge* (2011–2018) and *The Killing* (2007–2012). Hagberg's conclusion is neither revolutionary nor bold, but it is important and clear since scholars such as Tapper and Bergman have written extensively about the fall of the Swedish welfare state, though the book fails to make parallels to a broader discourse on hardboiled literature or the American Great Depression.

A thesis for my argument in this study is that the political theory and philosophy dominating an era becomes an important influence on the culture in that era, and a deeper perspective on how Chandler has had an impact on Swedish crime fiction is therefore needed. At least this is what I am aiming to achieve with this book.

The new conclusions which I am about to embark on here do not only concern the connection between Chandler and the Swedish wave of crime literature up until today, but also impact the theories surrounding this specific connection. In a deeper sense, these conclusions demonstrate how literature works intertextually—not just within an era, but also over time and, similar to Pepper, over continents in a globalized world, as a dialectical movement through time. The Marxist perspective of this book, therefore, deserves further exposition.

A Marxist Perspective

What do I mean by "A Marxist Perspective," and what relevance does this perspective have to the research on crime fiction? A quote from the preface to the first edition of *Capital Volume I*, written by Karl Marx in 1867, is perhaps an illuminating start for this discussion: "and it is the ultimate aim of this work to reveal the economic law of motion of modern society."[33] This exposure is probably just as effective in crime fiction as it is in political philosophy, and I suggest the reader bears this quote with them through this entire book. But first, it is necessary to clarify the meaning of a vast concept such as Marxism in this study.

To begin, it would be helpful to briefly explain the words "Marxian," "Marxist" and "post–Marxist," all of which will be used frequently in this study. "Marxian" denotes something that derives directly from the works of Karl

Marx, for example books such as *Capital* or *The Communist Manifesto*. "Marxist" is something that originates from the immense research on Marx, basically starting with the works of Friedrich Engels.[34] "Post-Marxism" refers to what Göran Therborn has described as "writers with an explicitly Marxist background, whose recent work has gone beyond Marxist problematics and who do not publicly claim a continuing Marxist commitment."[35]

So, what is Marxism then, really? Let us have a quick and dirty go at defining it.

The widest possible definition of Marxism is probably the one Carl Freedman employs in several of his works in which he analyzes literature through critical theory, mainly the article "Marxist Theory, Radical Pedagogy, and the Reification of Thought" (1987) and the book *Critical Theory and Science Fiction* (2000). According to Freedman, everything, from thinkers such as Immanuel Kant and G.W.F. Hegel, via Marx and the Frankfurt School, Sigmund Freud and Georg Lukács, up to Louis Althusser, Jacques Derrida, Michel Foucault, and a critic of postmodernism such as Fredric Jameson, the avowed disciple of Ernest Mandel, belongs to the huge discursive field called critical theory.[36] In this book I will employ almost the same perspectives as those of Freedman in my perspective on Marxism and post–Marxism, except for the nineteenth-century thinkers Kant and Hegel, who could hardly be called Marxist since they both predate Marx. However, critical theorists such as Theodor W. Adorno, Herbert Marcuse and Jürgen Habermas, and more politically oriented theorists such as Leon Trotsky and V.I. Lenin have been incorporated into my study, including a couple of women critics such as Chantal Mouffe and Rosa Luxemburg. Some of the Swedish crime writers this analysis concerns (Wahlöö, Mankell, Larsson) have even been active party members in different leftist organizations from the 1960s to the 1980s, so the political theory is important to study along with a reading of their works. Hence, I will use the term Marxism almost identically to Freedman's use of the concept of critical theory, which was once dubbed the grandchild of Marx.[37]

The basis for my perspective is also similar to what Carl Freedman suggests through his concept of "the regime of capital," which is obviously the context associated with the global era of capitalism. This creates a greatly enlarged theoretical terrain for the Marxist perspective and its methods.[38]

Furthermore, Freedman refines two distinct "lines" in Marxist theoretical work: First, the classical line of Marxism that begins with Engels and goes through the great revolutionaries of the early twentieth century—Lenin, Rosa Luxemburg, and Trotsky, and then further into the highly productive Trotskyan tradition with Isaac Deutscher, Roman Rosdolsky, and Ernest Mandel. This tradition has been devoted to the analysis of economics, politics and history with works such as Mandel's *Late Capitalism* (1972), Deutscher's three-volume biography of Trotsky (1954–1963), and Trotsky's own *History of the Russian Revolution* (1930).

The second line has been described by Perry Anderson as "Western Marxism," an intellectual current that started after the October Revolution in 1917, as a Western European response to the emerging Soviet Communism. This line begins with Georg Lukács's *History and Class Consciousness* and Karl Korsch's *Marxism and Philosophy*, both published in 1923 in German. This was a current, not a movement, not only consisting of thinkers such as Lukács and Korsch but also diverse intellectuals such as Antonio Gramsci, Walter Benjamin, Ernst Bloch, Max Horkheimer, Galvano Della Volpe, Herbert Marcuse, Henri Lefebvre, Pierre Macherey, Theodor W. Adorno, Jean-Paul Sartre, Lucien Goldmann, Louis Althusser and Lucio Colletti, Fredric Jameson, and Terry Eagleton.[39]

A post–Marxist current from the 1980s onward consists of names such as Ernesto Laclau, Chantal Mouffe, Étienne Balibar, Jürgen Habermas, Claus Offe, Axel Honneth, Manuel Castells, Régis Debray, Zygmunt Bauman, Pierre Bourdieu, Roland Barthes, and perhaps a giant such as Michel Foucault. A strong Marxist-feminist current from the 1970s until today could also be defined by names such as Evelyn Reed, Shulamith Firestone, Angela Davis, Nancy Fraser, Beatrix Campbell, Sheila Rowbotham, Valerie Bryson, Alison Jaggar, Gayle Rubin, and many others.

The labeling of texts and thinkers as post–Marxist is open to discussion and can be questioned. An example of this would be Swedish sociologist Göran Therborn, frequently referred to in this study, who has a firm past as a Marxist theorist since the 1960s, when he introduced thinkers such as Althusser and Marcuse in Sweden. A quick and simple search on Wikipedia suggests that nowadays he is writing on "topics that generally fall within a political and sociological post–Marxist framework."[40] Although, when reading one of Therborn's recent books, *The Killing Fields of Inequality*, there is basically nothing that qualifies him for going beyond, or leaving behind, Marxist thinking. Therborn himself doesn't even consider himself a post–Marxist either when given a direct question on the subject.[41]

Another example is Foucault. There are probably those who don't consider him to be in touch with Marxism at all, but I believe that he can be labeled as post–Marxist. In his youth he was a member of the French Communist Party, and the intellectual milieu in France during his school years was without a doubt dominated by Marxism and phenomenology. Two of Foucault's teachers were high profile Marxists such as Louis Althusser and Jean Hyppolite. Andrew Pepper's distinction of Foucault as a close-to-Marxist analyst of the operations of power and the implications for subjects or citizens in the modern state suggests this as well.[42] However, later Foucault saw Marxism and liberal humanism as his prime critical targets.[43] The post–Marxists referred to in this study will be Mouffe, Bourdieu, Habermas, and Foucault.

I will, to some extent, employ all of these Marxist traditions, lines, or intellectual currents in this study. Both the political scientist Lenin and the historian Trotsky will be mentioned and referred to, in addition to the economist Mandel, who has produced one of the most interesting studies on crime fiction where he identifies capital as a socio-economic force, and the philosopher Chantal Mouffe, whose theories on contemporary politics in Europe concern concepts such as "radical democracy" and "post-politics" rather than "class" or "revolution."

Crime fiction stories are invariably more socially revealing and concerned than any other narrative genres, and they offer underexploited opportunities for a Marxist analysis of modern culture. I don't know whether Marxism and crime fiction have ever before been examined together with the same level of focus and detail that I bring to both kinds of discourse. Michael Tapper is probably the one scholar who has carried out the most interesting studies on the subject from a Swedish point of view. Ernest Mandel's older study *Delightful Murder* is even more thorough from a Marxist perspective, but lacks the Swedish crime literature and my focus on post-industrial and post-political conditions.

The relationship between crime fiction and Marxism is certainly well established. My modest claim to originality (despite this book and its analysis owing much to other works) mostly concerns the establishment and discussion of a theoretical connection between Chandler's hardboiled school, as paving the way for Marxist criticism *within* the crime genre, and the Swedish wave of crime novels from the mid–1960s through today. To expose and explore this Marxist criticism, to some extent inherent in all the novels in this study, is a prime objective of my study. The crime novel is a privileged and paradigmatic genre for Marxism in our time, just as Georg Lukács claimed that *The Historical Novel* was during the nineteenth century as he was mapping it against the larger social, economic, and political history of the modern era, and as Carl Freedman claims that the science fiction novel has been during the twentieth century. According to Freedman, "science fiction is of all forms of fiction today the one that bears the deepest and most interesting affinity with the rigors of dialectical thinking." Thus, his point is that we can learn a great deal about the work of science fiction authors such as Philip K. Dick, Ursula Le Guin and Stanislaw Lem by studying it together with the theoretical production from Marxist theorists like Mikhail Bakhtin, Ernst Bloch and Theodor Adorno.[44]

Likewise, it is my claim that we can learn a lot about the works of such crime fiction authors as Per Wahlöö, Henning Mankell, Stieg Larsson, and Arne Dahl by studying them together with the theoretical frameworks of writers such as Theodor Adorno, Herbert Marcuse, Lev Trotsky, Michel Foucault, Jürgen Habermas, and Karl Polanyi. Or Karl Marx, for that matter.

Understanding these two modes of discourse together can reveal a great deal about the thinking behind the modern crime fiction that readers all over the world consume today.

Furthermore, the purpose of my Marxist perspective in this book is twofold.

First, it is important to understand how Marxist-influenced writers and their stories have for decades been the basis for a huge fiction industry generating billions of dollars in a global literary market today, with stories on the failing of capitalism resulting in murders, economic crimes, wars, suicides, arduous narratives of unspeakable human suffering, and the starvation of millions of people. This, somewhat ironic, paradox—the Marxist writer becoming a millionaire with the help of capitalism—is an inevitable part of the Swedish crime fiction boom foregrounded by names such as Henning Mankell and Stieg Larsson. Walk into virtually any bookstore in any airport and their paperbacks are on the shelves. Their Marxist commitment, as well as their deft writing filled with political and moral fervor, got them onto those shelves and into the big bookstores all over the world.

Second, the Marxist perspective in this study also displays a certain view of history as portrayed through the novels of these writers, which is mainly a Marxian world. That is, a world in which the writer's perspective is influenced by emphasizing the prophecies and writings of Marx, dominated by theories of economy, reification, alienation in society, and the diversified problems of the capitalist mode of production. These essential capitalist tendencies as described by Marx, and the capitalist dynamic that underlies all these tendencies, have been called "the unceasing expansionism of capital" by Carl Freedman and consist of elements such as

> the tendency to reduce the entire globe to a single market; to promote economic monopoly; to widen inequalities between those who extract profits and those who depend on wages and salaries; to revolutionize, constantly, the techniques of production; to remake entire societies in the image of capital; to eradicate or corrupt cultural and political forms that in any way hinder the march of profit.[45]

This, of course, is relevant today and describes how our notion of society is being transformed constantly by capitalism. Cultural historian Alan Wald has expressed this concern in one of his articles on Marxism and noir fiction:

> No one knows better than socialist activists of the twenty-first century that each generation must face its own "crisis" of Marxism. But we don't face this challenge to our theory and social movements just as we please. The way we remember our past governs our own dreams for the future. Above all, at a moment like today, when thousands of newly radicalizing young people know pretty much what they are fighting *against*, but are unclear about what they are fighting *for*, there is no point in simply pummeling the gates of history with one's fists. Sooner or later, we look to the past for shared, or at least recognizable, political experiences that might be retrofitted and rebooted; tactics

and strategies that have succeeded or failed; causes and explanations for economic and social trends that have persisted or morphed; and even role models, candidly reported, for how to live our chosen lives as Marxists.[46]

Historical events such as the Great Depression, the decline of New Deal liberalism,[47] the emancipation of the European colonies during the 1950s and 60s, the Marxist radicalization of the 1960s and 70s, the Vietnam War(s), the crisis of Marxism, the rise of postmodernism around 1980, the untrammeled march of capitalist exploitation across the world in the globalized era, the belligerent War on Terror during the 2000s, and the Great Recession in 2008 are all processes that have their own place in the Marxist perspective of this book. Writers analyze and describe events that surround them, influence them, and ultimately affect them, their comrades, and their families. In this way, these events, processes, or whatever you want to call them, turn into culture. Writers of crime fiction mainly study the world through the lens of crime. When reading Swedish crime fiction you learn how this capitalist world is being constituted through economics, theory, practice, and philosophy. For a writer such as Mankell, this fact is of moral importance. In order to struggle against the oppressors in our world you have to get enlightened, you have to know what the world looks like—what is right, and what is wrong. That is why Karl Marx wrote a deeply detailed theoretical work such as *Capital*. To learn how the world was consolidated is exactly what Mankell and many of his radical comrades aimed at during the 1960s, and Marxism eventually became the answer, and the tool, for obtaining this information.

As a result of this Marxist perspective I will also employ a number of concepts that are often used in Marxist social theory and philosophy. Consequently, the reader will encounter words such as reification, alienation, dialectics, critical theory, revolution, false consciousness, capitalist-commodity production, discourse, exchange-value, surplus-value, instrumental reason, and technocracy. But don't worry—I will elucidate these concepts as we go along. For example, the somewhat unusual term "*excursus*" will show up now and then. I have employed this term deliberately, in a similar way that Freedman does.[48] The term was originally borrowed from Horkheimer and Adorno's work *Dialectic of Enlightenment*, in order to emphasize that my analyses are not intended to provide proof (in any empiricist sense), but rather to extend my arguments.

Finally, the reader might ask, what on earth is *Marxist Noir*? Well, this ought to have its answer by now. But the concept certainly deserves a short exposition here anyway. This term is borrowed from the above mentioned cultural historian Alan Wald who (most likely) coined it in the 1990s when he studied the forgotten and purged works of "lost" leftwing authors during the American 1940s and 50s. Some of these writers survived the McCarthy persecutions of the 1950s and became famous Hollywood screenwriters or novelists, adapting to the capitalist social order; some of them, like John Steinbeck, became renegades, eventually dismissing socialism. Others were forgotten, thrown into the junkyard of history. In a letter, Wald explained to me how he arrived at the term:

> It seems as if the term "Marxist Noir" popped into my head while I was working on some talks in the 1990s—Marxist Literary Group, Left Forum. So it is possible that I heard someone else say it or that I read it, but I can't think of any particular sources. Mostly I was reading about Film Noir and Marxism, and I saw a connection to Leftwing pulp writers—especially those who had a relation to film (Maddow, Fearing) but others as well. I think the idea of an "urban landscape of Marxist Noir" may have been my first formulation. So I wouldn't want to steal credit from anyone else but I don't recall another source for that phrase—especially in relation to fiction.[49]

In this study I have adopted the concept of Marxist Noir and transformed it to fit the Swedish crime literature, and one purpose of this book is to work out a theory of Marxist Noir, and its continuation *Post-Marxist Noir*, which both have their parallels in social theory. In his essay "Marxism in Noir," Wald discusses what the second element in this word constellation, *Noir* (the French word for black, usually applied in film theory), actually is: "an authentic genre, a tradition, a school, a point of view, a vision, or just a style," and he concludes that it "to some of us seems more radically modern than ever."[50] He continues to describe the literary side of Marxist Noir:

> In writing, the language of noir is hardboiled and the sentences are plain and declarative à la Hemingway, a terse manner that tells the facts. It's not the refinement but the force and fascination of the narrative that pulls the reader in. Usually this is to an existential nightmare about entrapped people, economically adrift, trying to escape punishment for crimes they know nothing about, but law breaking that is often the upshot of decadent corruption on the part of the upper classes. It's fair to say that noir was a crystallization of the anxieties of the age that came right in the middle of what African-American Marxist writer Richard Wright deemed, "the most fateful of centuries."[51]

Current crises of capitalism in the post–9/11 era and the War on Terror, the climate crisis, and the emerging feeling of a doomed age in the shadow of increased nationalist and fascist movements, Donald Trump, Vladimir Putin, and the eternal wars in the Middle East should definitely provide modern *noir* authors with immense material for new stories with a Marxist backdrop "to galvanize the public sphere of their generation into consciousness," as Wald puts it.[52] This is also what has happened in Sweden since the 1990s—and is still happening, as this study will reveal.

Concerning Ideology

The concept of ideology is important for the understanding of the political meaning of Sjöwall-Wahlöö's work and the contexts in which it was composed.[53] Therefore, I will pause here and briefly discuss the Marxist notion of ideology according to some thinkers who had a great influence in Sweden during the 1960s and 1970s. Besides Karl Marx, this discussion concerns mainly highly influential philosophers like Herbert Marcuse and Louis Althusser. Moreover, these notions are some of the tools that we are going to use in the analysis of Sjöwall-Wahlöö, since their novels often concern ideology and what ideology does to individuals in relation to crime and crime investigations.

According to Marx, "ideology is the system of ideas and representations which dominate the mind of a man or a social group." The French philosopher Louis Althusser further stresses that ideology for Marx is "an imaginary assemblage (*bricolage*), a pure dream" existing outside the history of individuals.[54] This conception is not a general Marxist one, though. As we shall see, there is another notion as presented by Marcuse. But first we have to go further into the thoughts of Althusser.

Althusser was introduced to Swedish readers as early as 1966 through the journal *Clarté*, and later the journal *Zenit* became the foremost Althusserian platform of the Swedish New Left.[55] *Zenit* was also the first journal to introduce Marcuse to Swedish readers, in 1966.[56]

Althusser's conception of ideology does not include political ideologies as systems of thinking (following Destutt de Tracy from the late eighteenth century), but more as world view—for example, religious, political or philosophical views that make our world understandable. Marcuse's notion of ideology as false consciousness, therefore, is something other than Althusser's conception, in which a philosophical term like truth is irrelevant.[57]

The Althusserian concept of ideology is about how humans live their lives as conscious "actors" in a world that is more or less meaningful to them. He discards Marx's alienation theory as ideological.[58] Therborn describes Althusser's view on ideology as a medium where consciousness and meaningfulness is working, a mostly *unknown* process that shapes the human mind.[59] Althusser broke with the Marxist conception of ideology as a collection of ideas and thoughts when he saw it as a social process without a subject consisting of calls, or as he put it, "interpellations," to the human subjects (individuals) inside material social matrixes.[60] When every individual answers the interpellation they also confirm their own identity, and through this process every identity also has a given social coherence that makes it meaningful.[61]

Althusser's "break" with the old Marxist tradition was a critique "from the left" against the Stalinist ideology of the Soviet Union during the 1950s, when Russian leader Nikita Khrushchev made an abrupt turn to the right in criticizing Stalin's murderous reign of terror. In this, Althusser also distanced himself from Marxism as put forward by Marcuse and others, with the individual in the center of ideology instead of structures, processes of power, and economy.[62]

Althusser often came back to the motto of Lenin: without theory, there is no revolutionary practice. The philosophy of Althusser can be said to be a true participation in the struggle instead of sitting in an academic institution speculating with critical theory, e.g., the idealistic philosophy represented by philosophers such as Horkheimer and Adorno.[63]

Ideology, to Althusser, is something unbiased, created by the dialectical process, just like history. Individuals do not have anything to do with it. Or, as Althusser puts it, "an ideology always exists in an apparatus, and its practice, or practices. This existence is material."[64] Ideology is controlled by what he calls "Ideological State Apparatuses," for example the church, the state and its institutions. Each of them is the material realization of an ideology.[65] Ideology appears through practices and rituals, not the reverse, according to Althusser. These rituals could be the mass in a church, a funeral, a soccer game, a day in school, or a political party meeting.[66]

This view on ideology has, in philosophical terms, been called *antihumanistic*, which means it does not put the individual but the structures at the core of the ideological process.[67] In fact, the individual is quite unimportant in this machinery; ideology is the very power that "interpellates" individuals and controls them, not the reverse.

The Frankfurt School, where Marcuse was one of the foremost philosophers from the early 1930s, had been interested in the writings of the younger Marx that were discovered during the 1920s, and in which the theory of alienation is central.

The human individual is the center of attention in the philosophy of Marcuse. He and the other critical theorists in the Frankfurt School developed, contrary to Lenin and Althusser, a non–Marxist thinking to *develop* Marxism with elements from Sigmund Freud and Max Weber. Althusser, on the other hand, thought that science could be demarcated from ideology, and not a result of it as Marcuse did.[68]

Marcuse continued along the lines of the old tradition from the Frankfurt School of the 1930s, in which German fascism was dissected, and during the 1960s he used the same critical methods on modern day capitalism in the United States, where he had lived since the mid-1930s and studied phenomena like bureaucracy, media manipulation, and alienation.

To conclude: Althusser's focus on ideology is the structure; Marcuse (and the Frankfurt School) views the individual as creator *and* victim of ideology. Human beings in society uphold ideology through economy, politics, art, culture, aesthetics, religion and so on. According to Althusser, ideology is an objective process that interpellates individuals in society.

The tracks of these two incarnations of Marxist ideology are initially always present in the texts I will discuss in this study. Now, before diving into the analysis of Chandler's writing, let's turn our gaze onto these texts and my theoretical inclinations for a while.

Material and Theory

In this study, I will be focusing closely on what I believe are the most significant, definitive works of the Swedish crime fiction genre, from both ideological and genre developing points of view. The selection has naturally also been influenced by my own personal interests and areas of specialized competence. The starting point, therefore, is the work of the Swedish crime writer Per Wahlöö. The Swedish crime fiction tradition concerned in this study evolves from Wahlöö, and as we shall see, the link back to Chandler goes through Wahlöö and on up to the modern crime writers of Sweden.

The works included in my study contain a wide array of titles, read by millions of people, a mass culture phenomenon permeated with political ideas, both Marxist *and* neoliberal. I argue that these novels become the stem on which modern-day crime fiction blooms. Primarily, the texts focused on in my study are the following novels: *Murder on the Thirty-First Floor* (1964) and *The Steel Spring* (1968) by Per Wahlöö, and *The Man Who Smiled* (1994) by Henning Mankell. I will also include later works of the Swedish crime boom: *The Girl Who Kicked the Hornet's Nest* (2007) by Stieg Larsson; *The Girl Below the Street* (2007), *Two Soldiers* (2012) and *Three Minutes* (2016) by Anders Roslund & Börge Hellström (known as Roslund & Hellström); *The VIP-room* (2014) and *Sthlm Delete* (2015) by Jens Lapidus; *Chinese Whispers* (2011), *Musical Chairs* (2012), *Blind Man's Bluff* (2013), and *Last Couple Out* (2014) by Arne Dahl; *The Rabbit Hunter* (2016) by Lars Kepler; and finally, *The Crow Girl* (2016) by Erik Axl Sund (although other works will, of course, be mentioned).

The Swedish literary scholar Sara Kärrholm argues that Swedish crime fiction up to the 1960s has been lagging twenty to thirty years behind, compared to English or American ideals.[69] And if you take a look at Swedish post-war crime fiction, with Per Wahlöö and Maj Sjöwall (known as Sjöwall-Wahlöö) as the first hardboiled encounter taking up the Chandler legacy, Kärrholm's theory sounds just about right. The American hardboiled (and social-critical) crime novel broke through in the 1930s, and the corresponding Swedish one occurred in the mid-1960s.

Hagberg has remarked on how the original hardboiled writers depicted Los Angeles as a dissolving paradise and on their similarity to the modern Nordic followers of today who write about the declining welfare state. He further states that a careful reading of Chandler can say something about our society today.[70] That is also my approach in this book.

According to Ludmilla Jordanova, historians should "unsettle their audiences, provoking them to think harder and deeper about the human condition."[71] I would like to stress the importance of this view on historical research, but also the notion of historical knowledge—like the novels of Raymond

Chandler, for example—as social constructions within cultures and communities. Consequently, the times in which these texts were written are important to my conclusions, especially the human conditions in the shape of economic systems and ideologies in the United States (during the 1930s and 1940s) and in Sweden (during the 1960s, 1970s, 1990s and 2000s).

John Scaggs has also emphasized this question. According to Scaggs, the police procedural (a sub-genre that concerns police characters and their daily work against crime, a genre to which most of the works in this book belong) implies a more general transition to realism. The realist mode is not just the investigative process of the police, but also the themes, characters, actions and setting of the novel.[72] And since most Swedish crime fiction belongs to the realist mode, which has been central to this tradition since the 1960s, I conclude that the settings and historical context are instrumental to the development of the story and its legacy.

Like Andrew Nestingen, I would like to talk about Swedish crime fiction as a genre going through different transitions along with the historical context.[73] Some examples of these historical transitions are: the rise of the Cold War during the 1950s, the centralization of the Swedish police force in the 1960s, the economic decline in the 1990s (with results such as racism and mass unemployment), and the neoliberal wave of market forces during the 2000s. The same kind of context and transitional historical events could be discovered in the evolution of the American crime novel, which has influenced Swedish writers over the years: the rise of organized crime in the post-Depression 1930s, the focus on social theory and Marxist critique during the 1960s, and greater emphasis on globalization, economics, and neoliberalism during the 1990s and the 2000s. According to Sean McCann, hardboiled crime fiction became the symbolic theater where the dilemmas of New Deal liberalism, as it evolved from the 1930s through the 1950s, could be staged.[74] "The criminal violence that runs through the city appears an emblem of its very political order."[75] An even more interesting perspective—with a Marxist twist—has been made by Mike Davis, who emphasizes the impact that European exile film directors and philosophers have had on the hardboiled noir genre. According to Alan Wald, some German filmmakers and other leftwing radicals had invaded the Hollywood backlots as early as the 1920s to develop the studio system and start a colony of their own: Erich von Stroheim, Fritz Lang, Ernst Lubitsch, Otto Preminger, Michael Curtiz, Nicholas Ray, and William Dieterle. They were directors of films or pro-communists from the New York radical theater, or European refugees who identified with the European anti-fascist left.[76] A decade later, flocks of intellectuals fled Europe when the Nazis had their "Machtübernahme" in 1933. Writers, movie auteurs, composers, philosophers, and other intellectuals settled in the Sunshine State. Davis mentions names of leftist creators who transferred the works of James

M. Cain and Raymond Chandler into a kind of "Marxist *cinema manqué*"—names such as Edward Dmytryk, Ring Lardner, Jr., Ben Maddow, Carl Foreman, John Berry, Jules Dassin, Dalton Trumbo, and Joseph Losey.[77] At the same time, almost the entire Institute for Social Research in Frankfurt, known as "The Frankfurt School," came to the U.S. with social researchers and philosophers such as Theodor Adorno, Max Horkheimer, Herbert Marcuse, Leo Lowenthal, Friedrich Pollock, and Otto Kirchheimer. The new Marxist critical theory of these scholars had a profound impact on American sociology and the intellectual climate in the U.S. Davis, therefore, is closer to a Marxist interpretation of the hardboiled genre than McCann is, and I am going to consult them both in this study. But a basis for my analysis is that the hardboiled crime fiction genre soon developed into *a leftist genre*, with a clear leftist perspective. There are, of course, exceptions, especially in the early days of the genre, such as Mickey Spillane or James Hadley Chase, or nowadays, the king of modern "post-noir," James Ellroy.[78] But the roots of the genre, with Dashiell Hammett as the main source, definitely offer a socialist reflection of the world.

There is one shared theme going straight through the stories that I am about to explore here: the social and political criticism stemming from a view of the world as a place gone wrong. Or, in even more detail: this book is about these writers' *shared notion* of society, rather than the general historic depictions of these societies. I would say that all of these writers—from Chandler to Arne Dahl—in some way also blame capitalism for this modern problem. Wahlöö, Mankell, and Larsson in particular could be connected to this Marxist analysis of the world, as they were all members of different communist movements at some time in their lives. Chandler could be included in this list, too, since he adopted much of Dashiell Hammett's notion of power and crime—and unlike many other writers in the 1920s, Hammett was a radical Communist (however, mostly *after* he had finished his major works).[79] Therefore, the view on society, the world we are living in, and most of all, the world and ideology these writers depict in their works are the prime subjects that we are going to investigate here.

The preliminary emphasis in this study will be on Chandler, and even more so on Per Wahlöö, since he and Maj Sjöwall are considered to be "the godfathers of Scandinavian crime fiction" by the Norwegian crime writer Jo Nesbø.[80] Wahlöö's influence on Swedish crime fiction—especially together with his writing partner Maj Sjöwall (writing team Sjöwall-Wahlöö)—is huge and unequivocal. They reformed the Swedish crime story during the 1960s and 1970s with a new clarifying social perspective on criminals and crimes as something created by a sick society masquerading as a socialist welfare state. But there is one novel that Wahlöö wrote before the Martin Beck series (1965–75) came to life: the science fiction thriller *Murder on the Thirty-First*

Floor (1964). In that novel Wahlöö, for the first time—in a clear way—used his own influence from Chandler and developed it into a gritty urban story about the decay of the Swedish welfare state.

"It must be realistic as to character, setting, and atmosphere. It must be about real people in a real world," Chandler wrote in one of his notebooks.[81] That is probably the most important precondition for writing a hardboiled crime fiction novel. Reality, and the people in this reality, must be actively included in the plot. Both Chandler and Wahlöö shared this view, as well as the idea that there was something fundamentally wrong in this world where greed, power and abuse were growing, especially in the big cities. So, that is where we are heading next in this study, as a starting point: into the gritty urban realm of Raymond Chandler.

1

A World Gone Wrong
Raymond Chandler

Raymond Chandler's hero, private detective Philip Marlowe, drives around in the mobile city with the fluidity encouraged by the city's network of roads and highways into every new enclave where different people live. He is the first motorized detective in the most motorized city in the world. The car takes him from the coastal environments of Bay City (Santa Monica), up into the hills of Pacific Palisades or Beverly Hills, down to the rough Bunker Hill or downtown areas, and the reader follows right behind him, learning things along the way about a world gone wrong—a world where class differences are as clear as the sunny air over the Hollywood hillsides (at least in the 1930s). The stories about Philip Marlowe, and perhaps above all about Los Angeles, are the beginning of one of the most commercially successful literary genres the world has ever seen. How could this genre—a clear favorite among capitalist booksellers and publishers—become a decisively Marxist genre? That is something we will explore in this chapter.

Raymond Chandler was born on July 23, 1888, in Chicago as the only child of Florence Dart Thornton Chandler and Maurice Benjamin Chandler. His mother was an Irish immigrant and his father was born in Philadelphia. Later on, his father was absent in Raymond's life, and his mother moved to England with her son in 1895. Chandler went to school in England, and in 1909–11 he worked as a journalist, first at the *Daily Express*, later at the *Westminster Gazette*. In 1912, he returned to America and lived in Nebraska for a short while, before settling in Los Angeles.

By that time, Los Angeles was a growing city, originally consisting of several small villages and cities along the Pacific coastline in Southern California. It was a city built on decentralization and premised on the virtues of the small unit, dedicated to an ideology of individual freedom and ruled by a tiny coalition of leading oligarchic families. McCann concludes that interwar

L.A. was a city that aspired to centerlessness, but still the entire city was governed by the concentrated power from oil tycoons and landgrabbers from the booster era.[1] Basically, L.A. is the prototype for the postmodern city. It is the perfect physical illustration of what Jacques Derrida referred to with his phrase "the center is not the center," which means that "the concept of centered structure … is contradictorily coherent." Hence, a center that is contradictory is no center. The western way of thinking (as well as the cities) was based on a notion of a center in the structure, but Derrida argues that there has been a "rupture" in this notion of structure.[2] This centerlessness is the archetype for all modern American cities created during the twentieth century. Another postmodernist, Thomas Pynchon has described Los Angeles in a similar way in his typically mysterious novel *The Crying of Lot 49*: "Like many places in California it was less an identifiable city than a grouping of concepts—census tracts, special purpose bond-issue districts, shopping nuclei, all overlaid with access roads to its own freeway."[3]

This labyrinthine city—where the crime fiction plot is just as labyrinthine, thus becoming the symbol of Derrida's increasingly complex view on thought and the world—is the arena for Chandler's stories. They are all, to some extent, and in his own words, about "a world gone wrong, a world in which, long before the atom bomb, civilization had created a machinery for its own destruction, and was learning to use it with all the moronic delight of a gangster trying out his first machine gun. The law was something to be manipulated for profit and power."[4]

Raymond Chandler might be understood as the Joyce or the Proust of the modernist detective novel, Carl Freedman argues in a general stylistic periodization where he dismantles modernism and postmodernism. According to this model of analysis, Chandler's heir Ross Macdonald is a postmodern crime writer, with plots and scenarios resembling Chandler's, but with a Freudian twist.[5] One may also argue that Chandler is the Los Angeles parallel to French novelist Balzac, whose novels ripped the veil off the French big-city class society, just as Dickens did with Victorian England. As we shall see later, even the Swedish crime fiction author Per Wahlöö had the same function of political awakening in the Swedish 1960s.

David Fine describes Los Angeles as a completely different city than New York, Chicago or San Francisco: "It was a city that appeared to have no center and hence no periphery" with architectural styles that spread across the entire history, like "a giant improvisation" or an "unreal city"—"a fragile and temporary place that could be torn down at any moment if it didn't collapse first in an earthquake"—like the image of a movie studio, with its fake walls and temporary streets.[6]

There is a movement in American literature—from Mark Twain and Jack London to Joyce Carol Oates—that tries to avoid sentimentality, to keep feelings tight. Chandler's social-psychological gaze is engaged in the surroundings, in observing the world, not the inner state of humans, Asplund argues.[7] Consequently, he was an anti–Freudian writer, just like Hemingway or others in the same American stylistic tradition. This also shaped Chandler's view on society and the powers controlling it in Los Angeles, where he lived for the longest period in his life. Fredric Jameson argues that Chandler's way of observing and thinking derives from the interwar period, and that the geographical and intellectual place of this imagination, Los Angeles, makes his social content anticipate the realities of the 1950s and 60s, since L.A. is a kind of forecast and microcosm of the country as a whole.[8]

From the very beginning, Los Angeles was a tough place, first as a Spanish colonial town, then as the end of the trail to the American Wild West. The first building in L.A. was a jail, and traditional ingredients after that were whorehouses, weekend murders and frequent lynchings of Chinese and Mexicans. According to Frank MacShane, the city soon fell under a repressive rightwing coalition where hard-handed businessmen directed the elected officials and the police.[9]

When Chandler arrived in L.A. in 1912 it was a small outpost on the Western trail, but quickly grew to an urban sprawl under the pressure of the commercial success of the oil barons and the film industry, and soon Los Angeles became one city consisting of several municipalities from the flat basin that stretches from the Pacific to the mountains. The rich people lived in Pasadena, Westwood or Beverly Hills, the poor blacks in Watts, the Mexican Americans in East L.A.[10] Right from the start, segregation was present.

L.A. is a relatively new city without the history of a place like Chicago or New York. Or, as Frank MacShane puts it, "The city lacks an identity of its own and the buildings show it."[11] L.A. is to Chandler what London and Paris were for nineteenth-century writers such as Dickens and Balzac, where the cityscape is a big, unmissable part of the story. In fact, without L.A. Chandler's stories would verge on the impossible, since they are a historical consequence of the actual milieu. Or in the words of writer and satirist Morrow Mayo, written in 1933: "Los Angeles, it should be understood, is not a mere city. On the contrary, it is, and has been since 1888, a *commodity*; something to be advertised and sold to the people of the United States like automobiles, cigarettes and mouth wash."[12]

According to John Cawelti, the setting of the hardboiled story "is a world of lurking dangers ... an urban world," where the detective is exposing the unholy alliance between business, politics, and organized crime.[13] Chandler echoed the broad political atmosphere of the New Deal era, McCann argues, when he placed greater emphasis on class issues and economic reform than on culture and ethnicity. The federal government would need to protect the weak from the strong. Chandler then turned his focus towards a critical social theory that railed against the abuse of the public spirit, and invoked a different form of political association to criticize the decadent elite of the nonproducing class, religious charlatans, dope doctors, gangsters, gigolos, corrupt cops, and the idle rich.[14] McCann states that Chandler, in some kind of "pseudo-Marxism," "paints capital as a vampiric force driven to steal the labor power of honest workingmen." That is the central image of several of Chandler's novels: Behind all the great men—General Sternwood in *The Big Sleep*, Harlan Potter in *The Long Goodbye*—lies the wealth from dried-up oil wells and morally decadent business transactions such as the great land grabs in the beginning of the century. Or, as McCann puts it, "in Chandler's world, wealth stems less from production than from predation."[15]

Chandler had to relocate the genre from country to city in order to tell his stories of society as an urban maze of the new economic world of Southern California. He also recreated the protagonist as an outsider, a person who had to operate as an outlaw to solve mysteries and crimes. In the traditional "whodunit," the detective was often a part of the bourgeois world, and the criminal was the outsider. In contrast, Chandler called for a new kind of realism. Later Per Wahlöö, Henning Mankell, Stieg Larsson, and Roslund & Hellström would do the same, as we shall see. Chandler also stated another decisive credo for the future of the genre: Important writing could be fashioned in popular genres.[16] This Chandler legacy was followed by Per Wahlöö in the 1960s, and later on by Sjöwall-Wahlöö in their Martin Beck series. This is the very recipe for a broadly read critique of our modern way of life today.

Los Angeles has been the most fertile ground for the harshest critique of the culture of late capitalism, particularly the anarchy of the market forces and the tendency to degeneration of the middle-class stratum, which has been the persistent theme from the novels of Nathanael West to the cinematic stories of Robert Towne: "The most outstanding example is the complex corpus of what we call *noir* (literary and cinematic): a fantastic convergence of American 'tough-guy' realism, Weimar-expressionism, and existentialized Marxism—all focused on unmasking a 'bright, guilty place' (Welles) called Los Angeles."[17] Los Angeles is the ultimate nightmare at the end of American history (as reproduced in noir), and Davis sees the city as a polarized terrain and the object of a wild ideological struggle.[18] Yet Chandler was not the only writer adopting this critique of the city at the end of the trail. The entire hardboiled concept consisted of crime writers familiar with this milieu, but also writers with a proletarian vision of California: John Steinbeck, William Saroyan, Hans Otto Storm, James M. Cain, Horace McCoy, and George Hallas. Upton Sinclair wrote his novel *Oil!* (1927) about the Teapot Dome scandals of the Harding Administration that drew on the events of the 1920s oil scandals, like the Signal Hill strike, when portraying the rise and fall of an independent oil tycoon.[19] David Fine describes this hardboiled fiction of Los

Angeles during the 1930s and 1940s as an "antimyth" to the old optimistic booster myth of the city as a sunshine paradise: "In the iconography of hard-boiled depression fiction, the end of the American highway was also the end of the dream. Where the continent runs out, the dream runs out with it."[20] The corruption was there from the very beginning—it was the place where the road to the future ends; the coastal highway is ultimately a *cul-de-sac*, a dead end.[21]

Chandler and the Communists

I am going to argue in this book that the leftwing presence in hardboiled crime fiction is substantial. From the very beginning the genre might have been dominated by something else, though, when the old Western story evolved into the private-eye story. In the 1920s, the writers of *Black Mask* magazine wrote stories that appealed to reactionary groups such as the Ku Klux Klan, and one of these writers, the founder of the modern hardboiled crime story, Dashiell Hammett, had a background in the infamous anti-labor detective bureau Pinkerton, although he later became a convinced Marxist and member of the Communist Party. J.A. Zumoff has written an interesting essay on the subject of Hammett and his communist activities, stating that "Hammett firmly established the detective story as a form of social criticism, yet he also ensured that the genre could assume different political profiles."[22] The most famous one of these profiles (at least in Sweden), and the one we are about to embark on in this book, is definitely the leftist profile. Zumoff also stresses that Hammett *did not* become an organized Communist during his writing career, but rather at some point in the second half of the 1930s when his political evolution also reflected the leftist radicalization of many others in the intelligentsia.[23]

John Scaggs has come to a diametrically opposed, but equally interesting, conclusion on this matter:

> The ideological power of the hard-boiled mode is almost certainly one of the reasons for its appropriation on political grounds, and it is curious to note that the defining text of this most American of forms, *Red Harvest*, is, as the title suggests, a powerful socialist criticism of the relationship between capitalism and gangsterism. Hammett's imprisonment during the McCarthy period for his suspected involvement with the Communist Party only serves to reinforce such a reading.[24]

In the 1930s, capitalism seemed doomed to either collapse or fall into fascism, while communism gained a larger number of supporters within the intelligentsia—Zumoff mentions the "increasing breakdown of bourgeois respectability."[25] A writer such as Upton Sinclair denounced corruption and tied his muckraking to socialism.[26]

In his work *Delightful Murder*, the economist Ernest Mandel is one of the few Marxists who has analyzed crime novels. But his most famous book, *Late Capitalism* (1972), has been regarded by many scholars as the most important work of economic theory since Marx's *Capital*. Mandel's conception of "late capitalism," the current era of capitalism, includes two important innovations: first, the growing economic importance of nuclear, electronic, and cybernetic technologies, and second, the increasingly elaborate attempts to manage the national economies by both state and private means—for example, the arms industry and the permanent war economy that has existed in the United States since World War II.[27] Using this theoretical approach, he argues that the classic bourgeois crime novels contribute to the obscuring of the class nature of the criminal justice system, and he stresses the fact that bourgeois legality, bourgeois values, and bourgeois society always triumph in the end as they represent soothing, socially integrating literature, despite its concern with crime, violence and murder.[28] According to Mandel, French nineteenth-century author Honoré de Balzac related the rise of professional criminals to the rise of capitalism and the consequent emergence of unemployment.[29]

But the idea of a "soothing" literature certainly does not comply with Hammett's novels. They are disturbing because they are completely irrational. "Crimes are insoluble," Zumoff writes, and bourgeois order does not prevail in the end.[30] However soothing, the hardboiled crime novel also shed light on many social issues, all the way from Hammett's 1920s up until today's Swedish crime fiction with its roots in the radical socialist environment of Los Angeles.

This is also the political milieu wherein Raymond Chandler wrote his novels and short stories. But we have to ask ourselves if Chandler himself was a Marxist, since the master of the genre, Hammett, was a Communist later in life. Chandler did not dislike Hammett even though he was a Communist; on the contrary, he held Hammett in high esteem, or as he wrote in 1949, "He was tops. Often wonder why he quit writing after *The Thin Man*. Met him once only, very nice looking tall quiet gray-haired fearful capacity of Scotch, seemed quite unspoiled to me."[31] In a letter from 1951, Chandler also wrote: "I certainly owe a good deal to him."[32] But exactly how then did Chandler think about highly controversial issues such as Marxism, communism, and the Communist Party during this period, when the 1940s turned into the 1950s?

Most scholars nowadays would agree that Chandler was a liberal rather than a Marxist. As we have seen, McCann, in one certain regard, is calling Chandler a "pseudo–Marxist."[33] According to Tom Hiney, Chandler's second biographer, Chandler was politically non-partisan, suspicious of most institutions, not least of which the FBI and Hoover, and at the same time he believed in a strong army. But he also thought many of the Allied generals had performed badly in the war. He disliked the Church. One time a reader had suggested that Philip Marlowe was a Marxist, and Chandler answered that Marlowe "has the social conscience of a horse. He has a personal conscience, which is an entirely different matter.... Marlowe and I don't care who is President, because we know he'll be a politician." Chandler thought that communism was just a fashion in America and just as corrupt as Catholicism underneath.[34]

Nonetheless, his novels are packed with underlying criticism against themes that also applied to Marxist writers: the wealthy oil tycoons ruining the country, social tensions caused by urbanization and industrialization, political and police corruption, and increased air pollution.

In a letter to the literary reviewer James Sandoe in September 1949, Chandler's view on communists is quite clear. In it, he wonders how people that he would tend to like become communists: "It is obviously neither viciousness nor stupidity. How after the Katyn Forest and the Moscow Treason Trials, the Ukraine famine, the Arctic prison camps, the utterly abominable destruction of Berlin by the Mongolian divisions, any decent man can become a communist is almost beyond understanding, unless it is the frame of mind that simply doesn't believe anything it doesn't like."[35]

Eighteen months earlier, in January 1948, Chandler had written another letter to Sandoe explaining his view on Hollywood screenwriters that were being interrogated by the zealous Committee on Un-American Affairs of the U.S. House of Representatives. Chandler states that it is not illegal to be a member of the Communist Party and that the Hollywood studio bosses should accept this fact or their business would get smeared when they fired these screenwriters. Or, as Chandler put it: "although I have no sympathy for them [the Communists] and don't think anything very awful will happen to them, except that they will spend a lot of money on lawyers, and the worst kind of lawyers, I reserve my real contempt for the motion picture moguls who in conference decided to expel them from the industry."[36]

By 1951, Chandler's notions of communism had not changed much. In a letter to the literary agent Bernice Baumgarten he explains, "You can't laugh Communism off just as a dirty conspiracy. You have to justify its intellectual appeal to some very brilliant minds and destroy it nevertheless."[37]

It is obvious that Chandler is connecting communism to the Soviet Union and its politics and the Cold War. Chandler might criticize America, the oil industry, and the general corruption in the police force—and he certainly does—but he would not go as far as to become a Marxist. In another interesting letter to his friend James Sandoe in December 1948, Chandler criticizes the U.S. financial and legal system at the same time as he states that he is not a socialist:

There is something tragically wrong with a system of justice which can and does make criminals of honest men and can only convict gangsters and racketeers when they don't pay their taxes. Of course to be fair I must also admit that there is something wrong with a financial system which insures that every corporation executive during a time of depression will risk going to jail a dozen times a month in his efforts to save his company. I personally believe, and I am not a socialist or anything of the sort, that there is a basic fallacy about our financial system. It simply implies a fundamental cheat, a dishonest profit, a non-existent value.[38]

Nonetheless, Chandler's literary notions and criticism on contemporary America open up for Marxists—and others, both on the left and the right wing of politics, as we shall see later on in the case of Per Wahlöö and the birth of the modern Swedish crime novel.

Autopia

L.A. was already in the interwar years what Frederic Jameson calls "a new centerless city" where people had lost touch with each other because everybody lived in their own locked geographic compartments.[39] Chandler saw the city grow during the 1920s when he was working for the oil company J.B. Dabney, and the commercial experience in the oil industry helped him see what was going on. During those days, L.A. was the place to be for an oil man. One fifth of the world's oil was being extracted in the L.A. area in places like the Signal Hill oil field, where J.B. Dabney and many other oil corporations had their characteristic forests of oil towers reaching for the sky by the hundreds. The oil industry was the big thing in L.A., and it had great influence on power over the city. This is also why L.A. became the biggest car city in America—or in the world, for that matter—during the 1930s when Chandler's stories started to appear. It is probably no coincidence that the first prewar freeway, the Arroyo Seco Parkway, was laid out in 1939, the same year in which Chandler's first crime novel *The Big Sleep* was released.[40]

The development of the car society of America, and Southern California, is symptomatic of the American 1930s where ruthless car corporations and oil companies joined up together in what some call "the American streetcar conspiracy." A car-culture, that is never really commented on nor criticized, is the frame of all Chandler's novels, because it is a given part of the milieu, and therefore Chandler neither approves nor disapproves of it.[41] But it is also a crucial part of the historical context he was working in and that formed his stories and his view on big crime.

In 1935, the federal government approved the Public Utility Holding Company Act, a new law that forced transit companies out into the open market, without subsidies from the state. Many of these companies died at the end of the Depression, if they were not assisted by General Motors—who got pointed out as "the man behind the mirror" for getting the law approved. In 1936, GM formed National City Lines and began to buy transit companies all over the United States. The idea was to convert the use of streetcars into diesel buses. Soon both big and small cities across the U.S. started to buy buses from companies like Brill, Ford, Mack, and GM. The transit corporations partnered up with other commercial interests. In Los Angeles, Pacific City Lines was partnered with Standard Oil. These partnerships eliminated streetcar lines in cities like Baltimore, L.A., Oakland, Philadelphia, and St. Louis.[42]

After World War II, streetcars began to fade away fast, since more cars on the road meant more gas sales, which meant more gas taxes to fund more roads—a lot of roads—all over America. The construction of the highways had everything to do with the extinction of the public transit systems in the United States.[43]

This is the world of Raymond Chandler—a world in which big corporations run the development of society towards a more corporation controlled market economy, more money, and in the end—as we shall see with Per Wahlöö—more pollution, probably what Mike Davis calls "the anarchy of market forces."[44]

In his 1971 classic book *Los Angeles: The Architecture of Four Ecologies*, architectural historian Reyner Banham uses the concept of "Autopia" to talk about Los Angeles and its freeways. According to Banham, the freeway system is a totality, "a single comprehensible place, a coherent state of mind, a complete way of life." He refers to the freeway system as a "totality and extremity" in comparison to highways in other countries, such as England.[45]

This Autopia is a great paradox, according to Banham. On the one hand, the door-to-door transportation of the car is in accord with individual freedom. However, on the other hand, this transportation system includes "the almost total surrender of personal freedom for most of the journey."[46] Furthermore, commanding authorities "direct the freeway driver through a situation so closely controlled that ... he will hardly notice any difference when the freeways are finally fitted with computerized automatic control systems that will take charge of the car at the on-ramp and direct it at properly regulated speeds and correctly selected routes."[47]

But the concept of Autopia is by no means a critical conception in Banham's analysis, although one could easily think so. On the contrary, he seems pleased with what he calls *the fourth ecology of L.A.*, the freeway system. Yet we must not forget that Banham touches on a critical way of thinking when he points his finger at this paradox. Marxist sociologist Herbert Marcuse, who spent his final years as the head of the philosophy program at the spectacular new sea cliff campus of the University of California at San Diego, had a similar critique (which actually was *critique*) against the freeways some thirty years earlier, when Chandler wrote his first novels. In an article called "Some Social Implications of Modern Technology," originally published in the German *Zeitschrift für Sozialforschung* in 1941, he writes about "a man" who is about to travel to a distant place with his car and meet a countryside that is shaped and organized by the highway, where numerous signs and posters tell the traveler what to do and how to think, where to park and what to look at. A world where others have organized everything and what Marcuse refers to as "the structure of technological rationality," where rationality has been transformed from a critical force to adjustment and resignation. "The facts directing man's thought and action are not those of nature which must be accepted in order to be mastered, or those of society which must be changed because they no longer correspond to human needs and potentialities. Rather are they those of the machine process, which itself appears as the embodiment of rationality and expediency."[48]

The car is where the Los Angeles citizen is most himself, Banham suggests: "an existential limbo where man sets out each day in search of western-style individualism," to quote writer Brock Yates.[49] Marcuse, on the other hand, made a horrifying observation about the individual and the automobile thirty years earlier in his 1941 article: "The average man hardly cares for any living being with the intensity and persistence he shows for his automobile. The machine that is adored is no longer dead matter but becomes something like a human being. And it gives back to man what it possesses: the life of the social apparatus to which it belongs."[50]

At this very spot, Autopia turns into Dystopia.

American Fascism

Hagberg has noted that the contrasts and the tension between the dark and the light in the city of Los Angeles—with the paradise-like appearance on the one side, and the violence, corruption and ethnic antagonism on the other—makes it the perfect place for hardboiled crime fiction stories. In Chandler's novels, the entire city seems to have undergone a fall from grace, something innocent and beautiful has been lost, Hagberg states and further argues that this feeling permeates the stories entirely, with a dissolving moral.[51] In his often quoted essay "The Simple Art of Murder," Raymond Chandler states this view of the American world in his stories:

> The realist in murder writes of a world in which gangsters can rule nations and almost rule cities, in which hotels and apartment houses and celebrated restaurants are owned by men who make their money out of brothels, in which a screen star can be the fin-german for a mob, and the nice man down the hall is a boss of the numbers racket; a world where a judge with a cellar full of bootleg liquor can send a man to jail for having

a pint in his pocket, where the mayor of your town may have condoned murder as an instrument of money-making, where no man can walk down a dark street in safety because law and order are things we talk about but refrain from practicing; a world where you may witness a hold-up in broad daylight and see who did it, but you will fade quickly back into the crowd rather than tell anyone, because the hold-up men may have friends with long guns, or the police may not like your testimony, and in any case the shyster for the defense will be allowed to abuse and vilify you in open court, before a jury of selected morons, without any but the most perfunctory interference from a political judge. It is not a very fragrant world, but it is the world you live in.[52]

Furthermore, Chandler argues in "The Simple Art of Murder" that the old writers of traditional detective stories—most notably Agatha Christie and Dorothy Sayers—are "too little aware of what goes on in the world."[53] This shows the importance of a realistic approach (based on facts, documents and other unbiased material filled with social awareness, delivered in straightforward prose) in depicting what is going on behind the deceitful facade of society, where the highest powers are ruled by crooks and businessmen—sometimes in one and the same person. According to David Richter, Chandler's view of the underworld is that it is merely the underside of the legitimate world, where businessmen and tycoons rule over society with money and crime, and ultimately there is no real difference between these two worlds. Chandler saw this in real life when he worked for the oil company J. B. Dabney who, according to Richter, habitually swindled landowners out of their oil royalties. Chandler helped some of his friends with a lawsuit against his former employer after being fired in 1932.[54]

However, it is possible to see something of a Marxist turn in the texts of Chandler—although he probably was not a Marxist at all, but his thinking about the system of Southern California and the people caught up in it (just like he himself was from time to time) resonates with Marxist critique, as I have mentioned before. According to Frank MacShane, Chandler was sometimes accused of ignoring social conditions in his books, but from *The Lady in the Lake* (1943) it was evident that the novels started to embrace the political and social realities of Southern California. The novel concentrates on those individuals who are caught up in the system of Southern California, not those who direct it, but those middlemen who are "forced to conform to the style and habits of a materialistic world." In one sense Chandler becomes almost a Marxist thinker at this time, when he points out that materialistic circumstances control people—except for Marlowe who is a free agent. Or as MacShane puts it, "What Chandler shows us is a society of men and women trying somehow to keep their lives together, but always under pressure and therefore susceptible to violence."[55]

Mike Davis has formulated the critical ambitions of the hardboiled school as follows:

As the Depression shattered broad strata of the dream-addicted Los Angeles middle classes, it also gathered together in Hollywood an extraordinary colony of hardboiled American novelists and anti-fascist European exiles. Together they radically reworked the metaphorical figure of the city, using the crisis of the middle class (rarely the workers or the poor) to expose how the dream had become nightmare. Although only a few works directly attacked the studio system, *noir* everywhere insinuated contempt for a depraved business culture while it simultaneously searched for a critical mode of writing or filmmaking within it.[56]

The poor citizens of Chandler's L.A. vent their frustration by wasting their lives in bitterness, and the rich by numerous excesses. It is a world where, just as with philosopher Thomas Hobbes, misbelief is the very principle that dominates society and social relations. Hobbes uses the concept of *the state of nature*, "the natural condition of mankind," where the nation or a state-like organization does not exist, a condition of permanent insecurity where the human life is lonely, poor, brutal and repulsive.[57] According to Zumoff, the novels of Dashiell Hammett echo the social vision that the bourgeois society could only uphold with the help of violence when the gap and tensions become too big, when the Lockeian liberalism have become its antithesis, the Hobbesian state of violence.[58] Or as Hobbes explains in his work *Leviathan* (1651): "To this war of every man against every man, this also is consequent; that nothing can be unjust. The notions of right and wrong, justice and injustice, have there no place."[59]

This state of violence is also one of the historical American tendencies, from the very beginning, when Calvinist outcasts and criminals fled Europe across the Atlantic to form what became the United States, up until the violent Wild West era of the late nineteenth century. John Calvin had a huge influence on future Americans when he reformed the dogma stating that a human life was predetermined beforehand by a terrible God, to the dogma that the individual human being was appointed to success in society. This dogma included the notion of a life in rigorous asceticism. In this Calvin breaks completely with the ecclesiastical anti-commercialism of Martin Luther and paves the way for the triumph of capitalism.[60]

The seventeenth-century philosopher Thomas Hobbes wrote about "the savage people in many places of America, except the government of small families, the concord whereof dependeth on natural lust, have no government at all, and live at this day in that brutish manner."[61] In other words, the country has always—at least during its white occupation—been permeated by violence, and L.A. was one of the most violent cities during the 1920s Prohibition era, only superseded by the wave of crime in Chicago where gangsters like Al Capone, Dutch Schultz, and John Dillinger held a reign of terror for years. Ernest Mandel makes an interesting parallel between organized crime and capitalism during this period when he emphasizes the concentration and centralization of capital in general and the logic of organized crime and its takeover of bootlegging, prostitution, and gambling in cities such as Las Vegas, Havana, and Hong Kong. The more capital flow there was in this business, the bigger profits for new investments, which explains the growth of the organization and its geographical spread.[62] Capitalism and organized crime were growing phenomena, basically fed by the same things: money and greed. Or as Chandler puts it: "Because it's gambling and it breeds gamblers and when you add it all up there's one kind of gambling—the wrong kind."[63]

Chandler's notion of organized crime, as quoted above, eventually turned up in *The Long Goodbye*, in a scene where Marlowe is harassed by a gang of thugs and the cop Bernie Ohls saves him from a violent situation:

> We don't have mobs and crime syndicates and goon squads because we have crooked politicians and their stooges in the City Hall and the legislatures. Crime isn't a disease, it's a symptom. Cops are like a doctor that gives you aspirin for a brain tumor, except that the cop would rather cure it with a blackjack. We're a big rough rich wild people and crime is the price we pay for it, and organized crime is the price we pay for organization. We'll have it with us a long time. Organized crime is just the dirty side of the sharp dollar.[64]

The words "Crime isn't a disease, it's a symptom" are probably the closest one could get to Chandler's social theory—a discerning formula with political power that later on would influence leftist writers of hardboiled crime fiction.

The West had always been more arduous, crude, and violent than the more civilized East with its big sea coast metropoles (with a clear city center in the middle) such as New York, Philadelphia, Chicago, and Boston. In the West, the white man killed Indians or Mexicans to build the transcontinental railway, to dig for gold, or drill for oil. The cities popping up in this wasteland were no different than the irredeemable wasteland itself. The ruling power was capitalism as portrayed in John Steinbeck's *The Grapes of Wrath* (1939), where fascism grows out of capitalism with huge faceless banks confiscating the property of poor Oklahoma families, making them go West to get exploited by the affluent plantation owners of Southern California.[65] The novel, widely regarded as an example (one of many) of The Great American Novel, is the story of a dispossessed community of farmers, driven away from their bit of land in Oklahoma by the ruthless march of industrial progress and as a consequence of the Dust Bowl drought that destroyed their crops.[66] The big corporations that own the land these people have lived on for decades decide that the time has come to mechanize agriculture, and so overnight the bulldozers demolish smallholdings and cabins that represent many years of hope and labor.

The image of power, capitalism and fascism as the backbone of America is particularly clear in one defining scene. In chapter five of *The Grapes of Wrath*, there is a driver of a huge bulldozer that is acting on orders from the bank that owns the land where a tenant is standing with his gun, waiting to take revenge on the men who are driving him away from his land. The only one he can actually shoot is the driver of the bulldozer. The tenant tries to understand this predicament and starts a conversation with the driver, gun in hand. He wants someone who he can point his gun at, but there is no one responsible anywhere, no enemies but the system itself, and the tenant bursts out, "But where does it stop? Who can we shoot? I don't aim to starve to death before I kill the man that's starving me." And the bulldozer driver, a former petty farmer himself, now plowing other farmers' land for the bank that owns it, answers the tenant: "I don't know. Maybe there's nobody to shoot. Maybe the thing isn't men at all. Maybe like you said, the property's doing it. Anyway I told you my orders." And the tenant is getting confused, saying, "We all got to figure. There's some way to stop this. It's not like lightning or earthquakes. We've got a bad thing made by men, and by God that's something we can change."[67] This scene becomes an illustration of what Lenin suggested as the turning point between the old and the new capitalism during the twentieth century in his book *Imperialism: The Highest Stage of Capitalism* (1916). In this important work, which originally consisted of a series of articles written just before World War I, Lenin, for the first time, fully developed the strategic vision and the political practice connecting Marxism and the capital-labor conflict with anticolonial and other struggles for national self-determination.[68] Furthermore, he describes an economic displacement, from the reign of capital in general to the reign of a financial oligarchy, and the concentration of ownership to the owners of purely financial capital as an essential part of this transition. According to Lenin this condition, imperialism or reign of financial capital, as he calls it, is the highest stage of capitalism with its total domination of faceless owners of capital.[69]

Like their fathers before them, these displaced citizens of America set out on the migrant trail to the West, but not to find a land of plenty in the Golden West, but to become outcasts and slaves in the nightmarish world of huge plantations where workers were getting exploited and families were being reduced to even more poverty than before, deserted into the hands of the fascist plantation stooges of Southern California.

Five years before the poor farmers from Oklahoma, with the Joads among others, rolled into the Central Valley, James M. Cain had written about the California highway as the road that goes nowhere, the obvious metaphor for the deceptive California promise, as David Fine puts it.[70] In other words, Steinbeck's road saga of post–Depression migrant workers takes us straight into the political backdrop of Raymond Chandler's novels.

This is also probably the "Mafia-capitalism" that Chris Hedges mentions—the end of the line of the self-regulated free market—and something that economist Karl Polanyi refers to in his work *The Great Transformation: The Political and Economic Origins of Our Time*, published in 1944. In his book, Polanyi describes the devastating consequences that grow out of the free market economy in countries such as Great Britain, Nazi-Germany and the United States: the depressions, the wars, and totalitarianism. To Polanyi, fascism was rooted in a market society that refused to function, and that a financial system without government control always devolved into "Mafia-capitalism."[71]

After 1930 the liberal market system experienced a crisis, and a few years later fascism became a world power. The condition of the market system was the number one indicator for the upcoming role of fascism during the 1930s, Polanyi argues.[72] According to him, the United States was one of the countries that, during the 1930s, was preparing for war and then also got rid of liberal capitalism, just like other countries of the New Deal: Germany, Italy, and Japan.[73]

Polanyi describes fascism as something that is dependent on those who are in charge, the men in power, probably the distinguished gentlemen of the upper class or in the boardrooms of the huge corporations.[74] The faceless powers in Steinbeck's novel, of course, come to mind—the backbone of America.

These matters were raised by Marxists in the 1930s and 40s, recognizing the racist structures of the West as totalitarian, questioning whether fascism was the monstrous "other" of liberal capitalism or if Nazism was not the negation of the Weimar Republic but its continuation *in extremis*, as Alan Wald puts it. Furthermore, questions were raised by Marxists whether the Nazi genocide and Stalinist crime were the representatives of a singular "rupture" with Western civilization: "Or do the links between the holocaust, colonialism, slavery, and the war against decolonization, suggest that totalitarian tendencies might be at the very heart of what is misnamed 'liberal democracy'?"[75] These questions have been thoroughly investigated by many of the Marxist Swedish writers of crime fiction since the 1960s, using the hardboiled mode to display moral and political concerns, as we shall see later on.

President Franklin D. Roosevelt recognized the danger of political and economic decline and unbalanced power in society, and wrote to Congress on April 29, 1938, a memorandum with the title "Recommendations to the Congress to Curb Monopolies and the Concentration of Economic Power." There he wrote:

> [T]he first truth is that the liberty of democracy is not safe if the people tolerate the growth of power to a point where it becomes stronger than the democratic state itself. That, in its essence, is Fascism—ownership of Government by an individual, by a group, or by any other controlling private power. The second truth is that the liberty of democracy

is not safe if its business system does not provide employment and produce and distribute goods in such a way to sustain an acceptable standard of living.[76]

In the spring of 1938, Chandler started writing his first novel *The Big Sleep*, published in February 1939, where he points a finger at those who are responsible for the corruption of society: the big tycoons of the oil industry (like his former employer Joseph Dabney) and other people from the upper-class life of Los Angeles.[77] In essence, these are precisely the people who govern the state in just the way that Roosevelt warns about in his message to Congress in 1938, and those invisible rulers who cannot be held at gunpoint in Steinbeck's novel.

In one of Chandler's most extensive studies of the corrupt world gone wrong in post-Depression United States, *The Long Goodbye* (1952), rough tycoon Harlan Potter explains the Roosevelt warning in a clear and upright kind of way:

> We live in what is called a democracy, rule by the majority of the people. A fine deal if it could be made to work. The people elect, but the party machines nominate, and the party machines to be effective must spend a great deal of money. Somebody has to give it to them, and that somebody, whether it be an individual, a financial group, a trade union or what have you, expects some consideration in return.... There's a peculiar thing about money.... In large quantities it tends to have a life of its own, even a conscience of its own. The power of money becomes very difficult to control.[78]

In a short, clear-eyed description, Harlan Potter is being portrayed as "a coldhearted son of a bitch. All Victorian dignity on the outside. Inside he's as ruthless as a Gestapo thug."[79] Again there is a connection between the view of rich corporation barons, leaders of the new economy, and the ruthless Nazi regime. Chandler makes this connection; Wahlöö and the New Left do, too, in the 1960s. Mankell, Larsson, and Dahl also make this connection later on in their stories of the new Swedish neoliberal economy. Polanyi's model of explaining the Mafia-capitalism of fascism clearly fits in with the pattern of the social criticism of these novels.

The Dawn of Marxist Noir

The hardboiled crime fiction novel is created in California during the 1920s and 30s by writers such as Dashiell Hammett and Raymond Chandler. Their social theory of the world of Southern California as a lost paradise becomes the very archetype of the future crime fiction to come. It was there, in the California sun, where the mixture of the critical theory from the philosophers and sociologists of the Weimar diaspora, such as Marcuse and Adorno, met the new Dickensian hell of underclass poverty in America, the corruption of the post-Depression and Prohibition era all rolled into one. Novelists such as James M. Cain and John Steinbeck wrote something that was contrary to the myth of El Dorado, and they repainted it as its anti-thesis, where the dream gets stranded on the coast of California, a regional literature which smashed the inflated image of Southern California as the promised land. For German philosophers such as Adorno, Horkheimer, and Marcuse, Hollywood was nothing less than "the mechanized cataclysm that was abolishing Culture in the classical sense," as Mike Davis puts it.[80]

If the genre is not leftist from the very beginning, it certainly becomes so a few decades later with writers such as Albert Maltz, Ben Maddow, A. I. Bezzerides, Daniel Mainwaring, Dashiell Hammett, Chester Himes, Richard Wright, Willard Motley, Thomas Pynchon, Joseph Wambaugh, and Robert Towne, texts such as *Chinatown* and *Blade Runner*, and the Chandler and Cain movie remakes.

Culture historian Alan Wald, author of *Writing from the Left* (1994), stated in an interview that the contribution from leftist writers to the crime fiction genre, what Wald refers to as "Marxist Noir," is almost monumental. But he also stresses the fact that it would be misleading to theorize any aspect of crime writing as a "left creation," yet he is still prepared to say that there is a heavy leftist presence in noir production:

> In general, I think we can go so far as to say that there are certain aspects of the crime genre that especially lend themselves to a Marxist imagination—the urban setting, the theme of corruption by wealth, the possibilities of having a diverse range of characters (in terms of class, color, gender), the problem of the state, and so on. And clearly there have been many left novelists and screenwriters in the pulp/noir/crime genre who availed themselves of opportunities to make anti-capitalist observations through appropriate dramatic techniques and characterizations, with varying degrees of success. On the other hand, ideologues who go to these works in search of stories about conversions to Marxist ideology, the depiction of frankly Communist heroes, the use of episodes to openly express solidarity with the USSR, and so on, as the signs of a Communist presence, are bound to be disappointed.[81]

"Marxism doesn't embalm history; it seeks to join a living past to present changes," Wald argues in another article.[82] This stands as proof of the genre's richness, possibility of interpretation, and its durability. But the hardboiled crime fiction novel would not have its biggest triumph as a leftist genre in America. Instead, the mold of Marxism and hardboiled crime fiction traveled across the Atlantic Ocean and transformed into something else that by the end of the century would boomerang its way straight back to the U.S. as a pure leftist political genre. One of the first writers to make a real impression in this new leftist genre was Swedish, and his name was Per Wahlöö. What were his connections to Chandler and how did he display his Marxist critique? Those are some of the questions we are going to address in the next chapter.

2

The Accord
Per Wahlöö and Sjöwall-Wahlöö

In a newspaper interview in 1962, just before the release of his third novel *A Necessary Action*, Per Wahlöö confirms the great influence of Chandler on his writing, stating: "If there was any influence on my writing in *The Chief* [his first novel, never published in English], it came from [Robert] Penn Warren. I have always admired him and Raymond Chandler. After [his second novel] *The Wind and the Rain* there was talk about Hemingway, but at least I am not aware myself of any influence from him. Chandler has pointed out by the way that he himself, Hammett, Hemingway and W.R. Burnett all made their debuts in the same year and that the similarities in style were a product of the times and milieu."[1]

Hence, American prose actually had a crucial influence on Wahlöö's writing, and perhaps Chandler is the most important inspiration concerning the crime fiction writing of Wahlöö from the mid–1960s onwards. Andrew Pepper has stressed that the radical political crime novel had its first high point of transatlantic cross-pollination and exchange of ideas during the 1950s and 1960s, when the American writer Chester Himes moved to Paris and interacted with a Marxist crime writer such as Jean-Patrick Manchette.[2] Pepper suggests in his study *Unwilling Executioner: Crime Fiction and the State* that this fertile exchange included Sjöwall-Wahlöö as well.[3] However, the bond between Chandler's world and the milieu depicted by Wahlöö is part of the scope for exploration in this chapter.

One of the early insertions of Chandler into Swedish crime fiction, that also has a bearing on our time, is Per Wahlöö's novel *Murder on the Thirty-First Floor*, originally published in Sweden in 1964 and released for the first time in the United States in 1967 by Chandler's old publisher Alfred A. Knopf.[4] The notion of a corrupt contemporary world, later developed in Wahlöö and Maj Sjöwall's Martin Beck series, was introduced for the first time in this nearly forgotten novel that was re-released in 2012 in a new English translation by Sarah Death.

A year later, in 1965, Sjöwall-Wahlöö's first famous Beck novel *Roseanna* was released, and a couple of years later the Swedish crime fiction duo conquered the world market with their ten realistic procedurals mostly set in Stockholm. The novels of Sjöwall-Wahlöö have sold over ten million copies, become international bestsellers, and are widely regarded as classics and the ultimately defining works of the genre.[5] However, this study will commence with Per Wahlöö and the works he wrote before the Beck novels.

Wahlöö was born in 1926. His father, Waldemar Wahlöö, was an editor and journalist at one of the big papers in the south of Sweden, and his mother, Karin, was a housewife. The family moved from Gothenburg when Per Wahlöö was two years old and eventually ended up in the university city of Lund. Wahlöö worked as a reporter between the years 1947 to 1964 on newspapers and magazines such as *Sydsvenska Dagbladet, Kvällsposten, Veckorevyn, Folket i Bild* and *FiB-aktuellt*. His areas were crime, sports, movies, literature, and theater. He was also a freelance writer for a number of different newspapers in Sweden during the 1950s and spent several years in fascist Spain rambling through the countryside villages trying to write and work while studying the oppression of man inside the totalitarian system. Two of his early novels, *The Wind and the Rain* (1961) and *A Necessary Action* (1962, a.k.a. *The Lorry*), capture the fascist reality of Spain during the 1950s. It is during this period that Wahlöö becomes a leftist writer.

Wahlöö met Maj Sjöwall in 1962 when they were working as journalists in the same building in Stockholm. He was already married, with a daughter on the way, but he still had an affair with the almost ten years younger Sjöwall. They started writing together in secrecy. The following year, in 1963, they partnered up, moved together and started to plan their future writings, a huge series with ten novels about some police officers in Stockholm. Just as with Balzac's *La comédie humaine* (*The Human Comedy* [1898–1902]), Sjöwall-Wahlöö's series was going to be a comment on crime and the social order of society in Sweden. From the very beginning, the series went under the Balzacian name Novel of a Crime (*Roman om ett brott*). In later translations for the English and the American market, it has simply been called the Martin Beck series, since the character Martin Beck is the main protagonist in all of their ten novels.

The interest in Sjöwall-Wahlöö exploded in 1971 when they won the Edgar Award from the Mystery Writers of America for their fourth novel *The Laughing Policeman*, originally released in 1968. Two years later, in 1973, director Stuart Rosenberg brought the story of a mass murder on a bus to the silver screen with Walter Matthau as Martin Beck, although his name in the movie was Jake Martin. All the novels of Sjöwall-Wahlöö were translated and published in several editions in America, but before that Wahlöö's own political thrillers had been published in the English language. One of the first novels was *The Assignment*, originally released in 1963 and published in English in 1965. The same year, his novel *Murder on the Thirty-First Floor* (1964)—the first hardboiled crime novel of the new Swedish wave—was translated into Russian and became an immediate success.[6] The following year, 1966, *The Assignment* was published by Alfred Knopf in the U.S. and the critics did not like it at all. In February 1967, three years after its original release in Sweden, *Murder on the Thirty-First Floor* turns up on the American market—and becomes a triumph with the critics. So when Sjöwall-Wahlöö became a huge success in 1971, Per Wahlöö had already been there and was an established name.[7]

Beekman notes that Chandler's diction is a mixture of colloquial and poetic language, resulting in a style that is never fully realistic, yet always concrete. This is a hallmark of the American style, all the way from Herman Melville to Hemingway: "a direct style of communication which is clear and precise without sacrificing poetic beauty."[8] Wahlöö developed this style in his early novels and took it with him into the Martin Beck series later. Since then, this concrete way of writing has been a hallmark of the Nordic Noir tradition. For example, in one of his early novels, *The Assignment*, the first words are: "The car was a 1937 eight-cylinder Packard. It was black, like the soldiers' uniforms and the American motorcycles in the escort. The time was three minutes past eight in the morning, and it was already very hot."[9] The prose is direct and filled with details and facts. As are the first lines in *Murder on the Thirty-First Floor*: "The alarm was raised at exactly 13.02. The chief of police phoned the order through personally to the Sixteenth Police District and ninety seconds later the alarm bell sounded in the operational rooms and administrative offices on the ground floor."[10] Wahlöö's interest for details, documents and facts continues in all of his novels. No poetry, no magic, no inner monologue—just pure realism.

According to crime fiction aficionado John-Henri Holmberg, Sjöwall-Wahlöö's first novel *Roseanna*, released in late summer of 1965, was no immediate success in Sweden. The critics found it too gritty, too depressing, too dark, and too brutal. Gradually, however, their novels became a literary best-selling phenomenon.[11] Holmberg talks of the breakthrough of the hardboiled style in Swedish crime fiction during the 1960s as a coming of age, where younger generations—who grew up with American hardboiled crime novels published in cheap paperback editions, rather than the bourgeois Agatha Christie mysteries of their parents—fully enjoyed the social criticism in the American style.[12]

But before we embark into the Chandler legacy in Swedish crime fiction during the 1960s, we have to understand the background of Wahlöö's fascination for Chandler, which was a fascination filled with paradoxes and conflict.

Wahlöö's Criticism of Chandler

Per Wahlöö started reading Raymond Chandler during the 1950s in small, cheap English paperback editions. In Wahlöö's private bookcase, stored in the apartment of his second wife Sylvia (they were married 1957–1963), we can see well known titles such as *Farewell, My Lovely*, *The Lady in the Lake*, *Pearls Are a Nuisance*, *Pick-Up on Noon Street*, *The Big Sleep*, *The Long Goodbye*, *Trouble Is My Business*, *Playback*, *The High Window*, and *The Little Sister* in English editions. Wahlöö even had *Das Hohe Fenster* (*The High Window*) in German. Although Chandler is one of the great inspirational writers for Wahlöö, his connection to the old master is somewhat complicated.

During the 1950s, Wahlöö was working as a crime reporter and literary critic in the city of Malmö in the south of Sweden, later as a freelancer on other Swedish papers, mostly in Stockholm. In several of his newspaper articles on the extensive Swedish debate about violent literature, comics, and science fiction during the 1950s, Wahlöö mentions writers such as Raymond Chandler and Dashiell Hammett as "the dragon seed" to even worse followers in the hardboiled genre. He mentions pulp writer Mickey Spillane as an epigone with a sense of twisted violence and banality. However, during the 1960s Hammett, and especially Chandler, became one of Wahlöö's greatest inspirations. It is therefore interesting to look into what he wrote about these writers during the 1950s in the Swedish debate about violent literature and comic books. In one of the articles, he opens with a long exposition on Hammett's significance for the genre:

> For Hammett has for all time carved his name on one of the more shadowy sides of literature history in his capacity as an introducer of the "hardboiled" crime story. He himself was a discarded detective from the notorious Pinkerton bureau, and his books were some sort of racy parodies on detective novels in their established form. They were works with skillful and evident feeling for milieus, and they expressed, almost in passing, an excessive portion of cynicism and brutality which until then was unparallelled. Hammett was not entirely a bad writer, and there was within him, just as with the best of his sympathizer, Raymond Chandler, a certain amount of self irony, which in fact forgave quite a lot.... With that he also delivered the dragon seed, that richly fertilized by centuries of brutalization bears fruit today with an alarming abundance.[13]

So, how does Wahlöö take a stand *against* Hammett and Chandler at this time? His piece called "An Ordinary Swedish Boy" (En vanlig svensk grabb), quoted above, is one of the first articles he wrote on this subject. It was published in 1954, and these hardboiled role models of his would emerge in several other articles to come. Nevertheless, in 1954 Wahlöö was very critical of the hardboiled school, and accordingly even Hammett is one of the stooges of the culture industry traditionally blamed for having vulgarized, or even ruined, the reading habits of Swedish youngsters. Still, in another article, published three years later, Wahlöö's view on the matter is somewhat clearer:

> The success of Hammett and Chandler however soon leads to an epigone never seen before. The war and the brutalization so common in that time soon went on to the extreme consequence of this school, the exceedingly horrible Mickey Spillane, whose works recently have sold in millions of copies in the United States. Spillane is, with his distasteful dual personality between violence, quasi-religiousness, and sexual sadism, the very spokesman of private vendetta. Both directly and indirectly his books inspire to the persecution and oppression of dissidents.[14]

Throughout these articles, the moral tone is high. Wahlöö talks of this kind of literature as "the weapon of the entertainment industry" and as "a menace to society," and says that violent literature infiltrates and has an unsound influence on youngsters. Ernest Mandel stresses the connection between the development of organized crime and urban violence in America during the 1930s and 40s, with the evolvement of a new kind of mass produced crime fiction literature during the 1940s and 50s that primarily focused on violence and sadism. Mandel mentions Mickey Spillane, but also James Hadley Chase and William Irish, who wrote stories where torture, cruelty, and murder—*in its own right*—were the main parts of the mysteries. Novels such as James Hadley Chase's *No Orchids for Miss Blandish* (1939) became a huge success and reflected a sick society with social alienation, literary decay, and deeper changes regarding language and the capitalist mode of production. The lack of argument, subtle plots, and mystery, as opposed to pure action, resulted in an often reactionary—or even pre-fascist, or semi-fascist—ideology mixed with an increasing cultural decay and anti-intellectual tendencies amongst the readers.[15] This was also the conception of crime fiction literature sustained by Wahlöö during the 1950s. Perhaps he saw the need for a vitalization of the hardboiled genre. Somewhere in all this we can at least recognize the birth of the first thoughts that later transformed into a new kind of leftwing hardboiled detective story—a Marxist Noir—with elements of critical theory. This brings us to explore the Marxist notions of the Swedish 1960s.

Crime Fiction and Critical Theory

By the start of the 1960s, the political agenda of Per Wahlöö had changed radically. After being a rightwing agitator in the daily press during the 1950s, he became a convinced Marxist during a long stay in fascist Spain in the middle of the century. Wahlöö became an even more convinced communist during the 1960s when he saw how bourgeois-capitalist newspaper tycoons, such as the Swedish Bonnier family, handled the leftwing journal where he was working. At the end of 1962, Wahlöö's employer, the weekly labor journal *Folket i Bild*, was sold to the huge Bonnier corporation by its previous owner, the Social Democratic Party and the labor movement. In the wake of this affair, Wahlöö wrote his satirical novel *Murder on the Thirty-First Floor*, set in a tall newspaper building in central Stockholm, garbed in a slightly futuristic setting. It is the same kind of *1984*-ish noir future as written by authors such as George Orwell and Aldous Huxley, and at the same time it depicted a contemporary modern world very much inspired by the same American capitalist society we have seen depicted in the novels by Raymond Chandler. We can see the same corporate fascist structures as those that appear in the stories of Chandler, Steinbeck, and numerous other American authors—a hard, modern, shiny steel structure of industrial progress working against a Marxist awakening of the people. The ideologies are dead and the great power structures of society have all fused together into *the Accord*, where the labor movement, the monarchy, the state, and the corporations are all in bed together against the people.

Wahlöö's purpose with this story is similar to the one that Maj Sjöwall describes for Sjöwall-Wahlöö's common Martin Beck project known as Novel of a Crime: "under the official image of welfare-state Sweden there was another layer of poverty, criminality and brutality. We wanted to show where Sweden was heading: towards a capitalistic, cold and inhuman society, where the rich got richer, and the poor got poorer."[16] But the novel's principle criticism is that of the capitalist monopoly press, which here shows itself as the strangulation of the freedom of speech. In the long run this becomes a problem, even a hindrance, for democracy. Popular 1960s Marxist philosopher Herbert Marcuse wrote: "The products indoctrinate and manipulate; they promote a false consciousness which is immune against its falsehood."[17] When critical theory resurfaced in the 1960s, Therborn argues, it was in the context of media-prominent anticolonial revolts and the rise of a mass student body. The classical texts were published for the first time for a wide audience, and Marcuse's book *One-Dimensional Man* (1964) was perhaps the most prominent of those works.[18] Written in the United States, within a strictly American context and addressed to a wide audience, it was published the same year as *Murder on the Thirty-First Floor*, but the philosophy Marcuse presented was hardly new. It had developed from his more than thirty years of research under the wings of the Frankfurt School with its roots deep in the European philosophy of Kant, Hegel and Marx. In his book, Marcuse presents the notion of society as an economic-political rectification (standardization), just as Wahlöö does in his novel. This rectification, in turn, guarantees the manipulation of human needs which, of course, is reminiscent of the idea of the Culture Industry that Max Horkheimer and Theodor Adorno discuss in *Dialectic of Enlightenment* (1947). Their book describes how Hollywood movie industry has melted together with the propaganda machine of a reactionary ideology that broadcasts the system code for survival in industrial society. Mike Davis has made the connection between critical theorists—and intellectual exiles of the Weimar diaspora—such as Horkheimer and Adorno, and the rise of hardboiled noir fiction: Their exile in Southern California ultimately transformed the terms for understanding the devastating impact of modernism, and Adorno saw "Los Angeles as the crystal ball of capitalism's future ... the death agony of Enlightenment Europe."[19]

The connection between hardboiled crime fiction and the critical theory of the German exiles during World War II is interesting, and I am going to stay with it for just a while longer. Horkheimer and Adorno were two of the brightest stars from the Frankfurt School—the Institute of Social Research at the University of Frankfurt, an institution formed in the mid-1920s that had Marxist theory permeating all its work. When Hitler grabbed power in Germany in 1933, these intellectuals fled the country and eventually formed a colony in Los Angeles. In 1941, when Adorno arrived in Hollywood, this colony consisted of individuals such as the writer Thomas Mann, communist playwright Bertolt Brecht, composer Arnold Schoenberg, Adorno, Horkheimer, and many others. In this cultural wasteland, Adorno and Horkheimer saw a kind of history-lessness and vulgarity. Clearly—as in a crystal ball—the European enlightenment culture was sinking like Atlantis. The enlightenment had become a huge fraud led by Hollywood movie stars and studio tycoons. From their residences in the green hills of Pacific Palisades, Adorno and the others could see the entire Pacific Ocean, but also Hollywood, across Wilshire Boulevard, and all the way to the downtown area with its art deco towers. Eventually they saw a downtown area in decay where streetcars had disappeared and where the huge cinemas along Broadway started to deteriorate. In their famous opening section of the chapter "The Culture Industry" in their book *Dialectic of Enlightenment*, Horkheimer and Adorno write, in an almost Chandlerian image,

> Even now, the older houses just outside the concrete city center look like slums, and the new bungalows on the outskirts are at one with the flimsy structures of world fairs in their praise of technical progress and their built-in demand to be discarded after a short while like empty food cans. Yet the city housing projects designed to perpetuate the individual as a supposedly independent unit in a small hygienic dwelling make him all the more subservient to his adversary—the absolute power of capitalism.[20]

This place, Hollywood of the 1940s, was the definitive milieu that had inspired Adorno and Horkheimer to write *Dialectic of Enlightenment*, released in 1947.[21] In an interview, historian Martin Jay said that the American culture gained a lot from the presence of these German intellectuals. Jay specializes in the German exiles during the war and emphasizes that there was no real distinction between higher culture and pleasure for these intellectuals (this was not the case for American intellectuals who were interested in more moral concerns).[22] Ultimately there was no longer any gap between European philosophy, critical theory, or even Aristotle, on the one hand, and hardboiled crime fiction on the other. In the Hollywood melting pot of the 1940s, everything seemed to blend.

Although the founding fathers of critical theory actually lived not very far from Raymond Chandler, in Pacific Palisades, there are no clear links between these two different cultural strata.[23] Still, the ideas they share are basically the same, and it is likely that these ideas—the view on Los Angeles and modernism as the future of capitalism and the seed for fascism and decay—existed in the air of debate, discussion, and contemporary cultural discourse at the time. Adorno wanted to develop a philosophy that contributed to the social critical consciousness of humans, and that is basically what the hardboiled crime genre also wanted to achieve, especially in the 1960s when the interest in social theory really exploded in both America and Europe. A critical human consciousness was the prime objective of Adorno and Horkheimer, but they never saw crime fiction as the bearer of this mission, instead they regarded the "Crimie" or the Western, with their genre standardizations, as part of what they called the Culture Industry—i.e., in the long run as bourgeois culture making humans cling to their life in the shadow of capitalistic power structures.[24]

The harsh world of these thinkers, perhaps most notably Marcuse, can be seen in both American hardboiled noir fiction and in the works of Per Wahlöö.[25] In some cases the prose of Wahlöö is even strikingly similar to the philosophy of Marcuse—or Adorno's theories on the Culture Industry, for that matter. Let me illuminate this with the following example from *Murder on the Thirty-First Floor*:

> What they were attempting to do was to bring all the different points of view closer to each other. Perhaps it wasn't such a bad notion, but the methods that were being used to realize it were built almost entirely on hushing up any antagonism and difficulty. They lied away the problems. They glossed over them with constant improvements in material standards, and hid them behind a fog of meaningless talk pumped out via the radio, press and TV. And the phrase that covered it all was, then as now, "harmless entertainment."[26]

Just like in sci-fi literature, Herbert Marcuse is talking about the Utopian, and the importance of working out alternative conditions of society. The dialectical thinking, in this case, should then lead to an abstraction—an estrangement—of the empirical reality whose very existence could then be questioned. The distinguishing feature of Marcuse's theory on "advanced industrial society" is its effective suffocation of those needs that demand liberation.[27] It is a nation that lives in the shadow of the Cuban Missile Crisis and an emerging Vietnam War, whose very opposite in world politics is being constituted by the Soviet Union and is being threatened by the power game between these military super powers. That is also the exact kind of state being unveiled in *Murder on the Thirty-First Floor*—an existence where the foreboding threat of human extinction is central in thinking and philosophy.[28] Marcuse is talking about the "unification of opposites" that becomes an obstacle for social change.[29] It is a world in which giant corporations have joined up with trade unions in cynical lobby groups and cartels, in which the natural opposition between labor and capital is being shrouded by "the Accord" made necessary by economical force—an existence in which the increase of automation in advanced industrial society leads to inevitable powerlessness and the dispiritedness of the workers.[30] The similarities to "the Accord" in *Murder on the Thirty-First Floor*, with its alarming figures for low birthrates and high rates of suicide, are striking. Wahlöö presented an even stronger similarity with the world of Marcuse four years later in his revolution novel *The Steel Spring* (1968), presented in more detail below.

Marcuse mentions the transcendent capacity of the theater against the system in a line penned by another Hollywood emigrant during the 1940s, Bertolt Brecht: "To teach what the contemporary world really is behind the ideological and material veil, and how it can be changed, the theater must break the spectator's identification with the events on the stage." The only things required by this spectator are distance and reflection, Marcuse states and continues: "The 'estrangement-effect' ... is to produce this dissociation in which the world can be recognized as what it is."[31] These cultural expressions—just as the best hardboiled crime fiction—may well recall the pulp fiction slogan of the 1940s and 50s: "the idea as hero."[32] At least that is the main purpose of the crime fiction of Per Wahlöö: to make the reader conscious of the world behind the ideological veil.

Ideologically, Wahlöö's notion of history, of course, also joins the Marxist narrative of history as chronological transition from capitalism to socialism, and the story of contemporary time as a crisis of capitalism. The Swedish New Left saw Sweden as a bourgeois, bureaucratic, centralized, authoritarian, and capitalistic society populated by passive and alienated humans bound to the eternal wheel of consumption. The Marxist-Leninists took up a critique in the line of Lenin's theory on monopoly-capitalism and thought of Sweden as a monopoly-capitalistic fascist state in great need of a purge revolution, much like the Culture Revolution in China, in order to get rid of the Social Democracy that had governed the country since the early 1930s. The fact that the Social Democratic party cooperated with capitalism was one of the cornerstones in the leftist critique during this period.[33]

Sjöwall-Wahlöö have displayed their leftist critique of Swedish society in several interviews. By 1973 they had published eight novels in their Beck series, and the political tone of the novels had increased since the mid–1960s when they got started. Their view on society was as follows:

> It is quite obvious that a large part of the youngsters feel very unsafe—they lack a base in their existence. Labor does not seem meaningful for the young people, they wonder why they should work. There is no feeling of solidarity, no feeling that the state is myself and that we should all work together to improve society. The ideal would be a society where everybody knew what they are working for and that we all work for each other.... We want a socialist society. There is no template for how it should be created. Each country has to find its own recipe. But here, among us, we believe that good opportunities should have existed. An independent country, economically affluent through its natural resources. If we had had a decent planned economy it would not have needed to be like this. The mixed economy will lead to disaster. In this competitive society, where so many people get treated unfairly, we will never be able to create a feeling of solidarity. What is needed are changes so profound that they might just as well be called revolutionary.[34]

Critical theory is a basic element in the crime novels of Wahlöö and Sjöwall-Wahlöö since they describe the impact of modernism and industrial progress in a critical way. Just like Chandler, they were living and writing in a "car society," where the automobile was becoming more and more central in the lives of citizens. What impact did this "car society" really have on the stories of Wahlöö?

Swedish Autopia

The central character in Wahlöö's novel *Murder on the Thirty-First Floor* is the bleak cop Inspector Jensen, a traditional white-collar worker of the faceless dictatorship, the vacuity in person, or as Pepper labels him, "an apparatchik of a totalitarian order."[35] Basically he is one of those henchmen Steinbeck's farmers probably would have pointed their gun at without reaching the core of fascism. Jensen gets to investigate a bomb threat against the tall newspaper building where all the media power is set. During his investigation, he cruises through a world gone wrong, very reminiscent of Chandler's "car society" in Los Angeles. And if L.A. had the Streetcar Conspiracy and the huge corporations conspiring to build motorways all over the country, Sweden had a clearer plan for what it actually meant to be a "Car Society"—sanctioned by the government itself.

The setting of the hardboiled story, according to Cawelti, is "a world of lurking dangers ... an urban world," where the detective is exposing the unholy alliance between business, politics, and organized crime.[36] The Swedish model of this conspiracy involves the state and its administration, the bureaucracy, and economic interests behind it all, rather than gangsters such as Al Capone, responsible for violence and corruption in the American 1930s. The notion of the urban jungle and the modernization of this inhuman milieu is one of Wahlöö's main themes.

During the 1950s Sweden became the most motorized country in Europe, mostly because the Swedish government in the early days of the century implemented a plan to create a "Car Society." This society was fully developed by the end of the 1960s and was seen as an ideal for the future.[37] The ideas for this mass motorization came from American traffic engineering that had been at work since the 1940s with the Interstate Highway System in the United States. And just as in the U.S., market interests from the car and oil industries stood firmly behind the new road plan in Sweden that the Social Democratic government adopted in 1959 with the purpose of accommodating mass motorization.[38]

The Swedish Road Federation (founded in 1948 by the car and oil industries) managed to set the agenda that defined the car after the war. And this was not a problem at the time, since the "Car Society" was seen as the future, and basically no one saw the problems of environmental pollution. That came later, during the 1960s.

Chandler also addresses these issues in his later novels. Right from the beginning, when *The Big Sleep* was released in 1939, the construction of Los Angeles's first highway, the Arroyo Seco Parkway, started with its stretch from downtown Los Angeles to Pasadena. The highways and the detective moving around in a car along the Pacific Coast and in the system of highways is one of the compulsory genre clichés nowadays. As we have already seen, the city of Philip Marlowe soon became the most motorized city in the world. The number of cars in L.A. was at an incredible level already in 1925—one automobile per 1.6 persons. Other cities in the United States would not reach that number until the 1950s. Also, in 1928 Bullocks Wilshire, the first department store exclusively for motorized L.A., citizens, opened with a huge parking lot.[39] Jameson weaves the city structure into the novels of Chandler as he writes: "The detective's journey is episodic because of the fragmentary, atomistic nature of the society he moves through."[40]

Clearly air pollution had started to worry people in the 1950s. In *The Long Goodbye*, Chandler mentions that the "valley had a thick layer of smog nuzzling down on it. From above it looked like a ground mist,"[41] "and the acid sting of the smog had crept as far west as Beverly Hills. From the top of Mulholland Drive you could see it leveled out all over the city like a ground mist. When you were in it you could taste it and smell it and it made your eyes smart."[42] Wahlöö's criticism is similar in his second Jensen novel, the sequel to *Murder on the Thirty-First Floor*, released in the revolutionary year of 1968, *The Steel Spring*: "Hoar frost veiled the concrete surface of the motor-

2. The Accord 57

way, and the greyish air, poisoned with exhaust fumes, lay like an enormous bell over people, cars, roads and built-up areas ... the polluted air now extended fifty or sixty metres into the air."[43]

Wahlöö's criticism of mass motorization, a Swedish Autopia, in *Murder on the Thirty-First Floor* also concerns philosophical questions such as alienation and the commodification and consumer culture of the modern world. In fact, cars will make people unhappy in the long run, hence the notion of Sweden as a necropolitan state,[44] a state of many suicides, where the car culture is central:

> The experts at the Ministry of Communications had long since solved this statistical conundrum. The decrease in collisions and material damage could to some extent be accounted for by better roads and enhanced traffic surveillance. More important was the psychological factor: people had become more and more reliant on their cars, treating them with greater care and reacting almost subconsciously to the thought of losing them. The rising number of deaths was explained by the fact that most fatal crashes were really to be classified as suicide. Here, too, the psychological factor played a decisive role: people lived with and for their cars, and also wanted to die with them.[45]

Like in the United States, the Swedish car and oil industries had strong links to the government. Behind the market interests in Sweden was the International Road Federation with participating commercial interests such as Ford, General Motors, Opel, Fiat, International Harvester, Sacony Vacuum Oil (Mobil), Caltex, Shell, Michelin, Goodrich, Goodyear, Dunlop, Pirelli, and Caterpillar.[46] A "Car Society" was, of course, pure business planning for these multinational companies and fitted perfectly in what Blomkvist refers to as "the prevailing zeitgeist of postwar modernism."[47] This zeitgeist is the very ideology that Wahlöö puts forward in *Murder on the Thirty-First Floor*:

> The structure of society started to change, first slowly and imperceptibly, then at breakneck speed. The welfare state and the Accord were referred to increasingly often, until the two were seen as indissolubly linked and mutually dependent in every way. At first there was nothing to cause concern; the housing shortage was solved, crime figures went down; the youth question was being tackled. Meanwhile, the long-anticipated moral backlash started, as punctually as the Ice Age. Not especially worrying, as I say. Only a few of us had our suspicions. I assume you know as well as I do what happened next.... The most worrying thing for us, of course, was that all publishing activity was being gathered into the same camp, that publisher after publisher and paper after paper were being sold to the same group of companies, always with financial profitability as the deciding factor.[48]

Blomkvist stresses that the construction of a "Car Society" was also an ideological transformation of society. The private car, to own one's automobile, had an ideological role in the creation of a peaceful, liberal, and free Europe. The car "was not only an expression of free individual spirit: it fostered the individual and developed the personality in a liberal way."[49] Furthermore, he notes that huge train systems are associated with dictatorships such as those of Hitler and Stalin, or even social democratic governments such as the one in Sweden, for that matter. In other words, *the car was a creator of the liberal individual*. The car symbolized movement (and progress) for the individual man, trains symbolized adaptation to the masses, time tables, authoritarianism, and oppression. A private car was also the very symbol of progress, modernity, and welfare. This is where Wahlöö's notion of society meets up with Blomkvist: "car use became a basic premise in modernist architecture and city planning."[50] Or in the words of Marcuse, some twenty-three years before Wahlöö, in his aforementioned essay "Some Social Implications of Modern Technology," containing thoughts echoing straight back at us today, in our Facebook-crazed time: "Technology ... is thus at the same time a mode of organizing and perpetuating (or changing) social relationships, a manifestation of prevalent thought and behavior patterns, an instrument for control and domination."[51]

The ideas of Marcuse actually permeate the essence of Wahlöö's entire novel. On several occasions, Inspector Jensen is driving through an uninteresting landscape shaped by the motorways and the industrial surroundings, or through derelict suburbs draped with high concrete block buildings in decay. Everything is drenched in the distant roar of the cars on the motorway. It is the Swedish "car society" that Blomkvist is writing about, inspired by the American way of life, and the very same type of "car society" that Chandler's Philip Marlowe is driving around in—a world of endless highways, endless lines of cars, endless cities where people feel bad because the modern environment is killing them. It is Horkheimer's, Adorno's, and Marcuse's modernism and enlightenment spirit gone awry. Although at the same time the individuals in this society are increasingly dependent on their cars, television sets, and gadgets, psychologically bewildered and committing suicide at a rate that made Sweden internationally infamous in the 1960s. This was a cliché in the 1950s, mostly caused by American journalists and writers, so finally, also in 1964, the American psychiatrist Herbert Hendin released his book *Suicide and Scandinavia: A Psychoanalytic Study of Culture and Character*, and Swedish newspapers wrote a lot about the suicides during this time.[52] In the works of Wahlöö, and especially in the books he wrote with Maj Sjöwall later, the idea of a huge crime being committed against the individuals in Swedish society is central. What did this idea consist of, and what is its relation to Chandler and the Marxist philosophy of the time?

The Parallax View

According to Chandler and Wahlöö, the world is a conspiracy by huge corporations and tycoons, bringing fascism and Mafia-capitalism as seen by

Karl Polanyi into the open. Both Chandler and Wahlöö are describing a rough place, whether it is Los Angeles or Stockholm. The big crime is within the structure, the government, the corporations, the economy and (at least according to Wahlöö) the liberal ideology. In Wahlöö's second novel about Inspector Jensen, *The Steel Spring*, the complete image of this conspiracy is explained by a police doctor, one of the few individuals in the novel who possesses a revolutionary mind:

> Capitalism's a crime in itself. But it's a paper tiger. If anyone drops a spanner in the works, it's got nothing to fall back on. People are indifferent to it. They know nothing and understand nothing beyond the narrow sector of their own training. And the alienation makes them incapable of establishing connections.[53]

Of course, this is also the credo of Sjöwall-Wahlöö's Martin Beck mysteries: the exposure of the Social Democratic government as a bourgeois Accord in close cooperation with big corporations at the expense of the working class and socialism. The novels of Chandler and Hammett likewise employ the familiar perspective of the hardboiled criminal as a highly respectable member of society which the detective tracks down to "the rich and respectable levels of society and exposes the corrupt relationship between the pillars of the community and the criminal underground."[54] This is true, perhaps, even more so in the writings of Wahlöö. This perspective, with a little help from Slavoj Žižek, could be called *the parallax view*, which Žižek describes as, "the apparent displacement of an object (the shift of its position against a background) caused by a change in observational position that provides a new line of sight."[55] The crime novel, since Chandler and Hammett, has had a firm place as a producer of this parallax view.

Nonetheless, the stories of Wahlöö are naturally far more drenched in leftist political propaganda than the stories of Chandler. Wahlöö was a political writer in a time when political change was huge—a young generation witnessed the fallback of the colonial empires of several European countries in Africa and Asia, the Vietnam War was on the rise, and Marxist philosophy and the original writings of Marx were widely read and analyzed. Wahlöö managed to combine these things into his texts, and that made them contemporary, read by thousands all over the world. Actually, Wahlöö started this alteration of the crime fiction novel as early as in 1962 in his novel *A Necessary Action*, where a murder plot is central to the story. Everything occurs around the murder of a sexually liberated Scandinavian couple. The protagonist of the story, down-and-out German painter Willi Mohr, lives on a Spanish island (Majorca) and gets involved in the murder mystery. This opens his indifferent eyes towards the Spanish dictatorship of General Franco and his henchmen in the Guardia Civil. Mandel concludes that an alteration of the mass-produced crime fiction novel, of the classical type, could not have been done until the 1960s, when the colonial revolutions around the world—in Africa and Asia—and the impact of the Vietnam War, and the civil rights movement hit the Western world. That was the time when Indians became heroes instead of cowboys.[56] Moreover, that was the time when social criticism—in a clear Marxist fashion—became a commodity on a globalized literary market.

A Revolutionary Crime Novel

Per Wahlöö's 1968 novel *The Steel Spring* could be described as a long-winded monologue of revolutionary thinking typical for the 1960s Swedish leftist movement.[57] Specifically Marxist concepts such as *alienation* and *revolution* have a firm place in this book. While alienation had a primary function in the previous book about Inspector Jensen, *Murder on the Thirty-First Floor*, now, four years later, revolutionary frenzy soaks the entire narrative of *The Steel Spring*.

In this novel, Jensen (who is a precursor to Martin Beck) spends several months in the Soviet Union where he is having surgery for his ulcer (also similar to Beck). On his way back home, he is informed that something has happened in his native country, something that seems to be a revolution or a catastrophe. Jensen gets back home, starts to investigate the events and meets a devastated country with deserted, tarnished cities where some kind of holocaust or animus epidemic has paralyzed the entire civilization. Now his deductive skills as a policeman come in handy.

When reading this novel it is important to know that Jensen is by no means a nice or even sympathetic person. He is a zealously staunch pro-regime man, taking orders from the people currently in charge. This is the signum of all Wahlöö's characters, even Martin Beck. They are all the henchmen of power, telling the reader what is going on in society, and perhaps more importantly, they *illuminate what is wrong* with a society dependent on capitalism. Or, as the Danish literary scholar Niels Mors Nielsen called Beck in the 1970s, they are "a socialist filter function" ("socialistiske filterfunktion").[58]

In one important sequence, reaching over several chapters, Jensen listens to an incarcerated man from the socialist movement, who tells him what has occurred while he was away. In one lengthy monologue the man also tells Jensen about the Accord:

> The prevailing social practices were and are to be condemned. That the whole thing needed to be torn up.... Because the so-called Accord has never been anything but a bluff. It came into being because the old, supposedly socialist movement was losing its hold on employees and the working classes. And at that moment, the social democrats sold their voters lock, stock and barrel to the right wing. They entered into the grand

coalition, or Accord as it later came to be known. They abandoned socialism, made successive changes to their party program, and delivered the whole country up to imperialism and the formation of private capital.... I've studied these questions long and hard. To stop the country turning socialist, the social democratic party and the trade union movement deserted their most fundamental ideological principles. The leaders at the time had been in power for so long that they couldn't imagine losing it. What's more, they had discovered that even the labour movement and the mouthpieces could be run on a bourgeois-plutocratic model, with an eye to financial profitability for the few. The Accord's most deeply held principle was that everything had to make a profit. That was why this phantom political combination was entered into and its true nature hidden behind a hypocritical facade of clichés about higher living standards, mutual understanding and security. That everything was getting better all the time.[59]

This is also the prevailing problem, the main narrative of Sweden among the leftist movements during the 1960s and 70s. The long-time regime of social democracy, in power since the 1930s, had betrayed their own principles, consequently a revolution was needed. Or, as the Irish revolutionary-socialist leader James Connolly once said: "Revolution isn't a runaway train; it's the application of the emergency brake."[60]

Consequently, students, intellectuals, and radical parts of the labor movement ran the leftwing forces in Sweden at the time. The working class had been soothed into a sleeping condition by radio, TV, and meaningless glossy magazines. "[T]hey had almost an entire nation of sheep," Wahlöö writes in *The Steel Spring*, continuing: "until people only knew they had a car and a flat and a TV set and were unhappy. Knew it was more tempting to commit suicide or drink themselves to death than go to work."[61] Wahlöö describes the Accord philosophy as "a criminal attempt to make people accept the universal meaninglessness that had resulted from a crazed political and sociological experiment,"[62] and the regime's main role was to not wake people "up from their dream world of material affluence and strictly contained anxiety."[63]

That is classic Marxism, in the midst of a crime fiction novel with obvious dialectical aspirations. Wahlöö was an organized Communist at the time, so his heroes were not only Marx, but also names such as Lenin and Stalin. The prevailing maxim was the much quoted one from Lenin: "Without revolutionary theory, no revolutionary practice." According to Althusser, this means that only a correct understanding of Marx's theory can result in successful action.[64]

These political and philosophical preferences of Wahlöö have never been clearer than in *The Steel Spring*. It is one of the few crime novels (in Sweden, a straight bourgeois genre at the time) with instant dialectical aspirations from this age, and the collective class struggle (rather than the desperate individual outbursts of violence as ideological struggle in Sjöwall-Wahlöö's later novels) and the theories of Lenin seem to foreground the narrative.

So let's stop here for a moment in order to explain the complex and very often (mis)used term *dialectics*, according to Marxist theory. The German philosopher Peter Sloterdijk has, cynically enough, called it "The dream of a productive contradiction that everywhere moves through thesis and antithesis to higher syntheses."[65] The origins of Marxian dialectics as a concept, or an ontological method, came from the German nineteenth-century philosopher Hegel, and consisted of a model where one put arguments against each other in the order of *thesis—antithesis → synthesis*, displaying the contradictions and antagonisms that drive development further. The result should be new knowledge or historical progress. Hence, dialectics is the Marxist method for social progression within a society. Marx, on the other hand, used this concept as a way to see the contradictory elements *within* a certain situation or a process. Or, in the words of David Held, "What distinguishes the dialectical method is its recognition of the insufficiencies and imperfections of 'finished' systems of thought. The dialectical method is a critical method for it reveals incompleteness where completeness is claimed."[66] Ironically enough, later Engels and other Marxists developed this into dogmas that changed the original concept into one sterling philosophy called *Dialectical Materialism*, especially used within Soviet-Marxism.

Returning to the novel *The Steel Spring*, Marxist aesthetic criticism has traditionally proceeded along two separate lines, Martin Jay suggests. The first line is the Leninist *Tendenzliteratur* (partisan literature), deriving from the writings of Lenin, codified by Stalin's head of information, Andrei Zhdanov, which finds merit only in those works displaying unabashed political partisanship, a literature conceived in combat with aesthetic formalism around the turn of the century which later culminated in the sterile orthodoxy of Stalinist social realism.[67] This line is partly conducted by Wahlöö in *The Steel Spring*. The second line follows the lead from Engels who valued art less by the political intentions of its creator than by its inherent social significance.[68] The texts of Sjöwall-Wahlöö could be seen as a combination of the two, since their explicit idea was to sneak in political messages *within* a construction of a popular genre. However, this is not the case with *The Steel Spring*, hence its more prevalent political conclusion, especially concerning the revolutionary narrative. As a contextual curiosity, the novel was released about a month prior to the great election of 1968, when Wahlöö still was a member of the Communist Party. In one key scene, Jensen meets the radical "police doctor," a stern communist that most certainly speaks with the voice of Wahlöö himself. In one moment, this person explains to Jensen why the leftist movement hates the police, why it has to be replaced, and what a revolutionary situation is:

> The police do have to exist, of course, but your form of police has always been a willing tool of capitalism and the plutocratic ruling class. The police are too indoctrinated by

those ideas to be open to reform. It's the same with the military. Even a socialist society needs police and armed forces, however. Socialist police and socialist armed forces, to be more precise. And that's why the old organisations need to be eradicated and replaced with new ones. So that's why I don't like you. On principle.... Once the reactionary forms of the police and military stop functioning for some reason, something happens which is known in the jargon as a revolutionary situation. Somebody has now been kind enough to wipe out the police and the military. We assume it happened unintentionally, and the forms taken by the process were disgusting. Not even the minority among us that went on most eagerly and rabidly about creating a revolutionary situation can be feeling particularly satisfied or delighted.[69]

This paragraph contains at least two ingredients that I will explain with the help of Alan Wald's concept "Marxist Noir": Marxism and the role of the police as a gatekeeper and preserving force in a capitalist society.

In one famous article, Lenin explains his conception of *a revolutionary situation*, which is somewhat similar to the idea of Wahlöö:

The colossal superiority of the Russian strikes over those in the European countries, the most advanced countries, demonstrates, not the special qualities or special abilities of Russia's workers, but the *special* conditions in present-day Russia, the existence of a revolutionary situation, the growth of a directly revolutionary crisis. When the moment of a similar growth of revolution approaches in Europe (there it will be a socialist and not a bourgeois-democratic revolution, as in our country), the proletariat of the most developed capitalist countries will launch far more vigorous revolutionary strikes, demonstrations, and armed struggle against the defenders of wage-slavery.[70]

And he continues further:

Russia is experiencing a revolutionary situation because the oppression of the vast majority of the population—not only of the proletariat but of nine-tenths of the small producers, particularly the peasants—has intensified to the maximum, and this intensified oppression, starvation, poverty, lack of rights, humiliation of the people is, furthermore, glaringly inconsistent with the state of Russia's productive forces, inconsistent with the level of the class consciousness and the demands of the masses roused by the year 1905, and inconsistent with the state of affairs in all neighbouring not only European but Asian—countries.[71]

Wahlöö's version of the revolutionary scenario espouses from the ideas of Lenin, whose theories on the difference between revolution and evolution opposed the orthodox German Marxist Karl Kautsky. Engels and Kautsky, arguably the first Marxists, stressed the continuous process of progress, an historical evolution, and Lenin asked himself whether there was a place for the revolution at all in this scheme. All change consists of a progressive struggle between opposite forces (dialectics, as I have explained above), and sometimes this struggle also results in radical changes—hence, the revolution. In Russia, the revolutionary situation of February–October 1917 was one of those radical changes in history, when the Bolsheviks skillfully used the political vacuum to seize power.[72] According to Lenin's transition theory, the revolution is a leap, from capitalism to communism, where the leap itself becomes a stage of its own, a phase, in the chain of transition.[73]

In *The Steel Spring* it is also clear that Lenin's idea of the avant-garde, as expounded in his book *What Is to Be Done?* (1902), is predominant since it is *the doctors* that seize power in the political vacuum that is created in the epidemic situation, putting all police, military, and politicians out of play. This is one of the very foundations in Lenin's revolutionary theory—that the revolution should be initiated and controlled by a certain group of intellectuals, a political *avant-garde*, rather than obsolete and populistic obscure strata such as "the proletariat," "the people" or "the working class." Lenin's idea is therefore controversial, and very far from Marx's own notion of the revolution as something created and carried out by the working class themselves: "All previous historical movements were movements of minorities, or in the interest of minorities," Marx and Engels state in *The Communist Manifesto* (1848), and go on: "The proletarian movement is the self-conscious, independent movement of the immense majority, in the interest of the immense majority. The proletariat, the lowest stratum of our present society, cannot stir, cannot raise itself up, without the whole superincumbent strata of official society being sprung into the air."[74]

However, Lenin's theory was adapted specifically for the Russian situation, where many radical intellectuals lived in isolated enclaves in Western Europe, while the people lived under the dictatorship of the Czar. Marxism for Lenin was articulated as a finished tenacious party theory, a teleological process, that saw the theories of Marx as an absolute truth.[75] For the revolutionary characters in *The Steel Spring*, this theory is being put into practice and turns into the beginning of a dialectical liberation process that is far from finished. The final words of the novel, a short dialogue between Jensen and the police doctor, suggest that this process probably won't be easy:

> And now you're going to socialise this society of ours?"
> "You can bet your bloody life I am, Jensen. And it's not going to be easy. Plenty of bad thoughts are going to be thought."[76]

What Wahlöö is displaying in *The Steel Spring* is by far the perfect crime, a juncture in history, on the brink of a communist revolution, with a professional detective/cop as protagonist, using his deductive skills to enlighten the readers in revolutionary theory and practice. We are witnessing a world on the verge of its own extinction with technology in the center, referring to real historical events such as the Cuban Missile Crisis and the controversies of nuclear power and chemical warfare in Vietnam as thematic backdrops. *The Steel Spring* can be seen as both a science fiction novel (with its dystopian, slightly futuristic setting) and as a crime novel (a cop as protagonist, a mystery to solve) but one thing is for certain: it constitutes the peak of 1960s Swedish

Marxist Noir, and the ideas imbued into the narrative are the very fundament of the renewal of the Swedish crime novel as commenced by the writing team Sjöwall-Wahlöö.

During this period, sexuality was increasingly connected to politics. Free sexuality turned into dreams and political ideas of emancipation, and, of course, Marxism was a crucial tool for this liberation process. We are now going to have a look at some examples of that in the Marxist Noir of Sjöwall-Wahlöö.

The Sexual Revolution

In the beginning of the 1960s, sexual topics gained increasing importance in Swedish public debate.[77] Controversial issues like sex education in schools, the deregulation of pornography and abortion, and youngsters'—perhaps especially young women's—right to their own sexuality were discussed in newspapers, books, on the radio, and on television around 1962 when Wahlöö was writing his books. In the mid-1960s, this debate suddenly stopped when the Marxist turn gained a larger interest in issues such as the Vietnam War and class struggle.[78]

Many of the characters we meet in the Beck novels are individuals convinced of the importance of Marxist thinking. The themes of sexuality and the political awareness of Wahlöö are strongly linked together. In fact, there is a clear connection between sex-drive and political awareness in the Beck series that stretches back to the early novels of Per Wahlöö. In Wahlöö's novels, sexually liberated women become the representation of political (think Marxist) awareness that initiate male characters into revolutionary thought—for example, Siglinde Pedersen in *A Necessary Action* (*Lastbilen* [1962]).[79] It is the story of Willy Mohr, an outcast German artist, drifter and former soldier, who has fled the destruction of post-war Germany to the sunny paradise of the Spanish Balearic Islands. He becomes a part of the Bohemian atmosphere amongst Scandinavian artists in a small *puerto* during the 1950s, just before the dawn of mass tourism, but all the time the fascist dictatorship is closing in on Mohr. When a Norwegian couple, of which Siglinde Pedersen is the woman, gets murdered by two Spanish fishermen, Mohr turns into an avenger and the Spanish Guardia Civil pulls him in and interrogates him at length.

Siglinde Pedersen possesses "an immediate attractiveness, which appeared shallow and which made people think of sexuality ... in this phantom world of suppressed emotions."[80] Her naked body stays in the mind of protagonist Willy Mohr and awakens his revolutionary thinking.[81]

The same kind of awakening comes to Manuel Ortega in *The Assignment*

(*Uppdraget* [1963]), who is initially working as a foreign diplomat in Sweden and then goes back to his own country and sees the oppression of native citizens and a police state that is waging war against a communist rebel movement.

When Ortega meets mysterious secretary Danica Rodríguez, he suddenly starts to think about sexual issues: "Why have I begun to think about these things so much?"[82] He starts thinking of her body: "When she walked away he stared at the thighs and hips. Earlier he had tried to decide whether she was wearing a bra but had been unable to come to any conclusion."[83] Finally, Ortega has sex with her at the same time that she opens his eyes to the oppression of poor people in the country where they live.

It is likely that Danica Rodríguez is some kind of ideal woman in Wahlöö's gallery—politically conscious, sexually explicit—but as a bearer of ideological enlightenment and sexual awakening. Or even more clearly expressed: Danica could be seen as the embodied revolution, and Ortega, who is a highly regarded diplomat, is a part of the bourgeois ruling class, whose hegemony and ownership of the means of production in society gets exposed by Danica's sexual Marxism.[84]

Another of Wahlöö's white-collar workers in a totalitarian state—just like Ortega—is Inspector Jensen, the prototype for Beck. In *Murder on the Thirty-First Floor*, he meets a sexually liberated woman opposing the repressive Orwellian society of the novel who reminds him of "women in pictures from the old days."[85] In the sequel, *The Steel Spring*, Jensen finally meets a nurse when he is at a hospital in the Soviet Union. This nurse resembles communist heroine Danica Rodríguez from *The Assignment* and *The Generals* (*Generalerna* [1965]). The nurse has the same effect on Jensen as Danica has on Ortega: "She did not smoke or use any cosmetics, but she sometimes smelt of soap."[86] He starts thinking about the nurse in sexual terms, a phenomenon, as in the case of Ortega, that is completely new to him: "He could not remember ever having thought anything like that before."[87] This newly awakened sexual awareness breaks through what Marcuse refers to as the repressive desublimation associated with a totalitarian society, and, upon his return to Sweden, Jensen's thoughts turn to politics as he witnesses a full-scale communist revolution.

Yet, somewhere in the Beck series, this sexual motif changes. In *The Laughing Policeman*, sexuality is associated with oppression rather than freedom and, at this point, sexuality becomes a commodity associated with the sex industries of prostitution and pornography. In this fourth installment of Sjöwall-Wahlöö, Beck and his colleagues investigate a mass murder on a bus. The man behind the massacre has also murdered a girl some 16 years earlier, and the crime has strong sexual implications.

In his analysis of *The Laughing Policeman*, Tapper concludes that, concerning the initial spectacular mass murder on the bus, there is "a parallel between two death machines in the eyes of Sjöwall and Wahlöö—the United States and the Swedish welfare state."[88] The killer is no longer a product of conformity that suddenly explodes in violence, like Folke Bengtsson in *Roseanna*, but instead the murderer Björn Forsberg in *The Laughing Policeman* is an incarnation of capitalism that soon gets the full brunt of Sjöwall-Wahlöö's criticism. Tapper sees this novel as a "transition between the Freudian implications of the earlier novels and the Marxist subtext of the later ones."[89]

What is interesting for us here is, of course, the female victim Teresa Camarão, a Portuguese immigrant with an explicit sexual appetite. She is one of Wahlöö's many literary nymphomaniacs, standing in the long line of Wahlöö's earlier sexually liberated women—and murder victims, Siglinde Pedersen in *A Necessary Action*, Roseanna McGraw in *Roseanna*, Danica Rodríguez in *The Assignment* and *The Generals*, Sigbrit Mård in *Cop Killer*, and in the final novel, *The Terrorists*, this kind of woman exists in Kristina Hellström (who does not get murdered but is transformed into a soulless drug-addict by a vicious porn-producer). An aspect that Tapper and other scholars have overlooked is that these women are all the very opposite of what kills them: the male patriarchal hegemony of fascist Spain and Portugal, American capitalism and the conformist welfare state Sweden. The killers, in turn, represent the conformity of the welfare state, brutal fascism or American capitalism and greed.

Marcuse's repressive desublimation takes over, and, in the late novels of Sjöwall-Wahlöö, pornography and capitalism become synonymous with rape and crimes against humanity. This change may be partly attributed to the Vietnam War, which exercised a profound influence on Swedish public debate in the mid–1960s, with the result that the New Left's interest in sexual issues became marginalized. In fact, the New Left often criticized early sex liberals for paving the way for the commercialization of sexuality.[90] Sjöwall-Wahlöö's most obvious response to this perception can be found in *The Terrorists* with its porn-film producer-villain.

According to Marxist theory, the individual is always under pressure from the socioeconomic conditions of society, conditions that will subdue the power of the working classes if they do not organize and take charge of the means of production.[91] Wahlöö's nurses, appearing in several of his novels—not just in the Beck series but also in his Marxist Noir thriller *The Steel Spring*—are often symbols of vibrant womanhood, freedom, and healthy sexuality. They become the perfect representation of the classic Marxist enlightened proletarian that consciously sees through the dark cloak of capitalist repressive desublimation, as outlined by Marcuse.

Dawn Keetley engages with this very important theme, positing that the image of the nymphomaniac embodies a "formlessness and disorder," not even fitting into the writers' carefully constructed social determinism in the Swedish class system: "Women's bodies thus constitute the blind spot of Sjöwall and Wahlöö's trademark political critique."[92] It is nonetheless possible to argue that the notion of sexuality in Sjöwall-Wahlöö's work is even more complicated than Keetley suggests.

Sexuality as the symbol of freedom and liberation has a long tradition in the novels of Per Wahlöö, dating back to the early 1960s, as we have seen. Contrary to many critics, both Keetley and Tapper have established that the early Beck novels are not, as was previously thought, apolitical.[93] In his analysis of *Roseanna*, for example, Tapper reads the corpse of Roseanna McGraw, pulled from the muddy water, as a representation of pornography, violence against women, and sexual murders—in fact, as everything that has been hidden and denied within the Swedish Social-Democratic welfare state.[94] Tapper also talks about mass culture—imported American pulp cinema and violent comics—as the inspiration for Folke Bengtsson's crimes as they constitute the voice calling into his empty soul. Behind such artifacts of mass culture, there are perverse social structures making the killer a litmus test for all the wars in the world, most notably the Vietnam War raging at the time. Bengtsson or, for that matter, Ingemund Fransson in *The Man on the Balcony* (1967), thus becomes the ultimate expression of a repressive and alienated normality.[95]

Keetley, on the other hand, talks about *women's bodies* in crime fiction as "the inexplicable cause, of men's crimes, embodying the 'natural' and uncontrollable impulses of both themselves and others."[96] This is something an attentive reader may recognize from the novels of Raymond Chandler, perhaps most explicitly in *The Big Sleep*, where sexually driven women (think the Sternwood daughters) set the plot in motion. It is, in fact, entirely probable that the figure of the nymphomaniac in Sjöwall-Wahlöö is transferred from Chandler, who was a central influence on Wahlöö in the 1960s.

The intellectual historian Lena Lennerhed notes that the Swedish sexual liberalism of the 1960s represented a "stand for the freedom of the individual."[97] The demands for free abortion, free access to pornography, less judgmental sex education in schools, and greater tolerance toward alternative sexualities was, she argues, important for the young generation during the first half of the 1960s.[98] Lennerhed concludes that Alfred Kinsey became a central character in the Swedish sexual debate when he asserted that "[m]en with an active sex life were … also more active on the whole"—a statement that challenged the psychoanalytic perspective of Freud who thought *sexual abstinence* would lead to greater intellectual activity.[99]

Marcuse, just like Kinsey, stresses the connection between sexuality and freedom. In *Eros and Civilization* (1955), for example, Marcuse argues that sexuality can create highly civilized human relations—the goal of his new post-revolutionary society where lasting erotic relations between conscious, mature individuals is central. Sexuality would then be integrated into the order of work and play.[100] "The sex instincts are *life* instincts," says Marcuse in *Eros and Civilization* and further argues that the struggle for existence is a struggle for pleasure.[101]

Reading the novels of Wahlöö (and Sjöwall-Wahlöö) through the lens of Marcuse thus explains the link between the often virile sexuality of Wahlöö's heroes and their leftist political radicalism. The sexual liberation theme, however, as previously mentioned, fades away in the later novels and is replaced with a more Marxist critique of the commodification of sexuality.

Keetley mentions "men's perceived loss of power" as the root of the serial murders in the early Beck series.[102] That might well be the case, but sexuality as the negation of dictatorship and patriarchal fascism is the one clear thread working its way through every book Wahlöö has ever written. Marcuse writes of the proletarian in the early stages of capitalism as "the living denial of his society."[103] Such sentiments accord with Wahlöö's views, not just of nurses and sexually liberated women, but also with his and Maj Sjöwall's misunderstood revolutionary killers, who will be analyzed in the next section along with the perhaps most important and defining issue of Sjöwall-Wahlöö and Swedish Marxist Noir: class.

The Renewal of the Swedish Crime Novel

In his consideration of the question of class consciousness in both American and Swedish society, J. Kenneth Van Dover has made an interesting parallel between Chandler's *The Big Sleep* and Sjöwall-Wahlöö's *Murder at the Savoy* (1970).[104] In the first chapters of *The Big Sleep*, Philip Marlowe is entering the mansion of General Sternwood, watching the upper class people and how they live:

> There were French doors at the back of the hall, beyond them a wide sweep of emerald grass to a white garage, in front of which a slim dark young chauffeur in shiny black leggings was dusting a maroon Packard convertible. Beyond the garage were some decorative trees trimmed as carefully as poodle dogs. Beyond them a large greenhouse with a domed roof. Then more trees and beyond everything the solid, uneven, comfortable line of the foothills.... We went out at the French doors and along a smooth red-flagged path that skirted the far side of the lawn from the garage. The boyish-looking chauffeur had a big black and chromium sedan out now and was dusting that. The path took us along to the side of the greenhouse and the butler opened a door for me and stood aside.[105]

Almost the exact same scene—obviously a homage—is depicted by Sjöwall-Wahlöö in their novel when an eccentric working-class detective,

Månsson, is entering the secret garden of the rich, watching a widow sunbathing in the nude, living the hedonistic lifestyle after her husband has been murdered.

> Månsson walked across the grass under the trees in the direction of the house. This took him between rows of blooming laburnum and jasmine and, as calculated, brought him to the back of the house, which was quiet and deserted, with closed windows, kitchen and cellar stairs, and various mysterious adjoining buildings. He looked up at the house but couldn't see much of it, since he was far too close. He followed the path to the right, climbed over a flower bed, peeked around the corner and stood stock-still among the showy peonies. The scenery was breathtaking in several respects. The lawn was very large and green, as well as an English golf course. In the middle was a kidney-shaped swimming pool lined with light blue tile, with clear green, shimmering water ... at the edge of the pool, Charlotte Palmgren was sitting, or rather, lying, naked, her eyes closed.[106]

Philip Marlowe, like Per Månsson in *Murder at the Savoy*, is a working man with a strong distaste for the idle upper class, Van Dover argues. But Marlowe is willing to engage with them as fellow human beings with their own desires and frustrations, while Månsson, by contrast, never even wavers from his uncompromising contempt for the lifestyles, the homes, and even the bodies of the rich.[107]

Sjöwall-Wahlöö made a similar homage, but slightly more discreetly, in the next Beck novel, *The Abominable Man* (1971), when Martin Beck is sitting at the kitchen table in the sparse apartment of the old-time policeman Hult in Chapter 13. In an interview, Maj Sjöwall confessed their theft of the scene: "we did something nobody has noticed. What Hult says about the police profession is a pure theft from Raymond Chandler's *The Little Sister*. The passage about when he comes home and sits down to eat while the corpse maggots are falling out of his sleeves is there. It is an homage to Chandler. He was a favorite writer."[108]

These examples show Sjöwall-Wahlöö's great inspiration from Anglo-Saxon authors, most notably writers such as Raymond Chandler, Julian Symons, Ross Macdonald, Patricia Highsmith, Hillary Waugh, John Creasy, Bill S. Ballinger, and Evan Hunter (Ed McBain). According to Sjöwall-Wahlöö, those writers got new readers to explore the crime fiction genre in the 1960s and 70s.[109]

In Sjöwall-Wahlöö's fifth novel *The Fire Engine That Disappeared* (1969), they even develop their protagonist Martin Beck in surprising directions. Idiosyncrasies such as constructing model ships or reading Raymond Chandler round out his character. In a typical domestic loner sequence, this could be witnessed:

> For dinner he ate cold meatballs, fish roe and camembert on pumpernickel bread, and he drank two beers. He also drank some coffee and cognac and watched an old Amer-

ican gangster film on television. Then he got his bed ready and lay in the bathtub reading Raymond Chandler's *The Lady in the Lake*, every now and again taking a sip of cognac which he had placed within reach on the toilet seat.[110]

But Sjöwall-Wahlöö did not only read crime fiction to create their works. A thorough check of their private library, saved for scholars in Sweden by the Swedish Crime Fiction Academy, exposes a surprisingly varying collection of non-fiction, often scholarly literature in the English language on different subjects. A couple of samples are William Camp's documentary novel *Night Beat* (1968), with its criticism of how police forces act in racially discriminated neighborhoods. That book could easily have inspired Sjöwall-Wahlöö's plot in *Cop Killer*. Truman Capote's *In Cold Blood* (1965) is a landmark in documentary crime writing and was read by Sjöwall-Wahlöö. The leftwing author Nelson Algren's *Chicago. City on the Make* (1961) is a documentary about the tougher side of the Windy City; George E. Berkeley's *The Democratic Policeman* (1969) was sent to Sjöwall-Wahlöö by their agent for a check-up; Donald R. Cressey's *Theft of the Nation* (1969) is an incriminating study of the structure and operations of organized crime in America. Sjöwall-Wahlöö only touched on organized crime a couple of times in their writing, most notably in *The Fire Engine That Disappeared*, released the same year as Cressey's book. Richard Krafft-Ebing's groundbreaking book *The Sexual Offender* also had its place on Sjöwall-Wahlöö's bookshelf, and at that time it was probably obligatory reading for every crime fiction writer. The book was a popularized version of the work *Psychopathia Sexualis*, the case studies of Krafft-Ebing concerning things such as the force of sexual instinct, facts of physiological fetishism, sexual perversions in seniles due to impotency or dementia, lust murder, sexual bondage, symbolic sadism, satyriasis, and nymphomania. These notions appeared in several of Sjöwall-Wahlöö's novels, most notably in *Roseanna*, *The Man on the Balcony*, and *The Laughing Policeman* where sexual issues are foregrounded in the plot. There are also more pulp-like books such as Phil Hirsch's (ed.) *The Law Enforcers* (1969), with its cheap paperback slogans on the back cover: "They are the men who stand between you and the killers, thieves and con men of every description who stalk the streets of your city.... They are the men who face death every day to guard your property and your life.... They are ... THE LAW ENFORCERS."[111] Sjöwall-Wahlöö's interest in organized crime showed itself in Ed Reid and Ovid Demaris' classic *The Green Felt Jungle* (1960), where the authors expose the gangsterism and corruption in Las Vegas below imaginative chapter headlines such as "Dawn of the Golden Age," "The Temples of Mammon," "Hoffa's Fountain of Pension Juice," "Sex for Sale," "Politicians for Hire," and "Jungle Warfare, Las Vegas Style." They also owned criminology literature such as William Prendergast's *Crime Scene* (1969), with stories on crime in Liverpool, and perhaps the most classic book of them all, Jürgen Thorwald's gigantic

Das Jahrhundert der Detektive: Weg und Abenteuer der Kriminalistik (1964), and his *The Marks of Cain* (1964) on the detection of crime from fingerprints and bullets.

As we have seen, Sjöwall-Wahlöö also read what we today would label True Crime, and not only Truman Capote, but also Brad Steiger's unsettling documentary *The Mass Murderer* (1967) about some of America's worst killers such as Charles Whitman, Richard Speck, Howard Unruh, Earle Nelson, Ernie Ingenito, Charles Starkweather, William Cook, Melvin Davis Rees, and Magdalena Solis. Whitman's shootings at the University of Texas in Austin in 1966 are easy to connect to the bus massacre in the beginning of *The Laughing Policeman*. Ingenito and Unruh were both avengers in retaliation for accumulated injustices and insults—real or imaginary, but still tenacious and violent. In some novels of Sjöwall-Wahlöö, criminals such as these are described as involuntary revolutionaries. They also read classic true crime books such as Gerold Frank's *The Boston Strangler* (1967) and Ludovic Kennedy's *Ten Rillington Place* (1961), both filmed (in 1968 and 1971, respectively) by director Richard Fleischer. A commercial poster for the film *Ten Rillington Place*, starring Richard Attenborough, actually appears in Chapter 10 of Sjöwall-Wahlöö's *The Abominable Man*.

The renewal of the Swedish crime novel was built not only on fiction, as you can see, but also on influences from scholarly literature, documentary books, true crime, and movies of the 1960s.

Van Dover argues that *The Fire Engine That Disappeared* marked something of a pause in the ideological advancement of the Beck series. However, he also stresses some social issues in the novel that arouse Sjöwall-Wahlöö, such as the pollution in the Swedish capital ("Stockholm has the most polluted city air in the whole of northern Europe"), the welfare system, riot control, and the Greek colonels.[112]

The American influence is evident in Sjöwall-Wahlöö's novels. In their first novel *Roseanna*, Roseanna McGraw is the only non–Swedish victim in the entire Beck series, which Van Dover notes as he discusses the fact that it could be a tribute to the American source of the police procedural genre. His further arguments deserve a quote:

> The humorous but efficient Lt. Kafka would not be out of place in Ed McBain's Eighty-Seventh Precinct. More important, just as the final Beck novel matches *Roseanna*, in duration, it also contains a major American presence, although of a quite different nature. And the victim in the last novel is the quintessential Swede, the Prime Minister. The progression is significant: the first victim is from outside the nation; the last one is from its center.[113]

In later novels, such as *Murder at the Savoy* and *The Abominable Man*, Sjöwall-Wahlöö's revolutionary art of the crime procedural culminates. The plot of detection, the police work, and the social criticism of the narrative are all integrated to reach their most effective balance in these two novels.[114] The stories were also published during one of the most political and radical times of Swedish society. The leftist political environment permeated the entire discourse and debate, and the time around 1970 has been called *the Leninist turn*. This is when Marxist critique turned into Leninist and Maoist divergence in the New Left. Sjöwall-Wahlöö left the political life (they had been members of the Communist Party since 1965) at this time and moved from Stockholm to Malmö, in the south of Sweden.

Class antagonism operates in novels such as *Murder at the Savoy, The Abominable Man, The Locked Room* (1972), *Cop Killer* (1974), and *The Terrorists* (1975). The killers in these instances represent the dispossessed, the outcasts that Marcuse is referring to when he mentions the bearers of the new revolutionary consciousness in late capitalist society, the disaffected former workers and non-workers, the oppressed blacks in America and in the colonies who act consciously or unconsciously to subvert the established order.

This became the new paradigm and what is referred to as "the criminal as victim" formula, which is a reversal of the old recipe for a crime fiction novel, where the criminal was an evil outcast that deserved the abhorrence of the bourgeois society and its citizens—the widespread middle-class. According to Marx, the criminal broke up the monotony and the safety of the bourgeois life, and this is, of course, something that Sjöwall-Wahlöö were well aware of.[115] In this sense, these characters (the criminals) also became revolutionaries in this brave new world where alienation, increased market capitalism, and a grave impact from the culture industry were topics that writers such as Sjöwall-Wahlöö wanted to stress in their mysteries. Basically it is the negative thinking from Hegel, via Marxists such as Adorno and Marcuse, put into crime fiction stories where every being expresses the dynamic unity of reality, that is the dynamic unity of opposites, the result of antagonistic conditions.[116] Critical theorists such as Marcuse used this method, via Marx, to explain how human individuals become what they are through the labor process, "man's act of self-creation," where the individual is struggling to fulfill anticipated needs. Private property is a negation to man's true nature, Marx said, and this was the doctrine Sjöwall-Wahlöö followed in their most revolutionary novels.[117] That is why their heroes—and criminals—are young girls living an alternative life (Rebecka Lind in *The Terrorists* and Monita in *The Locked Room*), scorned members of the working class (Bertil Svensson in *Murder at the Savoy*, Sture Hellström in *The Terrorists*), bitter ex-cops (Åke Eriksson in *The Abominable Man*), and young thugs (Krister and Ronnie Kaspersson in *Cop Killer*).

Perhaps Bertil Svensson in *Savoy* is the cardinal example of this type of criminal/victim, when he becomes conscious, realizing that his life isn't just filled with hard luck, but that he's been unjustly treated by the rich man Viktor Palmgren, or even a social group (i.e., the upper-class).[118]

> After he'd been evicted, forced to move, laid off from work and finally divorced, he would sit in his lonely room in Malmö thinking over his situation. It became clearer and clearer to him who was the cause of all his troubles: Viktor Palmgren, the bloodsucker, who lined his purse at the expense of other human beings, the big shot, who didn't give a damn about the welfare of his employees or tenants.[119]

By contrast, one should remember the corpus of Sjöwall-Wahlöö's first novels, where criminals display a more complicated political pattern, as loners and outcasts, and might more easily be mistaken for crooks from the old conservative detective story, where the criminal was an evil loner: the alienated women-hating molester Folke Bengtsson in *Roseanna*, slayer drunk Hans Gunnarsson in *The Man Who Went Up in Smoke*, child serial killer and pedophile (also alienated) Ingemund Fransson in *The Man on the Balcony*, the fascist-capitalist mass murderer Björn Forsberg in *The Laughing Policeman*, and drug dealers/gangsters such as Bertil Olofsson, Göran Malm, Max Karlsson, and Alfonse Lasalle in *The Fire Engine That Disappeared*.

Likewise, class issues also operate within the new centralized police organization, which has been pointed out by Pepper, quoting Eddy Von Mueller as he points out that law enforcement in the procedural mode (where police officers are investigating crimes according to legal regulations, such as Beck and his colleagues) "is an industrialized process ... there is a complex division of labor, marked by professional hierarchies and specialized training ... and like many industrial labourers, police officers are often alienated, both from their constituency (the public they are expected to 'serve and protect') and their ostensible masters."[120]

Finally, Søholm, author of the earliest and to date most extensive study on Sjöwall-Wahlöö, has identified four arguments for why the writers have chosen the police procedural genre in the first place: First, the criminals of the crime novel always appear in a coherent social context, and in relation to other humans. Second, the plot makes room for conflict—often triggered by a murder—which opens up the possibility of identification and analysis of causes. Third, in the crime genre the literature of the early 1960s had paved the way for objective and psychological realism. And fourth, the crime novel was a possible shortcut to a larger audience.[121]

Furthermore, Søholm states that Sjöwall-Wahlöö, in this, created an entirely new genre: social crime fiction (*samfundskrimien*), a new kind of literature where acts of crime are a part of the medium for a critical social depiction.[122] No scholar has yet called the works of Sjöwall-Wahlöö *Marxist Noir*, but essentially that is exactly what Søholm is talking about in his study. According to Søholm, a grand part of the work's strength lies in the precise description of the guilty system.[123]

Pepper makes a similar distinction that coheres with the basic elements for a Marxist Noir as he stresses Sjöwall-Wahlöö's use of a popular literary form which is anchored in a recognizable social reality "where the effects of capitalism as a mode of social organization are readily apparent."[124]

Towards a Swedish Marxist Noir

The Chandler legacy was picked up by Swedish writer Per Wahlöö in the 1960s when he had his reckoning with the old, dusty, bourgeois detective novel, and at the same time launched a renewal of the crime fiction genre in Sweden with international influences. The springboard is Wahlöö's novel *Murder on the Thirty-First Floor*, with its criticism of monopoly capitalism and the fall of the welfare state. A criticism against the Social Democratic government—from the left—is at the very center of Wahlöö's artistic evolution, where the hardboiled prose of his social fiction slowly peels off the mask of the power complex behind the Accord between the government and the capitalists. The novel interprets the contemporary time of the 1960s, on the verge of a Marxist turn, and displays a Marxian world with alienation and reification, where the increasing influence of capital, commodification, and industrial production exerts a commanding force on every single individual. But it was not until the sequel to *Murder on Thirty-First Floor* that Wahlöö really took Marxist Noir further, into the dialectics of crime fiction in *The Steel Spring*. That is a rare novel which presents the utopian image of the alternative to capitalist society: the communist revolution. As we shall see this is a crucial novel, and a landmark for Swedish Marxist Noir.

The detective novel should represent a moral truth, Van Dover states, and this moral truth should consist of a redefinition of traditional concepts such as innocence and guilt in the new societal context of the 1960s. The conservative ethic of the old whodunnits of the 1940s and 50s is transformed by Wahlöö, (and later on by Sjöwall-Wahlöö) into a revolutionary ethic—an inversion of the conventional formula where the perpetrator is the true victim, a killer not completely responsible for his misdeeds. This individual is not the representation of evil in the novels of Sjöwall-Wahlöö; instead, the true evil lies in a corrupt social structure—the police force, the big corporations, the government—which must be fundamentally altered by revolutionary thinking and action.[125]

This new formula basically changed the Swedish crime fiction novel forever, and scholars call it the *paradigm* for the genre in Sweden in the decades that follow.[126] When comparing the old detective story to the new procedural, they are in many ways obvious opposites of one another, forming a Marxian dialectic of capitalist modernity that resembles the very simple model as displayed by Therborn:

Advance	Contradiction/Conflict
Individualization	Atomization, alienation
Productivity development	Exploitation and distributive polarization
	Outgrowing existing relations of production
Capitalist extension	Proletarian unification and strengthening
Globalization	Anti-imperialist revolts.[127]

Some of these dialectical opposites—dichotomies—are presented below as I have identified them in the evolution from *then* to *now*, from old bourgeois detective novel to modern crime fiction:

Old Crime Novel (up to 1965)	New Crime Novel (from 1965)
Bourgeois (conserving)	Social-critical
Non-dialectical (static)	Dialectical
Introspective	Extrovert
Regional/Local	Global
National	International
Amateurism	Professionalism
Fantasy	Realism
Puzzle intrigue	Logical structure
Classlessness	Class distinction
Isolated setting	Varied setting
Unprogressive	Progressive
Non-developing protagonist	Developing protagonist
Focus on intrigue	Focus on social description
Small town	Big city
Slow course of events	Rapid course of events
"Gathering in the library"	Gradual dissolution
The criminal as a deviant	The criminal as a victim
Demonical view on crime	Sociological view on crime
Logic/Intuition—deduction	Science—deduction
Solo-detective (one)	Working-team (several)
Individual as criminal	Society as criminal
Small-scale	Large-scale
Classic literary style	Hardboiled style
Swedish/British	American
Retrospective	Prophetic

Chastity	Sexuality
Crimes against individuals	Crimes against structure
Ethics (good and evil)	Morals (right and wrong)
Idyllic	Decay
Domestic crime (at home)	Organized crime (in society)

In a famous, often quoted article, written by Sjöwall-Wahlöö and published for the first time in 1971 in the Danish daily paper *Politiken*, the crime writing duo have their own exposition on crime fiction and how they define the features of the genre:

> The detective novel written by the older, conventional school, had—and has—a society-preserving and conservative character. The absence of realism, which actually is a deliberate dissociation from reality, makes it the ultimate literature for relaxation. That is why this kind of detective novel carries on being written and read, but in our days often strongly situated in a very localized context. It does not want to disturb the reader or deliver annoying truths and it can also be read with blinkers by people who exclusively regard the literature as a part of the entertainment industry. But that is obviously no reason to disparage these books. They fill a clearly delimited need and the very best of them will always keep their place in the history of literature.[128]

Sjöwall-Wahlöö's view on society was filled with familiar Marxist tenets that created their plots and characters—in a total reverse to the old detective story. The hardboiled procedural—as created by Wahlöö, and later Sjöwall-Wahlöö—is decidedly a leftist genre because of its obvious interest in contemporary reality and what Marcuse and other critical theorists call the "advanced industrial society" and its capitalist mode of production.[129] This process has an economical, industrial, and environmental impact on the individuals in the late capitalist Western world that is an inevitable part of the hardboiled story: air pollution, big corporations getting even bigger, post–Depression crime, alienation, and reification (the production process which reduces social relations and all *things* into commodities). The perspectives of Chandler and Wahlöö are somewhat different from one another, but they both display an image of a Marxian nightmare of history. Marcuse showed that the problems confronting the emerging radical movements were not simply the Vietnam War, racism, colonial oppression or inequality, but *the system itself*. This issue is interwoven in Sjöwall-Wahlöö's novels in the Beck series, where a liberating potential is hidden within the oppressive social system, to paraphrase Marcuse. But the full-blown society of advanced industrial capitalism was in no way finished during Sjöwall-Wahlöö's active time (Wahlöö died in 1975).

The human individual is always central in the entire Sjöwall-Wahlöö series, from the early 1960s to the very end. The structures and social processes that Althusser stresses in his conception of ideology dominate the later novels, although alienation and other aspects of Marcusian theories are predominant in the early novels. At the same time, Sjöwall-Wahlöö's notion of the welfare state in the later novels resembles rightwing ideas from a conservative writer like Roland Huntford and his book *The New Totalitarians* (1971).

Revolutionary theory dominates the later novels with killers like Bertil Svensson and Åke Eriksson, and both Althusser and Marcuse are revolutionary theorists, although their revolutionary subjects are different from each other. Althusser has adopted Lenin's notion of the party elite taking charge of the process, leading the masses into communism. Marcuse mentions the outcasts, the unemployed, and the oppressed people in the colonies as those who need a revolution the most.[130] This idea is probably the one that is most similar to the political agenda in Sjöwall-Wahlöö's writings.

The next Swedish crime writer who would share a similar analysis of the world—a definitely Marxist one—and who hit the international book market during the 1990s was Henning Mankell. When he started writing his Wallander series in 1989, the Swedish decline had begun and the nightmare for Marxists during the 1960s and 70s had become pure reality. The Neoliberal era was here, and it would—in its own irony—make the Swedish Marxist Noir into a worldwide blockbuster phenomenon.

3

The Fall from Grace
Henning Mankell

Fog. It is early October 1993, and the fog is rolling in over the landscape in southern Sweden. The entrance of the fog in the works of Henning Mankell reminds us of the entrance of organized crime, the global dark wave of hooligans rushing in, crossing the border into this lost paradise of welfare politics. The very first word in Mankell's novel *The Man Who Smiled* (1994) actually is "Fog," followed by the haunting words, "A silent, stealthy beast of prey."[1]

The Man Who Smiled is the fourth novel about Mankell's Swedish police hero Kurt Wallander, a lonesome, overweight, middle-aged man stemming from the old Swedish welfare state.

Mankell's overall concern in his ten-novel series on Wallander is the fall from grace and how Sweden has changed in the 1990s, from being a rather isolated but healthy country of equality during the postwar years, to a worn-down state of economic depression, criminality, racism and smashed borders letting Eastern gangsters and European crime take charge of society. He once called these books "novels about the Swedish anxiety" and has emphasized their importance as a mirror of the European and Swedish 1990s and 2000s.[2] A reader of Mankell's novels encounters disparate themes such as racism (*Faceless Killers* [1991]), Russian corruption and its influence in the Baltic countries (*The Dogs of Riga* [1992]), the murderous South African apartheid regime and its fascist stooges (*The White Lioness* [1993]), the neoliberal politics and its eroding effects on the Swedish welfare state (*The Man Who Smiled* [1994]), the forgotten children and immigrants of Sweden (*Sidetracked* [1995]), early examples of third-wave feminist revenge in crime fiction (*The Fifth Woman* [1996]), transgender killers as the Other (*One Step Behind* [1997]), and the weakness of a computerized society (*Firewall* [1998]). These are the central themes of Mankell's Wallander series. In 2002 he released *Before the Frost* with

Wallander's daughter Linda Wallander as the main character, dealing with issues like religious fanatics in the wake of 9/11. Although different publishers released the novel with the series subtitle "A Linda Wallander Mystery," there were no additional stories about Linda Wallander, except on television.[3] In the final novel about Kurt Wallander, *The Troubled Man*, which was released in 2009, the protagonist gets Alzheimer's disease and disappears into the obscure mist of his own mind.

The international theme is always present in the works of Mankell. That is also the case in *The Man Who Smiled*, which puts issues such as illegal organ trade and the impairment of the public economy on the agenda. Mankell, who was a communist in the 1970s, clearly sees the economic decline of capitalism as a question of morals, which is also what makes this novel one of the most compelling in the Wallander series. Its thematic bond to the world of Chandler and Wahlöö is also the most obvious among the novels in the entire Wallander series, as we shall see.

Mankell and the New Left

Henning Mankell was born in Stockholm on February 2, 1948. He had a bourgeois upbringing; his father was a lawyer, but many of his forefathers were musicians. When he was two years old, the family moved to Sveg in northern Sweden, where his father worked as a judge. Mankell himself describes the environment in which he grew up as politically passive, conservative, but still very culturally liberal. So when he wanted to become a writer, his parents accepted his decision without any further ado.[4]

When he was 16 years old, Mankell dropped out of school and got a job as a seaman for two years until he moved to Paris. After a year and a half in the French capital, he moved back to Stockholm and started working in a theater. In 1973 he went to Africa for the first time, and in 1986 he became the artistic leader of Teatro Avenida in Maputo, Mozambique.

His books, over 40 titles through the years, from children's books to crime fiction and novels, have sold in 40 million copies and have been translated into 41 languages. In 2008, Mankell was the ninth best-selling author in the world.[5] He passed away on October 5, 2015, in Gothenburg, after suffering from cancer.

Mankell is a typical leftist writer who stems from the 1968 social movements, where many intellectuals born in the 1940s were engaged in political matters. Mankell was also a part of the Maoist movement, where the works of Chairman Mao Zedong were hailed—widely popular in Sweden during the 1970s. The Maoist approach is sometimes employed in his novels, which mostly take place in the countryside (where the revolution starts, according to Maoist theory). Other theories from the Maoist movement that probably inspired Mankell's novels included the idea that economic progress could never be made at the price of increased class differentiation and reduced solidarity, and the rejection of a political elite (as held by Lenin) taking charge instead of a mass mobilization of the people. Instead, the Maoists focused on the freedom movements in the "third world," mostly Africa and Asia, where the break between the Soviet Union and China was particularly evident, especially in the raging Vietnam War, where the struggle against U.S. imperialism reached its peak.[6]

Mankell even participated in one of the most iconic events of the Swedish 1960s: the occupation of the student union building in Stockholm in May 1968. But he was not one of the big protesters on that occasion; only 19 years old at the time, he worked in the kitchen, washing dirty dishes, while hundreds of students had their glorious revolution—for a couple of hours.[7]

In a 1978 interview, Henning Mankell speaks about his literary style and the age of leftist politics that Sweden was just then leaving behind, which he did not like: "I belong to the privileged generation that learnt from the FNL-movement [the anti–Vietnam War protesters movement]. To start thinking critically and to work politically, that gave more to the mission of writing."[8]

In his novel *The Madman* (*Vettvillingen* [1977]), Mankell has his political reckoning with a post-war Sweden and its cowardly history in relation to Nazi-Germany and the concentration camps for communists in the northern parts of the country. The novel is set in a welfare state where people are supposed to forget, keep quiet, and accept that all the traces and the guilt get swept under the carpet. It is a novel by the communist Mankell, who wrote a similar political novel in 1973, *The Rock Blaster* (*Bergsprängaren*), which is the story of an old worker, a rock blaster called Oskar Johansson, who is a real person from Mankell's own childhood. In the novel, Oskar Johansson recalls his tough life and the Swedish social democracy, a political dream astray in the modern accord, that has betrayed socialist ideology. This feeling changed people sometime during the 1930s or the 1940s, Mankell says in the 1978 interview, and before that "people hadn't yet been pulled up with their roots and transported into the capitalistic production."[9] Statements such as these also came from Sjöwall-Wahlöö, especially during the 1970s.

Pettersson (2010) emphasizes the new experiences Mankell had when he returned to Sweden in 1989 after several years in Mozambique, where he had been working with a theater in the capital Maputo. Back in Sweden, he started to write the first novel in the Wallander series, *Faceless Killers*, which was released in 1991. Mankell's view of the world was quite unchanged from his communist view during the 1970s, when the main notion was that everything crucial (the awakening of revolutionary consciousness, political revolts, etc.) happened in the poor countries in the third world. This view, and Mankell's own experiences, differed greatly from other Swedish writers, and Pettersson suggests that this also had an impact on the huge success following the Wallander novels.[10] Žižek also stresses this view, stating that "Mankell's true achievement: among today's writers, he is a unique artist of the parallax view"—that is to say, the two perspectives, that of the affluent Ystad and that of Maputo.[11]

Mankell worked mainly in a Swedish moral political tradition where writers such as Jan Myrdal, Sara Lidman, Göran Palm, and Sven Lindqvist were the dominating intellectual personas when he started his writing career in the beginning of the 1970s. Things such as solidarity and socialism were both deep moral questions to Mankell. Therefore, the epigraph by nineteenth-century French philosopher Alexis de Tocqueville in *The Man Who Smiled* is not an accidental choice: "It is not so much the sight of immorality of the great that is to be feared as that of immorality leading to greatness."[12] The words come from de Tocqueville's famous work *Democracy in America* (*De la Démocratie en Amérique*, 1835–40), where he warns about the dangers for freedom and individuality created by democratic mass society. This all-powerful bureaucratic organization that de Tocqueville had seen in the United States could be a threat against freedom for all people in society, but on the other hand he did not quite know what form this threat would take.[13] The neoliberal market economy, in the line of Polanyi's worst case scenario, could also be what de Tocqueville's theory leads to. I guess that we can assume that Mankell criticizes what he regards as de Tocqueville's worst case scenario: the state in the service of capital, according to Hegel's notion of the master-slave dialectic.[14]

By using this quote Mankell is, of course, referring to the moral disorder in society as his conception of modern-day society, where neoliberal ideas have struck down like lightning in welfare state Sweden, especially during the 1980s wave of neoliberal politics coming from the U.K. and the U.S. with the emergence of Margaret Thatcher and Ronald Reagan and the ideas of Milton Friedman's economic Chicago School. This market economy is a very nightmare for a socialist such as Mankell, where everything gets reduced into commodities. It is the society a Marxist such as Georg Lukács warned about with his theory of reification. The concept of reification originated from the social process when something a person has made or done is transformed into a commodity and a thing. This has already happened with labor, homes, health care, schools, and culture. Since the dawn of capitalism, this reification process has survived through the transformation of human needs, activities and relations into commodities on a market.

Critical theorists such as Adorno and Horkheimer, who, similar to

Lukács, had studied Marx's *Economic and Philosophical Manuscripts*, talked about the commodification of culture and the appearance of people's productive activity as something strange and alien to them. Lukács' concept of reification, developed in his obscure and mysterious collection of essays, *History and Class Consciousness* (1923), was one of the chief barriers to revolutionary consciousness. Reification permeates all spheres of life; it is not simply a subjective phenomenon, rather it arises from the new industrial productive process.[15] The market is limitless—and as we have seen with Wahlöö, perhaps even Chandler and Steinbeck, and absolutely with Polanyi—this kind of market economy soon collapses into fascism. *The Man Who Smiled* is the story about how Swedish business becomes another huge brick in this global world crime enterprise. Michael Tapper argues that *The Man Who Smiled* is a stepping stone between the threat of foreign invasion (in the first three Wallander novels) and the moral corruption of the decaying welfare state (in the latter ones), a story where neoliberalism has "revealed its true fascist face."[16]

The Collapse of Solidarity

The society gone wrong, turning into fascism, is one dominating notion that both Wahlöö and Mankell—and the entire Marxist-Leninist movement of the 1970s—warns us about. But there is also the return of Hobbes' sinister state of nature lurking in the background—that crime invades our world and soon becomes what Hobbes called the "war of every man against every man," the state of nature that existed before a strong state organization was created. The Hobbesian parallel in its Swedish edition does actually exist in one of the final Wallander novels, *Before the Frost* (2002), where Wallander's colleague Martinson suddenly bursts out:

> Crime has never paid as well as it does today, it seems. I've been researching this. To find an equivalent level of what we may call successful crime you have to look as far back as the fifteenth century, before Gustav Vasa pulled the nation together. In that time, the time of small city states, there was widespread lawlessness and criminality just as there is today. We're not upholding law and order now, we're only in the business of trying to keep the growth of lawlessness from getting any more rapid.[17]

This is exactly the kind of reflection that Wallander himself used to make in his own mind in every novel, stating the fact that Sweden has gone through a fall from grace during the past decades. Going back to Martinson's reference to the old king Gustav Vasa, who created the modern Sweden during the sixteenth century, this is actually the same period of time that Hobbes refers to in his work *Leviathan*, when he talks about the state of nature. In other words, the fear of a lawless land within modern democracy is something that has followed in literature ever since the days of Chandler.

The Man Who Smiled sets off on the sandy shores of the Danish beach resort Skagen, where Wallander wanders around in an alcohol-fueled depression after killing Russian thug-assassin Konovalenko in *The White Lioness* (1993). An old friend looks him up and talks about the suspicious circumstances in which his father has died. Some time later, this friend also turns up dead and Wallander returns to Ystad to investigate what has now become a double murder. Enigmatic big-business tycoon Alfred Harderberg seems to be involved and Wallander is soon on his trail, exposing intricate schemes against the Swedish welfare sector in the county office involving the illegal trade of bodily organs from South America.

Barry Forshaw calls Henning Mankell "the Trojan horse for foreign crime in translation." After the dark wave of Sjöwall-Wahlöö was released in the American and English book markets of the 1970s, Mankell was the first Swedish crime writer in centuries to hit the bookstores in the U.S.[18] Yet Mankell's recipe for his police novels was close to Sjöwall-Wahlöö's: to show the widening cracks of the welfare state and Swedish family life torn to pieces by deep psychological traumas.

Henning Mankell himself once said that the central idea behind his main character Wallander is to show how difficult it is to be a good police officer in a world of change, and that he cannot be a good cop if he does not evolve in the harsh reality in which he lives.[19] One evolution Mankell perhaps had in mind was the gradual inner change of Martin Beck in Sjöwall-Wahlöö's ten-novel series, where Mr. Beck goes from being an indifferent white-collar worker in a huge police organization, what Marcuse would call "a totally administered society," to becoming a conscious individual. That is, the negation to Marcuse's one-dimensional man, who recaptures his freedom and individuality after leaving his bourgeois wife and getting together with a new political aware woman.

This evolution, of course, is central to the entire Wallander series, and *The Man Who Smiled* is perhaps the most important brick in this construction. In this story, the connections from Raymond Chandler all the way up to Per Wahlöö and Sjöwall-Wahlöö tie together in Swedish crime fiction. The mission in all of these writers' novels is to explore and expose how crime has infiltrated the entire structure of society. In Mankell's books, this theory has reached even more complicated structures than in Sjöwall-Wahlöö's.

Michael Tapper has the feeling that Wallander's confrontation with capitalist villain Harderberg at the end, when they have a final word duel on morals and ideology, was snatched right out of a Chandler novel.[20] This is basically true, but the dialogue is more of a contemporary discussion of philosophy where the ruthlessness of Harderberg is exposed to the readers. "Truth,"

Harderberg bursts out, "Does it exist for a Swedish police officer? ... there's no such thing as an absolute truth or an absolute lie. There are just agreements. Agreements that can be entered into, kept or broken."[21] Harderberg's words sound just like the postmodern credo interwoven with some Marxian reification theory, and Nietzschean moral-nihilism, gradually sliding over into pure fascism: "Heathens ... see the highest level of goodness in mental greatness, bodily strength and all the qualities that make human beings frightening. Wise words that I always do my best to live up to."[22] Harderberg's philosophical and historical reference in this case is Italian writer Niccolo Machiavelli, who wrote his controversial work *The Prince* in 1516. In this work, Machiavelli presents an outline of how a despot should act to maintain his reign of terror. One might expect that Harderberg's admiration for Machiavelli could equally apply to a fascist dictator such as Mussolini. Strength, as mentioned in Harderberg's quote above, is one of the most admired qualities in fascist ideology. Actually, Harderberg is the very person who embodies what Shane McCorristine calls "the collapse of solidarity."[23]

> I look for business deals where I can find them.... If there's a market for kidneys, I buy and sell kidneys.... All I have ever done is buy and sell.... What happens before the goods come into my hands is no concern of mine. I don't even know about it.[24]

For Mankell, the tycoon Harderberg is clearly some kind of modern monster—if not *the* monster of our time. In the earlier quoted interview in *Bonniers Litterära Magasin* from 1978, Mankell develops his view on ideology and says, as an early antithesis to Harderberg, "That's when we must trust the common strength. Solidarity is not a way out—it's the only way! And resignation frightens me more than almost anything else."[25]

In the same interview, Mankell forebodes the harsh times of the 1980s and early 1990s in Sweden, when the leftist movement had its final major battle during the anti–nuclear-power campaign in 1980, the era of the yuppie started, and finally, in the 1990s, the Depression and the broken down Eastern bloc released phenomena such as racism, neoliberalism, globalization, and trans–European criminals, as described in the first Wallander novel *Faceless Killers*:

> Now the fear increases when the crisis gets deeper. You can't laugh the crisis of capitalism off anymore.... Nevertheless we can't keep our eyes shut to the fact that we are living in a pre-war time, a time where peace is just a break between two imperialistic wars of redistribution. At the same time big groups of people are being radicalized when their material existence is being threatened. And that's when the real struggle starts to form. And then we shall see how many in our situation, everybody with some kind of public opinion work, that are ready to stand up and be counted.[26]

A world ruled by economic forces, such as the one that grew out of the Depression of the early 1990s, is not a place for solidarity, and that is basically the quintessential question in Mankell's Wallander novels.

Mankell and the Neoliberal Project

The words of the tycoon Harlan Potter in Chandler's *The Long Goodbye* to Philip Marlowe, explaining the market forces and how the power of money becomes very difficult to control, echo through history when we listen to Alfred Harderberg. He is just another ruthless baron, drilling his business through the foundations of society. "I'm an actor on the stage governed by market forces," Harderberg explains to Wallander in the final sequence of the novel.[27] Shane McCorristine argues that society in Mankell's perspective, just as in Ian Rankin's Rebus series, has entered a post–welfare-state era "characterized by a sense of critical transition, a community that is envious of the past and uncertain about the future."[28] The postmodern, slightly nihilistic mentality of Harderberg is one indicator of this new age, but also how his crimes are made possible because of neoliberal politics—in some way foreshadowing the Trumpian post-politics of our time. In *The Man Who Smiled*, Harderberg is not the crook to start with, but rather the entire society governed by the ideology of New Public Management (and perhaps most of all, the Social Democrats in the government that opened the doors to this *marketification* in the 1980s)—a system where economy is the prime objective for the entire welfare state.

The French historian Michel Foucault, best known for his investigations of the microtechnologies of power, sees neoliberalism much as an art of control.[29] It is a system that makes capitalists and tycoons such as Harderberg into criminals on a global level. John Cawelti talks of corruption in the hardboiled narrative as "general and endemic to the social world of the story."[30] The criminal order rules the entire society, and entrepreneurs such as Harderberg become the heroes and rock stars of the new millennium in this neoliberal hegemony. Actually, he is the very person Franklin Roosevelt warned about in his 1938 "Recommendations to the Congress to Curb Monopolies and the Concentration of Economic Power." He is the prince of neoliberal economics who has evolved into the same kind of fascist tycoon that Polanyi and Steinbeck write about—he is the boss of Mafia-capitalism, the Al Capone of *fin-de-siècle* Sweden. And ultimately, Alfred Harderberg is one of those immoral men whose immorality has led to greatness, according to Mankell's epigraph from de Tocqueville. But the Capone reference is not just taken out of the blue. In *The Man Who Smiled*, Wallander's colleague Ann-Britt Höglund, investigating the death of an accountant, says to Wallander, "remember that a master criminal like Al Capone was caught out by an accountant."[31] In a neoliberal world governed by economy, who is the best detective? The accountant, of course!

Mankell's connection to the hardboiled novel and its roots in the American Prohibition era suddenly resound through the entire novel. Furthermore,

Höglund says, "They used to say that concealed behind every fortune was a major crime…. Why just 'used to'? Whenever you open your newspaper nowadays it looks more like the rule than the exception."[32] This was also one of the major notions in the novels of Sjöwall-Wahlöö, perhaps especially in books such as *The Fire Engine That Disappeared* and *Murder at the Savoy*. Mandel concludes that this type of crime—just like the crime fiction novel itself—is being created *within* the bourgeois ideology and that the capitalist system *itself* will reproduce it, over and over again. Together, these operators—the Mafia, the big corporations, the state—are parts of the same system.[33]

What we see here is a change of system that Foucault has identified as the relocation of the social space to the economic space. All institutions that earlier were located outside the space of economy—family, marriage, education, sports, upbringing etc.—have suddenly found themselves in the center of economy and then being submitted to its calculation of costs. Hence, the neoliberal individual is actually controllable and responds to the changes in the environment, even if these are artificial. Now this individual—the Economic Man—according to Foucault, also becomes a creature that knows how to manipulate its existence and learns to control it to its own benefits. In this way, the market becomes the controller of the state that is run according to the principal of supply and demand.[34] In this sense the state and the market are no longer opponents, rather they have become *partners* and the competitive spirit of neoliberalism is the only principal that can guarantee the rationality of the economy.[35]

One of the most important questions that Mankell raises in *The Man Who Smiled* is how the welfare state has gone through a transition during the early 1990s. It is the dark wave that has been sweeping through the stories of Swedish crime fiction since the 1960s and Per Wahlöö, but in Mankell's work it gets reborn. His critique on New Public Management concerning the County Council economy, which runs all healthcare in Sweden at the time, is extremely foreboding. Only a few doctors and some scholars of political science had written about this in the early 1990s (and probably nobody from the general public had actually read these texts). Mankell was the first crime writer to put this out in the open and obviously relate to it as a democratic problem—at least according to my interpretation of his de Toqueville epigraph in *The Man Who Smiled*.

In the novel, a former director in charge of auditing in Malmöhus County Council, Martin Oscarsson, explains how New Public Management works for Wallander:

> You have to remember that a county office is like a large business, or rather an industrial empire associated with a small duchy. Its main responsibility is health spending, but it oversees a lot of other things as well. Education, culture, and so on.[36]

Oscarsson explains to Wallander the far-reaching change that the administration has undergone in recent years, that public authorities should be managed as large business enterprises with increased demands of efficiency.[37] This is when Wallander hears about the central plot in the novel: a huge, four-million-dollar scam against the County Council by a private company with a lot of owners and a structure almost impossible to penetrate or even get an overview of. Big Swedish corporations such as Skanska and Volvo have been involved, but in the end one fraudulent owner is being exposed: the timid, reserved, and inexorable tycoon Alfred Harderberg—a man who lives a life of avarice while owning a great deal of business enterprises all over the world.

Basically, New Public Management is the notion that the state and the County Council could be more effective by imitating the private industry, the market, and business corporations. Besides Sweden, where New Public Management smashed down like an evangelical revival in different public administrations during the second half of the 1980s, very few countries converted into this reform enthusiastically: New Zealand, Great Britain, Canada, Netherlands, Norway, and Australia are the most well known examples that adopted it.[38] Perhaps the most extreme examples come from Great Britain and Australia, where even prisons are run by huge corporations.[39] An even more bizarre example is when United States fought the war in Iraq from 2003 and onward, with huge private entrepreneurs such as Halliburton and Blackwater carrying out some of the combat.

The journalist Maciej Zaremba points out the similarities between corruption and New Public Management; the striving for economic control and effectiveness turns nurses, doctors and police officers into cold bureaucrats, only serving their own means in the mode of production, to earn more money without aiming at quality.[40] Reification, as in Marxist theory, becomes reality and everything turns into commodities, although the social service they are providing cannot really be recounted into numbers. New Public Management creates a fantasy world of figures and control. Healthcare, for instance, is divided into several fake corporations where every company should fund their activities themselves. The result is, of course, that every company only does what earns them the most money. This has been called "a dysfunctional bureaucracy," fixated on extreme details in the control of the system itself.[41]

In 1988 Sweden actually changed its own constitution, Ahlbäck Öberg argues, when the Swedish parliament formally decided to introduce New Public Management.[42] In fact, it could be described as a control paradigm, or an Accord for *fin de siècle* Sweden, where the financial concept of the market was a cure for the inefficiency of the state bureaucracy. That is why *The Man Who Smiled* is the most interesting among Mankell's novels; it exposes the crime of the system itself. An invisible crime inside a system where criminals can hide out as businessmen without being seen. The question of Harderberg's illegal organ trade is thrilling in and of itself, but the ideology that makes it possible is New Public Management and the neoliberal idea of everything as commodities on a market.

Originally, New Public Management evolved from the harsh, market-friendly neoliberal criticism on the Swedish welfare state. Neoliberals saw this system as a cold and ineffective bureaucracy. This criticism was, to some extent, shared by the New Left of the 1960s and 1970s. The welfare state was seen as a blockage for individual freedom, and this very Swedish model had reached the end of the line in the late 1980s. Hence, the Social Democratic government once again abandoned socialism and chose a market liberal ideology. They probably had to do so in order to keep power, and that is also how neoliberal politics smashed socialism in Sweden once and for all. But it all came from the U.S. and the very time when Raymond Chandler wrote his novels. An ideology that changes the social structure of an entire country is one of the common issues of both Chandler and Mankell, or Wahlöö for that matter.

In the early twentieth century, the United States started to develop methods of measuring efficiency within the public administration in order to counteract corruption and incompetence. This coincided with Franklin D. Roosevelt's New Deal, the biggest welfare reform in America during the 1930s.[43] It is the same structure Karl Polanyi warned us about in *The Great Transformation*, where he spoke about fascism as "rooted in a market society that refused to function,"[44] and it is the "immorality leading to greatness" de Tocqueville warned about in the 1830s. The collapse of democracy into a ruthless elitist bureaucracy where responsibility is invisible, where private interest has turned the state into a criminal empire, recalls what Per Wahlöö wrote in *The Steel Spring*: "Capitalism is a crime in itself."

This leftwing critique in Mankell's novels coincides with the surrounding geopolitical landscape, which deserves a further exposition.

A Political Landscape

The narrative of a neoliberal capitalism that suddenly converts into fascism and crime frequently returns when studying Swedish crime fiction and its coherence with the stories of Raymond Chandler. The ideological critical deductions of Chandler, Wahlöö, and Mankell always strive towards this conclusion. In Sweden, the collaboration with Nazi-Germany during World War II is a recurring taboo area, and Mankell points his finger at it in several of his novels, from *Faceless Killers* (1991) to *The Return of the Dancing Master* (1999). The moral disaster that constitutes the link between the Nazis, fascism and capitalism was also an inherent criticism that the Swedish New Left movement during the 1960s slung towards the Swedish Social Democratic government at the time. A leftist movement which, as we are familiar with now, Mankell and Wahlöö both were a part of.

When Wallander thinks about the brave new world created by men such as Alfred Harderberg, he notes that "national boundaries have been replaced by ever-changing demarcation lines between different companies whose turnover and influence are greater than the budgets of many whole countries."[45] Again, the historical remnants of Roosevelt's warning about corporate power is there: at one point, Wallander thinks about the repugnant corporate power concentrated in the world as he examines a list of the ten largest companies in the world. The ones he mentions are Royal Dutch/Shell, a car manufacturer, an oil company, General Electric, and Exxon. "He tried to imagine the power wielded by these companies, but it was impossible for him to grasp what this concentration really meant."[46]

There is ultimately no big difference between the criticism in the 1930s and 1940s hardboiled pulp novel, from writers such as Hammett or Chandler, or the novels of Mankell, for that matter. They are all watching a new, fearful landscape appearing in front of them. It is the brave new world where faceless powers rule: the banks and huge corporations such as those appearing in novels by John Steinbeck or Upton Sinclair, or ruthless governments soaked in corruption like those of the Harding Administration during the American 1920s, the city of Los Angeles, and Chicago during the 1930s, when organized crime and the oil industry ruled the economy before the Great Depression. Those were the days when people could not afford to have morals.

Henning Mankell—according to this concept—is obviously writing hardboiled crime novels, although his stories are set in the picturesque countryside town of Ystad in southern Sweden, instead of the big city.[47] With Mankell, there is an abandonment of the urban maze and a stronger focus on small town milieus in Swedish crime fiction. That also makes him an exception in the hardboiled genre. Sjöwall-Wahlöö wrote stories drenched in urban culture and realistic depictions of the cityscape, with the decaying city as a screen for the darkest sides of humanity. Mankell, on the other hand, employs the familiar recipe for the small town mystery of the classic bourgeois crime novel, but the hardboiled themes are still there. The world is definitely a dark place, and crime has crawled its way up onto the long, sandy beaches of Ystad and into the Swedish countryside, across the porous Swedish borders from Eastern Europe, Russia, and Africa. History is always present in his novels: the fall of the Soviet empire, the deregulation of Swedish economy, the emancipation of African colonies and its baggage of neocolonialism, crime, war, and racism. Mankell knew about these things, not only for having lived in Africa for decades, but also from his political interest in these matters ever since the 1960s political radicalization.

On Henning Mankell's own webpage, he writes, "[the southern province] Scania is the place where Sweden ends, it can almost be compared to a kind of Baltic Texas. Borderlands have a very special kind of dynamic."[48]

From Ystad, the hometown of Wallander, ferries run back and forth to the European continent every day, and the problems of globalization, which Sweden is a part of, are constantly topics of the series since the borderlands have a tendency of enhancing these problems, Sjöholm argues.[49]

The landscape in the Wallander series is a place of permanent collisions between different dichotomies such as old/new and countryside/city. This is also the case in Chandler's fiction, where the old oligarchs of California and their huge mansions cling to the old way of life while the landscape around them is being transformed rapidly. The oil fields, with their tall forests of oil towers, such as Signal Hill, are being wiped out while cheap housing projects are taking over, extending the city of Los Angeles, making it the biggest postmodern project in history, swallowing every smaller city in its way.

Sjöholm mentions the landscape of Wallander as a *process* rather than a static place, where people meet, think and talk, and this creates a new meaning of this landscape through a social process.[50] Chandler's diverse city landscape likewise changes continuously—not just in the mind of the reader, but in a historical materialistic way because of the huge building expansion and land grabs in Southern California at the time when the books were written: all the freeways popping up at the time, the expansion of the middle-class, commercialism, the development of the capitalist mode of production, but also the epic dereliction of old downtown areas such as Bunker Hill, symbolizing the rot in the heart of the expanding big city. Chandler frequently puts his characters in cheap hotels, greasy diners, dusty, run-down office buildings, dingy apartment interiors, and ragged bars. And naturally all the inhabitants of these mysterious places are characters like shabby hotel clerks, cynical bartenders, red-lipped and white-teethed movie stars, prostitutes, rich widows, and their spoiled evil children or nephews. Geographically, the grandeur of the Sternwood mansion in *The Big Sleep* (Chandler's most anti-rich novel, as Mike Davis puts it) is not far from the trashy apartment buildings in the valley.[51]

Class issues are just as important in the novels of Chandler as they are in the Wallander series, and the landscape, with its topographical details of high and low, strengthens this class image. Details like the private roads leading to exclusive residential compounds patrolled by private police are not just important class distinctive ingredients of Chandler novels such as *The Big Sleep*, *The High Window*, and *The Long Goodbye*, they are also present in Mankell's *The Man Who Smiled*, which makes it one of the most obvious Chandlerian novels of the entire Mankell corpus.

Bergman refers to Mankell as the most important crime writer after

Sjöwall-Wahlöö.[52] With over 35 million copies of the Kurt Wallander series (2012) sold, he is the definitive successor to Sjöwall-Wahlöö, and he carries their political crime fiction project into the modern age of globalization and the post-communist era of Europe.

Pettersson argues that Kurt Wallander is just as unpolitical as Sjöwall-Wahlöö's cop Martin Beck because he notes the change in society, but he does not protest against it. While Beck can discuss this fact with friends and colleagues, and even get support from them, Wallander remains an introverted person who does not even bother to speak with his colleagues Höglund, Martinson, Hansson, or Svedberg. The collective was important for Sjöwall-Wahlöö, Pettersson further states, but for Mankell it is not. Wallander, in one person, becomes all the characters that Sjöwall-Wahlöö portrayed some twenty years earlier: the melancholic Beck, the tough rule breaker Gunvald Larsson, the overweight philosopher Kollberg, and the taciturn man of duty Einar Rönn.[53] Mankell moves between different American traditions—the loner detective (Hammett, Chandler, Macdonald) and the collective working group (McBain), and he mixes the open seaside countryside in southern Sweden, with its far stretching fields and long sandy beaches, with the big cities Malmö and Copenhagen. But Wallander seems to be most content in the countryside and eventually ends up in a country cottage in the final novel *The Troubled Man* (2009).

In the epilogue to the second Wallander novel, *The Dogs of Riga*, Wallander is thinking about his own lack of knowledge about the world surrounding him, what this world really looks like, and if this perception has been a complete lie.[54] The thought seems to frighten him since it exposes his naïve view of the world. This leads to an association with the old Marxist notion of our knowledge of the world as a lie, the idea of false consciousness, which cuts right back to Mankell's political roots in the New Left—a background that has followed him during his entire career and definitely formed his view of his native country, ever since his first novels. This is also something philosopher Slavoj Žižek mentions in his famous essay "Henning Mankell, the Artist of the Parallax View":

> There is, however, more in Mankell's work than a police procedural set in Bergmanland: he fills in the detective investigation frame not only with the expected existential-depressive stuff, but primarily with the social topic to which ultimately even the existential aspect is subordinated—in one word, the long and painful decay of the Swedish welfare-state.[55]

Henning Mankell could be seen as the foremost chronicler of this long and painful decay. Bergman mentions Mankell as the founder of *the European Turn* in Swedish crime fiction.[56] His books are saturated with the dominant presence of the internationalist perspective as discovered by young Marxists in the 1960s, in which Sweden is just a small imperialistic part in the rest of the world, and this perspective probably surprises many Swedes. The world is closing in on the archetypical cop Kurt Wallander in these stories—probably along with his spectators among the readers. However, some years after the original Wallander series was finished at the end of the 1990s, a chain-smoking political journalist named Stieg Larsson made the Chandler legacy and its flare for social criticism return to Swedish crime fiction in the 2000s. The urban maze once again became central to the postmodern Swedish crime novel of the new millennium.[57] And that is where we are heading next.

4
The Collapsed Dream
Stieg Larsson

By the time Stieg Larsson—a workaholic journalist of the leftist, antiracist magazine *Expo*—wrote his Millennium trilogy in 2002–03, the dark wave of the 1990s Swedish crime fiction had started to wear off. Henning Mankell's Wallander series was basically finished, with the final scraps and short stories published in *The Pyramid* (1999), and in 2002 the first, and only, Linda Wallander novel *Before the Frost* was published. But Mankell's Marxist Noir had peaked long time before that, in the mid-1990s, with novels such as *The Man Who Smiled* (1994), *Sidetracked* (1995), and *The Fifth Woman* (1996). In the beginning of the new millennium, the other king of crime fiction of the 1990s, Håkan Nesser, had also finished his long series about Van Veeteren. Spy fiction master and journalist Jan Guillou had concluded his ten-novel Hamilton series some years earlier and had started writing knight novels, the Arn series, about a crusading hero in the Middle Ages.

At this time, the big news was that crime fiction old-timer Leif GW Persson returned to crime writing in 2002, after a twenty-year intermission, with his extensive and deep dive into the traumatic mythology of the murder of Prime Minister Olof Palme in the two novels *Between Summer's Longing and Winter's End* (2002) and *Falling Freely, As If in a Dream* (2007). Persson is inspired by the so-called police lead, exposing a connection between the Swedish Security Police and the power struggle within the Social Democratic government. At the end of the 1970s Persson, who was a professor in Criminology and had worked for the government, debuted as crime writer after being dismissed from his lucrative post on the National Police Commissioner's office in Stockholm. His first novel, *The Pig Party* (1978), was a satirical procedural concerning a robbery against a post office in Stockholm and the advanced plot surrounding it. It had trails leading up to the Minister for Justice visiting prostitutes, a scandal that actually took place (the Geijer Affair and the Brothel Affair) and that had resulted in Persson getting sacked in the first place.

Persson writes realistic crime novels with a satirical twist in the line of Sjöwall-Wahlöö, and his return to the genre in 2002 quickly made him one of the best selling authors in Sweden. Nowadays he keeps writing novels at an impressive pace, while at the same time starring on the crime TV show *Crime of the Week* (*Veckans Brott*).

During this time, female crime writers also broke through in Sweden, and the "femicrimi" began to see the light of day. Both Mankell (*The Fifth Woman*) and Nesser (*Woman with a Birthmark*) had written novels with a feminist plot twist in the mid–1990s, when there was a huge feminist public debate in Sweden. In 1998, the first modern queen of crime (after Maj Sjöwall, of course), Liza Marklund made her mark with her novel *The Bomber*. Before her there were a number of major female writers such as Kerstin Ekman, Maria Lang and Ulla Trenter (wife of the hugely popular crime author of the 1940s and 50s, Stieg Trenter). But Liza Marklund wrote a more modern, deliberate, conceptual genre crime fiction with fast-paced plots and domestic narratives in a contemporary, page-turning prose inspired by the melodramatic style of soap operas. She was a tabloid journalist who had made her debut in 1995 with the semi-documentary *Buried Alive—A True Story*, the story of a woman getting violently persecuted by her husband. In her Annika Bengtzon series, the protagonist is a female journalist who becomes the detective solving the mysteries. A huge wave of female crime writers followed Marklund, with names such as Helene Tursten, Karin Alvtegen, Anna Jansson, Inger Frimansson, Åsa Nilsonne, and Aino Trosell. At the same time, the reputation of Mankell had started to grow immensely abroad, and eventually his novels hit the American market and became a worldwide success. Several Swedish crime fiction authors were translated and published abroad but the boom, as we know it today, had not started quite yet.

Such was the Swedish crime fiction market when Stieg Larsson wrote his novels. The new genre was totally dominated by old leftwing intellectuals (Mankell, Nesser, Guillou, Persson) and feminists (Marklund, Alvtegen). Larsson actually saw his novels—all three of them written in one long stretch— as market investments, his future pension, since crime fiction was far more lucrative than being an editor for an antiracist magazine such as *Expo*.

The final result over a decade later: over 85 million copies sold worldwide, 24 million in the U.S. alone.[1]

Perhaps Stieg Larsson's Millennium trilogy—*The Girl with the Dragon Tattoo* (2005), *The Girl Who Played with Fire* (2006), and *The Girl Who Kicked the Hornet's Nest* (2007)[2]—represents an even darker shade of Sweden than that portrayed by Mankell. In the novels of Larsson, Hobbes' state of nature is almost here, and just as in Chandler's writing, there are no ordinary people anywhere in the stories—just thugs, cops, ruthless serial killers, violent motorcycle gangs, a mysterious superheroine, lots of reporters, a mad psychiatrist, and hordes of government agents. It is truly the collapsed dream of the Swedish welfare state that has turned into a nightmare filled with murder and abuse of power.

Stieg Larsson (1954–2004) was fifty years old when he got his first novel, *The Girl with the Dragon Tattoo*, approved by one of Sweden's biggest and most renowned publishers in 2004 (actually the same publisher as Sjöwall-Wahlöö, and the crime duo's editor Lasse Bergström was one of the first to recommend Larsson for publication). Then Larsson suddenly died of a heart attack. His death has shot him into mythical proportions, and made his stories become a part of his own fascinating life. He had been a reporter during the 1970s, with a background in the Trotskyite communist movement, and started the antiracist magazine *Expo* in the mid-1990s. His life could be spelled out as work, work, and more work. Perhaps he worked himself to death, living a hard life with lavish and imprudent amounts of junk food and too many cigarettes. The tragic and fascinating Stieg Larsson saga is well known all over the world by now.

Germany was the gateway to world success for Swedish crime writers in the 2000s. It was the eye of the needle that all Swedish writers had to pass through on their way to international stardom in countries such as the Netherlands, France, Spain, and Italy. The most prominent of them even made it into the British and American markets, just as Mankell had done. In 2004 Larsson was introduced at the influential Frankfurt Book Fair, and the platform for Swedish crime fiction had already been built.[3]

Larsson's novels were published in Great Britain by MacLehose in early 2008 and quickly became a worldwide publishing phenomenon. Henning Mankell's novels had been translated into English since 1997 and in some way plowed the way for Swedish crime fiction during the 1990s.[4] Both Mankell and Larsson were telling bleak stories of alienation and hopelessness in modern day Sweden. By now, Larsson's novels are probably one of the most remarkable successes ever experienced by a Swedish writer. The Millennium trilogy is widely mentioned in the same context as a number of other bestseller phenomena of the 2000s: J. K. Rowling's Harry Potter series, Dan Brown's *The Da Vinci Code*, Khaled Hosseini's *The Kite Runner*, E. L. James' *Fifty Shades of Grey*, and Stephanie Meyer's Twilight series.

All of Larsson's novels have been turned into movies in Sweden, and the first novel became a successful Hollywood film in the United States. They have also been made into comic books, and the Nørrebro theater in Copenhagen, Denmark, even made a play out of the initial novel *The Girl with the Dragon Tattoo* in 2010.[5]

Holmberg refers to Stieg Larsson as the leader of Swedish crime fiction in the English-speaking countries that led to an increasing number of other Swedish crime fiction authors being translated and introduced all over the world. By contrast, this is a development which Sjöwall-Wahlöö's success never led to. Therefore, Larsson has had a more profound effect on the crime fiction market than his predecessors from the 1960s and 70s.[6]

Along with Stieg Larsson's Millennium trilogy, the Swedish urban crime fiction narrative truly had its comeback. Dan Burstein describes the big city as being the true star of the show in the novels of Stieg Larsson where Stockholm is the stage for everything, just like Raymond Chandler's Los Angeles or Sara Paretsky's Chicago are the implicit stars of their novels.[7] However, this study's first aim is to show in what way Larsson was a political writer. In order to do that, we have to take a brief look at the radical environments and literary ideas that shaped him. The times were the radical 1970s, but Larsson's leftwing awakening was, as we shall see, a bit different than that of Mankell.

The Collapsed Dream

John-Henri Holmberg specifies three important crime writers that Larsson admired most: Dashiell Hammett, Raymond Chandler, and Ross Macdonald (pen name for Kenneth Millar). One of their central themes is loneliness and alienation in a modern world—themes that also fit well into Larsson's ideological credo. According to Holmberg, Larsson viewed Chandler as the greatest writer of them all, writing about dark images from the twilight side of society. Larsson especially saw *The Long Goodbye* as one of the greatest American novels ever written, up there with Hemingway and Steinbeck: "Nowhere else ... has the collapse of the American dream been as nakedly exposed."[8] John Scaggs argues that the hardboiled novel is a powerful ideological tool and acknowledges Hammett's *Red Harvest* (1927) as the defining text, a socialist critique of the relationship between capitalism and gangsterism.[9] In the new millennium, Stieg Larsson has become the defining writer of the collapsed dream of Sweden in the international market.

And what was this collapsed dream? Having once been a Trotskyite Larsson was, of course, critical towards the Social Democratic government, just as all communists were in the 1970s. Still Tapper, on the contrary, has noted that Larsson's attitude towards the Social Democrats is in stark contrast to the demonized image propagated by Stalinists such as Sjöwall-Wahlöö and the Maoist Henning Mankell. Instead, Larsson finds virtuous examples of humanism and egalitarianism among Social Democrats such as Lisbeth Salander's former guardian, lawyer Holger Palmgren. But there are also some good examples of cold-blooded careerists, such as the attorney Richard Ekström in the final novel.[10] One reason for the milder view on Social Democrats could be that Larsson grew up in a Social Democratic home—both his parents were members of the party—but being an oppositional figure, Larsson chose his own way.[11]

A number of crises in the 1970s increased this criticism and eventually strangled it when Marxism in general had its huge crisis around 1980. Let me get back to the ideological crisis of Marxism later and stay on for a while with the historical events that have had an influence on the novels of Larsson.

The global recession in 1973, also known as the Oil Crisis, was perhaps the first big blow against the leftwing movement. By then Stieg Larsson was a member of the anti-Vietnam War movement in Sweden; he was 19 years old and already a politically conscious person. The recession, what Robert Brenner has called the "long downturn," an era subsequent to the post-war boom,[12] resulted in a radical restructuring of the world economic system, which led to a crisis and the abandonment of the Keynesian-Fordist policies of the Western world and the initial bankruptcy of the communist countries. A new system of flexible accumulation increased the importance of international finance capital, the globalization of labor markets, accelerated migration of cheap foreign labor, the weakening of the trade union movement, and rationalization by new technology. Milton Friedman's Chicago School of economics was the intellectual center of the capitalist Western world, and Ronald Reagan and Margaret Thatcher implemented this neoliberal ideology in the U.S. and in the U.K. This new system eventually seemed to produce its own crises through uncontrollable mechanisms, and it disabled the heir to the Marxist proletariat, which meant that nobody was actually in a position to challenge the system from within.[13] This post–1973 restructuring of capitalism had its cultural correlate in the rise of the post–Fordist system, and the cultural condition reflecting these conditions has come to be known as postmodernism.

During this time, in 1973, Sweden had its own Watergate scandal known as the IB Affair. IB—the Information Bureau—was a military intelligence organization within the Social Democratic Party that spied on communist insurgents (students, hospital staff, personnel within the state bureaucracy). The top secret organization was exposed spectacularly in 1973 by journalists Jan Guillou and Peter Bratt in the communist journal *Folket i Bild/Kulturfront*. Guillou went to prison and started to sketch a series of spy novels that he wrote during the 1980s and 90s, the Hamilton series, thoroughly inspired by Sjöwall-Wahlöö as the novels depicted a society in transformation over one decade (1986–1995). The IB Affair, of course, increased the paranoia and the criticism against the Social Democrats in the leftwing movement, where Stieg Larsson was active at this time. As we shall see, a similar secret organization figures in Larsson's final novel, *The Girl Who Kicked the Hornet's Nest*.

The next event of importance was a monumental national trauma for

Sweden: the murder of Prime Minister Olof Palme in February 1986. A crime leading to the biggest crime investigation in the world, a massive labyrinthine of material just made for the postmodern era. The murder became a huge, mysterious crime in the center of a traumatized nation. Pettersson argues that right there, in the background, one could sense a displacement in people's way of looking at the surrounding world, that a togetherness and trust had been lost, a sense of justice failed, that something broke in Sweden on February 28, 1986.[14] A couple of years earlier, in 1984, the gruesome murder of a prostitute, Catrine da Costa, also took place in Stockholm and resulted in a feminist debate, since the crime showed a contempt for women never seen before. da Costa had been chopped up in pieces that were found in black garbage bags on a deserted lot just outside the city's center, much like Elizabeth Short in James Ellroy's *The Black Dahlia* (1987). Her head, genitals, inner organs and one of her breasts were never found. The police deemed the dismemberment to be a professional job, and the case became a modern parallel to Jack the Ripper some hundred years before. Two doctors—one a forensic pathologist—were arrested, but murder could not be proven, just that one of them had handled the dead body at some point.

In the late 1980s the nationalist, former Nazi BSB movement (Preserve Sweden Swedish) also got started. Today they are known as the Sweden Democrats and have had tremendous success in the Swedish elections and gained places in the parliament in 2010. Their popularity grows from year to year, and they are not alone. In all European countries, extreme rightwing parties enjoy success in the era of discontent and nihilist politics. Donald Trump has had a similar role in the United States.

Two other events that shaped contemporary Sweden and Larsson's antiracist work in the early 1990s were the horrors of the so-called "Laserman," John Ausonius, an immigrant-hating loner who shot several people in Stockholm in 1991–92; one of them was killed, with a rifle equipped with a laser sight. He was eventually arrested and is still imprisoned.

At around the same time, a new racist populist party gained a lot of support in the 1991 elections: New Democracy (Ny Demokrati) led by a rich entrepreneur from the Swedish nobility, and an equally rich owner of a record label. The tone in the public debate was soaring with racism. It is almost certainly true, as Pettersson concludes, that something was being lost in Sweden at that time. The outlines of a collapsed dream started to grow rapidly, and the critical idiom represented by the crime fiction genre was the best way to tell the story, of course.

Since the rollback of the Russian Revolution, during the post–1992 era, the political right basically won. They have had free-trade agreements such as NAFTA and GATT, which granted the unfettered international movement of capital, priority over labor rights, and environmental conservation, and they achieved a granting to the bond market of a practically absolute veto over federal tax policy and public expenditures. Still, in several other areas, the cultural areas, the rightwing propagators have gone backwards—in realms such as gender, sex, and race equality, women's liberation, feminism, antiracism, and so forth. That is why we can observe a huge backlash across the Western world right now, with Donald Trump, nationalist and fascist movements gaining popularity all over Europe. Freedman argues that culture is the area of social production where the rightwing failed to impose its dominance.[15] Looking at crime fiction today, his statement is still valid.

Further context lands us in the summer of 2001, when the EU Summit was held in Gothenburg and George W. Bush was one of the attending world leaders. The demonstrations from leftist movements were huge. Syndicalists and communists met up with hordes from the anti-globalization movement and black-clad anarchists. The police had all their troops in place, and everything went haywire when heavily armed police forces intervened against innocent participants and later anarchists started throwing rocks and set piles of rubbish on fire in the streets. In the midst of the chaos, one activist got hit badly by a police bullet, but he survived. The Gothenburg Riots were probably the last gasp of the anti-globalization movement in Sweden, and by the time of 9/11 it was totally punctured when the War on Terror was initiated by the Bush Administration. The neoliberal era had conquered, but it did not start that summer in Gothenburg.

Neoliberal politics had started pouring into Sweden during the 1980s; in 1991 the Social Democratic government lost the elections, and a Liberal-Conservative coalition took its place. That was to be the opening of the floodgates of neoliberal reforms. Of course, this showed up in contemporary crime fiction. Henning Mankell's first crime novel *Faceless Killers*, released in 1991, mirrors the Swedish public debate on immigrants and violence against refugees and, as we have previously seen, his novel *The Man Who Smiled* reflects the new type of crimes marching in with neoliberal politics. Stieg Larsson wrote several non-fiction books on the subject of extreme rightwing politics and the different groups affected by this growing phenomenon. In his novels, the neoliberal hegemony becomes the backdrop for the stories about Lisbeth Salander. But before embarking on Larsson's stories we have to ask ourselves how the arena of politics changed from the 1960s, when Larsson became politically conscious and active, to the 1990s, when his Marxist youth turned into a more antiracist and feminist orientation.

From the Crisis of Marxism to Postmodernity

Marxism had its huge crisis in Sweden during the second half of the 1970s, and famous intellectuals such as Lars Gustafsson, Göran Rosenberg,

4. The Collapsed Dream   101

and Svante Nordin gradually left Marxism behind and became liberals. For example, the prominent author and intellectual Lars Gustafsson, who had been a profiled Marxist since the 1960s, cherished individualism and the intellectual work that could only be made by an independent artist seeking the truth—as opposed to work being made within the structures of authorities and institutions.[16] In the 1960s, the dichotomy of the individual against the structures of power was central to many leftwing intellectuals, and the power structures were represented by capitalism, the Social Democracy, and the United States. Later, this critique transformed into something else. Suddenly, in the 1970s, it turned against the growing welfare state that was seen as an oppressive Soviet-style authority with the purpose of eliminating free intellectuals, democracy, and civil rights.[17] The greatest threats against the free individual, according to Lars Gustafsson, were the public sector and high taxes.[18] Consequently, many of the old leftwing revolutionaries cherished neoliberal thinking with its focus on the individual and the market during the following years. Nordin points to 1975 as the paradigmatic year for a new kind of skepticism towards Marxism, and this skepticism would eventually be named postmodernism.[19]

The international leftwing movement encountered several crises over the years, undermining Marxist thought and the social idea of a utopian alternative to capitalism. This included such events as the Soviet takeover in Czechoslovakia in the spring of 1968 (probably the single most important event of that time for the future of Marxism), the dictatorships springing from the chaotic and lengthy Vietnam War (the Khmer Rouge of Cambodia and the aggressive North Vietnamese army), the cruelties and new direction of post–Mao China, and the genocide in Cambodia during the second half of the 1970s.[20] Moreover, this was the time for Soviet-exile writer Aleksandr Solzhenitsyn's alarming documentary of the Stalin camps, *The Gulag Archipelago* (1974), which became a catalyst for the reckoning with communist ideology in the West during the 1970s. In Europe, some of the extreme leftist movements had transformed into violent terrorist groups such as the Red Army Fraction and Baader-Meinhof gang in West Germany, and the Red Brigades of Italy. Still, Larsson kept working in the Trotskyan movement well into the 1980s, but his interest mostly concerned the political theory.[21] According to Petterson, Larsson saw the Trotskyan movement as a clearer and freer alternative to the Eastern European Communism. He was attracted by the internationalism as well, and the open view on culture that had always been the trademarks of Trotskyism.

The Swedish Trotskyan movement was a relatively new political tradition in the 1970s, and it constituted a political alternative to (and a reaction against) the biggest leftist party at the time, VPK (Vänsterpartiet kommunisterna), since they were regarded as reformist, and against the Maoist

Swedish Communist Party, SKP (Sveriges kommunistiska parti), which was regarded Stalinist. Larsson's view on culture did not concur with that of the Maoist left, where classic social realism or the people's culture was important; instead, he got interested in the subversive movements within the popular culture, how tendencies in society were made visible through movies and books.[22] Freedman considers that the authentic critical Marxism has always been antithetical to Stalinism, especially within the Trotskyan tradition, which he sees as probably the richest variety of Marxist thought insofar as specifically political and political-historical writing is concerned in its theoretical discourse.[23]

Trotsky's writings belong to a subsequent scientific tradition along with some of the great works spawned directly from Marx's *Capital* (1867), in the classical Marxist tradition, Rosa Luxemburg's *The Accumulation of Capital* (1913) and Lenin's earlier mentioned *Imperialism: The Highest Stage of Capitalism* (1916). During the 1970s, some of the socialist thinkers got connected to genocides and terrorism. In that way, Trotsky could hardly be criticized in the same way as Stalin, or Mao, for the atrocities of communism, since he was expatriated from the Soviet Union in 1929 and then murdered (by the agents of Stalin) in 1940, and that might have been a good reason for Larsson to keep alive his interest for his theories.

Larsson wrote numerous texts for the Trotskyan-Marxist journal *Internationalen* (The International) published by the Socialist Party in Sweden during the 1980s. He started to write as a young radical without getting paid and kept writing well into the 1980s when his Marxist interest was gradually replaced with antiracism as the new arena for struggle in society. During the 1980s, these two themes intertwined and evolved as parallels in his writing. His first article published in *Internationalen*, written under the pen name Severin (the name of his grandfather the communist) concerned Jules Verne and the bourgeois roots in his science fiction that hailed a capitalist machine society.[24] In Stieg Larsson's final article in *Internationalen*, "Glasnost in the Streets of Moscow—As a Warm Wind" published in 1989, he wrote about the falling Eastern bloc and the Soviet Union, and he expressed strong hopes and support for a democratic socialist development in the Soviet Union.[25] The texts published in *Internationalen* also reveal Larsson's stance as a Marxist, Trotskyite, and revolutionary during the 1980s, when almost the entire New Left of the 1960s had been shattered into pieces. In an article published at the end of 1983 that Larsson co-wrote with two other party comrades, they express their view on the socialist struggle at the time. The annual congress was about to take place for the Socialist Party, and the article expressed an internal debate where Larsson, et al. craved a sobering up of some of their somewhat unrealistic comrades who thought that Swedish workers were ready for the big class battle against the capitalists, and that the Socialist Party

4. The Collapsed Dream   103

was the very unit to lead the way. Larsson, et al. insisted that these revolutionary romantic members in the party should sober up, take a good look at reality and hold back on the grandiose revolution babble belonging to the old days. In fact, the Socialist Party had very few members, they had little influence on the working class and the public debate, and the article argued that this should be considered when deciding the tactics for the party in the future.[26]

The critique against the Social Democratic government is central in this debate. The working class in Sweden had been sedated by centuries of accord—the cooperation between the labor movement and the labor government on the one hand, and the capitalists on the other—and this fact makes it impossible to see the Swedish workers as a mob running out with hayforks ready for the revolution, Larsson, et al. argues.[27] The old methods and tactics of mass mobilization of the workers were outdated already in 1983, according to Larsson. This makes him a realist, rather than a revolutionary romantic, and eventually he found a new path to follow in life where Marxism had its place, although it stood firmly side by side with antiracism and feminism.

Stieg Larsson had grown up with his grandfather Severin Boström, who was a stern, Soviet-style communist and had been incarcerated during World War II because of his political preferences and for his stubborn opposition against the Nazis.[28] Later in his teens, Larsson became a member of the Trotskyite organization the Communist Workers Union (Kommunistiska Arbetareförbundet), and Holmberg suspects that the choice of Trotskyism, instead of Maoism or Marxism-Leninism, which was far more popular at the time, was due to Trotsky's aesthetics being much more inclusive than that of other socialist ideologues. The blind obedience and dogmatism in many of the other political leftwing groups repulsed Larsson, and in the Stalinist or Maoist groups only social realism was permitted. And Larsson was a huge fan of American crime fiction and science fiction. He loved the movies by Stanley Kubrick, Sam Peckinpah, and Sergio Leone and thought the hardboiled noir classic *Chinatown* by Roman Polanski (written by Robert Towne) was one of the greatest films ever made.[29] His eclecticism and varied taste for popular culture—which stood in stark contrast to the contempt for American imperialistic culture as seen by the Marxist-Leninists—eventually landed him as a postmodernist crime fiction writer, serving long and winding, almost *Pynchonesque*, plots to the Swedish public. Politically he was *more* of a radical feminist and an antiracist in the early 2000s than a Trotskyan communist. When the 1980s faded into the 1990s, Larsson gradually stopped paying his membership fee to the local party section; eventually it was dissolved and he left the Trotsky-Socialist Party (Socialistiska partiet, before 1982 named Communist Worker's Union).[30] According to his old party comrade Håkan Blomqvist, it was in the Trotskyan movement of the Fourth International that

Larsson learned to converge the perspective of socialism with democracy, feminism, antiracism, and internationalism. As a young boy, he had participated in study circles of revolutionary Marxism where the reading of Ernest Mandel, Trotsky, Lenin, Marx, and Rosa Luxemburg was central to developing social critique instead of dogmatism.[31]

When reading the works of Trotsky, especially his works on literature and art, one can certainly understand why Larsson was fascinated by this aesthetic theory. Alan Wald have summarized Trotsky's literary values as "a liberal attitude in principle to all literature, an openness to the artistic merits of creative work without regard for the author's political views."[32] In one of Trotsky's central works, *Literature and Revolution*, originally a series of articles in *Pravda* that he wrote over two summers and published in the form of a book in 1923 while he was leading the Red Army against White Russian and invading foreign troops, he argues that it is absurd to pretend that art should be insignificant to our time. What actually happens is prepared by people and gets carried out by people—it affects human individuals and ultimately changes them. This concerns all art, Trotsky says in stern opposition to Stalin's rigid conception of art and literature, where art is an instrument in the hands of power.[33] However, Larsson's conception of literature and culture was probably similar after having read the works of Trotsky, which were widely translated into Swedish in the late 1960s. Moreover, Trotsky writes about individualism in opposition to the Soviet focus on the collective and argues that the revolution must presuppose the central idea that the collective human being has to be lord over himself.[34] In fact, it is crucial to get rid of all mechanical influence from the Stalinist bureaucracy on all forms of spiritual creation.[35]

Trotsky's notion of literature's importance and function as social theory is thoroughly displayed in his essay "The Social Roots and the Social Function of Literature" where he writes, "art is always a social servant and historically utilitarian ... it enriches the spiritual experience of the individual and of the community, it refines feeling, makes it more flexible, more responsive, it enlarges the volume of thought in advance and not through the personal method of accumulated experience, it educates the individual, the social group, the class and the nation."[36]

To Trotsky, the translation of art into the language of politics does not indicate a desire to dominate art by means of decrees and orders, as Stalin did, and later as even the stale communist regimes of Eastern Europe did. The new art must, according to Trotsky, "plough the entire field in all directions" and the aesthetics are indeed influenced by, and dependent on, social conditions.[37] According to Alan Wald, in his writings on art Trotsky "vigorously and boldly sought to theorize a relationship between the cultural legacy of bourgeois society and the politico-cultural tasks of the epoch of the transition to socialism."[38] Instead of a distinct proletarian culture during the transition phase of the dictatorship of the proletariat, Trotsky advocated a complete eclecticism.

Larsson probably read these ideas and got inspired by them since they promoted his interests in a variety of genres such as science fiction and crime fiction literature. Trotsky was obviously an advocate of differentiated inspiration, and not a dogmatist of social realism.

This, too, was the credo of post–Marxist theorists such as Michel Foucault, Jean-Francois Lyotard, and Jean Baudrillard, whose theories had a huge influence on culture in the post-industrial era which, according to the former far-leftist Lyotard, started sometime during the 1950s. According to the French Althusser-disciple Foucault—who rejected the notion of the subject as a philosophical unity—knowledge is power, and power is knowledge. Foucault wanted to show how sciences such as medicine, psychiatry, sociology, and criminology have always been in the service of power throughout history, to regulate and normalize, and to repel everything deviant or threatening.[39] In his analysis of *The Girl Who Kicked the Hornet's Nest*, Tapper terms the torture-like mental treatment of Lisbeth Salander, by the Section's loyal psychiatrist Peter Teleborian, "a feminist version of Michel Foucault's theories of modern punishment as directed against the soul and not the body. She is to become 'the disciplined individual' ... a compliant woman."[40] One of the probable inspirations for Salander's violent revenge fantasy could have been Helen Zahavi's famous postmodern crime novel *Dirty Weekend* (1991), which Knight suggests was "a postmodern move to disrupt textual certainties as much as masculine self-confidence in one of the true originals of crime fiction."[41]

In postmodern theory, individual truths and projects have replaced the idea of grand narratives, continuous linear progress, and one universal motion of history, such as modernists saw it. All these notions ultimately lead to oppression. Instead, there is an absence of a single highest authority. This was also a post–Marxist conception. Jean Baudrillard argues that there are no proletarians in the reality of postmodernism—there are only consumers of symbolic values. Thus, he takes the commodity theory of Marx several steps further and, at the same time, he releases his ties to Marx by stating that there are only symbolic values on commodities, created by the advertising industry, and, in the long run, the capitalistic system itself. This postmodern reality is a mere simulation, Baudrillard says, and he dismisses the moral character of the consumer criticism of the 1960s Marxists, where false and manipulated needs hid the genuine needs.[42] The serial killers and men who hate women in the novels of Larsson all belong to this "simulated" reality dominated by exchange values and commerce, just like Bret Easton Ellis's killer yuppie Patrick Bateman in perhaps the most postmodern novel of them all, *American Psycho* (1991). In this novel, the first lines read, "*Abandon all hope ye who enter here* is scrawled in blood red lettering on the side of the Chemical Bank near the corner of Eleventh and First."[43] Similar to the Millennium trilogy, *American Psycho* exposes the corruption and greed engendered in 1980s politics and high living, displaying a nihilist reality and the collapse of solidarity in a post–Marxist world. This American influence of culture was profound on Larsson, as already mentioned, and perhaps the often violent and grim stories produced by huge bestselling authors in the U.S. fitted Larsson's taste best. He was definitely a product of the dark, fast-paced genre works developed by such writers as Thomas Harris (Hannibal Lecter series), James Patterson (Alex Cross series), Jeffery Deaver (Lincoln Rhyme series), James Ellroy (Lloyd Hopkins series and the L.A. Quartet), Michael Connelly (Harry Bosch series), Sarah Paretsky (V.I. Warshawski series), Val McDermid (Carol Jordan and Tony Hill series), and even John Grisham with conspiracy novels such as *The Firm* (1991) and *The Pelican Brief* (1992). Besides this, there are other important elements in Larsson's literature we have to consider, and one perspective diligently foregrounded in scholarly research on Larsson is feminism.

The New Order: Feminism and Technology

Larsson made a remarkable political journey during his life, from Trotskyite communist, to post–Marxist, and further to becoming a ragingly intense antiracist and radical feminist, eventually, basically (like many other old leftwingers), dumping the class matters overboard. Tapper argues that Larsson has changed the entire perspective of the crime fiction genre with his novels, similar to what Sjöwall-Wahlöö did with their Marxism-Leninism when they reversed the old conservative detective story into urban crime stories focusing on social circumstances. Instead, Larsson shifted the Marxist credo from the 1960s to a radical feminist analysis of society.[44] This is especially evident in the first part of the Millennium trilogy, *The Girl with the Dragon Tattoo* (which is titled *Men Who Hate Women* [*Män som hatar kvinnor*] in Sweden), where a statistical quote opens every new part of the book, for example in part one: "18% of the women in Sweden have at one time been threatened by a man," or in part two: "46% of the women in Sweden have been subjected to violence by a man."[45] Larsson took these statistics from the scientific report *Battered Lady—Men's Violence Against Women In Gender Equal Sweden: A Scope Investigation* (*Slagen dam—Mäns våld mot kvinnor i jämställda Sverige, en omfångsundersökning* [2001]) by Eva Lundgren, Gun Heimer, Jenny Westerstrand and Anne-Marie Kalliokoski at the University of Uppsala in Sweden. This makes Larsson's focus and leitmotif quite clear, and the transformation from being a Trotskyite in the 1970s and 80s led him to the postmodern theories of radical feminists such as Beatrix Campbell, Sheila Jeffreys, Kate Millett, and even the controversial Valerie Solanas. Barry Forshaw makes an interesting note on this, stating that Larsson "is in tune with the feminist writers of an earlier era whose attitude to male sexuality often evoked violence and violation as part of the experience."[46] Larsson was definitely a radical feminist who thought women are oppressed due to their gender. According to Kate Millett, in her book *Sexual Politics* (1970), sexual relationships between men and women in a patriarchal society are an expression of men's power abuse. The erotic encounter between men and women cannot be an encounter between equals until the patriarchal structures have been smashed, and sexuality has gone through a total transformation.[47] Beatrix Campbell argues that the sexual revolution of the 1960s and 70s, when Larsson had his political awakening, was basically an awakening for men who, hidden behind the words of Marxism, consolidated their power over women, when she writes that the sexual revolution was "about the affirmation of young men's masculinity and promiscuity; it was indiscriminate, and their sexual object was indeterminate (so long as she was a woman). The very affirmation of sexuality was a celebration of *masculine* sexuality."[48] Therefore, of course, it is very tempting to see Lisbeth Salander as a conscious emancipation and revolt against this order that, in many ways, was created by the leftist pals of Larsson during the age of the revolution.

The public debate about violence against women, and so-called honor violence, exploded in Sweden in the beginning of the 2000s. Two events became central for Larsson and his conception of feminism: the murder of Melissa Nordell in Stockholm in November 2001, and the killing of Fadime Sahindal in Uppsala in January 2002.[49] This hatred against women had nothing to do with religion or ethnicity, Larsson's close friend and colleague Kurdo Baksi has stated—men hate women, men want to own women, men fear women, and men want to control women.[50] This radical notion was shared by Larsson in one of his most important articles on the subject, "Swedish and Un-Swedish Violence Towards Women," originally published in 2004.[51] He was also a huge fan of female crime writers such as Minette Walters, Elizabeth George, Patricia Cornwell, Liza Cody, Sue Grafton, the aforementioned Val McDermid, Dorothy Sayers, and Sara Paretsky. Several scholars have emphasized Larsson's influence from the 1980s feminist turn of the crime genre when female authors "took the social concerns of the American hard-boiled tradition, stripped away its sexist elements, and recreated the detective hero in a feminist mode," as Barbara Fister explains it.[52] On one occasion in 1992, Larsson even carried out an interview with Elizabeth George.[53]

Larsson's weapon of choice in this feminist battle against the male patriarchal structures, of course, is the very popular Lisbeth Salander. She is a complex character, skilled fighter and computer hacker, qualities that are often reserved for males in the crime fiction genre. Considering that Chandler's sleuth Marlowe is a reflection of the most typical American hero à la Hemingway—with their drinking habits and complexity towards women—Wahlöö's character the Nazi Tadeusz Beck in his novel *The Wind and the Rain* (1961), or Willi Mohr in *A Necessary Action* (1962), are quite the opposite, although connections can be made between them. Perhaps the fact that they are shards of life rambling about in post-war Europe makes them Hemingway archetypes of some kind, two individuals from the lost generation. David H. Richter argues that Marlowe is a fantasy figure who is not walking in someone's leash, consequently embodying a fantasy about freedom and independence.[54] The very same could be stated about Stieg Larsson's feminist, aloof but unfettered heroine Lisbeth Salander. She is the perfect crossover between a superhero and the clever computer sleuth of the 2000s young generation. No one can touch her, as she is the cunning, street-smart, survivor in the neoliberal urban jungle—just like Marlowe. The path of Salander is the individual path, the path of vengeance. Her popularity echoes the revenge fantasies of the new middle class with their heads crammed with imagined insults that require immediate action, as the Danish writer Carsten Jensen puts it. Jensen concludes that Salander could be seen as an omnipotent dream in the shape of a victim of violence. She starts off as a character from a fairy tale for the digital era and ends up as Jesus, complete with burial and resurrection, when she gets thrown into a grave in the second Millennium novel, *The Girl Who Played with Fire*, with three bullets in her body, one in the head, and gets buried alive. Ultimately, just like Uma Thurman in Quentin Tarantino's *Kill Bill Vol. 2*, Salander rises after digging herself up from that deep hellhole.[55] According to Larsson's fiancée Eva Gabrielsson, the Salander character was inspired by comic books such as *Superman* and *Spiderman*, supernatural heroes that Salander could have been little sister to, and certain parts of the hacker world she belongs to can be found in books such as Bruce Sterling's *The Hacker Crackdown: Law and Disorder on the Electronic Frontier* (1992).[56] Her computer skills resemble those found in protagonists in science fiction novels, and sometimes she seems to embody the computer world, becoming an indivisible part of the machinery, and as critical theorists such as Marcuse perhaps would define it, she would also be a part of the neoliberal ideology, reworking it from within like Trotskyites used to employ their permanent revolution. The notion of an intimate relation between technology, revolution, and a new way of thinking leading up to emancipation was central to Marcuse and other critical theorists, such as Andrew Feenberg. "The totalitarian universe of technological rationality is the latest transmutation of the idea of Reason," Marcuse argues in *One-Dimensional Man*,[57] and in 1941 he also stated that technology was a mode of changing "social relationships, a manifestation of prevalent thought and behavior patterns, an instrument for control and domination."[58] Critical theorist Jürgen Habermas argues that modern day technocracy is concealed behind a facade of objective necessity that makes it more ideological than all previous ideologies. At the core of technocratic consciousness there is instrumental reason and domination, which accords well with Marcuse's view, and in the long run Habermas is talking of a new level of rationalization at which decision-making could be completely delegated to computers.[59] This is probably the world in which Lisbeth Salander is the perfect antidote. A rebel individual fighting the system on its own terms, like a human computer virus. Though it is uncertain whether Salander's goal for the struggle is the same as that of philosophers such as Marcuse or Habermas: emancipation from domination for everybody. Still, Larsson seems to be far more optimistic concerning these matters than a postmodern theorist such as Baudrillard. The techno-revolutionary optimism of Marcuse is more Larsson's style in the Millennium trilogy. Like a cyborg, or a robot, Salander is born into this system of oppression, where neoliberal ideology, technology, and male patriarchs reign totally. And this is why Salander is a decidedly political figure in the Swedish crime fiction world. Like Martin Beck or Kurt Wallander once was, she is the perfect guide in this modern technological political landscape, constituting the feminist counterstrike on the new order.

Game Plan: Within the Maze

The detailed depiction of setting is, according to Bergman, one of two distinguishing features of Swedish crime fiction (the other feature is the melancholic detective with health problems).[60] Hence, the city becomes an additional character in the stories, and perhaps Stockholm is the most featured city of them all. Stockholm is the setting in nearly all of Sjöwall-Wahlöö's novels, in Stieg Larsson's novels, and certainly in the novels of Roslund & Hellström and Jens Lapidus, as we are about to see. Furthermore, Bergman refers to the city as an urban maze "used to illustrate the difficulty of establishing knowledge and an overview."[61] A modern example of this is Stieg Larsson's novels, where the city is being contrasted with the countryside. Emancipation and freedom occur within the urban maze, according to Larsson. That is the place for diversity, freedom of expression, individual emancipation, tolerance, open-minded relations, and unrestrained sexuality such as homosexuality, trans-ethnic sexual encounters, or BDSM.[62] The countryside in the novels of Larsson is a dangerous place filled with worn-down industries, ominous small towns, deserted summer cottages, and evil motorcycle gangs. It is the place of the hidden crimes of the past, such as old Nazi connections from World War II and the obsessive serial killings of Gottfried Vanger and his son Martin Vanger in *The Girl with the Dragon Tattoo*. It is the place where patriarchal villains, rapists, and killers such as Zalachenko and Nils Bjurman hide out in *The Girl Who Played with Fire*. An older use of these dichotomies was made by Per Wahlöö, who exploited the contrast between opposites in his crime fiction novels, and perhaps more clearly than ever in *The Steel Spring*, where the countryside becomes the symbol for (socialist) freedom and the urban maze of Stockholm implies death, destruction, and pure horror. The city was the very opposite of freedom in the left-wing movement of the 1970s, which resulted in a "green wave" when young people left the city environment to grow their own organic food in the countryside. The city was a polluted and dangerous milieu filled with crime and horrors, and it made Martin Beck dyspeptic; the violence in the city also made Sjöwall-Wahlöö's most humane (and socialist) hero Lennart Kollberg leave the police occupation in *Cop Killer*.

Yet, the sick city had been an emblem for much longer than that; for example, it was a recurrent theme in the works of Dickens, as well as in those of Dostoevsky, who was one of Wahlöö's favorite writers. Particularly in *Crime and Punishment*, where the city of Saint Petersburg appears as a swelling boil of puss, and just like Southern California and Los Angeles in the novels of Chandler, this world is characterized by social injustice. When Marlowe goes up into the mountains in *The Lady in the Lake*, he experiences a cleaner, more pristine, and calmer side of California. The city in Larsson's novels do not have the same symbolic meaning, still they are the pictorial landscape where most of the stories occur. Stockholm is more of an arena, an enclosed scene for a conflict, where readers can relate to a familiar geography, with famous spots such as Götgatan on Södermalm, where tourists nowadays can take a Larsson walk conducted by the City Museum. Larsson's stage, his game plan, Stockholm, is also the place where historical crimes have been committed. Some of them have already been mentioned: the IB Affair, the Geijer Affair, the da Costa murder, the Palme murder, and of course it is the prime stage for the biggest crime of them all—Sjöwall-Wahlöö's big crime, the Social Democratic government and its betrayal of the working class in Sweden. Still, for a postmodern writer such as Larsson, Stockholm is above all a game plan for some of his favorite crime novels. It is a legendary, intertextually important field that writers from every generation have to colonize, even today.

Geographically, Larsson's paranoid scenario spins across the entire country, from the northern parts and its deserted small towns (where he grew up himself), to the big city of Stockholm (which he moved to in the late 1970s to become a journalist). In this widespread geography, the reader witnesses a rapidly growing number of murders, crimes against women, exploitations by neoliberal politics, and big corporation CEOs exposed as criminals in the new economy. It is all transformed by Stieg Larsson into a gritty, huge novel in three parts, with some of the most labyrinthine plots ever seen in a Swedish crime fiction novel. Larsson brings the postmodern era into crime fiction and simultaneously creates a concept for future novels to come. Yet the main concern in the works of Stieg Larsson are the issues he used to engage with as a journalist: racism, abuse of power, and feminism. The stories are well researched, containing elements almost reminiscent of non-fiction and journalistic material where the readers are supposed to get the feeling that everything is correct and checked in detail, just as in the novels of Frederick Forsyth, or Sjöwall-Wahlöö, for that matter.

But Larsson commenced his fiction writing much earlier than the Millennium trilogy. To understand the roots of his literary style and political concerns, we are now going to make a quick analysis of one of his first short stories and then move on to the third, and most politically important, Millennium novel.

Excursus: "*Brain Power*" *and* The Girl Who Kicked the Hornet's Nest

In what follows, I embark on some very short analyses of the general themes in Stieg Larsson's fictional writings. His short story "Brain Power" (published in 2014 for the first time since 1972) shows that Larsson, at the age of 17, was already concerned with issues such as the abuse of power and the abrogation of civil liberties by the elite.[63] The story centers around Michael November Collins, and it is set in the future (approximately 102 years after the year when Larsson wrote it, which would be 2174). This future is the kind of future well known to science fiction readers all over the world. It is the same kind of familiar, creepy, totalitarian dystopia displayed in George Orwell's *1984* (1949), Ray Bradbury's *Fahrenheit 451* (1951), and numerous other nightmarish sci-fi stories. The character of Collins is a former competitive athlete, and the government wishes to take his body and remove his brain to replace it with the super-brain of the dying science genius Hans Zägel. The doctor in charge tells Collins, "It demands your absolute obedience. If you refuse, you will be arrested for obstructing the government."[64]

When Collins becomes aware of this encroachment on his head (he has to die while his wife and children are left behind), he tries to escape. The escape sequence is also typical of this kind of sci-fi story—the runaway from a fraudulent totalitarian regime and its stooges, trying to suppress its own citizens. Of course—also according to genre rules—Collins gets caught, and then he is finished. At the time, this was a very customary ending in sci-fi stories and conspiracy movies deriving from the paranoid Nixon era of the

1970s. Think *Klute* (1971), *Serpico* (1973), *The Parallax View* (1973), *Executive Action* (1973), *The Conversation* (1974), *Three Days of the Condor* (1975), *All the President's Men* (1976), *Capricorn One* (1978) and others, where the clandestine power structures eventually, always, in some way or another, win or slip away. Happy endings were out of date totally, and this dystopian image also corresponded to the gloomy 1970s reality with the Pentagon Papers, the Watergate scandal, and the acts of cruelty during the Vietnam War, and the highest officials getting away with it (except for Richard Nixon who, of course, had to resign in 1974).

This early story of Larsson's is filled with criticism of authority and power, and at one point the protagonist Collins says, "But the police are supposed to protect people's lives." And the doctor explains, "They do exactly as the government tells them. And in this case, Zägel's life is more important than that of an athlete."[65]

Stieg Larsson's fiancée Eva Gabrielsson, whom he met at an anti–Vietnam War political rally in 1972, has written about their common interests in politics and science fiction. Gabrielsson even made a translation of Philip K. Dick's *The Man in the High Castle* into Swedish in 1979. For those who are not familiar with the story, it is about what the world would have been like if the Nazis had won World War II. Moreover, Gabrielsson and Larsson shared favorite writers in the genre: Samuel R. Delany and—quite surprisingly—Robert A. Heinlein.[66] (Surprisingly since Heinlein is known for being an openly rightwing writer.)

The themes of a huge government conspiracy and the abuse of an exceptional individual (Lisbeth Salander) are two central elements in the stories of Larsson. The short story "Brain Power" shows that this paranoid display of governmental control was there from the very beginning in Larsson's writings and thoughts. It is basically an obligatory ingredient of the sci-fi genre, and Gabrielsson has noted that the Millennium trilogy actually could have been a great series of sci-fi novels with Salander as a cyborg, instantly connected to the Internet.[67]

Now, let us take a giant leap to 2007, when Larsson's third Millennium novel, *The Girl Who Kicked the Hornet's Nest*, was published in Sweden. Later on, it was published in English for the first time in 2009 by MacLehose in Great Britain and became an instant hit, since the two earlier novels had plowed their way through the international crime fiction market for a couple of years by then. The novel corresponds nicely with the early themes of Larsson's sci-fi stories during the 1970s: government abuse of power, control, conspiracies, and secret agencies within the welfare state. By now, the reader has followed protagonists Mikael Blomkvist and Lisbeth Salander for over a thousand arm-straining pages and are familiar with their story. Larsson's overall concern is to expose the patriarchal structures of the welfare state, and in

4. The Collapsed Dream

The Girl Who Kicked the Hornet's Nest he goes deeper than before. This time it is not just about old capitalists and a serial killer (as in the first book), or an ex–KBG defector hidden away by the Swedish secret police (Säpo) to build a criminal empire and who murders reporters (as in the second book). This time, Larsson makes a steep dive into the core of the democracy and takes a look at the demarcation lines of the Social Democratic regime. About a hundred pages into *The Girl Who Kicked the Hornet's Nest*, we have a summary of the violent events in the earlier novel along with a couple of helpful conclusions:

> The problem is that none of this could have happened if Säpo weren't involved somehow. It's possible that Zalachenko really was a Russian spy who defected and was granted political asylum. It's also possible that he worked for Säpo as an expert or source or whatever title you want to give him, and that there was a good reason to offer him a false identity and anonymity. But there are three problems. First, the investigation carried out in 1991 that led to Lisbeth Salander being locked away was illegal. Second, Zalachenko's activities since then have nothing whatsoever to do with national security. Zalachenko is an ordinary gangster who's probably mixed up in several murders and other criminal activities. And third, there is no doubt that Lisbeth Salander was shot and buried alive on his property in Gosseberga.[68]

One key character that shows up in this third novel is old-time agent Evert Gullberg, one of the founders of "the Section": "Gullberg, formerly Senior Administrative Officer at the Security Police, was now seventy-eight years old and had been retired for thirteen years. But intelligence officers never really retire, they just slip into the shadows," as Larsson puts it in his extensive description of Gullberg and his life in the shadow of the organization.[69] So let us stay with this interesting character for a while. Gullberg has spent his entire life in "the secret service of the social democratic welfare state. Which was an irony, since he had faithfully voted for the moderates in one election after another," except in the 1991 election when Gullberg voted for the Social Democratic leader Ingvar Carlsson, the successor to the murdered Prime Minister Olof Palme, since he thought the conservative leader Carl Bildt was a political catastrophe.[70] In 1964 Gullberg had been one of the officers in the new Section for Special Analysis, SSA (the Nazi connotations are probably no coincidence), in daily parlance "the Section," which was called "the last line of defense." The model was the secret strategic organization within the CIA created by the legendary James Jesus Angleton.[71] Gullberg was also one of the officers cleaning up the shambles after the IB Affair in 1973, when two leftist journalists exposed the secret spy organization working for the Social Democrats, and he was a member of the extreme rightwing organization Democratic Alliance, which despised communists and supported the Vietnam War during the 1960s and 70s.[72] In short, Gullberg was the nightmarish kind of bureaucrat the New Left saw as an enemy of the people during the 1970s.

Another officer from the old days, along with Gullberg, is Fredrik Clinton, the head of the Section, who says: "We're the ones who don't exist.... We're the ones nobody will ever thank. We're the ones who have to make the decisions that nobody else wants to make. Least of all the politicians."[73] Clinton is one of the terminal forces behind the patriarchal structures punishing Lisbeth Salander, but he is dying throughout the entire book, and by the end his disintegrating body seems to symbolize the same disintegration as in the old Social Democratic welfare state: "That is how it goes. We are born. We live. We grow old. We die. He had played his part. All that remained was the disintegration."[74] This disintegration does not seem to worry Larsson, though. In fact, it is probably the prime objective for his permanent revolution, and in the final chapter Mikael Blomkvist explains the Larsson plan to the reader: "When it comes down to it, this story is not primarily about spies and secret government agencies; it's about violence against women, and the men who enable it."[75] And that is where the very key words of Larsson are being displayed: "the men who enable it"—the men behind the technology, the power, the ideology, the organizations and institutions of the welfare state. Larsson is using the spy thriller genre, and all its dark and fascinating memorabilia, to tell a feminist story in the end. In fact, this world is the very same as Marcuse's conception of the historical rise of a technological world which overpowers and controls its subjects. Hence, it is also a Marxist view presented by Larsson. His Trotskyite roots are showing up in the subtext of the novel. According to Trotsky, the established order, the existing power, "status quo," are just brief moments in history. Trotsky's entire existence is constantly being characterized by an indestructible revolutionary optimism.[76] Change is possible—or even so, inevitable in the long run. "The permanent revolution" is his theoretical solution. Salander embodies this revolution in several ways.

In one of Trotsky's books, translated into Swedish and published in 1969, and probably read by Larsson, Isaac Deutscher describes the concept of "the permanent revolution" as the core of Marxism, a concept formulated by Marx in the mid–1800s, after the revolutionary year of 1848. In the beginning of the 1900s, Trotsky reworked the concept as the solution to a problem that Lenin had pondered upon for over a decade: How could a revolution, led by a socialist working class against a bourgeois opposition, still, in the end, result in the establishment of a capitalistic order? Trotsky's solution to this problem was his conclusion that the dynamics of the revolution could not be limited to one definite stage, and once it all got started it would sweep away, not only Czarism, but also weak capitalism. What got started as a bourgeois revolution—such as the French one in 1789—would then end up as a socialist revolution. This revolution also had to blast the borders of Russia if it would succeed. Trotsky saw the revolution and the national state as incompatible concepts. The revolution had to become transnational, international, and, in the words of our time, even *global*, to survive.[77] In that sense, Trotskyism is a cosmopolitan revolutionary theory that was condemned by Stalin. Lisbeth Salander embodies this, as I have mentioned: She is a diversified and transnational character, with connections to the entire world, and in this sense she is also optimistic in relation to the notion of change in a neoliberal world. Watching her from this Marxist perspective, she is certainly a promising update of Trotsky's permanent revolution.

But equally, the world of Larsson is a postmodern depiction of reality, as in the words of Carl Freedman: "the era in which capitalist modernization is so thoroughly triumphant that, owing to the lack of that contrast on which visibility depends, it becomes somewhat difficult to see."[78] It is also the era that Lenin described as the imperialist phase of capitalism.

Finally, the end of "Brain Power" is a dystopian one, as it should be in the depressive climate of 1970s science fiction. But how about the ending in *The Girl Who Kicked the Hornet's Nest*? Everybody, except for the bad guys, do nicely, and that is probably the recipe for its huge success. It is a dark and deeply disturbing story in many ways, but finally Larsson sheds some optimism over this gruesome Swedish reality. There are good guys working for a better world out there: namely, Mikael Blomkvist (the journalists), Torsten Edklinth (the good bureaucrats), and Lisbeth Salander (the anarcho-feminist hackers out there fighting abuse of power). Salander is the perfect Marcusian revolutionary subject, in all its optimism as presented in critical theory, born within the oppressive apparatus, jacked up to its own internal system, taking control over it, overriding it, and becoming the ultimate hero of the neoliberal era in the end.

The production of this type of hero—the revolutionary hero, the criminal hero, etc.—could also be studied from a Marxist perspective, and that is where we are heading next.

Inversion of the Hero

In Per Wahlöö's novel *Murder on the Thirty-First Floor*, the author makes an interesting choice as he is presenting a more-than-zealous protagonist meant to be despised by the reader: a cold police bureaucrat out of touch with the more sympathetic parts of society. In Wahlöö's novels *the idea is the hero*, as we have seen, and the main character is not a hero in the old sense of the word. On the contrary, his purpose is to guide the reader into the bizarre realm the writer wants to depict as a contemporary critique. Ernest Mandel mentions the erasing of demarcation lines between law and lawlessness in Robert Ludlum's *The Road to Gandolfo* (1975), where crime finally seems to pay off. This renders the entire crime fiction genre topsy-turvy, and questions such as what is legal, what is not, who are the crooks, and who are the heroes no longer have clear answers.[79] In fact, in the new crime thriller of the 2000s, the questions of legality are not important at all. Carsten Jensen stresses that the crime fiction of Henning Mankell, with his pondering detective Kurt Wallander, is completely out of date. Instead, the broad middle-class that reads Larsson's revenge fantasies about Lisbeth Salander feels an almost infinite urge for violence, revenge, and a hero who runs amok rather than uses the skills of deduction. Guilt is not important in this new thriller genre, Jensen argues; instead, the pretext it gives for violent action without guilt is of importance for the middle-class readers. According to Jensen, Salander is Wallander's real daughter (instead of Linda), and with her there is a shift in the genre paradigm, from rights of principles to revenge fantasies, from self-sacrificing duty to emotionally grounded anarchy, from the idea of the law to the tribute of a narcissistic feeling of omnipotence.[80]

In the works of Wahlöö, the central issues are moral ones, and the reader learns to answer them as the narrative unfolds. The unsympathetic protagonists are just there to point out the (Marxist) direction for this limited reader. The idea of an inverted hero was probably to, and I quote Alan Wald, "galvanize the public sphere of their generation into consciousness."[81]

In order to operate in a certain socio-economic climate, saturated by neoliberal capitalism, the crime fiction hero has evolved through the years, and Mandel argues this evolution has been a circular one. According to him, there was a tendency during the 1980s to make the killer into a hero, and this signifies a return to the origin of the crime novel, the picaresque novel with its noble lower class bandits.[82] This evolution of the crime hero is in fact in full motion even today, where almost every Swedish crime author has their own hero with a criminal past. Lisbeth Salander is the one who got the ball rolling in Sweden, but Jan Guillou had his bourgeois military Carl Hamilton in the 1980s, a CIA trained and Navy Seals educated Swedish agent who actually murdered for the state, and eventually became a serial killer in the final Hamilton novel in 1995.

Mandel traces the revenging hero to the 1960s Modesty Blaise series by Peter O'Donnell, which is probably one of Stieg Larsson's sources of inspiration for Salander as well. Blaise, too, had a difficult past and used selective criminal events to do good. According to Mandel, this kind of hero, outside the boundaries of law in society, depends on a change in climate and a growing skepticism towards law, order, and society. These stories also employ a cynical view of police work and the downfall of capitalism; the society is regarded as being rotten to the bone.[83]

Alan Wald argues that there are certain aspects of the crime genre that especially lend themselves to a Marxist imagination, and a diverse range of characters, in terms of class, color or gender, is one important aspect besides the usual contents such as urban settings, corruption by wealth, and the problem of the state. Moreover, through appropriate dramatic techniques and characterizations, Marxist writers make anti-capitalist observations, but the depictions of openly communist heroes are unusual.[84]

Neither can Salander be seen as a pure Marxist hero. Her looks suggest that she is a part of the anarchist movement, resembling those rock-throwing youngsters seen when the world leaders gathered at the huge summits in Genoa, Seattle or Gothenburg in the end of the 1990s and the beginning of the 2000s, when the anti-globalization movement was strong and powerful. Critic Göran Greider makes a similar suggestion when stating that she belongs to the anarcho-socialist movements of the 1970s and 80s and that he has seen the likes of her in leftist demonstrations during the past thirty years.[85] Larsson's description of her, when the reader is just getting to know her in the first novel, is a taciturn young girl all dressed in black:

> Salander was dressed for the day in a black T-shirt with a picture on it of E.T. with fangs, and the words "I am also an alien." She had on a black skirt that was frayed at the hem, a worn-out black, mid-length leather jacket, rivet belt, heavy Doc Martens boots, and horizontally striped, green-and-red knee socks. She had put on make-up in a colour scheme that indicated she might be colourblind. In other words, she was exceptionally decked out.[86]

Obviously she is dressed in the goth-vegan-leftist style that youngsters started to wear some time during the 1990s postmodern fashion boom, with its crossover dressing culture; nothing really seemed to be what it actually was, but it was definitely more complicated than that (or at least *wanted* to be more complicated). Tim Parks has called Salander "a taciturn young woman of punk appearance flaunting aggressive" and has argued that her complexity makes her a "victim, superhero, and torturer" all at the same time. Parks also remarks that with all of this Larsson has "stepped out of any feasible realism into a cartoon fantasy of ugly wish fulfillment," concluding that the heroes in the Millennium books are "comic strip material" because they are in no real danger at any moment.[87]

Likewise, Salander is full of paradoxes. Definitely no vegan, she has the unhealthy lifestyle of the hacker stereotype: smoking, eating junk food, drinking, and probably doesn't shower very often. She doesn't eat organic vegetables or demonstrate her wish to smash capitalism. Instead, she works for a private security firm doing personal research in the first novel, she undergoes breast augmentation surgery in the second novel, and she does not seem to fight a collective struggle in the socialist sense of the word.[88] Since she is being attacked as an individual, she also defends herself as an individual. According to Mandel, the crime novel consists of an individualistic bourgeois ideology, which is probably why Salander is a success among contemporary readers.[89] Although she is an ideal bourgeois hero (in the sense of her personal agenda for the struggle), she fights the patriarchal structures on her own, with a little help from the novel's true protagonist Mikael Blomvist. The ideal of the strong self (and even as a personal brand) is the prime conception of the perfect individual in modern day Sweden. Salander moves around as she likes, she does not seem to have any problems with money (she's a hacker and can steal as much as she needs), she moves outside the law and the capitalist system, yet she uses the system to get what she wants. Basically, Salander is the typical postmodern hero, or in the words of Carl Freedman, she is "a scandalous mixing of high and low [that] strives to break decisively with the category of the aesthetic ... favoring a protodeconstructive stress on the marginal, the fragmentary, and the heterogeneous."[90] Her notions about the police and the law are similar to those of anarchists, and Larsson declares this as follows:

> Salander was not like any normal person. She had a rudimentary knowledge of the law—it was a subject she had never had occasion to explore—and her faith in the police was generally exiguous. For her the police were the hostile force who over the years had put her under arrest or humiliated her. The last dealing she had had with the police was in May of the previous year when she was walking past Götgatan on her way to Milton Security. She suddenly found herself facing a visorclad police officer. Without the slightest provocation on her part, he had struck her on the shoulders with his baton. Her spontaneous reaction was to launch a fierce counterattack, using a Coca-Cola bottle that she had in her hand. The officer turned on his heel and ran off before she could injure him. Only later did she find out that "Reclaim the Streets" was holding a demonstration further down the road.[91]

Reclaim the Streets (later known as Reclaim the City) was an urban movement during the 1990s and early 2000s, mostly consisting of young people who opposed globalization, transnational capitalism, and the increased mass-motorization in the cities. Most of them were leftist activists and some were anarchists, and on several occasions the clash between activists and the police forces became violent, especially in Sweden. Götgatan in Stockholm, the place of the Millennium office, was a central spot for the perhaps most famous one of these battles. Yet Salander, as we have seen, is not a part of this collective activist struggle, because, according to Larsson, she is not that political aware. Her struggle is the individual striving for freedom and truth (and revenge), even though her appearance has been hijacked from the leftist street movement of the 1990s. Mandel has made a comment on individual heroes and sees them as a limitation of the crime fiction genre. This type of hero belongs to the main pattern of the genre, Mandel argues, and as long as a writer accepts this pattern, he or she can only achieve a partial social awareness among the readers. The novel never fully takes the leap and emancipates itself from bourgeois ideology; it can only expose and intensify the crisis of this ideology.[92]

The Swedish literary scholar Nina Björk has written an interesting passage on the inversion of Salander's hero. According to Björk, Salander is not a strange hero at all in the modern culture of the Western world. She is merely the bearer of a hugely traditional view of the human qualifications that create a hero. "Is it not the lone cowboy, the lone ranger, the action man, the strong man—in short, the ultimate hero, that stands before us in new shape?" Björk asks rhetorically.[93] The only fact that makes her appear new and fresh in the crime genre is that Salander's role has transposed, from being a male to a female hero—a simple gender shift, that is. If Lisbeth Salander had been a man she would have been ridiculous, Björk argues, but instead she turns into someone we admire in a world where the man can no longer uphold the old views on what constitutes a traditional hero.[94] Instead, a woman (obviously tomboyishly enough) can.

The *Zeitgeist* of Autopia—or the "Car Society"—is the creator of the liberal man in novels by Chandler and Wahlöö, and a similar statement could be made about the example of Salander and technology. Even if she is not completely an individual fighter, she still signifies the struggle between oppositional *forces* (such as the Pirate Bay and Napster communities on the Internet, etc.) and the technological *rationality* (the huge corporations and the state) as once defined by Marcuse. Critic Magnus Peterson has made an interesting note on this technology as an inevitable part of the story in Larsson's novels:

> In the Millennium trilogy, the boundary between private and public blur while the intertwining of different media and genres intensifies. Communications in Larsson's fictional universe are constantly and strikingly mediated and indirect: e-mailing, texting, programming, scanning, bugging, word processing, and talking on cell phones. When people speak face-to-face, we can be sure that the dialogue is soon interrupted by one of the ubiquitous media technologies.[95]

Questions of technology and identity in the modern world are continuously being displayed in today's crime fiction, and these themes, of course, have their place in the inverted crime story as well. Mandel mentions Robert Ludlum as a writer who consciously inverts the modern crime hero. His novel *The Bourne Identity* (1980)—with its hero clearly working outside the demarcation lines of law and order just like Salander, in this case (in the era of identity politics)—seems to be the ultimate postmodern crime fiction novel. The hero wakes up on a fishing boat suffering from retrograde amnesia after being shot several times and does not even know his own identity. He seems to be the self without a center or a past. The rest of the novel (and several other novels in the series) contains the breathtaking rollercoaster ride of his search for his true identity. Basically, Bourne is the embodiment of two Marxist concepts. First, the false consciousness, as stressed by Adorno, after being brainwashed by the CIA (capitalist ideology). Second, he wakes up being Foucault's rejected subject symbolizing the break-up of the self in a disorganized, fragmentized world.⁹⁶ Lisbeth Salander makes a similar journey, and in the final Millennium novel the full-blown image of her damaged life is exposed to the reader. Still, the deconstruction of her past is displayed to the reader rather than to herself, as is often the case in novels by Chandler and Macdonald. They frequently use characters with double, or even triple identities, and the main theme in their novels is basically always the return of a character's past that threatens their existence in the present. Larsson deliberately used this formula since he had read hardboiled crime writers since early childhood, and the theme is one of the most reliable in modern crime fiction, having been firmly introduced in Sweden by Sjöwall-Wahlöö in the 1960s.

Salander has been connected to several characters in popular fiction through the years, from being "a gamin, Audrey Hepburn look-alike, but with tattoos and piercings, the take-no-prisoners attitude of Lara Croft, and the cool, unsentimental intellect of Mr. Spock," as *New York Times* critic Michiko Kakutani writes, to a new incarnation of French assassin *La Femme Nikita* of the 1990s movies and the television series in 2010.⁹⁷ Nina Björk argues that Salander has an avoiding, almost dissolving, identity, and that she is totally independent of a firm identity. As a sexual human being, she cannot be categorized as either homo-, bi-, or heterosexual. Consequently, the idea of a real identity has been annihilated in the elite hacker society that Salander is a part of. In that world, they mainly know each other under gender-neutral names such as Plague, Wasp, or Six Of One. Anybody could hide behind these names, no matter their gender, ethnicity, or religion, etc.⁹⁸

An email conversation between Larsson and his publisher Eva Gedin at Norstedts on April 30, 2004, unmasks the underlying ideas of the character:

> Lisbeth is an exception simply because she is a sociopath with psychotic traits and she doesn't function like normal people. She therefore doesn't have the same perception of what is "right" or "wrong" as normal people, but she also suffers the consequences.⁹⁹

In the same conversation, Larsson develops his thoughts on the inversion of his heroes as follows:

> I tried to create protagonists who are radically different from the usual characters in detective fiction.... That's why Mikael Blomkvist doesn't have ulcers or problems with alcoholism or existential anguish. He doesn't listen to opera or dedicate himself to some strange hobby like model aeroplanes or something similar. In general he doesn't have any problems and his main characteristic is that he behaves like a stereotypical "whore," something that he himself recognizes. I also consciously inverted the gender roles: in many ways Blomkvist plays the part of the "bimbo" while Lisbeth Salander has ways of behaving and qualities that are characteristically "male."¹⁰⁰

Yet, how about Mikael Blomkvist, evidently the dream character for Larsson himself: a crusading journalist (true) and a ladies' man (not likely)? Furthermore, an intriguing question could be whether Blomkvist is actually a Marxist or something else? Salander is probably not, since her revolutionary consciousness has not yet awakened. Blomkvist, on the other hand, has a background from the 1970s when he went to school (later the College of Journalism in Stockholm, which was famous for being a leftist institution back then), at a time when leftist politics permeated all areas of society, from children's books to television and public debate. Still, Salander has not found any distinctive leftist proofs in his life when she presents the thorough report on Blomkvist that she has made for the Vanger family lawyer Dirch Frode in *The Girl with the Dragon Tattoo*:

> *Millennium* is generally viewed as critical of society, but I'm guessing the anarchists think it's a wimpy bourgeois crap magazine along the lines of Arena or Ordfront, while the Moderate Students Association probably thinks that the editors are all Bolsheviks. There is nothing to indicate that Blomkvist has ever been active politically, even during the leftwing wave when he was at secondary school. While he was plugging away at the College of Journalism he was living with a girl who at the time was active in the Syndicalists and today sits in the parliament as a representative for the Left party. He seems to have been given the left-wing stamp primarily because as a financial journalist he specialises in investigative reporting about corruption and shady transactions in the corporate world.[101]

Right here it is clear that Larsson wants to distance Blomkvist from himself. Blomkvist was born in 1960, Larsson in 1954. That is only a six-year difference, but in Swedish political history those six years are crucial. Larsson was fourteen when he joined the Marxist movement in 1968, when Blomkvist would have been eight. When the leftist movement in Sweden started to wear off during the second half of the 1970s, Blomkvist was too young to get involved. This lapse in time between author and protagonist is probably deliberate. Larsson does not only want to distance himself from Blomkvist— although some of the most important characteristics (the crusading journalist, the leftist magazine, the preference for coffee shops and junk food, etc.) are picked right out of Larsson's own life—he also wants to distance Blomkvist from Marxism. Greider has made an interesting note of this and mentions a taboo in contemporary Sweden of calling Larsson a socialist, in contrast to him being a feminist and antiracist, which is much more acceptable.[102] Making Blomkvist a Marxist is the same thing as making him a political crusader instead of a feminist crusader seeking equality and justice for women (which makes him a hero, and not an enemy of the capitalist system) rather than seeking equality between classes (which makes him a communist, hence a crook with all the guilt of *the Red Danger* on his back). And a writer who strives after popularity, writing in a popular (hugely commercial) genre such as crime fiction, does not openly declare that he is a socialist. On the other hand, there could be a million other reasons for this lapse between Larsson and Blomkvist. In fact, Larsson's novels *are* more feminist, they *are* more antiracist, than they are Marxist. Still, without his background in Marxism during the 1970s and 80s, there would not have been any *-ism* left at all, and certainly no dark stories of the collapsed dream, either.

To conclude this discussion, we are now turning our attention to the newly written sequels that are currently flooding the market.

The Lagercrantz Sequel

On August 27, 2015, ten years after the original release of *The Girl with the Dragon Tattoo* in Sweden, the world saw a new, fourth, Millennium novel, *The Girl in the Spider's Web*. It was the biggest book release in the world that year, and in the U.S. its front cover advertised "A Lisbeth Salander Novel.... Continuing Stieg Larsson's Millennium series," rather than just a new Millennium novel.[103] It was written by the Swedish author and journalist David Lagercrantz (born in 1962), famous for his autobiographical accounts of notable rebellious, and disparate, names such as Swedish soccer player Zlatan Ibrahimovic and British mathematician Alan Turing.

In short, the plot unfolds as follows: In the new story, once again the crusading journalist Mikael Blomkvist meets up with hacker heroine Lisbeth Salander. Blomkvist gets a phone call from a source claiming to have information vital to the United States. A tangled web of spies, cybercriminals, and governments around the world is what Blomkvist discovers along with Salander, whom he asks for help. Someone is ready to kill to protect the big secret they are tracing: that a crime organization—the Spiders—led by Lisbeth Salander's sister Camilla, plunders tech companies of ideas and new technology worth astronomical sums of money. Swedish professor Frans Balder picks up their tracks and subsequently gets eliminated. Finally, Lisbeth Salander tracks her sister down and finds out that Camilla has inherited the father's—Zalachenko's—crime organization from the first three novels.

In the summer of 2013, Lagercrantz was asked by the Larsson Estate Moggliden and Larsson's publisher Norstedts to write a fourth, free-standing sequel to the Millennium series. The meeting was strictly confidential, and Lagercrantz had to sneak in the back way to the publisher's office in Stockholm; they used secret code words in their emails, and Lagercrantz wrote the entire novel on an off-grid computer to avoid the risk of being hacked. The manuscripts never got emailed but were sent on USB-memory sticks by personal couriers to the publisher.[104]

Lagercrantz has a quite different background from Stieg Larsson. He belongs to the Swedish nobility, and his father, Olof Lagercrantz, was a huge authority within public debate and literature for decades. Lagercrantz also lacks the political activist background of Larsson, which is clear when reading the fourth installment in the Millennium series, which focuses more on mathematics and the technology of surveillance than on feminism, antiracism or Marxism. Lagercrantz's upbringing was filled with higher learning, reading all the classics, and crime fiction was not a part of that. He is repulsed by the violence in some works of crime fiction, but is intrigued by the intellectual part of the deduction process in works by Håkan Nesser and Dennis Lehane.[105]

By the time Lagercrantz put out his first Millennium novel in 2015, the first Millennium trilogy had sold 82 million copies by 50 publishers worldwide.[106] Quite an accomplishment for a Swedish debutant. So the question we have to ask ourselves right now is how Lagercrantz's novel compares to the original Larsson installments?

Naturally, Lagercrantz's background makes it impossible to read his novel in the same way as the old trilogy. He lacks the Trotskyite background, the antiracist commitment, and the eclectic, postmodern style with its labyrinthine crazy plots. All that's left is basically a manic, imaginative workaholic.

One of the first reviews in the biggest newspaper in Sweden, *Dagens Nyheter*, was written by literature sociologist Johan Svedjedal who was not too impressed and stated that Lagercrantz was a literary actor who had mutated into a marketing man, entertainer and a brand of his own: the trademark David Lagercrantz and the trademark Millennium. The reviewer perceived the strong market forces behind it all, and a desperate but impossible will to please everybody. However, in the end all the ingredients are there: the abundant torrents of coffee, the body piercings, the secret and successful client mediating a mission to Mikael Blomkvist, the newsroom interiors at the Millennium magazine, the hacker attacks, the assaults on women, the revenge on the assaulters, the hunts and the guns blazing, the intertwining course of events, the chapters headlined with actual dates, etc. The plot contains elements such as organized crime, Russian Mafia, American computer surveillance, corporate secrets, and artificial intelligence. It is a little bit of *Rain Man*, a little bit of Julian Assange, and huge amounts of hacker culture, and the reviewer concludes that a power outage would devastate major parts of the plot in this novel.[107]

Crime writer Lee Child, reviewing *The Girl in the Spider's Web* in *New York Times*, starts by mentioning similar efforts in literature history, from John Banville reviving Chandler's Philip Marlowe, or Jill Paton Walsh doing the same thing to Dorothy Sayers's Lord Peter Wimsey, to the extraordinary industry in the wake of Robert Ludlum, who seems to have published more novels posthumously than when he was alive. Child concludes that Lagercrantz lacks Larsson's passion, radical instincts, and sublime madness. Child asks himself to what extent fictional characters are genuinely reproducible.

Furthermore, he is impressed by the Salander character and sees her as an invention "in the same ballpark as Thomas Harris's Hannibal Lecter. She's a classic antihero—fundamentally deranged, objectively appalling, lawless, violent and deceitful, but fiercely loved by millions of readers because she has good reasons for the way she is and a heart of gold."[108]

The first Lagercrantz sequel is almost impossible to analyze without stating the fact that it is an utterly commercial project, *created* to generate money. Lagercrantz may be a passionate and professional writer, but this is still a purely commissioned work, not stemming from the creative madness in Stieg Larsson's head, but from avaricious agents and publishers. The industry surrounding the publishing of *The Girl in the Spider's Web* was made into an industry itself. David Lagercrantz wrote a working diary for the whole process for his publisher in Sweden, and the diary was published in 21 international newspapers worldwide in August 2015, a couple of weeks before the release. In it, Lagercrantz tell his own tale of the "crazy" times—starting in May 2013 and ending in July 2015—through the work process. Right from the start he was aware of the fact that he was writing a commercial product even more commercial than most other books. When he came to the U.S. in May 2015 to meet the media at Book Expo America, the first thing he saw was a huge banner of his own novel. A minute later he sat down beside John Grisham to give interviews. After that he went to his hotel and gave more interviews to *USA Today, New York Times, Los Angeles Times* and *Hollywood Reporter*. It was all a monstrous publicity stunt, and the world press was going crazy.[109]

In this novel, technology and science get emphasized more than questions of antiracism and feminism. Let's take a look at a brief example. When Part 1, "The Watchful Eye," starts, there is a quote. Larsson frequently used quotes on statistics and facts with feminist issues. Lagercrantz's first quote is:

> The NSA, or National Security Agency, is a U.S. federal authority that reports to the Department of Defense. The head office is in Fort Meade, Maryland, by the Patuxent Freeway. Since its founding in 1952, the NSA has been engaged in signals surveillance—these days mostly in connection with Internet and telephone traffic. Time after time its powers have been increased, and now it monitors more than twenty billion conversations and messages every twenty-four hours.[110]

While Larsson worked within several Swedish traditions, such as the puzzle mystery novel, the police procedural, or the spy novel, Lagercrantz, on his account, emphasizes the scientific mood of the modern spy novel, and from that moment he starts building his own Lisbeth Salander mythology. Salander is a well-known character in this story, a celebrity—people recognize her, in a way similar to how Superman gets recognized when dressed in his red cloak and blue tights. On one occasion the character Needham, an American NSA agent, notes the following about Salander's nickname on the web, Wasp. He has been searching for references to the name and found that "wasp" is a

British fighter plane from World War II as well as a comedy by Aristophanes, and continues:

> But those references are all a little too sophisticated for a hacker genius; they don't go with the culture. You know what did fit? The superhero in Marvel Comics: Wasp is one of the founding members of the Avengers … with Thor, Iron Man, Captain America. In the original comics she was even their leader for a while.[111]

Salander's status as a superhero is thoroughly reinforced in Lagercrantz's version of her mythology. Hence, he is leaving Swedish realism behind with huge broad strokes and makes a colorful cocktail of science fiction and the control mechanisms of technology that Larsson would have probably enjoyed. It is a "sick world … in which paranoia is a requirement," as old-time cop Bublanski tells Mikael Blomkvist in one scene.[112] It is a world where Habermas' notions of an increasingly technological consciousness and instrumental reason seem to take form. Lagercrantz writes about the idea of "technological singularity," the state at which computer intelligence will have overtaken our own, also known as artificial intelligence.[113] The growth of technological control ultimately implies an organization in which technology becomes autonomous and dictates its own value-system. At the end of this process, Habermas sees a level on which decision-making is completely delegated to computers.[114] This does not imply the presence of critical theory in Lagercrantz's novel, but instead it is all about general questions as posed in science fiction novels since the days of Isaac Asimov in the 1940s and earlier. However, this is not the place for further analysis of *The Girl in the Spider's Web*. The saga of Larsson's Millennium trilogy is a saga of its own and it has had a tremendous effect on Swedish crime fiction all over the world; the saga about David Lagercrantz is a completely different chapter. In October 2016, the Swedish publisher Norstedts announced that Lagercrantz was writing a second sequel to the Millennium series. It was released on September 7, 2017, with the title *The Girl Who Takes an Eye for an Eye*. Another part of the story, a Millennium 6, is to be released in 2019. The new project goes on. How history will treat this phenomenon is something for the critics to deal with in the future.

End of the Line?

Andrew Nestingen remarks that the Millennium series adheres to the socially critical vision of the Scandinavian crime novel, but in an ambivalent way. According to him, the novels are built on a double movement: "Salander and Blomkvist fight neoliberalism by using its own tools more skillfully and more ruthlessly than the corporations; but, in so doing, they replicate the values, ethics and practices they ostensibly oppose." Nestingen calls this struggle against the neoliberal welfare state "vigilante individualism."[115] Furthermore, he sees this as a total reversal of John Scagg's claim that police mobilization fails in the tradition of the Scandinavian police novel—justice is not delivered by the state, but by the private individual. Nestingen, in this sense, talks about a *reversal* of the Martin Beck tradition when the market becomes the only arena where justice *can* be delivered.[116] One gets the feeling that Larsson is deliberately blurring the outlines of the new crime novel here. Scaggs argues that the crime solving procedure is a part of the ideological state apparatus of control, and that the genre of police procedural emphasizes regulatory authority and social control.[117] In Larsson's novels, this social control has been removed from the state apparatus and shifted into the private sector with companies such as Milton Security. This is an interesting shift in society that Larsson is pointing his finger at, and of course it is a paradigm in the Swedish society we are witnessing here, where the state is gradually being outnumbered by the private sector.

The neoliberal project is the backdrop for Mankell, and, moreover, it is what makes the Millennium trilogy possible. The critique works on different levels in the novels; it intertwines with the fast paced action, the amazing labyrinthine plots, the strong characters, and the postmodern intertextual play pervading the entire series. The "vigilante individualism" has since Larsson become somewhat of a new norm in Swedish crime fiction. Private initiative surpasses a police force in constant crisis with scarce means to solve crimes and fight crooks in modern society. The private eye (backed up by huge corporations) is coming back in Sweden, as we will see in the novels of Jens Lapidus, and the new forms or organization within the police force are also being portrayed in several novels, just as they once were by Sjöwall-Wahlöö.

The notion of the collapsed dream is the most important leitmotif in the entire wave of Swedish crime fiction since 1965. The nostalgic, pensive dream of the welfare state—or the memory (false or not), the idea, of it—becomes the big sadness and despair permeating the genre in Scandinavia. The decay of the welfare state is basically complete in Sweden today, but still politicians talk about the welfare state as if it were actually there. Crime fiction writers know this is just the phantom pains of the past becoming a huge lie in the present. The talk of the welfare state has transformed into rhetoric used as populism in the public debate. The neoliberal project has made its big score in creating an unequal society filled with rapists, killers, pedophiles, tax frauding capitalists, junkies, and youngsters moving into the cyber world where everything seems to be cozier. The critical idiom of the crime novel is perhaps the best cultural expression for displaying this downfall, and Larsson knew it, just as Marxists had known it for decades, from the American Marxists during the 1940s and 50s sneaking their criticism into their works, to Per Wahlöö, who openly declared his membership in the Communist Party and wrote Marxist agitprop novels during the 1960s.

As we have already seen, Stieg Larsson was not a leftist writer who romanticized the revolution; instead, he probably had a notion of critique and emancipation that concurred a lot with critical theorists such as Adorno, who thought the critique of humanity only can be a critique of what constitutes humanity at a particular point in history.[118] The critique is thereby bound to context, and that is why computer technology has a central meaning in Larsson's crime fiction, because his stories articulate meaning with the contemporary times of Sweden in the beginning of the 2000s, when computers had an increasing importance in almost all parts of life for people. Moreover, technology is an arena for emancipation and control, two old Marxist themes in literature and philosophy, elegantly picked up by Larsson for the new millennium.

Are the novels of Larsson the end of the line for Marxist Swedish crime fiction? One could easily launch a revealing critique against them. The novels have resulted in an industry bigger than Stieg Larsson could have ever anticipated: Swedish and American blockbuster movies, the new series written by David Lagercrantz, over 90 million books sold and counting. The Millennium phenomenon has fed many capitalists, and let's be frank here: Larsson was writing entertainment, and most of his readers across the globe have not analyzed his stories as I have done here. He is merely another one of those authors working in the moody tradition set by Sjöwall-Wahlöö, in which the political messages are thoroughly embedded in the rapid narrative, and there is a big chance that readers might miss the point while rushing to the next page, or chapter, or book. Let us just hope that the story about Lisbeth Salander stays in the mind for a while before they embark on the next project or series in the ever-growing Swedish crime fiction genre.

To answer the initial question in the paragraph above—are Larsson's novels Marxist?—I have deliberately avoided answering this question until now. Of course they are Marxist, as I have interpreted them above. Still, they are also feminist, and antiracist, and postmodern, and post–Marxist, and eclectic, and traditional. They represent the multitude of new Swedish crime fiction novels, where vigor and remembrance of the welfare state (and the leftist movement) are obvious elements. However, at the same time as Larsson broke through in Sweden in the mid–2000s, two other writers were setting off with a new series of gloomy, socially critical novels with a worm's eye view on the world. They are currently the most interesting writing duo, excavating the Swedish underbelly, who have also launched a triumphant comeback for the social perspective in the Marxist crime fiction tradition, and they are the ones that I am about to explore next: Roslund & Hellström.

5

Excavating the Swedish Underbelly
Roslund & Hellström

Roslund & Hellström's march to triumph has been a slow one. They have hardly enjoyed the rocket stardom of Stieg Larsson, or the international growing success of Henning Mankell. But still, perhaps their stories on the Swedish underbelly are even more urgent than the vivid, web-like plots of Larsson, or Mankell's global themes packed with moral issues. The trail from Raymond Chandler to Roslund & Hellström seems a long one, but there are several inescapable parallels between them, as well as huge differences.

First, Roslund & Hellström write in the hardboiled tradition. Their prose is concrete, tough, rough, and harshly poetic. The use of Hemingway's iceberg technique is obvious, and the narrative is played out like a movie in different scenes containing realistic, sparse dialogue and the intercutting of a screenplay. Second, their theoretical approach to characters and protagonists is a humanistic one, with the individual in the center of the story. Third, the big city is the backdrop of their stories. They deal with Chandlerian issues belonging to the urban crime story, such as political corruption and class differences in a modern capitalistic society.

The big difference is that Roslund & Hellström write about cops. Their genre is a mixture of classic, socially realistic novel and police procedural. There are no private eyes telling cynical stories in first-person in their novels. Perhaps the contempt for crime is larger in Roslund & Hellström's protagonist Ewert Grens than in Chandler's Philip Marlowe, who is not a servant of the law; instead he is an outsider, not belonging to either society or the law enforcement occupation.

Roslund & Hellström write crime novels with a personal concern for the new world we have created through history. Similar to Balzac, they believe the best way to expose the fraudulent image of this society is through the criminal underground.

A short biographical exposition will help us to understand the deep political devotion of Roslund & Hellström.

The Roslund & Hellström Track Tapes

There is actually a connection between Roslund & Hellström and Stieg Larsson, but it is not a literary one—rather a professional one in another sense. Anders Roslund has declared how he met Larsson during the 1990s when they both worked as journalists, covering the rise of extreme rightwing movements in Sweden:

> He [Larsson] was working then at TT, a Swedish wire service, like your Associated Press. I'd heard of him and we may have met incidentally in a pub, but we didn't know each other. We were both looking into the same organizations and the same people, and we began to talk on the phone, almost always about how to survive the death threats we both had received. We met later, but it was always for professional reasons; we never socialized. What I most remember is that I could trust him to give me straight advice when I ran into trouble because of my reporting. He was one of the few guys with real knowledge.[1]

Anders Roslund, born in 1961, is a longtime, prize-winning investigative journalist who worked a lot in the milieu of rightwing extremists and in prisons. During the 1990s, he covered the rise of rightwing extremists in Sweden for the National Swedish Television, SVT, and the daily news program Rapport. In the beginning of the 1990s he covered the hunt for the notorious "Laser Man" (John Ausonius), a racist killer in Stockholm.

Börge Hellström, who was born in 1957 and died of cancer in 2017, was a former drug addict and criminal who got sexually exploited as a child. Later he became known as a reformed ex-con and criminal justice debater who had served time in prison on two occasions. He was one of the founders of the noted rehabilitation and crime prevention organization called KRIS (Criminals Return Into Society), and just like Roslund he had a considerable network among criminals, which gave the writing-duo the opportunity to perform the thorough, often extremely time-consuming research they needed.

This odd couple met when Roslund was making a documentary on KRIS, *Lock Them Up* (*Lås in dom!* [1998]). They started talking to each other and became friends during the two years of making the film. They drank huge amounts of coffee during long hours of conversations and started to develop ideas for novels. One of the first ideas, that later became their debut novel *The Beast*, was built on one clear question: What happens when the father of a child who has been the victim of a pedophile decides to kill the perpetrator? This was to illuminate the Swedish sexual legislation, but also to put forth more existential questions such as: Does revenge give a real sense of redemption?[2]

Anders Roslund has also collaborated with screenwriter Stefan Thunberg on a new series of novels called *Made in Sweden*. So far, this crime duo has written two installments: *The Father* (2014) and *The Son* (2017). *Made in Sweden* focuses on one of the most notorious robber gangs in Swedish crime history, "The Military Gang" (*Militärligan*). The story, which is set during the 1970s, 80s, and 90s, follows three brothers and their ruthless father, who eventually become energetic robbers armed with military automatic weapons. Just as the novels in Roslund & Hellström's Ewert Grens series, *Made in Sweden* is a story about how Sweden shapes individuals who become criminals.

In Roslund & Hellström's first work *The Beast* (2004), the general theme, as we have seen, is how society should handle pedophiles. Two children are found dead in a basement. Four years later their murderer Bernt Lund escapes prison and kills another child. The father of the murdered child takes revenge in a frantic atmosphere whipped up by the media. His action leads to devastating consequences. In *Box 21,* also released as *The Vault* (2005), Ewert Grens comes across a Baltic trafficking gang, and his attention is captured by a Lithuanian girl who has been brutally whipped while she was being held captive in a Stockholm brothel.[3] In *Cell 8* (2006), Roslund & Hellström discuss the devastating consequences of the death penalty, with repercussions that reach from Death Row in Utah across the Atlantic into the world of some Stockholm police officers. In *The Girl Below the Street* (2007), there is a killer who hides among the outcasts living in the tunnels and the sewer-level underworld of Stockholm at the same time as 43 abandoned children turn up at Police Headquarters. Complex ethical discussions of responsibility, solidarity and homelessness serve as vehicles for exposing disturbing stories. In their international smash hit *Three Seconds* (2009), Roslund & Hellström portray the complicated life of undercover agent Piet Hoffmann, exposing issues such as drug smuggling into Swedish prisons, the moral responsibility that the police have against infiltrators and the corruption reaching high up in the Swedish government. In *Two Soldiers* (2012), they once again focus on the prison milieu with drug smuggling, escaping and murders. This time, the writers tell the violent story of two young criminals, Leon and Gabriel, and their way to the top of a ruthless crime gang in the suburbs of Stockholm, their spectacular escape from a high security prison and the way in which they hold an entire suburb hostage with their criminal activity. Roslund & Hellström's next effort, *Three Minutes* (2016), is a sequel to *Three Seconds* that gained them an undisputed reputation as Scandinavian crime kings in the United States. Their infiltrator Piet Hoffmann is back, hunted all over the world, fleeing with his family, at the same time as he has infiltrated the world's largest cocaine business in Colombia for the American Drug Enforcement Administration, DEA.

This hardworking writing duo has given several interviews in Swedish and to international media over the years. Their writing takes a long time; each book takes about 24 months of full-time writing to finish. "We use the specific knowledge we have, and that's what makes things happen. Reality is sad, black and sad. It is serious dark topics we take up, and I think you have to make it lighter in the form of a novel for people to be able to absorb the message," Börge Hellström says in one interview.[4]

The consequences of violence seem to be an overall topic of theirs, and this issue set in a new kind of landscape, the New Sweden, has been Roslund & Hellström's overall concern since the beginning of the new millennium. They also see their books as part of a social dialogue about crime and how to avoid it, dreading and dismissing the American solution with armed citizenry barricading itself into gated communities.[5] Anders Roslund has also said that it is no coincidence that Sweden is currently pumping out good crime writing; he attributes it to a loss of innocence that began with the assassination of Prime Minister Olof Palme in 1986 and continued through to the terrorist attack that killed a suicide bomber who blew himself up in a Stockholm street in December 2010. "Crime is no longer limited by borders; it is so universal," Roslund said, contrasting with the image of Sweden, which remained neutral during World War II, as a peaceful haven where politicians don't need bodyguards and nobody locks their doors.[6] In an interview two months later, Roslund also described the importance of the crime novel and its superiority to other genres: "Today, for some reason, the 'other novel' has left all descriptions of societal problems to the crime novel. All societal reflections are left to, and taken care of by, the crime novels. The Swedish crime novel is very much alive. There is not a crime fiction wave, which is sometimes said, but there is a crime fiction segment. A wave has peaks and valleys, crime novels are evenly demanded. I think that the establishment will have to live with that. The crime novel is a part of the Swedish narrative tradition, together with the classic novel about today's society."[7]

Roslund & Hellström's author role models definitely stem from the traditions studied in this book, packed with leftist critique. Börge Hellström holds the Swedish procedural couple Sjöwall-Wahlöö in the highest esteem for their voluminous use of dialogue, and Anders Roslund's admiration for the skilled craftsmanship of the American hardboiled writer Dennis Lehane is huge.[8] These influences are, of course, something we are going to look at in this chapter. But first, Roslund & Hellström are quite new to the American and international book market, and they have been stubbornly launched as crime writers in the tradition of Stieg Larsson. Considering that, I will discuss some of the media voices conveying this image to the public before embarking on Roslund & Hellström's writings.

Voices on "the Next Larsson"

When Roslund & Hellström were launched in Great Britain and the United States in 2008–2009 with their second novel *Box 21* (originally released in Sweden in 2005), the comparisons with Stieg Larsson were inevitable. Since then, basically every critic has compared them to Larsson, although the similarities between them are very few. Patrick Anderson in the *Washington Post* describes *Box 21* as a grittier novel than *The Girl with the Dragon Tattoo* and stresses the ugly scenes of forced sex, and that the novel ends mostly in despair, in contrast to Larsson's novel, which had a happy ending.[9]

In 2011, Roslund & Hellström's fifth installment *Three Seconds* hit the market in the U.S. and Great Britain. It was originally released in 2009 in Sweden and won several awards. It is probably the crime duo's best-selling achievement so far. A Hollywood movie has dragged its way through development hell for years ever since 20th Century–Fox bought the rights in 2010. It premiered in March 2019 with the title *The Informer* and a Swedish actor, Joel Kinnaman, in the lead.

Even in 2011, two years after the U.S. launch, they were seen as the second cousin to *The Girl with the Dragon Tattoo*, as *New York Times* critic Janet Maslin puts it. It is now obvious that the publishers (and the critics) are set on a desperate game trail for the "New Larsson," and Maslin's review of *Three Seconds* even has the imaginative and telling headline, "Stoking the Fire Larsson Ignited."[10] *The New York Times* review also contains a quick and entertaining analysis of the recipe of the Scandinavian Noir in seven words: "Guilty, Moody, Broody, Mopey, Kinky, Dreary and Anything-but-Bashful."[11] Maslin describes the social criticism in the plot as pointed at two Swedish authorities—the police and the Prison Probation Office, both necessary to supply drugs in Swedish prisons, which is what the Polish Mafia is doing in order to expand into "the closed market": "The book ascribes malfeasance to both sides, saying that 'the Police Service has for many years used criminals as covert human intelligence sources,' that the police conceal and deny this process, and that prison authorities quietly condone it."[12]

Los Angeles Times critic Paula L. Woods also mentions Larsson as quickly as she can, in her first sentence. Along with other critics, she is not too impressed by *Three Seconds*, stating that it suffers from "too much information, erratic intercutting and a heavy-handed style that not even an able translator like Kari Dickson can smooth over."[13] Carol Memmott of *USA Today* also drags up Stieg Larsson in her first sentence, saying the fans of Lisbeth

Salander "need a fresh fix of Nordic noir." "Gun play, explosions, betrayals and the ingenious ways drugs and weapons are smuggled into prisons give this novel ... an eau de testosterone level that's through the roof," Memmott concludes her review.[14]

An early review for the English-speaking market was Barry Forshaw's in *The Independent* in November 2010, when Larsson's publisher Quercus/ MacLehose Press launched *Three Seconds* in Great Britain. Forshaw says the book invites comparison to *The Girl with the Dragon Tattoo*: the same obsessive detail, the same corruption of the authorities, and "Larsson's tactic of the slow introductory chapters that suddenly shift into a higher gear." But he also mentions that Roslund & Hellström are very much their own men and that it doesn't matter whether they or Norwegian crime king Jo Nesbø are "the new Stieg Larsson" at the top of the Scandinavian crime fiction tree—that's something for "the bean counters at the publishers."[15]

Almost three years later, in 2013, Forshaw reviews Roslund & Hellström's next novel *Two Soldiers*, originally released in Sweden in 2012. This time, the tiresome Larsson parallels are washed away completely and Forshaw knights the author duo as "the hardest-hitting writers of the Scandinavian crime wave." But Forshaw is not as impressed now as he was some three years earlier. The book is far too long (the Quercus edition contains 669 packed pages), and at times it relaxes its grip; "it's a shame to have to record that slackening" he concludes, also criticizing the syndrome whereby publishers demand ever-longer crime novels, a critique Forshaw has also made of the Millennium trilogy.[16]

When reading Swedish reviews, the tone is somewhat different. For example, Nils Schwartz in *Expressen* criticizes Roslund & Hellström's invention of the fictitious town of Råby, a suburb to Stockholm that doesn't actually exist. Not even Swedish readers, or even citizens of Stockholm, necessarily know that Råby is a fictitious place as it is set in the city's periphery, mostly populated by immigrants and different ethnic groups. Moreover, Schwartz argues that Roslund & Hellström have invented the huge gang problems in the Stockholm suburbs and that *Two Soldiers* conforms to a modern media mythology that strengthens the social gaps making the gangs grow in the first place. Schwartz concludes that this alarmist scenario results in people being much more afraid than they should be, and when the writers don't see any other solution than resignation, they have become the ethical problem themselves.[17] However, not all Swedish reviewers had this harsh analysis of the novel. Per Planhammar of *Göteborgs-Posten* described the novel as disturbing and as an explorative journey towards a contemporary heart of darkness. There is a war without winners going on in the suburbs, and this strikes an emotional chord for readers, Planhammar writes. He concludes that the novel is one of the most important books of that year. It should even be obligatory reading in schools and the corridors of power, in prisons and social welfare offices.[18]

In order to find our way into the dark realm of Roslund & Hellström, we will start by taking a look at their hero, Ewert Grens.

Ewert Grens and the Realist Novel

Roslund & Hellström's protagonist Ewert Grens is another one of those grumpy, old-timer detectives we have seen rambling about in crime fiction for the past sixty years or so. He is not a sympathetic human being, but he is a good cop and, above all, he is on our side. He gets morally insulted by the crimes he investigates, since these crimes are also a proof of how rotten contemporary society has become since he started on the force in the beginning of the 1970s. But there are circumstances the reader understands and sympathizes with, even if he openly opposes female police officers, drinks huge amounts of coffee, and is basically one of those old men that everybody is afraid of. Anders Roslund has explained the general idea with this awful person, working day and night sniffing the trails of criminals:

> Grens is a name, but it's also the word in Swedish for limit, for a border. So his name means what he copes with every day. He's always asking himself: Who has crossed the line? Who's right? Who's wrong? Who's the victim? Who's the perpetrator? Or both? He is a limping detective inspector, aging and obstinate, the sort who never gives up, who pursues the truth as far as he can and then some more when he realizes that a handful of colleagues have known it from the start.[19]

Grens could easily be seen as the antithesis of the male cop genius that usually populates the crime fiction flora. His methods and conclusions are often wrong, and he is guided by prejudices and a morally doubtful sense of intuition. This makes him an interesting character, since he is no hero. Instead, he becomes a crucial part of Roslund & Hellström's complicated reality where the lines between the real perpetrator and victim in crime are somewhat ambiguous. Tapper implies that the police in the novels of Roslund & Hellström do not necessarily represent the solution to the crime problem; instead, the police might be an active part of it, sometimes even sanction it.[20]

In the preface to a new edition of Sjöwall-Wahlöö's second novel *The Man Who Went Up in Smoke*, Roslund & Hellström state that Ewert Grens is a modern follower to Martin Beck since they work in the same city, that very Stockholm that Beck left in 1975, and the same police headquarters; Grens is probably sitting in the same room, forty years later, in another time.[21] But whereas Martin Beck has a long marriage behind him that faded off and vanished into a new life with the Marxist Rhea Nielsen, Grens' marriage is more of a lifelong acerbic tragedy that explains his angry posture towards the rest of the world, his fear of going to sleep, of going home to the apartment, of living a normal life: a long time ago he and his wife Anni, who was also a cop, for a short time lived a happy life as husband and wife and colleagues. Their life together ended in tragedy sometime around 1980, twenty-five years before the Grens novels start, when they were both working in the riot squad, driving around in a squad car on the streets of Stockholm. Grens was the commander and driver of the squad car. They were in an accident when they were going to arrest a notorious thug and Grens' wife tried to pull him into the van but the thug pulled her out instead and Grens, by mistake, drove over her head.[22] After that, Anni Grens was put into a nursing home, out of reach from her devastated husband, who visits her every day. In the end of *The Girl Below the Street*, she dies and leaves an even more tortured Ewert Grens behind.

As a protagonist, Grens is the classic illuminator, the truth-seeker, the character we need in a socially critical story to understand what's going on, along with all the other witnesses from the underbelly of Swedish society, of course: the homeless, the probation officers, the junkies, the trafficked prostitutes, the criminals, the social workers, the welfare workers of the church, the parents in shattered families, the orphans. They are all there, in the works of Roslund & Hellström, telling the stories of our time. The authors themselves have explained the need for this type of novel on numerous occasions:

> ROSLUND: "In the 90s when violence against immigrants was on the rise, traditional novelists did not address those realities. So we crime writers stepped in to fill the vacuum. Here was a chance to write a good mystery, and to reflect on society, and obviously the audience needed and welcomed it. We Swedes have helped evolve crime writing well beyond the classic Agatha Christie closed-door police procedurals."
>
> HELLSTRÖM: "Our books reflect today's culture, and they have a duty to help us think about society's problems as well as individual violence: Why do people do it? Why does it happen here?"[23]

In this sense, Roslund & Hellström are the prime successors of Sjöwall-Wahlöö with their dense and deeply troubling stories where a documentary and journalistic style of writing describes a new world where we have stopped caring about one another. This reality, the collapse of solidarity, also scares Ewert Grens, and it likewise makes him furious. In *Two Soldiers*, the authors make Grens' view on morals and crime quite clear:

> He'd worked in the police in the capital for thirty-seven years and still believed in the same values as he had the day he collected his first uniform as a young cadet. Perhaps it was too obvious, too simple. Maybe it wasn't even particularly deep. *Anyone who aggrieves another party should have balls enough to pay for it afterwards.* That's just the way things were, the only way he could deal with him or her who had given themselves the right always to cause permanent harm.[24]

This moral concern also seems to correlate with the morals of the authors themselves. There are victims among criminals, people who have been sent to jail when they definitely should not be in a place like that. In the world of Roslund & Hellström, the victims are mostly children or women, as in *The Girl Below the Street* or *Box 21*, but as these two novels also reveal, these women and girls can also be the perpetrators, the killers in the unsolved puzzle. Roslund & Hellström's perspective on drug addicts is both understanding and irreconcilable. Mostly the junkies in their novels are described as egoistic idiots, trampling on other people just to get what they need, but they are also victims that don't deserve to be imprisoned; instead, they need care, not punishment. The murderers in their puzzle plots are diverse creatures snared into a violence created by fear, revenge, lust, anger, or greed. These murderers can be either real perpetrators or victims of a political system they don't seem to understand and therefore become unconscious players in.

The literary style of Roslund & Hellström is by far one of the most realistic approaches taken in crime fiction in modern literature. I am convinced that all of the writers in this study have a notion of reality—and the historical (mostly contemporary) context—that they see as an important (and even necessary) part of their stories. It is only a matter of how they choose to depict this reality. In short, these writers—from Chandler to Roslund & Hellström—are moving around in what James M. Cain has referred to as "the muddy waters of experience."[25] For example, this idea can be seen in the corruption in the 1930s and 1940s Los Angeles of Chandler, the soul murdering dictatorship known as the Accord in the works of Wahlöö during the 1960s, the 1990s Sweden on the verge of globalization as depicted by Mankell, the post-welfare state of the 2000s in Stieg Larsson's Millennium trilogy, and the modern hegemonic capitalism in Sweden with cracked-up suburbs and the criminal underground sunken into the institutions of society of Roslund & Hellström, and Jens Lapidus, the global crime and economic crisis of capitalism in the novels of Arne Dahl, etc. These views all share some common themes—they are dialectically interrelated, and that is what we are going to take a look at in order to explain Chandler's important influence on Swedish crime fiction up until today. We are going to further explore (though by now it should be quite obvious) how the thirty-year lapse that Kärrholm refers to has been caught up by the Swedish crime fiction prose, which has now become a world-leading literary industry. So far, Roslund & Hellström are the foremost examples of this *hyper-realism* where historical context, and the dialectical progress of the genre, have been molded together with an exquisite prose, sometimes on the verge of poetry, with the mixing of documentary journalistic effects with drafts from interrogation protocols, phone call records, emails, letters, investigations, and other sorts of evidence belonging to a police investigation. This approach was thoroughly applied by Sjöwall-Wahlöö in the 1960s, who used transcripts from interrogations and coroner's documents, while Larsson, in the 2000s, peppered his novels with hoards of emails and electronic communication.

According to Georg Lukács, the new realistic style of a nineteenth-century writer such as Balzac arises from the need to adequately display the new image of the social life. The individual and his/her relationship to class had become increasingly more complicated than during earlier centuries.[26] This complication, the class consciousness among the citizens, is basically different in every new generation, and hence every historical era needs its own culturally realistic approach. And even if Roslund & Hellström are definitely working within a very familiar genre (almost destroyed by the high production rate of its authors), they distinguish themselves from the rest with their hyper-realism, their consistent worm's-eye perspective, and their class consciousness. In one of their most definitive novels, *Two Soldiers*, this perspective is particularly evident, and that book could be described as the *Red Harvest* of our time. In this sense, Roslund & Hellström are Marxists. According to Marx's historical materialism, reality is conceived as formed and constructed through human practice and labor—hence the optimistic Marxist conclusion that systems and societies surrounding humans can be altered by humans. What surrounds humans are social products open to transformation: "What is true of the existing order need not be true of the next."[27] Following this line of thought, we might conclude that Swedish Marxist Noir is a realistic genre where historical materialism and the dialectics of crime fiction have significance for the foundations of both narrative and tradition.

Into the Heart of Darkness

Two Soldiers is the sixth novel featuring Roslund & Hellström's grumpy, gimpy old-timer Ewert Grens in the Stockholm investigative division. Just as with Martin Beck and Jensen in the novels of Sjöwall-Wahlöö, his bloated and dilapidated body represents the Swedish society gone wrong. The readers first got acquainted with Grens in 2004, when the crime writing duo's first book *The Beast* was published. Even back then Grens was old and shabby, with his wife living in a nursing home after having been run over by a car some years earlier. This tragedy runs through the entire series and lies behind much of Grens' pessimistic view on colleagues and people in society. He thinks the world was less complicated when he was younger and listens to famous Swedish singer Siw Malmkvist and her hit songs from the 1960s, which belong to the world he has left behind, and still longs for—a world and a time when he had his wife Anni, the only person who ever understood him. Some of the material possessions in his near vicinity enhance his nostalgia, perhaps mostly thoughts about his dead wife Anni, but also the old songs of Siw Malmkvist, and even the couch in his office:

> The brown corduroy sofa was too soft—especially on the nights when he slept several hours in a row—it was too short—with a stiff left leg that couldn't stretch out—and it was too warm—the fabric was worn and rubbed against his back. But he slept so much better there than anywhere else, he belonged in it in the way that it belonged in the room. It had stood there in the corner, as far from the wardrobe as the window, longer than most people had worked in the building.[28]

But all the time the modern world is closing in on him, with its horrible crimes that he has to face, often connected to deep moral questions on what is going on in New Sweden in the era of neoliberal politics, which was first penetrated in Mankell's Wallander series.

It is a new Marxian world, an extension of Mankell's and Larsson's political landscapes suitable for a Marxist interpretation. Carl Freedman has written a compelling description of this world, referring to Ernest Mandel and other Marxists:

> [C]apitalism today resembles Marx's abstract or "pure" model of the capitalist mode of production much *more closely* than did the capitalism that actually existed during Marx's own lifetime; the increasingly "totalitarian" character of capitalism as a world system paradoxically makes it increasingly difficult to feel or even to theorize either capitalism in general or particular capitalist societies as wholes (just as fish, for instance, presumably do not feel wet and, even if endowed with rational faculties, would have great difficulty in producing the concept of wetness).[29]

Furthermore, as the historical novel was a paradigmatic genre for Marxism during the nineteenth century, the realist crime novel—or in the case of Roslund & Hellström, *the hyper-realist* crime novel—could be equally paradigmatic for Marxism in our time as it describes the *Dickensian hell* of underclass poverty and the criminal underbelly of contemporary neoliberal capitalism. It is a world consisting of costs, economic calculations, increasing budget warnings, numb politicians, and marginalized suburbs rarely treated as priority number one. This is essentially what Pepper has called "capitalist noir": "the idea that the interpenetration of crime, politics, and business is now so pervasive that it produces a bleak, potentially totalizing imaginary whereby all expressions of deviance and violence, however shocking, can be understood as an inevitable symptom of free market rationality."[30]

This idea is especially evident in Roslund & Hellström's most class distinctive novel *The Girl Below the Street*, where the nexus between neoliberal politics and the cynical trade with children is exposed when forty-three Romanian orphans, street children from Bucharest, get dumped (as garbage) on a street in Stockholm, just a couple hundred yards from the police headquarters. The investigation leads to the dubious Child Global Foundation, a private consulting firm doing business by "taking care" of homeless children that nobody will miss in Romania, dumping them in big cities all over Europe. In fact, the Foundation consists of gangsters posing as a charity organization. Neoliberal politics in Romania has led to privatization of "the rehabilitation" of hundreds of Bucharest's street children. The firm gets 10,000 Euro (just over 10,000 U.S.D.) for each child, a total of 1,940,000 Euro for the 194 children the firm has undertaken to make a profit on homeless children: "The cost that the Romanian state deemed reasonable to get rid of the problem."[31] This is where the crime fiction mystery turns into some of the most hard-hitting social critique against the neoliberal economy one can read. In the seized computers of Child Global Foundation, the police have found neat and well-structured Excel documents with incomes in one column and expenses in the other, a document that ordinary corporations use for the sale of toothpaste or chairs or potatoes. But these were no ordinary commodities—they were children that not a soul was missing.[32] Children as waste, children as bookkeeping, as merchandise, commodities—the logical consequence of neoliberal politics in an economy that recognizes nothing of human value. In her analysis of *Box 21*, Katarina Gregersdotter makes a similar conclusion, stating, "The Western world is basically depicted as using its economic superiority because it can, and, in the novels, the women's bodies are transformed into commodities."[33] In the case of *The Girl Below the Street*, children are being transformed into commodities, and Gregersdotter's conclusion about the neoliberal *zeitgeist* of a free market is the same as mine: "capital comes before people, and ... a globalized economy can lead to the commodification of the body," and "gender, class, and ethnicity are depicted as factors which determine who can be bought and who can be raped."[34]

Two Soldiers is the second most class distinctive novel of Roslund & Hellström wherein they describe not forgotten street children the authorities want to get rid of, but rather an entire suburb that the authorities want to see vanish. The literal underground in *The Girl Below the Street* is a troubling voyage into the sublevel darkness, the ducts and tunnels below the Swedish capital, but in *Two Soldiers* the authors really step into the heart of darkness of Swedish society as a whole: the peripheral suburbs, and the urban enclavization of Stockholm, where crime flourishes and the rule of gangsters even erodes democracy in the end.

There are several similarities between these two novels. Both display closed spaces relatively unknown to most readers, and just like C.S. Lewis's magic Narnian closet, we are being led into this unknown, fearful darkness where social problems are being tucked away by the authorities. Both these novels show the huge class differentiation that has been institutionalized into the very structure of the urban space and almost becomes what Mike Davis refers to as "urban apartheid."[35]

Those whom nobody cares about, the people populating the underbelly of Sweden—the immigrants, the criminals, the youths, and the outcasts—are the main characters in the novels of Roslund & Hellström. Their nightmarish tale is a story that, even more so than Stieg Larsson, exposes the fall of the once flourishing welfare state. The big suburban areas from Wahlöö's *Murder on the Thirty-First Floor*, big concrete high-rises, cities without a soul made of steel and glass, return in this modern age of young criminals: "A world within the world. Identical concrete buildings that faced the E4 like a wall and everyone driving past at a hundred and ten kilometers an hour. They had nowhere to go as there was nothing to leave."[36] This modernist city structure, created in Sweden during the 1960s and 70s and called "The Million Program," has several weaknesses in times of socioeconomic strains: the geographic isolation, the lack of functional ethnic and demographic mixing, the sparseness, the grand scale, and uniformity of the property structure: "Råby was seldom beautiful to anyone who didn't belong there and on days like this the bright light peeled the last layer of color from the high structures and the concrete buildings became ... a grey, airless place."[37] So-called "self-clearance areas" in Wahlöö's *Murder on the Thirty-First Floor* come instantly to mind as a similar kind of place:

> The suburb was twenty kilometers or so south of the city, and in the category the experts at the Ministry for Social Affairs liked to call "self-clearance areas." It had been built at the time of the big housing shortage and consisted of about thirty tower blocks, ranged symmetrically round a bus station and a so-called shopping center.[38]

On one occasion, Ewert Grens talks to the sociologist Ana, who is also the mother of Leon Jensen (the main gangster in the story), as she describes the breakdown of an entire society left behind by the authorities:

> Where were you when the only big shop we had, the haberdashery shop, moved to Älvsjö two weeks ago, to avoid being constantly burgled here? Where were you when the last restaurant closed after the seventh break-in this year—I think they'd driven a car into the window? Where *the hell* were you when the ticket collector on the metro was murdered and Stockholm Public Transport refused to let their staff work here for a long time, when the post office closed down, when the ATMs were dismantled, when...[39]

She goes on further, becoming one of those formal moral voices the political novels always need:

> Your colleagues don't even bother to come here to investigate any more because *it's too dangerous*. We're encouraged not to go out after ten in the evening because *it's too dangerous*. The rights and obligations that are so important for all the other citizens in this country, that are talked about so much—how they should be upheld and maintained—they don't apply here ... because everyone, society, has long since abandoned us, moved away, bit by bit![40]

Both in *The Girl Below the Street* and *Two Soldiers*, Roslund & Hellström depict the remnants of a society where the authorities abdicated a long time ago, ignoring the problems nobody wants to handle: gang related crime, homelessness, street children, the neoliberal market centered economy, paving way for organized crime. In this sense, Roslund & Hellström's recurring motif of power and abuse reminds us a lot of Stieg Larsson's equally strong devotion to the subject: the chain of abuse is never broken, instead it is sanctioned by the pillars of society.

Mike Davis recalls the radicalizing gang subcultures, their escalating organization, their aura of fearlessness, and their ideology of armed vanguardism in Los Angeles as "the revolutionary lumpen proletariat," and defines implicitly an element of class warfare against the tireless accumulation of power (in the police, the political authorities, etc.).[41]

Criminal gangs—in our case, such gangs as the Råby Warriors, or Ghetto Soldiers as they later change their name to—have come to represent an escalation of intra-ghetto violence to *Clockwork Orange* levels (murder as status symbol, and so on), as Davis puts it.[42] In an interview, Anders Roslund said that in the work for *Two Soldiers* he witnessed a world where severe heavy crime is status, and that his aim was to explain why a twelve-year-old boy expressed that he *really wanted* to be in jail.[43] This boy ended up as the fictional Eddie in *Two Soldiers*, a totally alienated twelve-year-old drug dealer, too young to be punished by the law and therefore exploited by the gangs in the area.

Davis employs an interesting evolutionary description of gangs in Los Angeles—that also could be applied to *Two Soldiers*—as "a 'managerial revolution' in gang organization," occurring in several steps: first, as a teenage substitute for a fallen older organization, that later evolves into a hybrid of teen cult and proto-Mafia, and finally, as "the power resource of last resort for thousands of abandoned youth."[44] That is the current stage in the gang evolution, when the Swedish Police Commission, in a public report, states that around 5,000 young people below age twenty-one are at risk of being recruited into criminal networks.[45]

Back to the novel: When the authorities, with Grens at the helm, finally decide to intervene and chase the gangster leader Leon Jensen into the urban enclave of Råby, SWAT teams and all, it reminds us a lot of the painfully familiar scenarios of the Vietnam War, "the Marines hitting the beach at Danang in the beginning of LBJ's escalations," as Mike Davis puts it in a similar situation, when LAPD invades Southcentral Los Angeles to chase the drug pushing gangs.[46] Naturally, the entire operation goes awry as the police enter the home territory of the thugs they are chasing.

Flashback to *The Girl Below the Street*, where a similar situation occurs when Grens orders the SWAT team to enter the tunnels and sewers to chase a killer hiding down there. The very same, almost colonial, Vietnam-like situation appears there, and the reader learns that Ewert Grens is more of a clumsy general than the genial detective one is used to reading about in this sort of literature. That also makes him human, as he seems controlled by his moral compass and feelings along with the deduction and logic of the police work, which is more systematically executed by his team partners Sven Sundkvist and Mariana Hermansson.

Ewert Grens despises anyone who assumes the right to injure a life, but in *Two Soldiers* he makes an expanded—almost Marxist—reflection: it was the *circumstances* he despised, the ones that created the person who injured.[47] A similar Marxist reflection is made by the sociologist Ana, who states, "I'm thinking that if you are exposed to crime and see the benefits, then it's more likely that you will develop criminal tendencies, and if you're *not* exposed and *don't* see the gains, then the probability is smaller. And I'm thinking that if the exposure disappears altogether, if it doesn't exist ... do you understand me?"[48]

Naturally, Ewert Grens understands this predicament. His life's mission is to erase and investigate crime, but he also knows about the reasons for crime and sometimes he is ashamed of these reasons. He is the guilty conscience the authorities themselves lack (the local and national politicians, the social workers, the bureaucrats). In fact, there is also an interesting class distinction between Grens and the real power of justice in Sweden—in this case personified by the prosecutor Lars Ågestam, a younger and richer careerist of justice symbolizing the gap between the proletarian cop (from the muddy waters of experience) and the upper class that commands the citizens from above (working far away from reality). This class distinction is also clear in the novels of Sjöwall-Wahlöö, where the police force is seen as a proletarian under-class, and in the novels of Swedish writers such as Leif GW Persson and Jan Guillou, the Swedish Security Service, Säpo, is seen as the bourgeois upper-class side of the otherwise proletarian police force.[49]

The epigraph in *Two Soldiers*, picked out from the early Swedish crime classic *Doktor Glas* (1905) by Hjalmar Söderberg, gives a clue as to some of the issues the authors wish to illuminate:

> We want to be loved; failing that, admired; failing that, feared; failing that, hated and despised. At all costs we want to stir up some sort of feeling in others. Our soul abhors a vacuum. At all costs it longs for contact.[50]

However, the quote does not expose the structural criticism inherent in the novel, as we have studied above, as it merely exposes the individual scarcity of belonging to the rest of society, being loved and respected in a peripheral part of the big city—namely, the poor part of this city, in this case the fictional suburb Råby. Or, as a mirror, we could apply the quote to Ewert Grens and his lonely life and all the years of suppressed emotions he endures without really being conscious of it. But the quote is most likely to point at the two criminals, the soldiers, referred to in the novel's title, living a hard life in the outskirts of a city dominated by the new middle-class captured by the neoliberal agenda. In all its complexity, the poor suburban strata populating Råby probably longs for this middle-class life, the rich life of the people in the inner city with flats bought for millions in gentrified areas developed into reservations, or enclaves, for a new status-oriented upper-class.

Marcuse stresses in his work *An Essay on Liberation* (1969) that all needs and satisfactions in the advanced industrial society are permeated by the forced necessity of profit and exploitation. All the competitive achievements and standardized pleasures are just symbols of status, prestige, power, uprated virility and charm, commercialized beauty—this entire world kills the very disposition within its citizens and organs for the alternative way of life: freedom without exploitation.[51]

Knowing this, could the criminal gangsters in *Two Soldiers* be connected to a revolutionary logic in our modern time? Hardly, I would say. They are not quite the revolutionary subject of Swedish society, or what Marcuse meant by the prerequisite for a transformation to a higher stage of development— "higher" in the sense of a more rational and equal use of resources, a minimization of destructive conflicts, and an expansion of the limits for the kingdom of freedom.[52] The violence from the gangs in *Two Soldiers* is never a straightforward political action; instead, it functions as a much more oblique reflection of contemporary socio-economic arrangements, for example the notable absence of many important institutions: the state, administration of justice, parenthood, and the story basically incorporates all ingredients that suggests a sociological climate in close alignment with neoliberalism. That is, a society where authorities retreat and everyone is being reduced to consumers instead of citizens in a democracy. Consequently, the suburban gangs are being exhibited as an ever-growing disease—a sickness—in society:

> She had waited for them in a room in the social services office and gradually become a part of the sickness. The long queues of young boys—children—who instead of coming closer, only got more distant. They had just started out on their journey and would never change direction.... The symptoms of the disease had also worked their way into her body. Gang formation, criminality, alienation. Leon. Her son. And she had screamed and cried and watched and embraced, but the ones who gave the diagnosis, who had the authority and power, hadn't recognised the disease, understood how it developed, it was still happening outside *their* bodies and what cannot be seen does not exist and symptoms that are not stopped and continue to spread, slowly become death.[53]

These gangsters represent a craving—not for social change, equality, or liberty rights—hell, they already have that and don't need more of it—but for the greed of power, money, and all the bloated gadgets imposed by advanced capitalism: expensive cars, watches, weapons, computers, cell phones, beautiful women, power, and respect. They are deeply involved in the circle of male violence in the hope of achieving power. Instead of being the negation to the society in which they live—as the revolutionary proletariat, according to Lenin—they rather constitute a local enclave of something that resembles an oppressive and imperialistic dictatorship, or the "rogue states" as proclaimed by Noam Chomsky. In *Two Soldiers*, the adult world has been broken down a long time ago and twelve-year-old kids are running the dope business in the suburb Råby, longing to become one of the real gang members. They're "the most dangerous. Not the fat arses on motorbike," the authors argue. "These guys are younger, have more hate, they've invited themselves in and taken their place in the only way they know how."[54] Continuing:

> They take all sorts of risks, commit crimes constantly, every new thought and action is the start of another crime.... But never for their own gain. The drug deliveries, gun running, break-ins are not for themselves, but for the family, members who exploit these kids' desire to belong.[55]

In an interview, Anders Roslund once said that the Sweden he is depicting in his and Hellström's novels are the worst nightmare of Stieg Larsson: a society where extreme rightwing parties, with their roots in the Nazi movement, such as the Sweden Democrats, are growing rapidly, where immigrants get shot every day, as in the Stockholm suburbs and in Swedish cities of recurring gangster wars, Malmö and Gothenburg, and where the hate is poisoning the suburbs everywhere: "Knock on anyone's door who lives outside Stockholm: there's so much hate. And this is just the start, I think you'll see more riots in the suburbs. It's a new thing, and I hope I'm wrong, but my kids and their kids will grow up in a new Sweden, a different Sweden."[56]

Similar to the novels of Per Wahlöö and Maj Sjöwall, the stories of Roslund & Hellström represent the continuing narrative of a New Sweden. They bring back social and political criticism to the police novel after years of what Tapper describes as "backlash narratives of vigilante supercops fighting crime as terrorist evil in far-fetched puzzle plots," referring to Håkan Nesser's Van Veeteren series, the Beck movie series based on the characters of Sjöwall-Wahlöö written by Rolf & Cilla Börjlind, and the rightwing evoked Johan Falk movie series.[57] In other words, to expose the problems in the broken down post-welfare state, the crime novel is the best tool where history meets philosophy, where criminology meets sociology, where realism meets feelings and understanding of the mechanisms of life in a modern society.

Still, what are the solutions to the problems in *Two Soldiers*, according to Roslund & Hellström? Well, it is not really clear. One of the central characters in the novel is the sociologist Ana, the mother of gang leader Leon, and her solution is a rather radical and spectacular one. Together with a firefighter, who is constantly called in to put out the fires in Råby ignited by minor gang members every day, she blows up an entire building complex with explosives hidden in the elevator shafts by the gang members: "I have done what I can and those who gave up, those who said this is not our problem, sort it out yourselves, you're the ones doing each other harm, they will now be forced to come back."⁵⁸ Unfortunately (or perhaps not), the ending in *Two Soldiers* is as disturbing as all endings are in the novels of Roslund & Hellström: the reader gets filled with a sense of aloof hopelessness, witnessing a juncture in history, since the drug running goes on, the violence in the isolated suburban enclaves continues, the authorities do not seem to be able to solve the problems, and perhaps—God forbid—they don't even want to. Reading Roslund & Hellström, one senses an inherent lack of interest in the bureaucratic structure for solving the "urban apartheid" since the real problem lies *within* the system, and the system won't change itself voluntarily. That sounds like a revolutionary conclusion, so it is not very likely that Roslund & Hellström would draw it themselves.

Tapper describes *Two Soldiers* as a story about how crime, abuse and poverty become a lifestyle transferred from one generation to the next.⁵⁹ What the reader witnesses is just the consequences of a rapidly differentiated society with increasing class gaps, and violence and drug sales representing the symptoms of this sickness.

In the seventh installment of the Ewert Grens series, *Three Minutes*, Roslund & Hellström go even deeper into the realities of crime, into what they refer to as the very origins of crime: the dope jungle.

The Green Dope Jungle

The novel *Three Seconds*, about the super infiltrator Piet Hoffmann escaping prison in one of the most nail-biting sequences ever accomplished in Swedish crime fiction, eventually spawned a sequel, and in 2016 the almost equally arm-stretching *Three Minutes* was released in Sweden. *Three Seconds* sold in 1.5 million copies and was the definitive breakthrough in the United States for Roslund & Hellström.⁶⁰

The authors had worked on their Colombian contacts for four years when they suddenly got personal guidance into this epicenter of the drug trade business. Anders Roslund went to Colombia, but Börge Hellström was too frightened to go and stayed home. "I have never been so frightened in my entire life," Roslund states in an interview as he continues, "and I have seen a sham execution in Israel."⁶¹

Roslund got to participate in certain situations and met key individuals that were seriously dangerous with a strange sort of power. He got to see places you should not visit even in daylight and listen to authentic stories about threats and murders. His journalistic methods can, as he says, make the fiction come closer to reality than the documentary ever can.⁶² And that is probably the method employed by Roslund & Hellström in all of their novels.

Narcotics lie behind about 80 percent of all crime in the world, Roslund & Hellström say in an interview.[63] Narcotics are always present in the world of Roslund & Hellström—on the streets, in the prisons, everywhere. That made them want to explore another secret world not everybody can access. Sexual crimes, human trafficking, gang-related crimes, everything occurs with the backdrop of narcotics. To seriously write about the criminality of our time, one has to explore the one thing that gets almost everything else started, to the heart of crime, *to the criminality that drives all other criminality*, as the authors put it themselves. Half of it is true, half of it is made up—that is their recipe for the novels. They spend months doing deep research and always have first-rate sources and personal contacts from the underworld that no other writer gets a hold of.

Roslund & Hellström's critique of the legal structures, the police, and the government in *Three Seconds* continues in the sequel *Three Minutes*. Both novels are about top-notch crime infiltrator Piet Hoffmann, who infiltrates the Polish mob and the Swedish prison system in *Three Seconds*. In *Three Minutes*, he has disappeared from the Swedish face of the earth, as he is on the run with his family, to infiltrate Colombian drug cartels for the American DEA. The bleakly eccentric detective of Roslund & Hellström, Ewert Grens, is assigned to go to Colombia and save Hoffmann from being killed by avenging American troops after the kidnapping of the high-ranked state official Timothy Crouse, who is being kept in a cage in the jungle. Hoffmann is the only one who knows where Crouse is being held hostage and is about to trade his own life to save him. The climax, where Hoffmann effectively deletes the bad guys and saves Crouse (is he also a bad guy?), is the same type of fast-paced, high-pressure prose, constantly shifting gears, as in *Three Seconds*.

The focus in this novel is on the war on drugs, the barbarism of the drug cartels, and the American supported forces hunting criminals and a drug business they obviously cannot handle. In this sense, the novel is more of a political thriller à la Tom Clancy's *A Clear and Present Danger* (1989) than actual Swedish crime fiction. But still, the criticism against the Swedish police system is there. The police chief responsible for the infiltration, Erik Wilson, thinks of himself as a prisoner within the big structure of the police authority, an authority without any insight from the public.[64] But the main critique in the book focuses on what the narcotics and those who sell it are responsible for. On one occasion, Ewert Grens speaks for the authors themselves when he explains the statistics that there are a hundred thousand reported narcotic crimes in little Sweden every year, that narcotics drive all the criminality, everything that the police are involved with: "narcotics doesn't drive all criminality," Grens concludes, "it drives our entire society," and he asks himself if anyone really wants it to quit. So many people make a living of its consequences.⁶⁵

In one chapter, the authors repeat that the drug trade is the biggest industry of our time, turning over an annual amount of 2,250 *billion* Swedish kronor (approximately 284 *billion* dollars, according to the exchange rate of September 2017) with huge profits lined with violence, blood, bodies, the prostitute trade, and weapons. The drug organization actually *drives* the entire society.⁶⁶

"An image of the conditions and consequences of narcotics. With life subordinated to profit."⁶⁷ That is how the writers conclude their postscript in *Three Minutes*. The cocaine industry in Colombia is clearly connected to the global economy and to capitalism in this story. Organized crime does not hide out in the peripheral parts of society any longer, Mandel argues. Instead it, nowadays to an even larger extent, has its origin in the same socio-economic driving forces that control the accumulation of capital in general: private ownership, competition, and the capitalist mode of standardized commodity production. Hence, as Mandel concludes, a rich man's world is also a rich gangster's world.⁶⁸ This is evident when reading about how top mobsters in Colombia live in huge residences, just like rich CEOs and corporate tycoons.

Similar to Sjöwall-Wahlöö, Roslund & Hellström realize the major implications of the drug trade and the crime wave it causes all over the world. It is a global problem whose mechanisms and structures are the very same as legal big business corporations. It is controlled by profit, greed, and violence. Sjöwall-Wahlöö had the drug trade in focus in novels such as *The Man Who Went Up in Smoke*, where inter-European hashish smuggling appeared for the first time in a Swedish crime novel, and in *The Fire Engine That Disappeared*, where the highest criminals, the drug lords, never get touched by justice and the police. In *Three Minutes*, the drug cartels saturate the entire world structure and economy. You cannot get rid of them since they are an indispensable part of the economic structure in a capitalistic world, with the United States as the only remaining super power.

Mandel mentions a symbiosis between organized crime, corporate finance, and the state as he concludes: *abolish the institutions of market economy and this symbiosis disappears.*⁶⁹ It is not clear if Roslund & Hellström are willing to go that far, since they have never actually stated that the problem is within the market economy.

So let's recapitulate a bit and take a look at how Roslund & Hellström have shifted focus through seven novels over a twelve-year-period, starting with the smaller, individual criminal such as the sexual offender Bernt Lund in *The Beast*, and the man who kills him and gets prosecuted for it (a micro perspective). This is the very antithesis to the criminality in *Three Minutes*, where global and complex structures are in focus, an exploration of the economical "base" of criminality, as Marx probably would have put it (a macro perspective). The trafficking swindle with Lithuanian prostitutes in *Box 21* moves the criminality up a notch to another level, from individual crimes to some kind of structure involving foreign mobsters, commodifying and committing crimes against female bodies. In *Cell 8*, the authors write their first international novel, with the action partly set in the United States, with a severe critique of the death penalty. In *The Girl Below the Street*, Swedish society is back in focus with people, especially children, living below the streets of Stockholm and a European perspective with children as waste products (and commodities) in the neoliberal economy. In *Three Seconds*, they take Swedish crime writing to new topical and stylistic levels with hard, adrenaline-pumping, page-turning prose, and again their critique of the Swedish prison system is evident. In *Two Soldiers* and *Three Minutes*, they once again employ a painful children's perspective, as they did in *The Girl Below the Street*. In these three novels, Roslund & Hellström show how children get involved and exploited in crime in different ways, as victims who don't have the luxury to choose, just following the inherent demands of a capitalistic society where competition, prestige, money, and the commodification of all spheres of life radically change people's way of thinking. The Swedish perspective is almost entirely gone in *Three Minutes*, which is an international thriller. It could have been written by any of the big ones—Tom Clancy, John Le Carré or, for that matter, Swedish spy novelist Jan Guillou. Several critics have also witnessed this new mode of Roslund & Hellström, the capsizing into the adventure oriented James Bondish genre, and have remarked on it.[70]

Hence, what Tapper mentions as the "backlash narratives of vigilante supercops," a tradition that Roslund & Hellström's stories ultimately reacted against in the mid-2000s when they launched their own version of Marxist Noir, seem to be the concluding chapter of their Ewert Grens series. Is that where Swedish crime fiction is heading next? Unfortunately, yes—and no, as it will turn out. The main current is that of supercops and private operating initiatives in the shady demarcation lines between law and criminality and an increasing *bland* and *tepid* Marxism, as we shall see with Lars Kepler in one of the following chapters. Moreover, there is an interesting path with increased Marxism and a healthy analysis of the neoliberal economy since the global economic crisis at the end of the 2000s, foremost represented by Arne Dahl.

Making an Impact

"What you're afraid of has already happened," one of the caretakers says to Ewert Grens in the novel *Three Seconds* as he approaches the nursing home where his diseased wife once lived.[71] This is the everlasting credo of Roslund

& Hellström. It doesn't just stand as a quintessential sentence for Grens and his fears, but it is equally as much of a statement from the authors themselves: We live in this society and look what it has become! How could it turn out like this? And perhaps, the most important question of them all: What is the solution? Is it socialism? Hardly! It is too late for that. What you're afraid of has already happened. However, it could get better now. How? Fighting crime? Stubbornly, mercilessly fighting crime in society, and at the same time taking care of social outcasts, those ignored by the authorities, the very same substratum rhetorically recalled in Marcuse's *One-Dimensional Man*, in an age when fortune and economic growth are stated to be everything.

Roslund & Hellström have taken the legacy of Sjöwall-Wahlöö into the new millennium and created a modern Marxist Noir that works dialectically, in several directions at the same time, as all great political fiction writing should: the political left sees a society exposed in all its disgusting disarray—here, look at this and what we've done—and the political right sees the alarmist scenario of the downfall of the collapsed dream and calls for more police, tougher sentences, to fight crime whatever the consequences. Stieg Larsson was the antiracist and feminist debater who turned the spotlight onto violence against women and immigrants and the progress of extreme rightwing movements in Sweden and Europe. His agenda was revolutionary, with Lisbeth Salander as the bearer of a permanent revolution. What footprints in the public debate and contemporary politics will Roslund & Hellström leave after them? The risk for rightwing extremists to use their stories as proof of the alarmist vision of Sweden and its post-welfare state decay is there, of course. But the Marxist agenda is foregrounded in their books, and that makes them more than bestselling phenomena, selling in the millions all over the world. Anders Roslund has described his feeling of meaninglessness when he was working as a reporter, when everything he reported on—most notably, the evolution of the Swedish Nazi movement in the 1990s—felt fleeting as a breath of air; who cared? He never seemed to accomplish *real* change. Writing novels, though, gave him and Börge Hellström the breakthrough in the public debate they had wanted for so long. After the publication of *Two Soldiers*, they got a call from the Prime Minister Fredrik Reinfeldt (of the Conservative Party, Moderaterna) who wanted to discuss the gang crime in the suburbs and trafficking with the authors. Hence, one novel had a greater impact than decades of journalism.[72]

The Swedish ex-lawyer/writer Jens Lapidus has undertaken several novels where the American hardboiled mode is being successfully employed in contemporary crime fiction while not leaving the Marxist horizon one bit. Instead, its scope is widened, and deepened, as Lapidus tells the stories of organized crime and ethnic groups and their relationship to neoliberal economics in contemporary Brave New Sweden.

6

A Brave New Sweden
Jens Lapidus

Crime today is all about modern myths, and politics is all about the battle of reality, Tapper argues. Who is going to take charge of the great narrative on how we live and what can be made of it? The battle of reality has moved out of the economy and into culture simply because the world is being mediated to us through stories in films, books, and television. Tapper suggests that writers, critics, and debaters have a greater importance than past generations when it comes to influencing our view on society.[1]

Perhaps that is why Swedish crime writers have such a varied background. They can be journalists (Stieg Larsson, Anders Roslund, Jan Guillou, Katarina Wennstam, Liza Marklund, Karin Alfredsson, and numerous others), cops (Varg Gyllander, Anders de la Motte, Martin Melin, Hans Holmér), criminologists (Leif GW Persson, Christoffer Carlsson, Pontus Ljunghill), ex-cons (Kennet Ahl, Börge Hellström, Liam Norberg), psychologists (Åsa Nilsonne, Ingrid Hedström), Ministers of Justice (Thomas Bodström, Anne Holt in Norway), economists (Camilla Läckberg), screenwriters (Rolf & Cilla Börjlind, Hans Rosenfeldt), teachers (Håkan Nesser, Maria Lang, Martin Holmén, Tomas Arvidsson), film directors (Michael Hjorth), artists and librarians (Håkan Axlander Sundquist & Jerker Eriksson, known as Erik Axl Sund), social workers (Camilla Ceder), doctors (Karin Wahlberg), nurses (Anna Jansson), mathematicians (Carin Gerhardsen), playwrights and theatre directors (Henning Mankell)—or they can be lawyers (Malin Persson Giolito, Lena Ebervall & Per E. Samuelsson, Leif Silbersky). Just like Jens Lapidus, currently one of Sweden's most popular crime writers, who concurrently worked as a successful practicing criminal lawyer in Stockholm for years, occasionally holding lectures on law at police academy seminars.

The importance, and larger influence of the genre—both economically (many writers do actually get filthy rich from selling books) and politically—

might be one reason why so many different types of people, with diversified backgrounds, have started writing careers. Their professional occupation and insight into unique situations also make their writings unique. One such writer is Jens Lapidus. His writing skills are unquestionable, and his affiliation with criminal delinquents makes the outcome very fruitful—something Swedish readers have not quite encountered before.

A Swedish Ellroy

Jens Lapidus was born in 1974 in Stockholm. His father is a journalist and his mother a sociologist, and they both shared Sjöwall-Wahlöö's leftwing ideals.[2] Hence, Lapidus's interest in writing and social matters derives from his parents. After studying law at Stockholm University, he became a court clerk at the Sollentuna District Court, where he worked in 2003–2004, and then got engaged in business law at the noted law firm Mannheimer Swartling in Stockholm, where he worked until 2007. By then he had made his literary debut, and since then he has also been affiliated with criminal law at the bureau Försvarsadvokaterna (The Defense Lawyers).[3] In 2017, he quit his law career and started writing full time.

In several interviews, he has stressed the huge influence from American writers such as James Ellroy, Dennis Lehane, and Philip Roth, and the most influential novel he has read is Ellroy's *L.A. Confidential* (1990), the third installment in the famous *L.A. Quartet*.[4] However, according to Lapidus, Ellroy's best novel is *American Tabloid* (1995), the first novel in the *Underworld USA* trilogy.[5]

Lapidus's first novel, *Easy Money* (*Snabba Cash*), released in 2006, is a 500-page sprawling, funny and disturbing tale of neoliberal hedonism written as a hardboiled gangster novel, propelled by a "James Ellroyish laconic telegram prose."[6] His first book alone has sold about one million copies. Barry Forshaw identifies "the flavoursome use of language, written in an in-your-face combination of street argot and new world coinages" in his review of *Easy Money*.[7] Besides its innovative language (not hailed by all critics, though),[8] *Easy Money* is a story about criminality as an integral part of capitalist economy and how these two worlds meet in the luxurious nightlife at Stureplan square in downtown Stockholm. It is the classical dark tale of quickly rising gangsters, such as Rico in Mervyn LeRoy's film *Little Caesar* (1931), as played by Edward G Robinson, or Tony Montana in the popular garb of Al Pacino in Brian De Palma's remake of *Scarface* (1983), effortlessly speeding down the highway to hell. It is all about the microcosm of the Stockholm underworld as run by Yugoslavian gangster Radovan, rather than the macro perspective of Ellroy, where the entire American system of politics and police are corrupt and rotten to the bone. Still, the novels of Jens Lapidus are also political, but most of all they are contemporary. "It is always difficult to describe one's contemporary time. But in a few years we probably will see *Easy Money* as a time document of the beginning of the 2000s," Lapidus says in an interview.[9] It is a post–9/11 age where capital rules all parts of life (at least in Lapidus's stories). It adopts the same hedonist and nihilistic perspectives on the upper-class that we recognize from novels such as *Less Than Zero* (1985) and, above all, *American Psycho* (1991) by Bret Easton Ellis. The Ellisian gadgets are all there—the same manic interest in details, status, trademarks, consumer products, alienation, and the constant depravation of the rich as an ideal way of life.

Blurring the Lines of Business

When reading Jens Lapidus's novels, such as the Stockholm Noir trilogy consisting of *Easy Money* (2006), *Never Fuck Up* (*Aldrig fucka upp* [2008]) and *Life Deluxe* (*Livet De Luxe* [2011]), filled with people—mostly belonging to ethnic minorities in Sweden—from the city and its underbelly—gangsters, drug dealers, bookmakers, gamblers, and corrupt cops—you could easily draw a straight line from Raymond Chandler to Swedish crime (via the post-noir of James Ellroy, that is, since Ellroy and Dennis Lehane are the very inspirations for the works of Lapidus). Most of his protagonists are criminals, and there are no honest cops anywhere. In fact, there are no honest people anywhere in any of his novels. And if they do appear somewhere, they get exploited and swindled out of their money in different ways. Lapidus's depiction of the city is what David Geherin stresses as "a center of corruption and decay, a place where crime, pollution, and general degradation of life are concentrated."[10]

This city is mainly run by criminal gangs fighting with each other within the patriarchal structure of organized crime, just like during the post–World War I recession and the Prohibition era of the American 1920s. Lapidus's city is exactly the kind of world Sjöwall-Wahlöö warned about during the 1960s: a "Marxian world, populated by Hobbesian men," as Tapper concludes.[11] A world corrupted by capitalism and greed, totally infiltrated by the criminal underground, returning on several occasions to the works of Raymond Chandler, perhaps most explicitly as described in his essay "The Simple Art of Murder" and the novel *The Long Goodbye*, as we have seen.

In his analysis of *The Godfather* trilogy, the Marxist critic Carl Freedman identifies a connection between the gangster story and the origins of capitalism in what Karl Marx, in the first volume of his work *Capital*, calls "primitive accumulation." Freedman puts it briefly as "the moment of violence and crime that is foundational to capitalism and untranscendable by it."[12] Rosa

Luxemburg wrote an entire book on this particular subject, *The Accumulation of Capital* (1913), in which she interested herself in the capital accumulation that occurred *outside* of Western capitalism, in the colonies and other *pre-capitalist* societies that, under the heavy suppression of colonialism, got integrated into the new world economy whose dependence on the exploitation of humans and natural resources in other parts of the world increased rapidly during the late nineteenth century.[13]

This note, Freedman's account on primitive accumulation, is an important one and connects to what we have discussed earlier in this study—the Mafia-capitalism of Polanyi, the fascist exploitation as uncovered by Steinbeck—and it all adds up to one thing: primitive accumulation. So let's hold on for a while to this concept, which also is applicable to the novels of Jens Lapidus. Mario Puzo, who wrote one of the greatest gangster novels of all time, *The Godfather* (released in 1969), had the outspoken aim of branding the similarities between the bourgeois society and the criminal establishment in the United States along with the social critical tradition.[14] This aim could also be identified in the works of Lapidus, since his stories explore the blurring lines between business and crime, between the upper-class and the suburban *lumpen proletariat* trying to accumulate their own primitive capital through violence, drug sales, imaginative schemes, and endless crimes. According to Marx, primitive accumulation is not really an accumulation at all, since it is the very origin of capitalism in Europe, replacing the dying economies of the feudal order. Capitalism starts with capital, and logically there had to be some capital there from the start. So, where does this capital derive from? Marx's conclusion is that capital and property come from a process of fraud, theft and violence. It is the consciously repressed history of the privatization of common lands, usurpation of ancient feudal rights, forcible seizure and privatization of public domains, plus the genocidal discoveries of immense fortunes in Asia and Africa, and the building of colonial empires, which led to the creation of modern bourgeois private property.[15] Marx describes this stage of *proto-capitalism* as similar to a *divorce* between the producer and the means of production, introducing the wage relationship between wage worker and capitalist. Another, more intensive, literal, and mythological similarity that Marx emphasizes is that this process has the same function in the political economy as the original sin, *the fall from grace,* in theology.[16] Or, in the words of Marx himself, in the famous eighth chapter of *Capital*:

> The discovery of gold and silver in America, the extirpation, enslavement and entombment in mines of the indigenous population of that continent, the beginnings of the conquest and plunder of India, and the conversion of Africa into a preserve for the commercial hunting of blackskins, are all things which characterize the dawn of the era of capitalist production. These idyllic proceedings are the chief moments of primitive accumulation.[17]

Tapper concludes that this repressed history of fraud, violence, and theft that gave birth to modern-day capitalism is analogous with the greedy and ruthless gangster's rise to social success as seen in mob films and novels such as the Lapidus novels.[18] Consequently, this narrative also concurs with the birth of modern politics in the famous sentence formulating Mao Zedong's thesis, "Political power grows out of the barrel of a gun," which locates the origin of politics beyond itself.[19]

But there is also a theory going even further back in history than Marx's idea of primitive accumulation. In their study of Dashiell Hammett's most politically evident novel *Red Harvest*, Carl Freedman and Christopher Kendrick have identified an interesting parallel between gangsterism and fascism that could basically function as a theory about fascism itself, or as the authors themselves put it: "the *feudalization* of illicit power." For fascism, in the organized crime version, to exist there have to be some specific societal circumstances: the absence of strong, central, universalizing state power, the prominence of private and semi-private armies, the corresponding importance of personal loyalty between master and dependent, and perhaps most important of all, that this highly visible, dynamic polity can overshadow economy. The authors conclude: "all these features of the gangster polity are precapitalist and classically feudal."[20]

Hence, the concept of Mafia-capitalism, which also shows its face in our neoliberal era, is an alloy of three different social, ideological, and economical historical elements that has followed my discussion all the way from the start: capitalism, fascism, and organized crime.

According to Kerstin Bergman, money is the ultimate source of power in Lapidus's Stockholm. She writes, "Lapidus' criminal underground has infiltrated every part and layer of Stockholm; it is operating just below the 'surface,' thereby remaining relatively invisible to the casual observer." Lapidus portrays the surface as just a veneer: the superficiality embodied by the importance of status and power symbols—cars, weapons, exclusive parties, designer clothes.[21] Above all, these gangster stories dismantle the dichotomy between legitimacy and illegitimacy, between crime and non-crime, criminal business and legal business, blurring the lines between legality and illegality. Or, as Carl Freedman puts it,

> [W]hat is essentially at stake in the workings of organized crime is nothing more than capitalism itself. Indeed, Mafia-capitalism, precisely because of its illegality and its corresponding relative autonomy from the ordinary systems of government regulation, might be considered to be capitalism at its freest and thus capitalism as most strongly and thoroughly—and violently—itself.[22]

In this context, Marxism is definitely the best method for reaching a thorough and deep understanding of our modern world (and how to change it), where capitalism and capitalist civilization has reached their most elaborate stage in history with globalization. It is a world where the system in many ways has become invisible, and it requires a Marxist theory to reach a true understanding. Crime fiction, at its dialectically very best, is a tool for this Marxist theory. Its fundamental presuppositions—the labor theory of value, the distinction between use-value and exchange-value, the concept of the wage-relation, the concept of surplus-value, the distinction between variable and constant capital, the "secret" of primitive accumulation, commodity fetishism—are all important ingredients in the modern noir crime story, as was the case in the dawn of capitalism in the realist novels of Balzac or Dickens during the nineteenth century, or even the Swedish labor novels of the twentieth century.

In Sweden, Jens Lapidus and Arne Dahl are some of the most obvious contemporary Marxist, or (post–)Marxist, crime fiction theorists in this sense.

Lapidus himself has, in an interview with a Swedish leftwing paper, stressed the desire of readers to see rich people as unhappy and that he wants to expose the rottenness behind these facades. But still, he maintains that he does not have a specific political agenda concerning class-matters. "I don't really know what class means today," Lapidus says in true post–Marxist fashion, clearly recognizing class as a pre-discursive or non-discursive formation.[23] Class used to be the most important concept in Marxist and leftwing discourse, as Therborn puts it, but has been displaced in recent years since the post-industrial demography has dislodged it from its previous theoretical or geographical centrality.[24] Instead, Lapidus emphasizes the importance of the French post–Marxist philosopher Pierre Bourdieu's theories of social rooms, coded rules and values of society as important for his writing. "I just want to study people, get into them, learn to know them and enter their surroundings. Explore different subcultures that don't always show up on the surface. The brats on Stureplan are just as evident as a subculture to me as the kids in the suburban gangs."[25]

Bourdieu's theory on social and cultural capital has been described as symbolic and material assets, and there are different types of capital where the cultural capital signifies a cultivated language and knowledge of "higher" culture. What Bourdieu calls social capital includes both bonds between relatives and private and professional contacts. This connects to the field theory that interests Lapidus and which, in turn, describes a system of relations between different positions. Culture, and subcultures in this sense, could be seen as one separated field.[26]

It is Lapidus's exploration of these diverse environments and social elements—the subcultures—in society which we are about to embark on next, though without leaving the Marxist perspective.

Excursus: The Maksumic Series

Jens Lapidus's new series of novels, after the Stockholm Noir trilogy (2006–2011), starts with *The VIP-Room* (*VIP-rummet* [2014]) and continues with *Sthlm Delete* (2015). In these novels, he returns to the old image of the Chandlerian private eye protagonist when introducing lower-class ex-con Najdan "Teddy" Maksumic. He is the working-class chameleon, coming from below, with one foot in two different worlds: the gangster world of the disintegrating Stockholm suburbs, and the flashy milieu of the rich lawyer firm in the downtown area where he eventually, well into the first novel, turns into a private investigator. He is the socially transgressing connection between neoliberalism and its henchmen at the lawyer firm, and the gangster-capitalism of the ethnic minorities in the suburbs and the jails. Bearing in mind the huge influence of James Ellroy on Lapidus's writing, he could also be construed as a Swedish replica of Ellroy's energetic and inventive protagonists in several novels: ex-con Duane Rice in *Suicide Hill* (1986), loser burglar turned private eye Don Crutchfield in *Blood's a Rover* (2008), or the super forensic trapped in the darkness of L.A. police corruption, Hideo Ashida in *Perfidia* (2014).[27]

Just as in *Easy Money*, the entire Lapidus corpus connects crime and gangsterism with capitalism and the neoliberal project. Frank MacShane argues that the private eye is central in the tradition of American literature and that its popularity rests on the skeptical view most people have of human institutions. The private eye's very existence could therefore be seen as a criticism against the police (or bourgeois society, for that matter) for their incompetence and corruption.[28] It is probably this tradition Lapidus is leaning towards with Teddy Maksumic, a tough player with his feet in two worlds: the criminal (illegal) underworld, and the (legal) law firm that employs him for his shady services. Just like everyone else from his side of town, he also longs for a quick fix to upper-class heaven.

The stories in Lapidus's new series are set in the same cold and ruthless Stockholm as the earlier trilogy. Teddy is an ex-gangster who has been imprisoned for eight years for a kidnapping. When he comes out of jail, he gets consulted by a business law firm to make investigations concerning the dark gangster world of the Swedish capital. The similarities to Philip Marlowe are clear. Teddy's criminal, worm's-eye perspective on society introduces the reader to the upper-class decadence where crime flourishes among the yuppies and youngster brats of the rich. Once again, it is a world with a surprising lack of the everyday, nine-to-five-citizens we are reading about, the neoliberal nightmare *in extremis*, since crime and criminals permeate the entire narrative. We are witnessing the end of the downfall of the Swedish welfare state according to Sjöwall-Wahlöö and other Marxists in the crime genre. It is a neoliberal world run by private corporations, the Culture Industry, and organized crime. A true Marxist Noir.

In all its complexity, Sweden has turned into a new country where immensely powerful bankers and financial institutions rule, and employees no longer feel secure since job security only gets weaker and the social welfare systems (such as public health, social insurance and pensions) are more and more eroded in favor of flexible capital movements. Taxes are being driven to rock bottom so that money can be transferred unimpeded between different nations, corporations, and parts of the world. In this new, flexible, brave "New" Sweden, which has gone through a profound, paradigmatic economic transformation since the early 1990s, there are no classes, no collectives, not even institutions, just individuals, according to the dominating paradigm. Social phenomena such as unemployment are explained as a lack of initiative and go-getter spirit on behalf of the unemployed. These people have themselves to blame; corporations and authorities have nothing to do with it. Such is the prevailing *zeitgeist* of millennium Sweden, and this zeitgeist, as well as the individuals populating the social and cultural strata, fields, and rooms where it prevails, are also the social objects of exploration for Lapidus.

The characters in *The VIP-Room* are all parts in this Brave New Sweden, dominated by neoliberal politics, and they know it. The other hero of the series, besides Teddy, is young freshman lawyer Emelie Jansson. She derives from the ordinary small-town middle class, and her parents are something really unusual in a Lapidus novel—just ordinary, decent people. But even for this non-criminal middle class—strongly represented by Emelie Jansson and her parents—society seems to go in the wrong direction. Several times in the two novels where she appears, *The VIP-Room* and *Sthlm Delete*, she reflects upon the life of her parents who were born in another time, the 1950s, in the idyllic old Sweden. They were politically dedicated students during the leftist radical 1970s, in a time when ideas and ideology really mattered, and they fought against dictatorships in Latin America, mainly Chile, but also against the apartheid race politics in South Africa. But now, in the 2000s, the political commitment of Emelie's parents has long since abated, and her father has retired into a tragic world of drunkenness, while the mother has switched the ideas of solidarity into typical ideas of individual self-fulfillment, mostly concerning things such as mindfulness, home decoration, and health foods.[29] Basically, they are what Sean McCann describes as "prisoners of fantasy and delusion … ensnared in delusional visions of themselves and their world" when he refers to the ordinary citizen as seen by realists when the hardboiled detective story came about in America during the 1920s.[30]

The signs of new neoliberal Sweden run by Mafia-capitalism imbue these novels. And just as Stieg Larsson describes and expands on a Sweden that has undergone the neoliberal turn—something that Mankell foresees in *The*

Man Who Smiled—this is one of the main concerns in Lapidus's stories when he vitalizes Swedish crime fiction with new input. He has taken the police procedural and worm's-eye perspective in the novels of Roslund & Hellström one step further, and even eliminated the worn-out cop perspective. In Lapidus's stories, there is no room for old, worn-down, dyspeptic coppers sleeping on the sofa in the office, listening to music, drinking too much booze while running away from a nagging wife or children. Instead, these novels are populated by criminals, high and low, and their family problems.

Andrew Nestingen has remarked, "Just as the whodunnit could not respond to the social transformation figured by the rise of organized crime, the police procedural requires refashioning to respond to the transformation figured by neoliberalism."[31] This is obviously a fact for Lapidus as well. The refashioning marked by his novels certainly responds to a social transformation, as we have seen. For example, one of the big-time lawyers of the Leijon business bureau where Emelie Jansson works, Magnus Hassel, has been involved in several of the big battles that neoliberal ideology has fought against the social welfare state of the old brand: the merging of pharmacies and the selling out of health care—the dismantlement of the welfare state and its institutions.[32] This transformation of Swedish society is extra clear through the eyes of Teddy Maksumic, who has been imprisoned for eight years. What he is witnessing is the full-size process, the transformation, of all the parts of the globe into capitalist marketplace sectors. Everything is business, from schools to babysitters, from health care to the economic crimes of the stockbroking upper class.

Economy, money, and the way to make fast money go straight are the overall thematic quests of Lapidus's novels. One of the slick yuppies of *The VIP-Room*, Philip Schale, is a born brat of the sumptuous belts of central Stockholm. Lapidus describes his background as a luxurious upbringing into business and the capitalist elite of Sweden; he went to the few private schools that existed in Stockholm back then, where all the rich kids went, and Lapidus concludes by describing the deregulation of schools in Sweden, creating a new market for capitalists to invest in. It is a society where anybody can open up a school, market it, and get hordes of students—where every individual represents a bag of money according to the free choice system introduced in Sweden during the 1990s. Hence, if you attract students (and their parents), you get money from the city council; it is a safe profit machine with low costs and secured revenues.[33]

Lapidus seems to be a writer who worries about these devastating consequences of neoliberal politics as he investigates their consequences with the same kind of wide-eyed surprise of many Swedes. And why shouldn't he? Since the early 1990s, Sweden has been socially transformed like no other nation in the Western world.

Another hallmark of neoliberalism in the Maksumic series is the privately owned security company Redwood Security, which reminds us of the similar Milton Security in Stieg Larsson's Millennium trilogy. At Redwood, ex-cop and forensic analyst Jan works as a private CSI-expert with more resources than the police. In both Stieg Larsson's and Jens Lapidus's literary worlds, private initiatives are far more effective than help from the authorities—the police, the IRS, the Social Insurance Office. Another instant reminder of Stieg Larsson in Lapidus's stories is the notorious hacker Loke Odensson, who was imprisoned with Teddy. Basically, he is Lapidus's own version of Lisbeth Salander from the Millennium series, minus the violent-lesbian-goth preferences. He is the one who gets information for Teddy, as he hacks every network there is. Odensson is the technical genius of the series, sometimes resembling the same type of *deus ex machina* function as Salander.

But the gangster society is not just run by criminals—the state itself wants in on the deal as well. Sometimes Lapidus, through the voice of others, seems to want to tell us that Swedish authorities, in accordance with Roslund & Hellström, are just as bad, or worse—that they are in fact hypocrites. On one occasion, Teddy makes an incidental remark about the Swedish state-controlled gambling corporation that publishes pamphlets against gambling at the same time that they pull in millions from gambling addicts all over the country. Teddy thinks, "well, that's strange"—Svenska Spel (Swedish Gambling), a state owned monopoly corporation, wants to work to prevent gambling, and the places where they put out Jack Vegas slot machines are the neighborhoods that are the most socially exposed. The number of gambling joints is highest in places such as the Stockholm suburban community of Botkyrka and Strömstad in western Sweden, where people need every penny for other things, and lowest in districts such as Danderyd, where most residents belong to the rich upper class.[34]

This dark and depressing reality goes straight through Lapidus's entire work, in which he depicts a Sweden drenched in crime, ethnic and economical segregation, poverty and the eternal hunt for money. The novels illustrate a dystopian scenario where old bourgeoisie values get smashed by the rampant spoiled and rich youngsters of new Sweden, or as Tapper so beautifully describes it in the line of cultural historian Christopher Lasch, "The new bourgeoisie break away from the old one's education, discipline, work ethic and social responsibilities to a culture of stupidity, leisure, hedonism and self-realisation, much like the classical gangster. At the same time, financial capitalism is established and with it a new Klondyke of accumulating money disconnected from labour and production."[35]

In the sequel to *The VIP-Room*, *Sthlm Delete*, the story about Teddy and Emelie continues and Lapidus's social criticism escalates, though it is never the main part of the fast-paced story. *Sthlm Delete* is more of a streamlined crime narrative with bits of social criticism here and there. But the dark image of society proclaimed by Lapidus could also be seen as sufficient criticism in and of itself, following the line of Sjöwall-Wahlöö and Roslund & Hellström. Some examples are definitely worth taking a look at. In some parts the plot from *The VIP-Room* continues, through a meta-narrative, into *Sthlm Delete* and is being concluded in the third and most recent installment of the Maksumic series, *Top Dogg* (2017).

The main narrative regards economic crime in the top gangster world of Stockholm. An accountant named Mats Emanuelsson gets framed in *The VIP-Room* and the story about him continues in *Sthlm Delete*. He is an expert in laundering money, creating primitive accumulation for the mob, but he witnesses something he should not see: one of the customers has a computer filled with child pornography. It seems like a network of pedophiles is hunting him and eventually he disappears—he performs what is called a "Stockholm delete"—he vanishes from the face of the earth and goes into hiding. Several years later, Teddy and Emelie puzzle over the mystery of his disappearance.

The flash images of realism, class segregation and the lives of the filthy rich are being seen through Teddy all the time in *Sthlm Delete*. Outside a worn-down gambling club called Star Gamers, there is a beggar missing a leg sitting.[36] It reflects a reality concerning poor emigrants, mostly from Romania, settling in Sweden for some time to beg money for their relatives back home. Lapidus is definitely one of the few Swedish writers including this in his world, and the result is a stronger sense of reality and feeling of class segregation in the novel. Lapidus constantly moves between the highs and lows of society, exposing its vulnerable system creating social symptoms in modern society we don't seem to understand.

On the topic of *New Sweden*—with segregation, new poverty, hedonistic lifestyles, and altered consumer habits—several interesting observations are made in *Sthlm Delete*. At one point, Teddy's nephew Nikola is about to take a crack at a huge mall in the suburbs as he reflects upon the new landscape of big supermarkets that has changed the way Swedes buy their daily groceries; everywhere in Stockholm these huge malls have popped up and, all of a sudden, the Swedes are just like the Americans, Nikola reflects. They only shop at these big malls outside the cities with their boring parking lots, supersized shopping carts, screaming kids, and bread shelves reaching for miles.[37] This reflection seems to illuminate an important movement in the neoliberal era, going from a Swedish collective folk culture (i.e., watching TV or singing together, visiting public amusement parks or the cinemas with family or friends, etc.) to an individualistic consumer culture (i.e., shopping at the mall to get happy, implementing commodity fetishism in daily life, playing video games alone, surfing the Internet, etc.). In the end, this symbolizes a complex, continuous transfer of power from state institutions to private corporations that only serves the global financial elites of the world.

Teddy is perhaps the best social spotlight on the question of class in these novels. When he visits one of the upper-class neighborhoods in Stockholm, an island called Lidingö, he immediately compares it with middle-class places such as Solna and Hässelby with small houses and cozy Ford and Citroën cars everywhere. But Lidingö is several notches up on the class ladder (not fully, like even more sumptuous places such as Djursholm or Östermalm, but close enough). Lidingö is definitely one of the favorite preserves of the upper class, where rich people can play all on their own, socializing and breeding with each other. Basically, it's a place where they don't have to bump into people other than different versions of themselves.[38] This hugely segregated city landscape is an important backdrop in all of Lapidus's novels. He is an observant writer, curious, and probably amazed (perhaps horrified) by all this transformation that has occurred during his own lifetime; as we have seen, Lapidus was born in 1974, when the Swedish leftwing movement had its bloom and started its long downfall into the neoliberal gutter.

In another illuminating scene, Teddy reflects upon the *new* Stockholm, probably what Lapidus thinks of as the result of neoliberal politics in the post-millennium capital: Stockholm is the city that at least tried in the past—tried to make it better for poor people like himself. Now the city had sold out, with worn-down walls and train stations covered in graffiti. Those who could afford it traveled with app taxi companies, and even in the outer suburbs the housing prices were running immensely high. To get a loan, you have to be accepted by the bank, and the few existing rental flats are being traded by criminal networks. The beggars, so called EU-migrants, are a rather new unusual element on the Swedish streets since the beginning of the 2000s. They arrived mostly from Romania (especially during the 2010s), and they sit all over the sidewalks with their cups to get some change, but nobody looks at them. And Romanian and Nigerian hookers are selling their bodies in mini-brothels. Designer drugs are being sold on the Internet and can be delivered to your door at once. What went on in the streets in the old days now goes on behind closed doors, in apartments and houses, unofficially.[39] This closed world, where lots of crime occurs on the Internet instead of in the streets, could probably be what Pierre Bourdieu refers to when explaining neoliberalism as "the utopia of unrestrained exploitation."[40] New information technology—the Internet—has made numerous new crimes possible, which has also been thematically explored in most of the recent Nordic Noir, where organized crime and pedophile networks have moved into cyberspace. This, the interest and craze for new digital technology, "the electronic slum,"[41] Facebook, and other social media sites, mark a definite distance from the old crime fiction novel of the 1970s and 80s, when cops chased criminals in the streets, and the hookers and hand-to-hand drug deals had their place in the topographic urban landscape in the novels by Leif GW Persson and Olov Svedelid. It was a tough, worn-down Stockholm City with its epicentric nerve at the Sergel Square, among the huge bank palaces (the inhospitable concrete, steel and glass buildings of capitalism signifying the closeness between crime and capitalism, or in fact, as Per Wahlöö once put it in *The Steel Spring*, capitalism *as* a crime) with the odor of urine all over it, together with the sound of subway trains grinding against the tracks, and the oily smell of pollution from all the cars. The digital landscape, nowadays more usual in modern crime fiction, with its computer cops, hackers, callgirl webpages, secret drug networks, and pedophiles, has definitely become the new mean street since the Millennium trilogy and its triumphant commercial march across the world.

Rebooting the American Tradition

Kerstin Bergman argues that Swedish crime fiction started to abandon its American heritage during the 2000s, after an explicit trend in the 1990s with the urban police procedural, with Mankell as the main exception.[42] The new tendency is to abandon the Sjöwall-Wahlöö legacy, with an aching protagonist cop and the big smelling city lurking around him, for the neo-romantic trend that leans towards the British mystery story, mostly set in small towns and the countryside. This reduces the element of realism, Bergman argues.[43] Crime queens such as Camilla Läckberg, Mari Ljungstedt, and Denise Rudberg are household names and sell books by the tons where the bourgeois milieu and the middle- or upper-class problems are in focus. Yet, with Jens Lapidus, the Swedish crime fiction is more American and lower-class gritty than ever, probing into social problems with a hardboiled prose, only surpassed by the hyper-realism of Roslund & Hellström.

In the Lapidus novels, neoliberalism has turned into the new gangsterism, or Mafia-capitalism, in the line of Polanyi, who stated that a financial system without government control always devolved into fascism and gangsterism. Thus, one could say that Lapidus is one of the strongest followers of the Chandler tradition in Sweden today, with the private eye and the dark Marxian image of contemporary society as a world permeated by criminals, crime and the neoliberal idea where monetary and market concerns are central.

Ordinary, decent people have no place in a Lapidus novel, just as they are insignificant in a novel by Raymond Chandler. Stieg Larsson's collapsed dream and the underbelly view of Roslund & Hellström have been taken even further into the roots of hardboiled crime fiction, and perhaps the circle has been closed with Lapidus. As we recall, he is mostly influenced by American novelists such as Dennis Lehane and James Ellroy (which is also clear in his style of writing). This is where Swedish crime fiction has made a circular move and gone into its most extreme version—straight into, *and back*, to the American tradition.

In the next chapter, I will follow a completely different line of Swedish crime fiction of great concern for the development in Europe, the great questions of democracy, and the neoliberal influence on the nation state. The time has come for Sweden's foremost practitioner of the tradition known as "the European Turn": Arne Dahl.

7

Sleuths of the Post-Political Condition
Arne Dahl

In 1997, when Henning Mankell's Wallander series took some of its final breaths with the release of novels such as *One Step Behind*, and the year after, *Firewall*, a thirty-five-year-old literary scholar and highbrow writer named Jan Arnald felt that he wanted to do something other than writing narrow and somewhat ambiguous literature mainly marketed for the intelligentsia. Some years earlier, in 1995, he had written his dissertation on the Swedish leftist writer Artur Lundkvist, and five years earlier he had made his debut as a novelist. So he invented a new name, a new identity for himself, which resulted in the pen name Arne Dahl along with the release of the first novel in his Intercrime series, *Bad Blood* (1998).[1] Yet, it would be another thirteen years before his works would be published in the United States by Pantheon, an imprint of Random House.

Nevertheless, when Mankell walked away from crime fiction, Dahl basically took up the gauntlet as he started writing about international crime topics concerning the dramatic change of capitalist Western Europe and the post-communist Eastern Europe and Russia. Or as Dahl himself has stated in an interview, "I wanted to address the issues of society, show what happens when you demolish what once built the society: solidarity." Continuing: "The books were born from political rage. A rage over what happens in society, over neoliberalism and the devaluation of human dignity that nowadays counts financially and is not grounded on human value."[2]

In the novels of Dahl—using the words of Andrew Pepper—"crime is characterized not as an interruption or challenge to the smooth running of the system, or even a sign that the system is broken, but rather as an indication that everything is working perfectly well, that is, according to the logic of the market ... crime as capitalism and capitalism as crime."[3] Hence Pepper's term "capitalist noir" could easily be applied to the novels of Arne Dahl.

Swedish crime fiction scholar Kerstin Bergman describes *the European turn* as a "need for European perspectives and the obsolescence of the national police tradition," or a "Europeanization of the genre."[4] According to Bergman, national identity is now being contrasted with notions of European identity by novels employing settings beyond the Swedish borders and with transnational crime issues in focus.[5] In this respect, she considers Arne Dahl to be the prime successor to Henning Mankell, whose final Wallander novel *The Troubled Man* (2009) depicts the nation-focused policeman Kurt Wallander's departure as a standardized character in Swedish crime fiction, heavily symbolized by the old copper's disappearance into Alzheimer's disease. Instead, he is replaced by younger people whose identities are based on Europeanization and globalization. Bergman argues that this is a shift in the perception of how cultural identities are being constructed: "Traditionally, these identities have been seen as primarily rooted in folk culture, language, and national history, but today they increasingly come across as a result of the emergence of a common, transnational cultural and medial environment."[6]

From being a rather anonymous figure in the Swedish crime fiction flora, Dahl has evolved to become a megasized star who has sold over four million books and been translated into thirty-two languages.[7] He sometimes travels hundreds of days each year all over the world to speak in front of delighted audiences, and his novels are even being used as course literature at the University of Minnesota, where students read them in their original Swedish.[8]

Arne Dahl was born in 1963, and I would like to designate him as *the great organizer* within Swedish crime fiction. His two famous series build upon the meticulous construction of fictitious police organizations: first the A-Group in the ten-novel Intercrime series, which also contains one collection of short stories, then the Opcop Group in the four-novel Opcop quartet. These organizations are just as important constructions as his labyrinthine and well-disposed plots that reach all over the world, just like any other international thriller from writers such as Robert Ludlum, Ian Fleming or John le Carré. Arne Dahl, just like these names, moves around in a strictly political universe. His police groups are secret political constructions made to fight modern crimes spreading across national borders.

When he started writing crime fiction in the mid–1990s, he had not read a crime novel in years. He thought that was something he had grown out of and hence dismissed an entire genre. But then a couple of very influential films appeared: *The Silence of the Lambs* (1991), based upon the book by Thomas Harris, and David Fincher's *Seven* (1995), written by Andrew Kevin Walker. At the same time, he got hooked on TV series such as *Homicide: Life on the Street*, the precursor to *The Wire*, and he started thinking. Then he came down with influenza and started reading Kafka, but changed to reading Henning Mankell's first Wallander novel *Faceless Killers*, and suddenly he understood that the crime genre was a space for doing something really great.[9]

As a writer, Dahl is an ardent advocate of the collective working process in all his novels, with the exception of his most recent books. The Intercrime series concerns a national police task force, the A-Group, hunting down transnational crimes and criminals. Hence, there is no time for pondering overweight old-timers with marriage problems in his stories. The A-Group is an elite unit within the Swedish police force, and Dahl wrote an impressive eleven books about these characters between 1998–2008. They all deal with contemporary issues such as the Swedish financial world (*Misterioso* [1999]), neo–Nazis (*To the Top of the Mountain* [2000]), Swedish Nazi collaborators during World War II (*Europe Blues* [2001]), the invasion of Iraq in 2003 and the dependence on oil (*Requiem* [2004]), pedophiles on the Internet (*Hidden Numbers* [2005]), terrorism (*Afterquake* [2006]), and the international sex trade with plastic surgery on prostitutes (*Eye in the Sky* [2007]). Arne Dahl's texts are all in constant dialogue with world culture and literature, and the great masters of culture are ascribed parts in his own world of imagination. For example, the title *Misterioso* has been taken from a jazz tune by Thelonius Monk, *Metamorphoses* by Ovid is of great importance in the third Intercrime installment *To the Top of the Mountain*, and the final Intercrime novel, *Eye in the Sky*, contains echoes of the spy world of John le Carré and James Ellroy's *L.A. Confidential*. In *Afterquake*, Dahl completely erases the boundaries between high and low culture when he, as the critic Mats Johnson points out, gives the reader a thorough lecture on the history of Islam on one page, while dropping names of his favorite musicians—Radiohead, Talking Heads, and the jazz pianist Wynton Kelly—on the next.[10]

Dahl himself has witnessed the huge influence from Sjöwall-Wahlöö, and when reading his works this is rather obvious. In a 2001 interview, he commented on the difference in political ambitions in comparison with the old crime fiction duo: "There are of course many things in society today that upset me: a fixation with money, media stupidity, indoctrination inherent in advertising, dehumanization, and the lack of thinking, of empathy, of culture, and of history. But the ideological criticism is never primary—in that respect I feel a difference between me and Sjöwall/Wahlöö. To me it is much more important to write well than to write politically."[11]

In 2009, he wrote the introduction to a new American edition of Sjöwall-Wahlöö's most political novel *Murder at the Savoy*, originally released during the peak of the Swedish and international leftist wave in 1970. Dahl is twofold in his critique of *Murder at the Savoy*. On the one hand, he states that the literary creation has never been better. On the other, he dismisses much of the political message:

It's problematic because the book personifies the least appealing side of the leftist politics of 1968. I think that in some ways we can talk about the dehumanizing side of the Left. The extremely predictable depiction of the capitalist circles criticized by the book is unrelenting. The corporate executive who is assassinated at the Savoy in Malmö in the opening chapter is given virtually no redeeming or even human qualities. Although there is a satirical power in the portrayal, it leaves the reader with a bitter aftertaste. So this was what the dehumanizing side of the Left looked like when ideology took precedence over humanism, and when the end was allowed to justify the means.[12]

Dahl himself confesses to being a leftist writer, but dismisses the agitprop tendencies in some crime fiction, especially in the past with Sjöwall-Wahlöö as the main precedents. Instead of criticizing the system, he is more interested in showing how it is being transformed and how humans are being changed within this system.[13]

Dahl started reading Sjöwall-Wahlöö in his youth and today identifies many similarities with the legendary crime-duo:

> What was it that Sjöwall and Wahlöö accomplished with their series of books? What was it that struck such a chord in a fifteen-year-old boy that twenty years later it triggered his own production of crime fiction? I think it was the sense of suppressed rage. A fire—but at the same time a strictly disciplined fire. The slowly emerging awareness that rage which is uncontrolled and without direction will fall flat. Yet at the same time, the fire must be present, and it must be preserved. Maybe it was the desire to find a form for their anger.[14]

That anger is present in Dahl's novels, but it is also intertwined with playfulness, satiric descriptions, a full awareness of the genre conventions that he is consciously working against. Constantly breaking the boundaries of the crime fiction genre in the Opcop series allows Dahl to create his own universe within the existing reality, repeatedly intertwining the plot with the help of random coincidences—thus he is breaking one of the most pertinent laws of a crime author, becoming somewhat like a Swedish Thomas Pynchon or Don DeLillo, developing hyper-complex plot structures in contact with historical events. And these complex plots become the perfect metaphor for the boundless crimes of our postmodern era, for the dissolving neoliberal Europe and a world living in the shadow of the War on Terror.

The Opcop quartet could be regarded as an advanced conspiracy theory explaining the racist and post-political development in Europe as a consequence of capitalism: *Chinese Whispers* (2011) deals with private security firms and banks with larger muscles than small nations; in *Musical Chairs* (2012), scientific research and the military are being dismantled; in *Blind Man's Bluff* (2013), organized begging and the oil corporations' methods for preventing the development of electric cars are the main themes; and in *Last Couple Out* (2014), Dahl ties this entire bundle together as he takes the capitalist crooks to one final showdown.

The Swedish literary critic Nils Schwartz has named the Opcop series a "doomsday tapestry where humanity with voluntarily put-on blindfolds let themselves be lead to their own ruin. There are no free spaces, no sanctuaries, no hiding places, there is only greed, limited to the few, the more and more rich, more and more powerful, more and more ruthless people who do not shun any means to become even fewer, even more rich, even more powerful, even more ruthless to fight over the final petty entrance fees to Armageddon."[15]

In 2016 Arne Dahl released the first installment of his third crime series, *Watching You*, which was followed by *Hunted* in 2017, and *Turmoil* in 2018. These novels focus mainly on the small-scale investigation. There are no more huge collective efforts, and the protagonists are the rugged homicide cop Detective Inspector Sam Berger and a Security Service infiltrator with the obviously Joycean name Molly Blom (as always, Dahl is in constant dialogue with world literature). There are probably more novels planned in this suite.

Now, let's have a look at how Arne Dahl fits into the Marxist critique as employed by twenty-first century crime fiction.

Interlude: Marxist "Praxis" and Utopia

The time has come to have a brief encounter with one of the most crucial concepts in the Marxist lexicon: the relation of theory to practice, or "praxis," as it is called by Marxists. Great literature that is read by many people often has a significant influence on its readers' conceptual frameworks. At least this potential is there, and crime fiction authors are well aware of that. The authors analyzed in this book are such writers in an extreme way. They are politically conscious, some of whom are thoroughly Marxist and have deliberately written crime novels in order to influence readers to take a leftist political stand in society. They also have strong connections to different forms of socialism and Marxism over the years. Consequently, I am going to briefly discuss the real possibilities for novels to affect the future, or to even change contemporary society.

Marx's single most famous, and much-quoted, sentence—the eleventh thesis on Feuerbach—reads: "The philosophers have only *interpreted* the world, in various ways; the point is to *change* it."[16] This is Marx's most fundamental statement, and it has inspired millions of followers throughout history. What he is referring to is that materialism, as perceived before 1845 when Marx wrote this thesis, was not seen as a reality with humans and their social conditions in focus. The view of the old materialism was that of the bourgeois society, and the perspective of the new materialism is the human society, as Marx puts it in the tenth thesis of Feuerbach. The goal is to promote "praxis," the subjective perspective of humans, in order for them to change their situation.

A more recent author, Arne Dahl, has said that he only wants to illuminate problems created by neoliberalism so that readers can understand our complex reality. In another quote about Sjöwall-Wahlöö, he spells out that one has to be careful with the political message in novels:

> But the point is that the literary creation is never allowed to be subsumed by political proselytizing. The authors [Sjöwall-Wahlöö] never forget the conventions of time and space; they never forget that the novel has to place the characters in a particular setting and that it has to be done with a certain vitality—a vitality that always comes before ideology. Which is what you will discover if you read the books closely.[17]

Still, what about the idea of praxis? The Marxist usage of this term, which originates from Aristotle's *Metaphysics*, has been outlined by Martin Jay as "a kind of self-creating action, which differs from the externally motivated behavior produced by forces outside man's control."[18] In Marxism, this praxis is seen in dialectical relation to theory, and the revolution is the unifying entity between these two disparate concepts. And as I am about to argue, crime fiction is not generally a genre concerned with praxis in the Marxist sense. Instead, science fiction has taken that role in modern literature.

Carl Freedman argues that it is in the science fiction works of authors such as Philip K. Dick, Samuel Delaney, Ursula K. Le Guin, J. G. Ballard, Michael Moorcock, China Miéville, Octavia Butler, Kim Stanley Robinson, and many others, that we find the strongest link to Marxist critical theory.[19] The existence is not necessarily constituted as it appears to be, which is constantly shown by critical theory through the dissolution of the reified static categories in the ideological status quo. The existence does not have to be static (capitalistic) for all eternity. There is a potency for change, different ideas about society, and so on.[20]

In a similar way, Georg Lukács, perhaps the grandest inspiration for many of the Marxist Frankfurt philosophers, reasoned about the relationship between Marxism and the realist historical novel by Tolstoy or Balzac. Freedman reasons about basically the same relationship between the science fiction novel and critical theory.[21] Yet this relationship is by no means unambiguous, according to Freedman. He does not mean that all science fiction remains faithful to critical theory either and mentions a rightwing conservative American such as Robert A. Heinlein, or a liberal such as Isaac Asimov, who have found their utopia in entrepreneurial capitalistic visions of future societies.[22] In the same way that there is a dialectic between *then* and *now* in the historical novel (Balzac, Tolstoy, Dickens), Freedman argues that there could be a similar dialectical movement—only between *now* and *the future*—in the science fiction novel.[23]

Furthermore—and this is basically my point—he stresses that the similarities between sci-fi and critical theory are that both present alternatives to the status quo, to what seems to be permanent: the capitalist system. Sci-fi and critical theory break with the conformity and an uncritical acceptance of the existing hegemonic circumstances.[24] These ideas were prevalent in the 1960s, and the New Left had their utopian visions one grasp away when its unity split up, weakened, and was eventually overpowered by neoliberalism and a rampant anti-communism. Per Wahlöö's *The Steel Spring* is probably the one Swedish Marxist Noir novel that comes closest to presenting an alternative to the capitalistic status quo. In this novel, theory and praxis are being molded together into one grand revolutionary vision where the bourgeois society stands before its final dissolution. This is probably the intersection that Freedman calls the "Utopian possibility."[25]

The greatest problem for Marxist crime fiction is its lack of interest in defining this "utopian possibility," especially through *praxis*. Or perhaps this is not a problem, just an interesting observation that could be made when stating the obvious fact that crime writers merely interest themselves in *defining* the symptoms of the disease in the capitalist system. Most writers are probably totally disinterested in telling their readers how society *should be* and are only interested in portraying how it should *not* be. Similar to critical theory, Swedish Marxist Noir is more concerned with defining itself through critique, not by stating a doctrine or any other self-consistent way of thinking. It is a contrapuntal interaction with a changing social reality and other schools of writing. But we have to remember one point: most of these writers do not even go as far as stating a formal critique against the capitalist economic system or any of its symptoms. Stieg Larsson, Henning Mankell, and Roslund & Hellström do; Per Wahlöö goes even further in *The Steel Spring*, where he portrays a communist rebellion by a guerrilla movement.[26] In fact, most of the Swedish crime writers are not Marxists at all. They merely employ a Marxian image of society that also happens to appeal to rightwing movements and their description of reality, although the cure for the disease differs greatly between right- and leftwing propagators.

Still, my argument is that the writers in this study are leftist authors and the lack of praxis in their works still makes them the foremost representatives of Swedish Marxist Noir. Arne Dahl is one of the most prominent critics of how neoliberal politics as promoted during the 1990s have shaped our way of thinking as well as the radical change of institutions in the Western World in the post–9/11 era.

Marcuse mentions his concept of *Das Ende der Utopie* (the End of Utopia) in one of his lectures from 1967 as he stresses that the utopian image has had its day, since the predecessors of revolution do not actually take form until *during* the revolutionary process. They are probably not envisaged or determined at all when the revolutionary movement starts, but the material and intellectual forces have to be accessible in order to succeed, Marcuse argues when he speaks of *the end of utopia*. Nothing (and certainly no Utopia, land of the free) stands ready and complete beforehand but evolves in the process.[27]

Crime fiction—especially in the shape of Marxist Noir—is a realistic genre. Considering this, Marcuse's vision is also realistic. Perhaps that is why Utopia has no place in crime novels. Science fiction is not a realistic genre since it is mostly set in the future and speculates and extrapolates our contemporary reality. When crime novels propagate for a different society, they come in the shape of agitprop literature, or as downright fantasy, as in the case of *The Steel Spring*. Instead, the modern crime novel of today, at its best, contributes to a critical perspective and suggests less violence in society, less deregulation of the public domain, stronger protection for battered women, more solidarity, fewer drugs, and more social workers to prevent youngsters from becoming gangsters.

The number of topics in the crime fiction business is huge, and Arne Dahl packs his Opcop novels with it all. Now we are going to take a look at Sweden's foremost Marxist Noir writer today and how he expresses his critique.

The Neoliberal "Involution"

Arne Dahl is quite an unusual figure among today's Swedish crime writers. Most of them do not actually contribute to a political debate, most of them are probably moderately politically aware, and very few have Marxist concerns, as I have pointed out earlier. Equally, very few have real knowledge about how the political and economic systems today—or historically—work, especially the European systems of diverse complexity and perhaps the biggest bureaucracy in the world right now, the European Union and its different organizations. Most of the crime authors of today are journalists and certainly know how to tell a good story. They know the craftsmanship, how to construct a plot, how to write, how to make readers turn pages without getting bored or mentally exhausted, and sometimes they even have a message. Arne Dahl is something else. He possesses deeper knowledge about the human condition in a post-communist and neoliberal Europe wading through a tidal wave of escalating crises after 9/11. Liberal and conservative politicians and public debaters, journalists—even crime writers—might well speak about the obvious failings of capitalism, such as inequality, colonial warfare, poverty, global economic crises, the destruction of nature, and the global climate system, but, as Freedman points out, they never really consider these failings to be fundamental for the capitalist mode of production, or that the problems they address are more symptoms of a failing system than anything else.[28] In fact, the Marxist illumination of how history actually turned out in the 1980s (as explained by Therborn, among others) consists of several pieces of a huge puzzle: Social Democracy and its turn to competition in the public sector and a market economy, increased devaluation and the lowering of real wages, the acceptance of the liberal doctrine of uncontrolled international movements of capital, the inequality processes created by financial capitalism, the crisis during the 1990s with mass unemployment, deregulations of the welfare state, and so on.[29] Arne Dahl has been telling the story of the world rising from all this since the end of the 1990s, and the complex climax of our existence is displayed at its highest fulfillment in his Opcop Quartet.

The concept of "involution," as put forward by Mike Davis, deserves a place in the excursus of the Opcop series. According to Davis (who uses the term "urban involution" in his book *Planet of Slums*), this is a societal regression, the very opposite of a social revolution, i.e., an anti-progressive movement that keeps the urbanized poor people in the big cities of the world in constant competition over the last coffee grounds in the economy, slitting each other's throats over pennies.[30] Urbanization and its consequences never became what Marx built his theory around: a series of urban revolutions during the twentieth century. Instead, the involution reigned within the cities, and all the big Marxist revolutions of the past century basically occurred in the countryside with peasant workers as the revolutionary subjects (Russia, China, Latin-America), rather than the urban industrial proletariat. In this involution, which is central in the novels of Dahl since they all spin around European cities such as London, Paris, Hague, Berlin, etc., neoliberalism could be seen as the forerunner to the conservative backlash in countries such as Hungary, Greece, Poland, Denmark, etc., where immigration is being thoroughly criticized and even stopped by governments imposed on by extreme rightwing political parties. This condition has been described by social theorists and political scientists as "post-democracy," or even "post-politics."[31] Such is the political backdrop to the Opcop series, and we will discuss it further later on in this analysis.[32]

There is a continuation, a narrative bridge, reaching from the Intercrime novels to the Opcop novels. The A-group has been scattered to pieces; some of them carry on working within the Swedish police force, and some of them have been recruited to a top-secret, trans-European police cooperation within Europol. Paul Hjelm, one of the main characters from the earlier series, is head of the new Opcop unit within Europol, and one of his old-time partners has also been transferred to the headquarters in The Hague—the intellectual, rather mysterious and utterly thoughtful Arto Söderstedt from the A-group. In Stockholm, the former leader of the A-group, and Hjelm's fiancée, Kerstin Holm, is working together with the impulsive and energetic computer expert

Jorge Chavez and his wife, the interrogation expert Sara Svenhagen, as national representatives of Opcop. This new unit consists of police officers from all over Europe, stationed in The Hague with Hjelm as the commander, and they also have national units in each EU country. This means that Dahl has a widespread catalogue of characters to keep track of in the following four novels— a difficult task worthy of a contortionist. Among the members of the Opcop group in The Hague are several memorable and charismatic characters: Jutta Beyer, born in former East Germany, British ex–MI 5 agent Miriam Hershey, the tough French Muslim drug cop Corine Bouhaddi, mob-busting Lithuanian infiltrator Laima Balodis, the Greek corruption fighter Angelos Sifakis, and several others.

In the first installment, *Chinese Whispers*, a furniture enterpriser in Stockholm is doing business with the mysterious Italian mob organization 'Ndrangheta, an American trading bank is moving gigantic sums of money, the employees of a Chinese furniture workshop are sick, and during the G-20 Summit of April 2009 in London, a dying man whispers a strange phrase in the ear of Swedish cop Arto Söderstedt. Of course, all of this is weaved together in one big web where 9/11 becomes the epicenter of the narrative along with mysterious organizations such as the Calabrian mob, 'Ndrangheta and the private security/military company Asterion Security Ltd., with its equally mysterious organizer with the typical playful crime fiction name Ray Hammett (his real name is Christopher James Huntington, suspiciously similar to the famous, real-life CIA agent James Jesus Angleton). Shady and malicious security corporations are a somewhat new player in Swedish crime fiction, showing up first in the 2000s. One of Jens Lapidus' protagonists in his second Stockholm Noir novel *Never Fuck Up* is an ex-mercenary from the military corporation Dyncorp who turns criminal as a logical extension of his former occupation. Naturally, non-fictitious American companies such as Blackwater and Halliburton comes to mind as they actually were private corporations running the war in Iraq from 2003 on, along with several other companies with contracts from the U.S. Government and the Bush Administration. Asterion's founder and owner Huntington immediately makes you think of Blackwater's founder and owner Eric Prince, a rightwing ex–Navy Seal setting up a military corporation with his heritage millions. In the Opcop quartet, Asterion amasses a lot on its conscience: they torture an American bank woman to death in London, murder several British police officers, spy on a Latvian ministry, defend the private property of criminals, murder a Slovakian geneticist, open fire against Opcop personnel, spy on the Opcop organization, and get hired by a French oil corporation to murder a Danish scientist with a knife. Additionally, they have drones flying around the entire globe killing people, and in the third Opcop novel they try to assassin a French EU commissioner in Brussels.

This is the new landscape of crime fiction. Open borders have changed crime in Europe. That is the main reason for Opcop. The target for this new unit is the fight against transnational criminals all over the world. These criminals are not quite what we are used to in the crime fiction genre. Basically, they are in disguise and could easily be mistaken for legal enterprises, also working transnationally with greed as the prime driving force. This is something we notice early in *Chinese Whispers*, when Arto Söderstedt (who is an old Marxist himself) thinks about the financial crises of recent years, starting in the United States where it all exploded in 2008–09. It is certainly reminiscent of the act of a criminal, Söderstedt ponders: maximization of profits without thinking of the consequences. What kind of strange criminal act are we living our lives within?, Söderstedt asks himself.[33]

This runs straight through the entire novel. On one occasion Miriam Hershey, the British operative in the Opcop group, makes a clear statement that aligns with our earlier discussions of fascism stemming from capitalism and organized crime following the line of Polanyi. All crime sticks together with all other crime, she says, and her colleague Angelos Sifakis continues arguing about the different reasons for this: weaker national states, multinational corporations structured similarly to mob families (and vice versa), a drastic increase of kickbacks or threats against politicians, and a growing disinterest for democratic foundations among ordinary people or journalists.[34] At the same time this is happening, the leaders of the twenty richest nations within the World Trade Organization (WTO) gather at the G-20 London Summit, where they make the biggest transfer of capital (in fact, a robbery) of all time from tax payers all over the world to save the banking system, which did, in fact, cause the crisis itself. The biggest amounts of money the world has ever seen will go straight down into private pockets, and nobody will object.[35] At one point, a police officer even makes a Marx travesty, stating: "The state supports Capital so that Capital can exploit a small poor country to the last drop. And this in the twenty-first century. When we quite possibly should have been able to learn something from the twentieth century."[36] The Italian operative Tebaldi, with extensive experience from organized crime in his own country, says, "I have seen pure Capitalism close up. It's the Mafia."[37]

The criminal way of thinking is taking over the entire world, Sara Svenhagen declares at the end of the novel. The criminal way of reasoning is taking over the whole world. People who were perfectly honest twenty years ago are criminals nowadays, in exactly the same situations. Criminality has become the normal way of doing things, fiddling and cheating has become our way of life, she proclaims. Money is seriously taking the place of morals, replacing independent thinking. A big, immature cowardice is spreading out all over the Western world. Everything is just getting more and more superficial. There is no room anymore for pain and suffering.... There's no room for it in the delusive fake reality of a world focused on entertainment, Sara Svensson concludes.[38]

Reading *Chinese Whispers*, one gets drawn into this huge conspiracy scenario, a dark nightmare story of contemporary Europe. Dahl's perspective is on a macro level. We are staring down at a world map where his characters are moving around continuously, revealing the crumbling world going through one of the biggest transformations since industrialism during the nineteenth century.

In the second Opcop novel, *Musical Chairs*, Dahl exposes an unexpected revolutionary potential coming from within world literature.

Praxis and the Guilt of Communism

The dark scenario continues in the next Opcop novel, *Musical Chairs*, as well. Once again, we encounter several sets of events occurring in different parts of the world that eventually come together. The Opcop group investigates a possible serial killer who is murdering his victims on prison islands all over the globe and leaving quotes from the classic novel *The Count of Monte Cristo* (1844–45) by Alexandre Dumas. The victims appear to have some relation to Communism or Marxism. For example, one victim is a German journalist, educated at the famous Frankfurt School of Social Research. He became a leftwing radical during the 1970s when writing for magazines such as *konkret* in Hamburg, with Ulrike Meinhof, and *Agit 883* in Berlin with Holger Meins. Another victim is a EU politician from the Czech Communist Party KSČM, and one murdered man is a Marxist theorist in the Brazilian Communist Party. The serial killer appears to be an avenger with his motifs rooted in the deeply disturbing Nazino Affair during the Stalinist regime era of the 1930s in the Soviet Union. Around 6,000 people, "outdated elements," "classless people" and "déclassé and socially harmful elements" mostly consisting of kulaks, peasants, "urban elements" and petty criminals, were deported to the small island of Nazino at the confluence of the Siberian Ob and Nazina Rivers in 1933. The original plan was to resettle two million people in Siberia and Kazakhstan, but the result was catastrophic. No food was brought to this deserted island (except a huge pile of flour) and soon hunger prevailed, which resulted in cannibalism and the deaths of over 4,000 people.[39]

Obviously, Dahl is acquainted with the French historian Nicolas Werth's book on the subject, *Cannibal Island: Death in a Siberian Gulag* (2007). Werth is famous as an expert in communist studies, especially concerning the Soviet Union, and has also co-authored *The Black Book of Communism* (1997), which lays a heavy burden of guilt on communist regimes through history in the trail of the fall of the Soviet empire. The serial killer's grandfather was one of the survivors of the Nazino debacle, which was not condoned, nor approved, by Stalin in the first place. He ordered an investigation to take place when the affair was revealed to him. Still, the killer wants to make a statement after seeing how some of his communist colleagues at the University of Gothenburg cheered the 9/11 attacks in sudden revolutionary euphoria. After apprehending the Marxist-avenging serial killer, it appears as if another serial killer is busily at work as well—simultaneously. This killer is a tormented result of a military human experiment carried out by a group of scientists (at a top-secret section of a research institute) who are trying to create the perfect leader under the NATO umbrella to fight China in the future. But the experiment went wrong, and their superhuman starts killing the scientists in the project one by one. Once again, the mysterious private security firm Asterion Security Ltd. tries to find the killer, violently clashing with some of the Opcop agents.

What we are witnessing are the results of a global criminal world with 9/11 and the financial crisis of 2008 as the central events, triggering crimes of gigantic proportions by diabolical security corporations and private armies (Asterion), ruthless financial capitalists (Antebellum), greedy scientists and doctors (the Section) and the victims of their global crimes.

The character Arto Söderstedt, who once wrote an infamous Marxist thesis at the university, "Marxism in Everyday Life" (with its harsh conclusion that no one in a capitalist society is innocent), is the one character that Dahl uses to explain how the capitalist world works. In *Musical Chairs*, one of Söderstedt's monologues mirrors the foundational idea of the series as he exposes some of his experiences from his shady background as a Mafia attorney:

> I have seen one side. A world where capitalism and crime simply is the same thing. Where everything is about the intoxication of power, the feeling of being stronger than others, to be able to dominate over others. Where lack of empathy not only is a requirement for success, but also genuinely admirable. Biggest lack of empathy wins. I used to work for these kind of people. I was their spokesman.... The world around me—and not the least myself—started to smell rotten. Still, it is an experience I do not wish to be without. Thanks to it I gained a large sensitivity for lack of empathy. I can detect it everywhere, it seems, even where you least expect it. Lack of empathy does not only exist in the world of economy—even if that is the place where it is most effective—but also in hospitals, in schools, in social care and aid organizations, in the church, and naturally within the police force. Everywhere that the ability to put yourself into another person's place [figuratively speaking] actually serves a purpose.[40]

In this respect, *Musical Chairs* is a thoroughly political novel unfolding modern day capitalism, as well as the still controversial idea of the *Guilt of Communism* in the post–Soviet era, too often drenched in a neoliberal agenda, by such historians as Stéphane Curtois, Paul Johnson, Hélène Carrère d'Encausse,

Nicolas Werth, and Richard Pipes. The different members of Opcop have equally different experiences of communism, which makes their discussions interesting as they lead them to the final conclusion, to find their murderer. Jutta Beyer, Laima Balodis, and the Polish desk police officer Marek Kowalewski have all grown up in communist countries behind the Iron Curtain. Arto Söderstedt once belonged to the radical left as a protest against the world of capitalism that he had gained insight into; Angelos Sifakis was still young when the fascist Greek Military Junta was in power in the 1970s. Moreover, their unique experiences vitalize the entire team, which is probably one of Dahl's main sub-plots in the first place: the construction of the EU partnership in a small-scale allegory—as collective police work. At one point he even makes a (probably unintentionally) Leninist parallel as he lets Paul Hjelm explain the meaning of Opcop as "the vanguard, the avantgarde, the secret precursors," to investigate if it is possible to run police investigations on a transnational European level.[41] In the final Opcop novel *Last Couple Out*, Arto Söderstedt even expresses: "We are the sign of a unified Europe."[42] Still, Europol as a transnational organization actually exists, but Opcop, the operative unit within Europol, a European FBI, does not exist in reality. This is also one point where Arne Dahl differs from other crime writers. He holds a grand vision of both the nightmares of the European project, and its potential for solving huge problems such as virtually all types of global crimes.

Another political dimension in *Musical Chairs*—which actually deals with one of the central tenets of Marxism, revolutionary *praxis*—is the meeting with the character Marina Ivanova, a scholar of literature from the University of Gothenburg, and girlfriend of the first serial killer in the book. In her dissertation on the already mentioned novel *The Count of Monte Cristo*, she proclaims that the novel holds a deeper message concerning the rise of an activist consciousness. The subtitle to her book is "The Unconscious Revolutionary Structure in *The Count of Monte Cristo*."[43] Ivanova's (Marxist) critical awareness, and awakening, is an interesting trail to follow. Her Russian parents were anti–Soviets, hence her teenage rebellion became a leftist one. Or, as she explains in *Musical Chairs*,

> It was a political awakening. The nineties were a strange era to become politically conscious in. The great leveling of humanity had just begun. The docu-soaps, hypermedialization, Internet porn, the dismantlement of all critical thinking. You automatically ended up in a very small minority of thinking creatures. Thus, almost in some sort of sect.... In my youthful eyes the world under capitalism was utterly lost, without any redeeming features. The eternally bizarre fact that something as irrelevant as money was permitted to control every small part of our lives. Wisdom and learning had not the slightest meaning, empathy and sympathy even less, a monumental greediness started to spread out across a civilization in death throes. Nobody cared that public places started to get filled with beggars. Capitalism made sure we were busy with other things, namely to fill our own wallets. If the price got raised we had to spend all of our

wakeful hours hunting money. That was what they wanted—to create egoists—that was the only way to survive—and egoists were not supposed to care about the escalating inequality. That was capitalism's wet dream, the citizen as passive consumer. I was convinced that the only solution was a strong state without profits. All politics had to be reconsidered. The only people who ever had thought correctly were the communists.[44]

The leftwing perspectives are predominant in *Musical Chairs*, although the pure communist theories, such as the words by Marina Ivanova above, are probably dismissed in the overall agenda. Still, this novel discusses communism in the past tense, and neoliberal capitalism in the present tense, and as the future, except in one of the final chapters, where Marina Ivanova develops her activist theory of *The Count of Monte Cristo*, which evolves into an idea of *praxis* in the thorough Marxist sense as she states that violence is always reactionary, always worthless. Although the main character Edmond Dantès exercises some violence, that is not the purpose of the story, according to Ivanova. Instead, it is all about activism, to take oneself beyond one's limitations, to overcome what seem to be laws of nature. Mao's often quoted exhortation during the Culture Revolution in China, "It is right to make rebellion," certainly comes to mind. The theme of revenge in *The Count of Monte Cristo* is of subordinated importance; instead, Dantès becomes *absolute justice*, an inner feeling for doing the right thing that exists within every human being. The obvious instinct to flatten injustices is in the genes of all humans, Ivanova argues, but right now we happen to live in an age that doesn't follow the fundamental laws of human existence. Every time we steal an advantage, just as the contemporary times tells us to do, our organism reacts instinctively. Ivanova concludes: "The era of greed is just a historical parenthesis, and the afterworld will judge these decades hard."[45]

Somewhere here, in the monologue of Marina Ivanova, Dahl is closing in on the concept of *praxis* as he—a scholar of literature—hides it within one of the greatest classic novels of all time. "The true object of Marxism," Max Horkheimer argued, is "the fostering of social change."[46] That is, Marxism's goal is to transform the social order through human praxis. And I believe this is one of the most important issues Dahl wants to discuss in *Musical Chairs*, and just as his predecessors Sjöwall-Wahlöö, he lets some of his characters express a relevant critique against modern capitalist Europe. *Praxis* in the works of Dahl essentially means that the capitalist mode of production, the financial economy, the neoliberal hegemony, has made us *think* in a certain way. We are all customers in a huge global market. Some of us are even commodities in this market, as we shall see. The point is, we are all players in this massive financial system. Basically, this has made us more noncritical and blind to the development of power and inequality as we are supposed to become egoists, and develop our own individual life projects. Critical thinking, imposed by novels with hidden or, in some cases, even open Marxist messages, could then *reverse* this mental process, and that is probably what *praxis* means to Dahl, rather than a classic, Lenin-style revolution. It is an intellectual process that must eventually result in greater knowledge of the disadvantages of the prevailing system.

There is a fundamental idea in the entire Opcop quartet that gets more and more obvious as you read the novels: Just as in the Intercrime series, Dahl is consistent in the usage of a police collective, almost resembling a small-scale neo-socialist utopia where everyone is of equal worth, everyone is intelligent, they know their place, and they complement each other perfectly. In *Musical Chairs*, Dahl returns to the troublesome history of Eastern Europe, shut in behind the Iron Curtain for decades in numerous dictatorships since World War II. Resembling Mankell's *The Dogs of Riga*, which also gave us an interesting peek into the secret world of the post–Soviet Baltic countries, Dahl is always showing something profoundly new to his readers. He does not plow the same fields as other Swedish crime novelists. Instead, he dismantles the postmodern notion of the world where neoliberal thinking leads to increased instability, not just concerning economy, war and peace, but also regarding politics, transfers of people, a movable global labor market, etc. Corporations such as Asterion and Antebellum are representatives of this new neoliberal order, as they constantly show up in new disguises and accusations, murders, and crises, and the police hunt for them almost seems to wear off frighteningly quickly. In each book these companies transform into something else and show up, sometimes peripherally, but always with some connection to the new global crimes developing faster than the surveillance methods and techniques of the police. These corporations let themselves become extinct in order to reappear in a new form, as demanded (and made possible) by the neoliberal ideology. They are what the British political scientist Colin Crouch has termed "phantom corporations."[47] These corporations have obscure ownership models, change constantly, and use different kinds of employees such as freelancers or casual workers, thereby liberating themselves from having actual employed people. The phantom corporation appears in different disguises, changes form and uses accidental profiles that can be altered and replaced with something new. Their past history is deliberately difficult to follow, and their invisibility becomes a weapon.[48] The obvious inspiration for this is Blackwater, later renamed XE after the numerous violent debacles and killings of civilians in Iraq had smeared the original name. During this time, Blackwater appeared in the cloak of around 30 names chasing contracts in Iraq from the U.S. Government during the War on Terror.[49] After XE, the company changed its name again to Academic, and in 2014 they merged with their biggest former competitor in the security business, Triple Canopy, and the new name Constellis Group appeared. This evolution is very similar to what Asterion is going through in Dahl's Opcop series.

Crime walks hand in hand with this neoliberal order, following the same laws of instability, constantly ready to convert into something that seems harmless, but still making enormous illegal profits in an economy created to make fast money. A further development of this relationship continues in the third Opcop novel, and the image of Marxist Noir has to be altered into something else, consequently following contemporary European neoliberal ideology and the critique against it: The Post-Marxist Noir has arrived at *Blind Man's Bluff*.

The Rise of Post-Marxist Noir

The third Opcop installment, *Blind Man's Bluff*, goes further into the crimes being committed in broad daylight, in front of everybody's eyes. Once again, the Italian mob organization 'Ndrangheta seems to be involved, this time in the exploiting of thousands of slaves (most of them Romany people) around Europe every day—the beggars sitting outside shops, banks, on the streets in basically every city in Europe making millions for gangsters. The Opcop group is carrying out surveillance on a small team of organized criminals in Amsterdam in order to follow the money trail from the organized begging all over Europe. At the same time, a researcher gets knifed in the middle of a Stockholm street, and the police find out that he was a leading scientist developing a new type of battery for electric cars that would revolutionize the car market if it were finished. Dark powers are in motion as a French EU commissioner gets blackmailed with nude pictures from her youth. As usual, the trails all blend together in the end in a mixture of contemporary politics, the racist evolution of Europe (Hungary, Greece), and the unscrupulous criminal acts of global corporations.

This novel could clearly be read as a response to the reified raw material provided by European capitalism and its shady counterparts in the underworld. As always, Dahl is exposing the connections between these two worlds. In fact, what he is telling us is that sometimes there is no ultimate difference between the world of big business and crime. At one point, Paul Hjelm, head of Opcop, even reflects upon this fact, stating that "big business" nowadays is so big that the corporations are larger than most countries. Nations worldwide stand on the brink of bankruptcy owing big business money. Big business could easily sacrifice entire states, entire populations, for the benefit of its own stock dividends. What is the difference between these corporations and the Mafia, Hjelm asks himself rhetorically—paying taxes? Hjelm concludes that big business has learned a lot from the Mafia concerning familial forms of organizations and loyalty, the art of creating sects.[50]

The phantom-like security corporation Asterion Security Ltd. is hired by both the Mafia and a huge French oil company in the Opcop series. Who is the criminal? Dahl seems to ask himself constantly. And when the reader seems to know the answer, Dahl shuffles the deck once again, creating a new order. Yet, for us the Marxist view is the one we have to stress in the narrative and, as usual, Dahl has a spokesperson, or in this case even a spokeswoman, to ensure that readers comprehend the crazy world of post-politics in today's Europe. Her name is Marianne Barrière, and she is an EU-commissioner for environmental affairs. Paul Hjelm meets her in the beginning of *Blind Man's Bluff* as she explains the evolution of politics in Europe over the past decades. Later, he investigates an extortion scheme against her, initiated by Asterion who got the mission from the French oil corporation Entien to stop Barrière's legislation against the use of petroleum cars in the cities of Europe. She is an old radical, the reader assumes, and when listening to her we understand that she is potentially dangerous to all the diabolical antagonists of the Opcop series. Basically, Marianne Barrière is what Paul Hjelm reflects on as a politician who is filled with fervor for politics, who wants to create a better, more sustainable and equitable life for as many people as possible, beyond all the corruption, lobbyism, cutbacks, freedom of choice, and outsourcing, and back to the core of politics, as it should be.[51] In this respect, she seems to be a politician as required by post-Marxist theorist Chantal Mouffe, whose theory of "the political" contains ideas such as those that Hjelm reflects upon. In fact, Marianne Barrière could be a literary incarnation of Mouffe herself, although she is Belgian and not French.

According to Mouffe, "the political" is a field characterized by power, conflict, and antagonism. Her critique against liberalism is dominated by the thought that liberalism is weak because it denies the indestructible character of antagonism. It lacks understanding of the nature of collective identities. Hence, it cannot understand the pluralistic character of the social world consisting of conflicts and opposing forces without one simple solution.[52] Dahl seems to have read Mouffe rather intensely as he formulates his critique on neoliberalism. Some parts of *Blind Man's Bluff* could be copy and pasted from Mouffe's famous book *On the Political*, released in 2005 with the evolution of European politics in its focus. It is a big mistake, Mouffe goes on, to believe that the neoliberal globalization can be more easily fought on the level of the nation. Instead, Mouffe believes that the only alternative imaginable to neoliberalism could be developed on a European level.[53] The denying of class differences, the basic antagonism in society, and a politics beyond the model of left- and rightwing factions has paved the way for the extreme right gaining increased influence all over Europe since the millennium, Mouffe concludes, thus charting the political territory Dahl is operating within: the post-political condition.

The above mentioned British political scientist Colin Crouch has coined the concept "post-democracy" that very much resembles the theories of Chantal Mouffe, and Marianne Barrière uses this concept in *Blind Man's Bluff*. According to her, "post-democracy" is the political condition in Europe where politics increasingly becomes the same thing as either lobbyism or politics of violence, a through and through commercialized condition arriving after democracy.[54] Furthermore, Barrière connects this condition to neoliberalism, which has disintegrated all thoughts of community; instead, the world has become a competition where economic skills are promoted. Unemployment and marginalization create new frustrations in society, new communities resulting in extreme right movements as symptoms of capitalism transferred into ideology. Few have gained very much from this condition, Barrière states, as she continues that most people have lost even more and that these losers now have their vindictive revenge on democracy.[55]

Crouch coined the concept of post-democracy for the first time in his book *Coping with Post-Democracy* (2000), and developed it further in *Post-Democracy* (2004), where he describes it as a condition in which recognized democratic countries lose some of the most important foundations of democracy, such as freedom of speech, free elections, human rights, free public debate, and competing political parties. Instead, these countries evolve towards becoming pre-democratic oligarchic regimes, governed by experts and a small elite.[56] The post-democratic evolution (which could be seen as an "involution") is basically the consequence of Chantal Mouffe's post-political condition: a world run by globalization and privatization from huge corporations and their economic interests, a world where different strata in society lack common goals, where liberal individualism has split up classes and class interests, where public debate lacks antagonism, hence leaving space for extreme rightwing movements fighting against a believed establishment. In this world of *consensus*, big strata of society are left behind (the unemployed, "the precariat" with uncertain employments, the immigrants, the sick, etc.), which paves the way for racism and non-democratic movements. Likewise, Crouch stresses the anti-democratic forces of corporate power: "Large, global corporations have today acquired a power that cannot be accommodated by any theory of democracy. No other interests can rival their lobbying, as the behavior of the U.S. Congress regularly reveals. They are often able to determine a country's fiscal or regulatory policies by threatening to relocate. Their claim to being acceptable within democracies rests on the argument that they exist solely within the market, where the consumer is sovereign. But this cannot justify the way in which they wield political power."[57]

The post-democratic condition, according to Crouch, resembles the world in the Opcop series and has several severe consequences: the return of class society with bigger gaps between the rich and the poor, the marginalization of the trade-unions and a general fallback of the working class, the police and the state that retake their role as supervisors, the reduced redistribution of wealth through taxes, a weakened interest for politics among the poor who ignore elections and voluntarily resume their old historical position before the breakthrough of democracy.[58]

In this world, public elections become a game about trademarks rather than an opportunity for citizens and politicians to meet. This, according to Crouch, is the logical terminal point of a process that has become so natural that we do not even think about it any more: the democratic process, the outmost expression of the rights of the citizens, more and more resembling a marketing campaign with the same methods of manipulation used for selling commodities such as Nike shoes or computers.[59]

However, even though Crouch considers capitalism to be problematic, his conclusions never land in abolishing it, just in rendering it more democratic and effective. This fact makes it difficult to put a Marxist label on Crouch, or even a post–Marxist label, for that matter.

Marianne Barrière, in *Blind Man's Bluff*, is probably a little bit of Crouch, a little bit of Mouffe, and a little bit of Dahl himself.

Furthermore, in their conversation Barrière and Hjelm agree on the contemporary European problem: that they are fighting against powers that actually belong in the dark Middle Ages, a world without the Renaissance or the Enlightenment, the basic, the primordial, the logic of football hooligans, as Barrière says. A world that lacks irony, sarcasm, humor. Instead, it owns the absolute truth.[60] Hjelm, who has thought this over a lot, proclaims,

> The super-individualism of neoliberalism has created an acute need for communities, not the least because its victory was based on all the popular movements—the main enemy—having to be extinct, gladly eaten from within. They succeeded in sweeping away all the communities of the social democracy, the absolute loneliness of greed conquered, hence they left the field wide open for the false communities of racism, fanaticism, and the gangster world.[61]

Blind Man's Bluff is packed with these post–Marxist notions recognizable in contemporary Europe, and the scope of the Opcop series actually resembles the international novels of Per Wahlöö in the 1960s, with their intrinsic and advanced insights into different dictatorships, mainly with Spain as the role model. Still, Dahl is investigating post-democratic tendencies rather than dictatorships. While Wahlöö could write a nuanced description of the Franco regime, Dahl is taking us behind the frightening fascist borders of Hungary, or making us witness the chaos in Greece where black-clad Nazi street militias throw rocks and get organized politically in the Golden Dawn Party. It is a polarized world, with countries either entering the post-democratic decay (Great Britain, Germany, United States, Italy), or different evolutionary conditions of fascism (Hungary, Greece, France). In the midst of all this we have the Scandinavian nations—Sweden, Norway, Finland—as Nordic welfare states also in different stages of decay, leaving their solidarity and equality past behind, and with extreme-right parties gaining increased interest among the voters.

The European Union and its contemporary crisis seem to worry Arne Dahl a great deal in *Blind Man's Bluff*. In one important scene, he lets a French CEO of the huge oil corporation Entier S.A. reflect upon the EU as a lost peace project for the future:

> The European Union had by all means started as a peace project, at a time when still the memory of the constant European wars were alive, but nobody in his world doubted that the EU nowadays was a corporate-promoting organization, at first hand an economical federation of states who all actively worked to minimize themselves and sell out their properties to people who were better at running them. War was no longer immediate, revolutionaries had been defeated, and contemporary politics were all about paving the way for the corporations. The corporations were the future of the world. The corporations knew how to run the world.[62]

By now, there is no doubt about the political ambitions of Arne Dahl as we are about to undertake a study of his final achievement in the Opcop series, *Last Couple Out* (2014). In this novel, the post–Marxist project will have its conclusion and the very question we have to ask ourselves, both for the sake of the narrative and for the political vision of Dahl, is who, *or what*, the crook of this four-novel plot really is? It's time for the end of the story.

End of Story: X as in Marx

In Dahl's final Opcop installment, all the previous stories converge into one final battle, indicating that the quartet should be read as one huge novel consisting of 2,049 pages, rather than as a series of novels.[63] In this respect, it resembles Sjöwall-Wahlöö's Martin Beck series, Novel of a Crime, with its just over 3,000 pages in ten volumes. Nonetheless, Dahl's uniformity is greater, and the result is one coherent text. A novel such as *Last Couple Out* would then be pointless to read if you are not familiar with the main plots of the earlier books in the quartet. As we shall see, this final volume also employs a different Marxist view than that of the other books, going back to Marxian critique and notions on economy and philosophy.

Last Couple Out starts with a hacking plot against a biotech company in Stockholm where the secret recipe for a new drug gets stolen. Opcop grabs the case and the traces lead to China, where a top-secret hacking organization within the military seems to be responsible. At the same time, the Opcop members are being sent out all over the world in couples by their head Paul Hjelm. One team goes to China to investigate the traces from the hackers in Stockholm, one team goes to the Calabrian mountains in Italy to hunt down the Mafia organization 'Ndrangheta and to find out what happened to their colleagues Fabio Tebaldi and Lavinia Potorac, who have been hostages for two years. Another team goes to New York, and at the same time a new Opcop collaborator, a former French criminal, infiltrates the new incarnation of the mysterious Asterion Security Ltd. in the U.S. as it enters the stock exchange on Wall Street, gaining huge amounts of new financial capital for its new evil plan: to take global control of the drug traffic in Europe and the U.S. Hence, the old-school Mafia in Italy, which runs the drug traffic in the present, meets a new predator in Camulus Security Group Inc., led by the ever present, and equally invisible, Christopher James Huntington. Asterion has vanished from the face of the earth and mutated into this big umbrella corporation Camulus, owning a long line of different security corporations. Huntington is the evil villain in all of the Opcop novels, an ex–CIA operative running Asterion as a field agent himself. According to Paul Hjelm, Huntington is a "man of the future," working with high-tech methods enabling a company such as Asterion to adjust its history afterwards, just like the "phantom companies" Colin Crouch mentions.[64] In this respect, these companies resemble a modern *macro*-version of the changing identities of people in the plots of novels by Raymond Chandler and Ross Macdonald.

The post-political and post–Marxist theory has been toned down in *Last Couple Out*, and instead Dahl focuses on a plot that reminds us of some of the main works at the very heart of Marxian theory, concentrating on the extremes of value exchange and commodity fetishism as described in the first volume of *Capital* (1867). One of the plot lines that extends from *Musical Chairs* into *Last Couple Out* is the genetically designed children exposed in the second Opcop novel. One of them is the serial killer W, who got away in *Musical Chairs*. He was the perfect specimen generated by the Section's experiments, we were meant to believe. Still, in *Last Couple Out* he is alphabetically and technologically superseded by the even more malicious X (Xavier Montoya), the final, and perfect, mercenary. In this final installment, we get to know what these freaks are really made for. Actually, they are commodities, designed by Udo Massicotte, an Italian plastic surgeon who has made a secret military NATO-project (closed down in 1992 when the Cold War ended) into a new way of doing business. The humans designed are to be new, strong and ruthless future leaders, mercenaries, dictators, and assassins controlled by Huntington and his network of obscure security corporations situated all over the world. DNA samples of the Nietzschean *übermensch*, the master in Nietzsche's famous moral about master and slave, are used to make a new leader for the capitalist era. A world full of these superhumans is a world, as Arto Söderstedt calls it, "beyond fascism," but hypothetically it is "just business. Nothing else," as Massicotte explains in one of their numerous conversations.[65] As the plot unfolds, it is obvious that Huntington and his Camulus

Security Group Inc. are the prime customers as they are developing an army of their own to take charge of the drug trade all over the world, with X as one of the primary leaders, and waiting to buy the next generation being created in secret labs in China.

Commodity fetishism (the confusion between persons and things), as Marx mentions in the first volume of *Capital*, has been diagnosed by Carl Freedman on one level as "the central evil of capitalism as a whole." Capitalist projects such as wars and unemployment are dependent on this "ruthless process of objectification," the ability to treat men and women as if they are material. This dehumanization, Freedman argues, has been created by commodity fetishism.[66] Dahl takes this one step further, employing the commodity theory of Marx on human beings for sale, engendered to be soldiers or oppressors in the future, serving capitalism and neoliberal ideology. And reading the famous pedagogical opening lines in *Capital* we could ask ourselves, why not? Marx's theory could easily be a theory of commodities as wide as the future allows it to be: "The wealth of societies in which the capitalist mode of production prevails appears as an 'immense collection of commodities'; the individual commodity appears as its elementary form.... The commodity is, first of all, an external object, a thing which through its qualities satisfies human needs of whatever kind. The nature of those needs, whether they arise, for example, from the stomach, or the imagination, makes no difference."[67] This prediction of Marx seems to be right, just as Göran Therborn has stated: "the relative economic importance of the largest corporations has grown over the long historical haul—creating a concentration of capital."[68]

The fetish character of the commodity is something that Marx compares with religion, a non-thing, something unnatural occurring within the social game between individuals who become personifications of economic relationships. It is the specific superstition of capitalism that connects to how value is being created within the system. According to Marx, this process of production "has mastery over man, instead of the opposite," and this "bourgeois consciousness" appears to be as much "a self-evident and nature-imposed necessity as productive labor itself."[69] What Marx is saying is that commodification is something unnatural, originally strange to humans, but the economic system, capitalism, which is something quite new to our species, has been designed to make profits for those people who own the modes of production. These powers are the prime targets for Arne Dahl, as we have seen, and as we reflect upon the genetically constructed humans in *Last Couple Out* we must, once again, encounter the concept of "reification" which Marx mentions in *Capital* as something "mysterious": "It is nothing but the definitive social relation between men themselves which assumes here, for them, the fantastic form of a relation between things" Marx writes, and some fifty pages later he mentions "the conversion of persons into things."[70] Remember how Marx described the commodity in the first famous lines of *Capital*: *the commodity is first of all a thing*. Georg Lukács later developed these words into a widespread theory of reification in his work *History and Class Consciousness*, an interesting text that really kept itself under the radar of the strong influence from the contemporary Soviet Marxist discourse at the time. When social relations get swept away in the maelstrom of reification, the social life in society will appear as conformity. It seems to be impossible to dislodge the social reality since it now consists of things that are involved in certain trade relationships with each other. The world appears to be built by eternal, unalterable facts, and the conclusion is that everything has to be *as it is*. The emancipation from this solid status quo of capitalism goes through the awareness of the world as something else, a shaking and disturbing understanding for many people and ultimately a situation that could result in a revolution. The basis for the globalization of today is the very material process where everything is being enclosed within the world of commodities. The result is a total reification.

"Wait a second now," the reader probably thinks at this point. People treated as things is nothing new in crime fiction. No, I would say—I definitely agree. As we already have seen in this study—with Mankell, Roslund & Hellström—there are plenty of examples of how humans have been converted into things and commodities. In Mankell's *The Man Who Smiled*, criminals are trading with body organs, not to mention all the crime novels with human trafficking as a theme (the illegal trade of prostitutes, refugees, labor, slaves, women's bodies, etc.), where humans are made into bits and pieces of the commodity exchange. Reification is a central part of the theory of crime fiction; the criminal world is permeated with the same kind of ruthlessness and fixation on profit as, say, the world of transnational capital, banking, and international business. Yet, Dahl elaborates on this topic even further. His description of reified consciousness in the modern criminal Europe has only been discussed in science fiction novels previously. Modern technology, such as genetically designed *and produced* humans, is probably the most extreme and gruesome version of reification in today's crime fiction. In one chapter of *Last Couple Out*, the police officers study a contract, an agreement on human trade, which stipulates that the buyer must get an entire "generation" of commodities (children), and the buyer's name is Christopher James Huntington.[71]

Still, the theories of Marx (and Marxists) are the best way to understand this as a specifically capitalist phenomenon, since the commodity fetishism proclaimed in the novels of Dahl is specific for the capitalist mode of production and the bourgeois consciousness, and finally Marx himself delivers the conclusion in *Last Couple Out*: "At a certain stage of development, it brings into the world the material means of its own destruction," as Marx writes in *Capital*.[72] When reading Dahl while considering these lines, the genetically produced serial killer W comes to mind. In the final spectacular battle sequence in *Last Couple Out*, it is W who associates with Paul Hjelm and the Opcop unit as they destroy W's buyer, the security firm network of Huntington and the Nietzschean superhuman X.

Marxian concepts such as commodities, freedom, reification, and exchange value are central in the entire Opcop series, as we have seen. *Last Couple Out* sums this up quite well, I think. Dahl consciously connects the major trades of our time with politics and philosophy in his quartet: the security business, the biotech industry, the drug trade, the car and oil industry, and the defense complex in countries such as the United States, China, Great Britain, France, Belgium, Germany, Latvia, Sweden, Italy, Greece and so on. These novels basically collect into the story of how capitalism is destroying our world, and how the struggle against this destruction, in the name of democracy, has to be a collective struggle. Not necessarily a Marxist struggle perhaps, but definitely a collective fight, depending on a democratic view of the future, where a Marxist analysis is definitely the best tool to find the enemies hiding within the structures of democracy, business, banks, governments, and in different organizations.

Finally, there are at least two representatives of critical consciousness in the Opcop novels that we have to emphasize: *First*, Arto Söderstedt, the pale Finnish cop with a shady past in gangster circles and Marxist theory, who is without doubt a Marxist critic, showing up on the very first pages in *Chinese Whispers* as he reflects upon the G-20 Summit, the power struggle in the world, and how financial capitalism resembles the action of criminals. *Second*, Paul Hjelm, the head of Opcop, and the voice of the author himself, slowly reflecting on political matters in every novel—not as an outspoken Marxist, though, but rather as a typical post–Marxist, a watcher and critic of the postmodern complexity surrounding us in the confused realm of post–9/11.

The conclusion from Per Wahlöö's Marxist Noir novel *The Steel Spring*, written during the radical 1960s, stating, in the famous words of Mao Zedong, that capitalism is a "paper tiger," and that "people are indifferent to it," could not easily be transferred to the 2000s. Yet Wahlöö's other conclusion, from the same paragraph in the same novel, that "capitalism's a crime in itself," has become somewhat of a fundamental credo, the very theoretical springboard, of Arne Dahl and the entire Opcop quartet.

In the last sentences of Sjöwall-Wahlöö's final magnum opus, *The Terrorists*, the authors draw up the future to come in one single alphabetical symbol that the leftist politically conscious Kollberg makes use of in a type of Scrabble that Beck and his fiancée Rhea Nielsen play when they visit Kollberg in January 1975, talking about the Roseanna murder in 1964 and how violence is getting worse. Suddenly Kollberg bursts out, nuancing the political dimension on modern crime:

> "Don't sit there thinking about all that now. Violence has rushed like an avalanche through the whole of the Western world over the last ten years. You can't stop or steer that avalanche on your own. It just increases. That's not your fault."
>
> "Isn't it?"
>
> [...]
>
> "The trouble with you, Martin, is just that you've got the wrong job. At the wrong time. In the wrong part of the world. In the wrong system."
>
> "Is that all?"
>
> "Roughly," said Kollberg. "My turn to start? Then I say X—X as in Marx."[73]

Tapper concludes that now is the time when fiction ends and the new reality of the communist revolution begins "as the end of history draws near in the inevitable course of dialectical materialism."[74]

The same stubborn determination of a communist revolutionary near future can hardly be seen in the final words of the Opcop quartet when Paul Hjelm expresses the even more philosophical (and confusing, and post–Marxist) final sentence: "Everything is always about something else."[75] This sentence either expresses the mysterious and complex contemporary, post-modern and post-political, times with shady capitalist structures operating globally, always out of reach from the national and transnational police forces all over the world. *Or*, it expresses the trademark resignation moral (or the infusion for action) of Marxist Noir: the fact that the big ones always get away. Just when the Opcop grabs a hold of what is going on, the structures of crime mutate into something else, and suddenly, blink and it's gone: *Everything is always about something else.*

This is hardly the case with the crime writing duo up next, who follow the well-worn path of Stieg Larsson in their quest to be a relentless conceptual money machine, famous for their international straightforward Manhunter novels peppered with horror fiction, serial killers, and superheroes. These fat, glossy potboilers are marketed by literary agents, immediately grabbed and cherished by the great publishers all over the world, written for the screen and the international market, and they tell another story about the waning Swedish welfare state and society. We are now going to have a look at the high-brow authors turned into the fast-paced crime fiction couple behind the *nome de plume* Lars Kepler. It's time for the "Larssonists."

8

The Age of the Manhunter
Lars Kepler

It is late at night. It is summer in Sweden. The place is a seaside cottage just outside the small city of Falkenberg, along the sandy beaches in the southern parts of the country. It is the year 2009, and the mysterious *nom de plume* Lars Kepler has suddenly appeared during the spring and finally released a strikingly violent crime novel just before the start of the summer. The novel is called *The Hypnotist*. On this particular occasion, at the beginning of August, two reporters from the evening paper *Aftonbladet* knock on the door of the seaside cottage of two hard-working, culturally high-brow authors with surprisingly similar names: Alexander Ahndoril and Alexandra Coelho Ahndoril. They open the door, stare into the excited faces outside in the glow of flashlights, and at that moment their big secret is revealed.

Now, let's scroll back some months. *The Hypnotist* has not yet been released on the public market, nobody but literary agents and publishing staff have read the thing. It is spring in Sweden and the novel—once again, that basically *nobody* has read—has already been sold to 28 countries, among them the United States, Brazil and Japan. Besides this fact, the authors hidden behind the pen name Lars Kepler have received an advance of nine million Swedish kronor (approximately one million dollars). During this time, speculations are running wild in the Swedish press; who's behind the mysterious Lars Kepler? Not even the staff at the publisher, who are actually working with the book, know who's behind the name. Famous names such as horror writer John Ajvide Lindqvist, Kajsa Ingemarsson, and giant crime authors such as Henning Mankell and Jan Arnald (Arne Dahl) frequently show up in the discussions.[1]

Back to August 2009. The summerhouse. The journalists knocking on Lars Kepler's door in the middle of the night. Why are they that eager to expose the people behind a pen name? Well, in this case several issues are of interest. Even before the book was released the huge success was a new thing, of course, and then there were the large amounts of money involved. This was definitely something new, at least in Sweden, and an important sign that Swedish crime novelists had really hit the big markets in the world. Even more important, the year before all this happened, in 2008, Stieg Larsson's *The Girl with the Dragon Tattoo* had been released on the British and American markets—and it became a smash hit, thus paving the difficult way to international stardom for others. Suddenly, basically every publisher in the world who wanted to earn tons of money was looking for the "next Larsson." Eventually Lars Kepler was to be this "next Larsson," serving the hungry literary agents at the world book fairs a mouthful, since Kepler's entire authorship is literally more or less a business construction made to grab the Swedish crime fiction throne after the posthumous giant Larsson.

In *New York Times*, when *The Hypnotist* had hit a much-coveted place on the bestselling list a couple of years later, Kepler was named "the latest author-bot engineered by the Swedes to further their takeover of the global publishing industry."[2] International critics had called the bluff a construction while they read Kepler's brick thick novels, fluttering the pages at a hysteric pace. As did readers all over the world.

After exposing their real identities hidden behind the Kelper pen name, the crime-writing Ahndoril duo stated in a press release: "The basis for The Hypnotist was that we both love exciting literature and movies. The pseudonym Lars Kepler arose in the same moment we decided to try writing together. We wanted to separate this new authorship from our own. Since we wanted to be judged without preconceived notions the manuscript was sent anonymously to the publisher."[3]

The Ahndorils have stated their prime inspiration for their cop hero Joona Linna as Robert Ludlum's restless amnesiac CIA operative Jason Bourne, played in the movies by Matt Damon. One night, during the spring of 2008, they watched one of the Bourne films on DVD and afterwards they wondered if they could write such a story in a crime novel. A constantly exhilarating action film in words, that is. Thus, their initial question was: How do you transform Jason Bourne into a Swedish novel?[4]

As Swedish inspiration, Stieg Larsson has been important to many modern crime writers, including Kepler. The American style of plot and page turning structure, where the authors work a lot with pace, cliffhangers, and *peripéties* all the time, is the basis of Kepler's authorship rather than the narrative in itself, or the social criticism, for that matter.[5] They have stated several times that they want to write entertainment, and this becomes a paradox, as we shall see.

Social criticism—one of the most famous ingredients of Swedish crime fiction—is not the prime reason for their novels, Alexandra Ahndoril says in an interview from 2011, after the release of their third novel *The Fire Witness*: "At the same time we believe that a social perspective is inevitable. Writers do not have to have a party political agenda but the crime novel is very suitable for a general moral discussion concerning current topics in society. Such as privatizations in health care. You could say what you want, but the fact that there is an interest for profit in taking care of girls that have been treated badly is unpleasant."[6]

The Ahndorils have given a great many interviews through the years, and political issues often come up for at least two good reasons: first, the modern Swedish crime novel with its roots in Sjöwall-Wahlöö is an undoubtedly political manifestation; second, Alexandra Coelho Ahndoril has a clear political past in the Swedish Left Party (Vänsterpartiet), just as Sjöwall-Wahlöö had in the 1960s (back then the party was outspoken Communist). In 2010, she entered the lists to get elected for the parliament. "Humans aren't nice and good, therefore politics is needed," she said in an interview following the release of her third solo novel *Master* (*Mäster* [2009]) about the man who introduced socialism in Sweden at the end of the nineteenth century, August Palm. "The Left does not have anybody that can speak anymore. The link to history and the struggle have vanished into thin air. That I believe is very dangerous. We kid ourselves that we always have had wonderful lives. Or that we have wonderful lives because we are worth it, unlike others. But the welfare state is extremely new and fragile. It could just as easily be a parenthesis in history."[7]

In another interview, from the same period, Alexandra Coelho Ahndoril explains how Swedish society right now is going through a rapid reversal of class matters, that it is shameful to be poor again, as in the beginning of the twentieth century—the pre-welfare state era. In Alexander and Alexandra Ahndoril's separate solo-novels, they vent their frustration with the tools of socialist agitation, and in the same year as Lars Kepler saw the light, 2009, they released some of their most political novels: Alexander Ahndoril's *The Diplomat*, an act of accusation against the U.S. and Great Britain for starting the war in Iraq in 2003 for the sake of earning money, and Alexandra Coelho Ahndoril's aforementioned *Master*, a furious socialist statement. In their solo efforts they have been searching for an eloquent modern socialism, or as Alexandra has stated, "Above all I yearn for proof of international solidarity. We seem to think it's all right that guest workers leave their children and families to come here and work. I hope a new agitator will work with such questions. I think we have an inhuman society, in many ways."[8]

Alexandra Ahndoril had her worldview totally smashed when she was twelve and read Martin Gray's *For Those I Loved* (1972), which is about the Holocaust during World War II. This initiated an existential crisis for her, and since then she says she can't trust humanity: "This could sound naive, but that knowledge is a constant trauma for me," she said in an interview in 2011, continuing: "And perhaps it is there the crime fiction genre has its source in Sweden, the knowledge that we lied us away from World War Two, closed our eyes to all the horrible things that happened."[9]

Further, this commitment operates as an important backdrop to, and ultimately constitutes the political anatomy of, Lars Kepler. But before Lars Kepler actually entered the stage, the two Ahndorils already had their own separate writing careers, as I have mentioned before, and before we go on we have to take a look at these.

The Kepler Track Tapes

Alexandra Coelho Ahndoril was born in 1966 and grew up in Helsingborg, in the south of Sweden. Her mother is Portuguese, hence the name. She has no relation to the famous author Paulo Coelho. Her father was a sailor who met her mother in Portugal during the 1960s. In the early 1990s, Alexandra moved to Stockholm, where she started attending the Stockholm School of Drama (Teaterhögskolan) because she wanted to be an actress. Later she pursued a writing career and started working on a dissertation on the Portuguese writer Fernando Pessoa. Almost immediately upon she moving to Stockholm, she met her future husband, Alexander Ahndoril, who was born in 1967. As a solo author, Alexandra Coelho Ahndoril has written three novels, a trilogy on the dreams of humanity: religion, science, and politics. Her first novel was *Stjärneborg* (2003), about the Swedish astronomer Tycho Brahe. Brahe had a disciple named Johannes Kepler, hence the pen name Lars Kepler (the first name Lars is a polite nod to Stieg Larsson). Three years later, she released her second novel *Birgitta and Katarina* (2006), about the saint Birgitta and her daughter. The aforementioned *Master* was released in 2009, when the Kepler engine had started to wind up.

When the Ahndoril couple met in 1992, Alexander (who originally had the surname Gustafsson) was already a published author. At the age of 22, he made his debut in 1989 with the novel *The Real Woman* (*Den äkta kvinnan*). A line of experimental and arty novels followed, until his big breakthrough in 2006 with *The Director*, a novel about the Swedish filmmaker Ingmar Bergman. The director himself got angry and condemned the novel in public. In *The Director*, Ahndoril mixes facts, fiction, truth and lies in a controversial manner. The novel was released in English, as was *The Diplomat* (2009), a fictional account of the events surrounding the invasion of Iraq in 2003 by the U.S. coalition, and a Swedish diplomat (supposedly Hans Blix, former Director General of the International Atomic Energy Agency, and a highly regarded UN official monitoring the disarmament of Iraq pre–2003).

However, this novel could not compete for attention with *The Director*, and it was probably drowned out by the noise made by the Ahndorils' latest fictional creation, Lars Kepler.

The novels written under the Lars Kepler *nom de plume* consist of the Joona Linna series, and Kepler's literary agency presents the first effort, *The Hypnotist*, unabashedly as follows: "The No. 1 international bestselling phenomenon, *The Hypnotist* combines the addictive power of *The Girl With The Dragon Tattoo* with the storytelling drive of *The Silence of the Lambs*. This adrenaline-drenched tour de force is spellbinding from the very first page."[10]

No humble ambitions there. But does this husband and wife team live up to the expectations, or the boasting from their agent and publishers? A Facebook update in late April 2017 tells how Kepler sales have reached over 10 million books worldwide.[11] Large figures by Swedish measures, but hardly worth mentioning when taking a look at other writers in the same field: the Millennium books and their 90 million, David Baldacci's 100 million, and James Patterson's God-only-knows how many millions. But let's be honest here. With those kind of numbers, the writers must be doing something right. At least people read what they are scribbling down on paper, and they read tons of it every day. This, of course, was something that the Ahndoril couple knew—that writing fast-paced prose in the American tradition would sell. No complicated poetic language, not too many swirling plots or long chapters. "Keep the pages flickering" is their credo.

The Hypnotist starts off with a Thomas Harris–like intro displaying a small suburban house where an entire family has been slaughtered. Kepler's hero Detective Inspector Joona Linna, a former elite soldier turned cop, insists on being the one cop to investigate the murders. There is only one surviving witness and the killer is on the run. The hypnotist Erik Maria Bark is being called in to hypnotize the witness, a young boy, to get more information, hoping to discover the killer through his eyes.

The second Joona Linna installment, *The Nightmare* (2010), employs an acerbic critique against the Swedish armament industry. The body of a young woman is recovered on a boat in the Stockholm archipelago. The next day another body, this time of a man, turns up hanging from the ceiling in his luxurious Stockholm apartment. The two mysteries finally become confluent, and a professional assassin is found to be killing people off one by one.

The third output, *The Fire Witness* (2011), is a critique of the privatized youth care in a country that has been under neoliberal politics for years. At a rural home for wayward girls, a young woman is brutally murdered. Another girl is under suspicion for the killing, as she has fled through the dark forests of Sweden. But the secret hides another truth that leads Joona Linna into a confrontation with a figure from his past.

In *The Sandman* (2012), a man who, according to the records, has been missing for seven years is found walking alongside a railroad bridge in the midst of a cold winter night. He is believed to be a victim of the notorious serial killer Jurek Walter (think Hannibal Lecter unabashedly copied and pasted), currently isolated in locked psychiatric care. Linna investigates where the man has been all these years, and at the same time his colleague Saga Bauer infiltrates the psychiatric ward where Walter is incarcerated in order to find the man's sister, who's still missing.

Breaking into the horror novel genre with *Stalker* (2014), Kepler writes even more cinematically than ever. The police are sent a video of a woman being candidly filmed through a wall-to-floor window. The next day she is found dead, stabbed viciously by a knife, sitting in a pool of blood. A few days later another video is sent to the police, with another woman in the frame. Her husband is in shock, and in order for him to make a complete statement the hypnotist Erik Maria Bark is called in.

In 2015 Lars Kepler released the novel *Playground*, without the protagonist Joona Linna. This is not a crime novel but a mysterious, dreamlike novel about a wounded female elite soldier who explores the land between the living and the dead.

Kepler's sixth story with Joona Linna, *The Rabbit Hunter* (2016), was released in English in March 2018 by HarperCollins. This is also the novel I will study later in this chapter.

The critics' reception of all Lars Kepler's novels has been immense. I am just going to recap some of it here, from both Swedish and American critics. Carl Erland Andersson has written one of the most thorough notes on Kepler's first novel *The Hyptnotist*, which he sees as a novel written in an international style, according to a familiar pattern, made to be sold to other countries. This renders the novel a better technical achievement, but also an uninteresting one. Kepler's language is not noteworthy; instead it is neutral, and Andersson calls *The Hypnotist* a "fake novel" filled with pieces of scenery: "It makes convention of the controversial. Hence my feeling of vacuum in its center."[12]

Patrick Anderson of *The Washington Post* names *The Hypnotist* as a worthy contender of the "next Stieg Larsson" sweepstakes: "a serious, disturbing, highly readable novel that is finally a meditation on evil." Anderson draws parallels to Thomas Harris' landmark thriller *The Silence of the Lambs* and appoints *The Hypnotist* to "another memorable blending of evil and suspense."[13]

Laura Wilson, in *The Guardian*, writes that she "experiences a sinking feeling" when reading *The Hypnotist*, "another brick-sized Scandinavian bestseller-in-Europe" that thuds to the mat, "accompanied by a press release that invokes Stieg Larsson."[14]

Mindy Farabee, in *Los Angeles Times*, does not concur with the Larsson parallels: "although their styles might share a certain lurid, cinematic flair, Lars Kepler isn't exactly the next Stieg Larsson," and she also notes that the authors "hope to put a sexier spin on the Scandinavian procedural." A common point of critique, which Farabee shares with many Swedish critics, is that the novel primarily operates on the surface, "lacking the depth of fellow Scandinavians-in-crime such as Henning Mankell or Karin Fossum. Blink and it's gone."[15]

An even more detailed parallel to Stieg Larsson was made by Lev Grossman in *Time Magazine*, who introduced his twin review of *The Hypnotist* and Norwegian Jo Nesbø's *The Snowman* with this amusing confession: "I've never been a big fan of Stieg Larsson's work. I know: that's not a popular opinion. And I do acknowledge that haunted hacker Lisbeth Salander is a compelling character. But a 24-year-old woman with the body of a tween whose idea of a good time is donating anonymous sex to older men? There's a little too much of the fantasy gamine about her. That's not what I want my daughters to grow up thinking a powerful woman is. Plus, if I wanted to learn that much about Swedish tax law, I would consult a Swedish tax attorney." Still, some good has come out of this "Larssonous state of American letters," Grossman believes. Kepler is one of these good things, and he concludes his review with: "I imagine a cabal of nefarious Stockholm publishers loading bulk orders of Larsson onto cargo planes bound for the U.S. while they rub their hands together over a copy of The Hypnotist stamped NOT FOR EXPORT. It's that good. It's the hard stuff."[16]

The Swedish critic Magnus Persson, in *Svenska Dagbladet*, has identified the few—but for Swedish crime fiction, almost obligatory—elements of social criticism in *The Hypnotist* as reduced to some agitpropish wordings on the guilt of neoliberalism for the dismantlement of psychiatric care.[17]

Andrew Caffrey of the *Boston Globe* senses the engineered construction of the Kepler hero Joona Linna, stating, "he's the kind of character you can build a franchise around." Caffrey also thinks that Linna is the kind of fictional detective who grows on you—quickly. "Self-assured and whip smart, he has a quiet personality that masks a stubbornness and arrogance he uses to bull through situations that deter fainter colleagues."[18] The American influences are, as we will see, stronger in the later Kepler novels, and many critics have reacted to the strong violence in every novel. Lars Kepler as a commercial locomotive, riding across the Atlantic for success, is something that came right at the birth of the novels and has been thoroughly noted by the press. The adjustment to an American idiom is in fact central to the Kepler project, with its language and plots audaciously grabbed from movies and other bestsellers. The deep anxiety and moral madness of the serial killer genre is perhaps especially worth noting.

A Worn-Out American Tradition

The serial killer had long been a worn-out cliché by the time Kepler initiated their crime writing in 2009. Stieg Larsson had revitalized this phenomenon in his first novel *The Girl with the Dragon Tattoo* in the beginning of the 2000s, with his diabolical study of the serial killer Martin Vanger who, in collaboration with and as a continuation of his father Gottfried's deeds, kills his victims over a period of forty years. Still, even since then this mythological figure has shown up in different versions, mostly popularized by movies and crime novels in the 1990s. Michael Tapper mentions Hannibal Lecter as the big superstar of the 1980s serial killer flora, but also emphasizes that "the definition rather implied the grey conformist next door," and that in "fiction, the serial killer was the end station of the movement away from crime against property in the nineteenth century to crime against the body and identity: rape, kidnapping, torture and murder."[19] This criminal monster could be anybody, his victims anybody, and this would scare people more than anything else in the growing individualism of the late 70s and early 80s.

Barbara Fister has made an interesting distinction between the Swedish fictional serial killer (primarily in the works of Stieg Larsson) and the American version (think Thomas Harris and James Patterson). According to Fister, the serial killings of Gottfried and Martin Vanger in *The Girl with the Dragon Tattoo* are not merely moral aberrations, but "an extension of their political and economic belief system, one that justifies exploitation and oppression of all kinds."[20] This is fundamentally different from the standard of the American serial killer narrative, Fister argues, "which depicts sexual violence as an expression of the spiritual battle between good and evil."[21] Knight, on the other hand, connects the serial killer genre to a political status quo where crime is no longer a problem created by a political system. Instead, the gruesome danger is narrowed down to one deranged individual, "a threat as easily removed at the end of the narrative as it was sensationally developed at the start."[22] Furthermore, Knight concludes, when discussing Thomas Harris' genre-defining novel *Red Dragon*, that "the realisation of violence does not shake the certainty of the system or the self and this is essentially no more than a successful mainstream detective chase."[23]

Some of the earliest examples of famous serial killers in movies include Fritz Lang's *M* (1931) and Michael Powell's *Peeping Tom* (1960), or Alfred Hitchcock's *Psycho* (1960), and later even the obsessed tie-strangler in *Frenzy* (1972). These films also touch upon the horror genre with later entries (and numerous sequels) such as Tobe Hooper's *The Texas Chainsaw Massacre* (1974), John Carpenter's *Halloween* (1978), and Wes Craven's *A Nightmare on Elm Street* (1984). Early risers in the more crimish serial killer field are Richard Fleischer's *The Boston Strangler* (1968) and *Ten Rillington Place* (1971), and perhaps William Friedkin's *Cruising* (1980). However, the genre would ultimately explode in the 1990s, prepared thoroughly by two films based on novels by Thomas Harris: Michael Mann's *Manhunter* (1986, based on *Red Dragon*) and Jonathan Demme's *The Silence of the Lambs* (1991). Independent achievements that gained an increased cult reputation include John McNaughton's *Henry—Portrait of a Serial Killer* (1986) and the French documentary–like *Man Bites Dog* (1992). A vast stream of films followed, of which the most famous are Eric Till's TV-movie *To Catch a Killer* (1992) about John Wayne Gacy, Dominic Sena's *Kalifornia* (1993), Oliver Stone's *Natural Born Killers* (1994), David Fincher's *Seven* (1995), Jon Amiel's *Copycat* (1995), and Philip Noyce's *The Bone Collector* (1999).

Films seem to have inspired the Ahndorils most of all, but during the 1990s the serial killer genre also had its bloom in literature. Of course, documentaries and medial expositions of famous and convicted murderers such as Ted Bundy, John Wayne Gacy, Ed Kemper, Jeffrey Dahmer, and Ed Gein were very popular, and the literary wave started sometime around 1981 with the publication of Thomas Harris's *Red Dragon*, the first novel with the infamous psychiatrist-turned-serial-killer Hannibal Lecter. Later, Harris followed up with three more novels, completing a quartet: *The Silence of the Lambs* (1988), *Hannibal* (1999), and *Hannibal Rising* (2006).[24] All have been turned into films. Soon a tidal wave of serial killer novels followed, and I am only going to mention a few of them here. The selection is completely based on my own preference, but I imagine these are the works that finally settled the standard of the genre: James Ellroy's five novels *Clandestine* (1982), *Blood on the Moon* (1984), *Killer on the Road* (1986), *The Black Dahlia* (1987), and *The Big Nowhere* (1988) are all early examples in the crime genre. Patricia Cornwell's *Postmortem* (1990) is often mentioned as a classic of the genre. Bret Easton Ellis's *American Psycho* (1991) is not a crime novel but a postmodern account of the serial killer phenomenon.[25] Michael Connelly's *The Concrete Blonde* (1994), James Patterson's *Along Came a Spider* (1993) and *Kiss the Girls* (1995), Dennis Lehane's *Darkness, Take My Hand* (1996), Val McDermid's *The Mermaids Singing* (1995) and *The Wire in the Blood* (1997), and Jeffery Deaver's *The Bone Collector* (1997) are all modern classics in the fast-paced thriller genre that Lars Kepler is working in. An important later output during the 2000s would definitely be David Peace's extremely somber Red Riding quartet (1999–2002), a remarkable achievement in the postmodern British hardboiled tradition about the infamous Yorkshire Ripper, haunting the wastelands of northern England in the 1970s and 80s.[26]

These examples all have an American, or at least Anglo-Saxon, origin. What about Swedish examples? Naturally, there are some, but there aren't many, and ethical concerns about good and evil are not as prevalent as in the American examples. In Swedish crime fiction, the social concerns are often foregrounded: even if the killers are insane, they have been forced into a world of violence. Naturally, there are exceptions. The roots for this kind of manhunter novel are Sjöwall-Wahlöö's *Roseanna* (1965) and *The Man on the Balcony* (1967), both dealing with sexually deranged men killing women and children. The most famous ones during the 1990s, when the genre was in its heyday, are Henning Mankell's Wallander outputs *Sidetracked* (1995), *The Fifth Woman* (1996), and *One Step Behind* (1997); Håkan Nesser's Van Veeteren novels *Borkmann's Point* (1994), *Woman with a Birthmark* (1996), and *The Strangler's Honeymoon* (2001); and Åke Edwardson's *Dance with an Angel* (2001). Later memorable entries are Roslund & Hellström's *The Beast* (2004), Stieg Larsson's *The Girl with the Dragon Tattoo* (2005), and Erik Axl Sund's *The Crow Girl* (2010–12).[27] Hence, Swedish readers were already very familiar with this type of crime thriller when Kepler arrived with grim tales of evil and terror in the Swedish landscape.

Scaggs stresses that the serial killer motif in contemporary crime fiction (both the police procedural and the crime thriller) is the logical development of a process of escalation in the crime genre. The famous serial murders of Ed Gein, Ted Bundy, and Jeffrey Dahmer accounted for the development of the serial killer novel, and Scaggs foregrounds Thomas Harris's first Hannibal Lecter novel *Red Dragon*, filmed by Michael Mann in 1986 as *Manhunter*, as the original tour de force of the genre.[28]

The huge interest and, in many ways, successful hunt for serial killers in the United States, often conducted by the FBI, also derive from developments in psychology. It is no coincidence that Thomas Harris's heroes Jack Crawford and Will Graham in *Red Dragon*, and Clarice Starling in *The Silence of the Lambs* and *Hannibal* are educated in psychology and behavioral science. In Europe, Sigmund Freud's psychoanalysis, uncovering the hidden secrets of the mind through dreams, became popular in the beginning of the twentieth century. Psychology and behavioral science in the U.S. took another turn towards behaviorism. Behaviorism as a part of modern psychology has its origins in the early 1900s. It has evolved around the notion that all psychic life is to be seen as a measurable and recognizable behavior. A hidden secret world is something that does not exist, according to behaviorists. One such individual, and probably the most famous one in our time, is B.F. Skinner, who interprets all human behavior as an adaption to a certain environment. Everything a human does, therefore, is the result of three different histories of adaption: First, *biological* adaption, common to the entire human race and following adaption to its surroundings over a million years. Second, *cultural* adaption, where development of a certain culture is central. Third, *individual life history*, where a person gets impulses that result in a certain behavior through life.[29]

FBI investigator Robert Ressler coined the term "serial killer" "as a label for an 'abnormally normal' individual, an enigmatic and socially well-adapted chameleon very much like an updated version of Dr Jekyll and Mr Hyde, with no atavism visible on the outside."[30] Tapper concludes that, according to the Left, the serial killer could be connected to the narcissistic culture of modern-day capitalism with greed, hedonism, pathological narcissism, shallow personalities and consumer culture, a philosophy perhaps best shown in Bret Easton Ellis's novel *American Psycho*.[31] The violent attacks on women and the exploration of patriarchal culture and sadism in *American Psycho* and other serial killer stories have been attacked by feminists, but still, this critique has been toned down on the basis of posthumanist theory, Knight suggests.[32] Consequently, these violent depictions are now widely seen "as being a dark satirical rhapsody on the implications of gender and identity that is under pressure in a world where meaning is born by surfaces and commodities, identity is transitional and reconstructable, and emotions may only be seen as valid when they, and behaviour, become extreme."[33]

The serial killer could be anybody, strike anywhere, and has become a cultural symbol for the dread of encroachment in our private life, in our home and of our personal safety. Fear is the root of the ideology of the crime novel, Mandel writes, and crime fiction presupposes a certain kind of fear for death with its roots in the conditions of the bourgeois society. The fixation with death, seen as an accident, leads to a fixation with violent death and ultimately to a fixation with murder and crimes.[34] John Scaggs makes an interesting pass at the ideological perspective, implying that the depiction of serial killers could serve a more conservative notion in society:

> The reduction of criminality—specifically, murderous tendencies—to a pure and inexplicable monstrosity, as occurs in the figure of Hannibal Lecter in Thomas Harris's *The Silence of the Lambs* (1989), in James Patterson's *Kiss the Girls* (1995) ... has two important effects. First, it isolates such criminal and murderous instincts from all social, political, or economic causes, exonerating the social order of all responsibility regarding its deviant citizens. Secondly, it returns to the clarity of black and white distinctions in which evil, unlike the unsettling abject "other" of Julia Kristeva's theory ... with its distinctly uncertain boundaries, its pure "other," that is uncomplicatedly monstrous and inhuman.... The device of reducing the killer to something purely evil or animalistic restores an ideal status quo, and is a corresponding validation of the social order that is specifically not responsible for social aberration.[35]

In his review of Kepler's debut *The Hypnotist*, the Swedish critic Carl Erland Andersson addresses the social problems of depicting serial killers as entertainment figures in a novel. These killers perform their deeds according to an inner, irrational and twisted worldview, and the problem arising from this is a dismissal of the moral questions. The gravely disturbed serial killer is no longer responsible for his actions and can only be neutralized, killed, or locked in. Andersson mentions an example from Dostoevsky's famous crime novel *Crime and Punishment*. If his protagonist Raskolnikov, who murdered an old woman (and her sister) because she was a ruthless pawnbroker with ill-gotten riches from the poor, would be a psychotic instead of a rational human being, murdering according to a sensible logic, the entire novel would be deprived of all its existential and moral core; it would collapse. According to Andersson, there is no such moral core in Kepler's *The Hypnotist*. Instead, people murder and kidnap because they are more or less insane.[36] This, in turn, calls for more punishment in society and serves only the conservative impulses in politics and among the public. Hence, it is the opposite of what Marxist Noir is all about—that is, opening the eyes of the people in the search for another social and political society, illuminating situations of class struggle and what the capitalist mode of production is doing to us, and ultimately exposing the criminals that are running the world we all live in.

So, how does this genre that Kepler is working in, a genre filled with clichés, posthuman theory and bourgeois traps, as we have seen, correspond to the tenets of Marxist Noir, or a leftist message, for that matter?

Excursus: The Rabbit Hunter

In the sixth Joona Linna outing, Kepler grabs a hold of the reader from the first page. A long sequence, split over several short chapters, contains their unmistakable mix of messy violence and sexual deviations when a prostitute gets attacked by a man who turns out to be the Swedish Minister of Foreign Affairs. It is a classic horror scene filled with fear, rape and blood as she simultaneously becomes the witness of the murder of the minister. A killer has entered the house and shoots him at close range and then swiftly disappears into the night. The security police immediately think of it as a terrorist attack and act accordingly, interrogating the prostitute in one of those secret rooms that all security organizations have in a post–9/11 realm. Eventually, Joona Linna is on the case and the manhunt is on. The killer keeps murdering victims that have been to an exclusive private school in the Stockholm archipelago. A gang rape of a woman is one clue that Linna and his colleagues are following while the government is on the bellicose terror hunt trail. Eventually they are hunting a serial killer (not very unusual in a Kepler work), exacting revenge on the perpetrators that raped his mother, and this killer is a trained assassin with a past in the Navy Seals as a sniper. Consequently, he is the rabbit hunter.

Nothing is ever *real* in a Kepler novel. The relation to realism, which is a defining feature of Swedish Marxist Noir in novels by Mankell and Sjöwall-Wahlöö, is basically non-existent here. Instead, we witness a play with genres and consummated constructed pageturners written for the wider consuming mass-public audience who wouldn't open *Crime and Punishment* for the world. The serial killer is a recurring figure in the novels of Kepler, and the serial plot is extremely evident in *The Rabbit Hunter*. It is basically the opposite of a postmodern crime fiction novel; there is no actual complexity (not even a false one, as often in works of presumed postmodernism), no steep dives into contemporary political theory. Kepler writes in huge, open images made for a spoiled cinema audience, just as they did in the previous novel *Stalker*. Nor is there any trace of irony in *The Rabbit Hunter*—it's just pure *pace*. The entertainment violence and pornographic sequences are all clichés penned to titillate the reader and to make him/her turn to the next page. Yes, these are my own opinions, but they are also some of the defining problems in modern crime fiction, made for an international market governed by literary agents and mega-sized publishing houses, constantly merging with each other. I could go even further, stating that this is a problem created by capitalism and the cynical production process of modern literature, only that would perhaps go beyond the aims of this book.

Nonetheless, the writers take a firm stand in our contemporary age using characters well known to most readers already: smug television chefs, contentious homosexual youngsters, beautiful blondes who are excellent fighters sweating in tight clothes, high-tech cameras, computers steered by a clever hacker, a police organization sprinkling money on helicopters and special forces, terrorist hunts, underground secret interrogation rooms in the midst of Stockholm, and tons of weapons. Social criticism is completely secondhand for Kepler, as the Ahndoril couple have stated in several interviews. These novels are more of a playful diversion after watching violent Hollywood movies than a true attempt to depict Swedish class society in the traces of neoliberal politics in the 1990s and 2000s. Or, to be quite explicit: Kepler's writing *in and of itself* seems to be an obvious result of neoliberal ideology, with its deliberate search for a global market.

The killer in *The Rabbit Hunter* is a lone avenger, seeking redemption for individual injustice (the rape of his mother) rather than a class-conscious worker rising in sudden political and revolutionary awareness. He is more similar to the serial killers in Mankell's *Sidetracked* and *The Fifth Woman* than the revolutionary minds in Sjöwall-Wahlöö's *The Abominable Man* and *Murder at the Savoy*, who not only kill individuals but also hit an oppressive structure in society. Actually, the killer in *The Rabbit Hunter* is not even a serial killer, according to Kepler who calls him a "spree killer," as they make distinctions between different types of killers:

> A mass murderer carries out his deed in one single place while spree killers move around. A serial killer sexualizes his killing often, while a spree killer rationalizes it. He doesn't take any emotional breaks—and there's never ever more than seven days between two murders.[37]

Not even Joona Linna is a realistic construction, like Martin Beck or Kurt Wallander, who both embody the contemporary society and its flaws. On the contrary, Linna is a superhero, a crossover between Superman and Sherlock Holmes, and the Ahndorils confess to that. He is supposed to be that way. And he is probably not a socialist, like Sjöwall-Wahlöö's cops Lennart Kollberg and Gunvald Larsson. Linna is more of a reactionary hero, like Lee Child's Jack Reacher or Jo Nesbø's Norwegian rugged serial-killer expert Harry Hole. Still, one thing is perfectly clear: Lars Kepler is probably the number one (topical and commercial) inheritor of Stieg Larsson, and the Ahndorils are working in the school of Nordic crime writing that the American crime fiction expert Peter Rozovsky has dubbed "Stieg Larssonism." This phenomenon has been described as the combination of "potboiler thrills and righteous anger in a fat, sprawling tosh-filled package, often with 475 or more pages plus a didactic, statistics-filled epilogue in case the reader doesn't get the point—or in case he or she thinks the point was just to have some fun. That way the reader gets dirty thrills but feels morally uplifted at the same time."[38]

Bearing this in mind, the Ahndorils are "Larssonists" rather than Marxists. That means they are imitators, masquerading as heavy social critics, working within existing parameters of the genre, rather than creating new outlines and pushing boundaries.

For instance, their heroine Saga Bauer, as beautiful as a blonde princess from a famous Swedish painting, is Kepler's own incarnation of Lisbeth Salander. She is tough, a good fighter, and can handle weapons and rough situations better than anyone else. Nonetheless, although significantly less gamine than Salander, Bauer is a conventional police bureaucrat who complies with the organization she is working within. That is something that Salander would never be since she is an anarcho-feminist, constantly seeking her own independence and liberation. Still, the reality as described in the Kepler novels is the same (obviously fictitious) brutal and dark reality as in the Millennium trilogy, where nefarious serial killers, rapists, racists, corporate tycoons, and pedophiles lurk in society, in the suburbs, in the picturesque small towns, in the beautiful but still threatening archipelago, in the huge, luxurious apartments and estates in Stockholm.

The killer in *The Rabbit Hunter*, as I have already mentioned, is interesting, though, and I will conclude this excursus by having a brief look at the underlying political message of the novel.

In the political studies of crime fiction, there are a number of questions that can be posed to analyze whether a work is a (post–) Marxist Noir or not. One of the most important of those questions concerns the perpetrator, in this case who the killer is and what his or her motives are. In this instance, he (for the killer is actually male, which is not the case of the serial killer in

Stalker where she, statistically unusual enough, is a woman) is an avenging conscience, haunted by anger, insanity and post-traumatic war memories connected to an incestuous relation with his mother. Since the mother was once brutally raped by other private school students in her youth, the killer represents an avenging angel from the past, born to be what he has become (basically bred by one of the rapists): an assassin that strikes against the same upper-class that has violated and abused Sweden for centuries, and keeps doing so by controlling society and the coterie that glues them together. The killer becomes a striking cue ball, smashing the members of the coterie for a short while, and creates shards of awareness about how the invisible, informal structures, created at exclusive private schools in Sweden, become the foundations for future power in society.

The bourgeois ruling class and its abuse of the Swedish welfare state turns into a literal function in Kepler's narrative, and the symbolism is inevitable as it is *The Rabbit Hunter*'s utmost political contemporary credo. This is also where the Ahndorils' obvious leftwing sympathies show up in the novel. As I have mentioned before, there are bits of leftist critique in every Kepler novel (against the arms industry, privatizations, and so on), but it never goes deeper than this, as a hardly visible current overpowered by all the noise from the bestselling novel effects.

Paradoxically, Kepler is very obedient towards the genre and its worn-down clichés as they participate in the global conquest of readers. Still, the feeling after reading one of their potboilers is a striking sense of... void. The Marxism we are used to from Sjöwall-Wahlöö or Mankell is not quite there. Theoretically, the books are shallow, since neither of their main characters seem politically conscious, and the writers themselves are probably more interested in keeping their readers turning pages than taking a firm stand against capitalism or finding the borders of Utopia.

It takes a rather investigative study to expose the Marxist Noir in a Kepler novel. Yet, the facts remain: a Kepler novel probably feeds the conservative urges of the public rather than invokes a sudden revolutionary awareness in a leftist sense of the concept. Crime novels are about empathy and restoring order and chaos, as Alexander Ahndoril has stated in several interviews.[39] Restoring *what* order is the clear question we have to ask ourselves. Dialectics is not about restoring order, but rather disturbing it, or interrupting it, in order to obtain *something else*, something better, through a contradiction, a conflict. In the classic Swedish detective story, much inspired by Agatha Christie, the element of restoring order was central. Then the crime was an aberration within the bourgeois society where everybody lived happily in their little cottages, far away from big cities, from poverty, perversions, and war in other parts of the world. Crime was something that barged in and constituted a rupture in the order of things. Therefore, Ahndoril's statement could be read as a neo-conservative credo in a time when neo-conservatism thrives in Sweden. Knowing the leftist stance in Ahndoril's earlier novels, such an interpretation is difficult to take seriously, though. No, when Ahndoril is talking about fighting crime to restore order, there is a clear individual stance in this. Chaos and disorder are not necessarily a socialist revolt, or even a sign of post-dialectic societal movement. It could be, and in much crime fiction most certainly is, something that threatens freedom and democracy. That is probably the crime Ahndoril is referring to. There is a lot of darkness and evil in the world, he says in one of the interviews mentioned earlier.[40] This reality, which also frightens the authors themselves, is ultimately what they want to tell stories about.

In Kepler's novels, the journey away from Chandler's literary style of autonomous episodes has been completed. Considering that Chandler participated in the logic of modernism, which tends towards an autonomization of ever smaller segments, as Fredric Jameson argues, Kepler has strived towards bigger units, comprising the entire book as one singular unit with about one hundred chapters divided by dozens of *péripetiés*.[41] The novels of Kepler are not literary pieces of art in their own right; they are fast-paced reading machines, and if you act according to the famous Chandler credo—a novel should be possible to read even if you tear out the final pages—the entire unity collapses into meaninglessness, and ultimately there are no dialectics to show the way out.

Conclusion
The Dialectics of Crime Fiction

In this book, I have tried to show that there is a dialectic movement from *then* to *now* in crime fiction, primarily between the bourgeois detective novel (think Christie, Sayers, the English formula still dominating the trade in the 1940s), to a more socially concerned response containing elements such as realism and Marxism (think the Chandler era of the post–Depression 1940s, and up to the Swedish Marxist Noir of the post–1990s). The elements of social criticism, in both currents of modern crime fiction (the American and the Swedish) are reactions against a conservative, bourgeois, detective genre, reigning fully at the time (the American 1940s and the Swedish 1960s). Chandler's often quoted account of this, where he identified Dashiell Hammett (and the realist mystery novel) as the one who "took murder out of the Venetian vase and dropped it into the alley," outlines his famous reckoning with the bourgeois detective story in his essay "The Simple Art of Murder."[1] Per Wahlöö made a similar analysis criticizing the Swedish bourgeois crime novel of the 1940s and 50s when he created the first Swedish Marxist Noir novel in the mid–1960s, interjecting Marxist theory into the narratives. These two examples demonstrate the dialectics of crime fiction, from then to now, a dialectic movement that still progresses into our time with examples like Stieg Larsson and Arne Dahl.

Cultural historian Alan Wald has used the theories of Trotsky to explain a similar dialectic in culture as a whole that I wish to apply to Swedish crime fiction literature, where new styles grow out of old styles, as their dialectical negation:

> Instead of positing that each new cultural phase smashes and annihilates the culture that preceded it, Trotsky proposes a dialectical continuity in cultural history. Literary tradition proceeds by a series of reactions, each of which is united to the tradition from which it is seeking to break. Moreover, these developments occur not at once, but under

the stimuli of new artistic needs as the result of changes in the psychology of social classes attendant upon changes in the economic structure.²

Ultimately, there seems to be no way out of the world of lawlessness in today's society, and crime fiction, foremost Marxist Noir, as an important cultural expression, is the tool continuously mirroring the contemporary crisis of global capitalism during the War on Terror. Consequently, again referring to Alan Wald, who has pointed out five analogous elements between past and present that answer why our contemporary situation seems so familiar after a time lapse of seventy years. This leads us to an explanation of which social developments and anxieties are behind the noir fiction of the 1940s of Raymond Chandler and other writers, and a similar Marxist Noir in Sweden during the second half of the twentieth century through the *fin de siècle*, across the new millennium and well into the 2000s:

- The advent, unpredicted, of a poorly-understood and not-fully-appreciated new phase in the march of capitalist exploitation across the world (then, it was economic boom and postwar imperialism; now, neoliberal globalization and ecological crisis);
- A major interruption in the progress of the organized working class (then, the turn away from social unionism toward the consolidation of bureaucratized business unionism; now, the catastrophic decline in union membership and influence);
- A dangerous polarization in world politics in which rightward-moving liberal intellectuals are needed to give legitimacy to U.S. imperialism's ideological mask (then, the construction of "totalitarianism"; now, the manufacture of the Islamic threat and the war on terror);
- A domestic counterpart of foreign policy to produce a liberalism of fear and scapegoating (then, the suspicion of one's neighbor, teacher, or civil rights activist as a subversive communist; now, the wariness of "foreign-looking" persons and immigrants as potential terrorists);
- A persistence of sickening racial violence even after apparent political progress (then, the Fair Employment Practices Committee and the "To Secure these Rights" report; now, the election of a Black president and appointment of a Black attorney general).³

All of the writers in this study are trying to explain their contemporary eras with the help of crime fiction, and sometimes with the help of Marxism. Per Wahlöö was the first one, putting the social theory and social criticism of Chandler on the Swedish chart. His novel *Murder on the Thirty-First Floor* is the first Swedish Marxist Noir novel, but it was not until the sequel, four years later, that Wahlöö really took Marxist Noir further, into the dialectics of crime fiction, with *The Steel Spring*. It is a rare novel that presents the utopian image of the (then, in 1968, obvious) alternative to capitalist society: a progressive communist revolution.

Marxist Noir, at its best, acts as a preserve of human yearnings for that "other" society beyond the present one. Consequently, Henning Mankell's hero Kurt Wallander witnessed a receding movement, the old and solid society where he grew up falling apart from the pressure of something new and frightening: globalization, Eastern gangsters, immigrants, homosexuals, and the escalating violence against women. But in the works of Stieg Larsson, the entire welfare state itself has mutated and gone corrupt, the old and good society has become a modern and sinister place. This image of society induces a reactionary impulse within the reader, Hagberg argues, of a false dream that the good old days were much better than the modern society infested by crime, corruption and decay.[4]

"The inescapability of history," David Fine argues, "is the lesson of the Chandler/Macdonald California crime story, one that would be carried into the present by dozens of followers."[5] As we have seen, Sweden has been a truly fertile ground for this lesson. At this time, the new crime novel is even more complex and reflects our contemporary, postmodern society and its diversity. Issues of race, gender, and class are highlighted in both Swedish and American crime fiction. Those who were relegated to the margins in Chandler and Macdonald have now become major characters: racial and ethnic minorities, female police officers, and sexual minorities. Hence, this illustrates the need for the concept of Post-Marxist Noir. Nevertheless, postmodernism could be deceptive while it does not always serve the dialectical purpose of Marxist Noir.

Ekman (2010) mentions the concept of "false dialectics" when discussing the postmodern narrative. This narrative is illusory since it has a pretext for openness, movement and nuances, but in reality nothing is ever moving anywhere, no doors are being opened, and there is ultimately no way out at all. Adorno's concept of "phantasmagoria" could be applied as a "tendency to mask the social-psychological genesis ... by making it appear to be derived from 'natural' sources, a deception characteristic of much authoritarian thought."[6] The illusory movement in postmodernism is, in fact, only a static relativism, Ekman argues as she further states that when Marxists speak about dialectics they mean how society progresses through a process driven by pairs of contradictory opposites, that an apparently homogeneous conflict or contradictory free situation always contains its own antithesis, the seed for its own destruction. Therefore, it is important to identify these seeds. But when postmodernists speak about opposites, there is never any motion in these opposites; they don't move anywhere, they just exist. According to postmodernism, life is just one huge, static bundle of tension and conflict that makes you unable to understand anything.[7]

Hence, the dialectic method makes truth claims, it progresses and shows a way out, while postmodernism, or Post-Marxism for that matter, are dialectics *masquerading* as analytics, claiming to begin from scientific facts when in fact they begin from conclusions that are analytically either false or unproveable. Consequently, these conclusions do not constitute any threat against the existing order (that is, capitalism). Class conflict still remains the sole motor of history and radical social change in Marxist Noir. Another theoretical approach to this is what Carl Freedman calls "post-dialectical" theory. For example, he refers to Michel Foucault's investigations of the microtechnologies of power and Jacques Derrida's analyses of linguistic sedimentation commonly known as post-structuralism, and suggests a connection between neoliberalism and poststructuralism (i.e., postmodernism):

> If, however, this body of thought must be considered postdialectical rather than dialectical proper, it is not only because of the strategic distance that figures like Foucault and Derrida have usually maintained from Marx and Freud (and even leaving aside that, in the particular French intellectual formation relevant here, the names of Marx and Freud have often served as code words for Althusser and Lacan). More important, though not unrelated, is the suspicion that virtually all versions of poststructuralism have cast on the indispensable dialectical category of totality. This is the point of contact between poststructuralism and neoliberalism (or, sometimes, neoconservatism), a contact grotesquely illustrated in, for example, the editorial history of *Tel Quel*.[8]

Contrariwise to Marxist Noir, Post-Marxist Noir shows complexity for its own sake, but no social solutions; it shows dichotomies, but no way towards *praxis* in the Marxist sense of the word. Post-Marxist Noir is all about restoring order. Not necessarily a capitalist order, but instead it endorses a parallel order to progress that exists within our complex reality, such as the strive for electrical cars in Arne Dahl's *Blind Man's Bluff*, or the prevention of genetically constructed humans as commodities in *Last Couple Out*. Post-Marxist Noir does not prescribe giant leaps of social change through revolution, as Per Wahlöö does in *The Steel Spring*; it never prescribes radical social change, or pulling the emergency brake. Instead, the reader gets familiar with a radical criticism against capitalism, and questions of democracy, racism, identity, feminism, and politics are prominent instead of pure class matters of historical importance connected to issues of economy and the distribution of wealth. It never has the ambition to erase, or question, the fundamental conditional economic system of our time: capitalism. Class matters do operate in the novels of Lapidus and Kepler, where the hedonistic upper-class is being analyzed with their private schools and business coteries, which lead to corruption, murder, and pedophilia at the very heart of capitalistic power. Moreover, the eternal dependence on an income, on money, constantly pressuring the lower-class citizens, is splintered open: the constant car troubles of Wallander in Mankell's novels, the eternal hunt for cash and the yearning for status in the Lapidus novels. These are actual class matters that concern and have an influence on many people in real life. However, some of the novels in my study don't care to notice this, the most fundamental of all problems in a capitalist society, at all. For example, Joona Linna, the superhero cop in the novels of Kepler, never really has to think about how to get money for the rent. Stieg Larsson's Lisbeth Salander uses some of her computer magic and doesn't really have to work for a living in the two final Millennium novels. Some of these writers merely use class issues as an interesting tableau rather than depict them as actual, fundamental problems of existence within a hegemonic economic system.

Most crime fiction with social-critical ambitions tells how things *are*, instead of telling the reader how things *should be*. After all, restoring order means going back to the kind of society we are used to—that is, capitalism—before the crooks created a rupture, which means that most writers are proclaiming a capitalist order in the end. Still, it is an immensely difficult task to draw a line that separates Marxist Noir from Post-Marxist Noir. Social concerns are a dominant part of both traditions, and definitely a vital ingredient of these genres. Many writers claim to be socially concerned, and some of them—for example, Lars Kepler—who are analyzed in this study could be dismissed as "Larssonists," only imitating social-critical crime fiction writing to make tons of money. Still, many of these writers have leftist backgrounds; they proclaim social issues in their novels, but their stories feed the urge of a conservative ambiance in society as well as create an image of a corrupt, dark, and violent world where the struggle between good and evil, black and white, is prevalent. These stories contain leftist *and* rightwing elements, I would say, as did the novels of communists such as Sjöwall-Wahlöö and Henning Mankell. In their stories, there are elements of racism, anti-feminism, womanizing images, and criticism against the welfare state, of course inflicted by contemporary discourse. But, could this be read as "false dialectics"? Are the "Larssonists" and their postmodern approach to the crime genre in fact "false dialectics"? I believe the answer is yes *and* no. Their crime novels could create awareness of the social order in the world, but still, very few indications show that this would have political influence in a progressive leftist way. Sjöwall-Wahlöö wrote some of the best crime novels ever, with exciting plots and a leftist perspective on society, power, and crime. Still, the Left had its huge decline in the second half of the 1970s, concurrent with the big world economic crisis and the Martin Beck novels becoming a worldwide success. The fact that crime fiction is a monumental capitalist literature industry, made to earn money for agents, publishers, and ultimately the writers themselves, always comes back to us.

In the following, I will conclude this study by sketching some strategies for Marxist Noir and making some claims regarding how to categorize the writers discussed in this book by genre or type of writing. One question the reader of this study might like to have in mind when reading crime fiction in the future is the one I have been faced with for years: *How do you define Marxist Noir?* Some fundamental key questions could be helpful, and I have displayed some of them below. There are probably several more intricate questions one could address to any source material, in that case I would like to encourage the readers themselves to face them in their own inquiries.

- Who is the killer/perpetrator?
- What motive lies behind his/her deeds?
- What is the nature of the crime?
- Is the crime an act of emancipation or a sign of class struggle?
- Who is the crime being committed against?
- Is the criminal portrayed as a victim?
- How are the police described? Heroes? Bullies? Fascists?
- What role in society do the police play?
- How is society being portrayed?
- Are there signs of class struggle?
- Are class distinctions visible in the narrative?
- Do they play a central part in the story?
- How are they portrayed?
- What kinds of work do the characters have?
- Is the story a realist one, a portrait of contemporary society?
- On what level of power in society do the characters play out their roles?
- Does the novel, or a character in the story, ever question the fundamentals of capitalism?
- What are the social conditions in the novel?
- What does the historical development of society and class look like?

Social criticism is one of the defining features of Swedish crime fiction, and in the following I will try to name some of the most important writers with social or bourgeois agendas. As one might have expected, the social writers predominate:

Social Writers	*Bourgeois Writers*
Leif GW Persson	Camilla Läckberg
Henning Mankell	Mari Jungstedt
Arne Dahl	Denise Rudberg
Stieg Larsson	Jan Mårtenson

Social Writers	Bourgeois Writers
Roslund & Hellström	Håkan Nesser
Erik Axl Sund	Johan Theorin
Jens Lapidus	Kristina Appelqvist
Lars Kepler	
Cilla & Rolf Börjlind	
Ingrid Hedström	
Tove Alsterdal	
Liza Marklund	
Helen Tursten	
Karin Alvtegen	
Katarina Wennstam	
Kjell Eriksson	

A risky task, and a dirty job (but still, someone has to do it) is to make a thoughtful split between writers whose works contain predominantly Marxist or post–Marxist topics respectively. An attempt to categorize this (with great reservations for the fuzzy lines between the two, of course) would appear as follows:

Marxist Noir	Post-Marxist Noir
Henning Mankell	Arne Dahl
Per Wahlöö	Jens Lapidus
Sjöwall-Wahlöö	Liza Marklund
Roslund & Hellström	Stieg Larsson
	Lars Kepler
	Erik Axl Sund
	Ingrid Hedström

Now, what is the difference between Marxist Noir and Post-Marxist Noir, the readers of this book might finally ask themselves. I don't believe in presenting the differences in dichotomies, as I have done with, for example, new and classical crime fiction earlier in this study. The two Noirs are intertwined, and Post-Marxist Noir is certainly dependent on Marxist Noir. Therefore, I will avoid doing the same kind of schematics as I have done above with the writers.

Works of Marxist Noir contain Marxist tenets that are intertwined in the narrative in some way. Some of the most important tenets in the novels of Wahlöö and Sjöwall-Wahlöö are the elements of class struggle, alienation, reification, the proletarian view of power structures, or, as Althusser would say, Ideological State Apparatuses (the regime, government, the bureaucracy, the chief of police, and so on), and the criminal as a victim of circumstance in a society governed by a bourgeois regime. Some of these novels contain a solution, such as *The Steel Spring* with its outright revolutionary scenario. Some of them have an inexorable worm's-eye view on society, defending the poor and weak, as in *The Girl Below the Street* by Roslund & Hellström.

The Post-Marxist Noir, on the other hand, has a post–Marxist perspective on things. That means, once again in the words of Göran Therborn, that it retains the fundamental Marxian idea that human emancipation from exploitation, oppression, discrimination and the inevitable linkage between privilege and misery can come only from struggle of the exploited and disadvantaged themselves. It then continues by recognizing that the twenty-first century is beginning to look very different from the twentieth—not more equal and just, but with new constellations of power and new possibilities of resistance.[9]

The post–Marxist writers often have an explicitly Marxist background but have gone beyond (think, abandoned, and become disinterested in) original Marxist problematics, though still operating in a field with contemporary critique towards capitalism. Furthermore, they have developed and pursued new tendencies and new desires in society. For example, Jens Lapidus (who does not have a political or theoretical Marxist background) has an interest in groups, subcultures, and strata in society in the line of the sociology of Bourdieu, rather than class matters in a straightforward Marxist way. Or Arne Dahl, who has built his entire Opcop quartet on the question of democracy in Europe and its way into the future of organized crime and rightwing movements. Stieg Larsson is the prime propagator for questions on radical feminism, technology, and antiracism in his narratives and has definitely gone beyond the Trotskyite themes of his youth. Topics such as racism, feminism, linguistics, aesthetics, production of history, anthropology, psychoanalysis, culture, the eclectic play with genres and so on, are certainly defining features of Post-Marxist Noir. However, Marxist and Post-Marxist Noir are also opposite sides of the same coin, sometimes intertwining. Henning Mankell is that kind of a writer, working with old leftist issues such as class, alienation, economy, and the controversial Swedish Nazi heritage after World War II, while simultaneously asking high profile questions about New Public Management, privatizations, radical feminism, and the post–Soviet Europe emerging in the 1990s.

Still dominating the Swedish crime genre is the procedural novel, although new trends are opening new horizons. One interesting perspective, obviously influenced by American crime writing, is the recent vitalization of the criminal-as-hero formula (or hero-as-criminal, depending on which view one wishes to employ). More and more cops, private detectives, and crime heroes choose to work outside the boundaries of law. This is probably a development in accordance with the prevailing individualist *zeitgeist* of the new millennium where entrepreneurs, loners, private eyes, and even homeless people can be turned into heroes, representing new ideals in the post-democratic era. Wald argues that the social situation in the American 1940s—filled with strikes and a continuous feeling of social disarray—communicated a war between an impulse for change and the repression of that impulse. This was expressed in noir through sympathetic protagonists outside the law.[10] A similar tendency could be identified in the Swedish crime fiction of the 2000s. Arne Dahl's latest installments in his Berger/Blom series are excellent examples of this new wind. Cilla & Rolf Börjlinds' Tom Stilton novels, with an ex-cop-turned-bum who solves crimes, are other series on the march into the future.[11] Jens Lapidus's Teddy Maksumic is the typical transgressor of boundaries between the criminal underworld and legitimate society. Lars Kepler's Joona Linna has taken a step away from the police force and into the underworld—*and back again*—and even been to prison. And, of course, Stieg Larsson's and David Lagercrantz's Lisbeth Salander is the most imaginative—the germinal example of this type of hero. In the fifth Millennium novel by Lagercrantz, *The Girl Who Takes an Eye for an Eye*, she even goes to prison, handling all types of social milieus, like a chameleon. But, more importantly, like in the case of serial killers, these heroes constitute a step further away from realism—which we have seen has had such strong ties to Marxist Noir—towards a bourgeois (and postmodern) ideology of individualism. Still, let me state it once again: *The Marxist Noir crime novel is a realist genre*. This is something that I have constantly stressed in this book, and it is a characteristic that I will continue to emphasize. Consequently, the decrease in the realist elements in crime novels vouch for less Marxist critique, and perhaps more of the bourgeois or conservative elements where topics such as class matters, class struggle, commodity theory, and the results of the capitalist mode of production have a lesser function in the narrative.

So, where is Swedish Marxist Noir heading in the future? The great old-style crime fiction Marxists of our time are long gone: Stieg Larsson died in 2004, before he could witness his astonishing worldwide success, Henning Mankell died of cancer in 2015, and Börge Hellström (of the duo Roslund & Hellström) passed away in 2017. Per Wahlöö died back in 1975, at the very height of Marxism, and Maj Sjöwall (who is still alive as I am writing this) has not published crime fiction since the 1990s. Instead, the future seems to belong to the "Larssonists": highly effective, glossily packaged, and profiled producers of brick-thick potboilers, engineered to invade the American market with a (in all its irony) putative promise of social criticism behind the equally gloomy and shiny facade. False dialectics, marketed as social criticism—that's the future of Swedish Marxist Noir. Only, remember the initial quote from Marx: "and it is the ultimate aim of this work to reveal the economic law of motion of modern society."[12] Old Marxist authors of the 1968 revolutionary generation and "Larssonists" may stay around a while, but they will eventually disappear. Instead, new forms of revealing crime stories will come to life, and perhaps they will be better suited to galvanize future generations into consciousness than today's potboiler thrillers.

Epilogue: "There is no analysis"

Finally, there is one interesting, and slightly glowing, name in the dark that I wish to mention and analyze before this study is over: Erik Axl Sund. Sund is the *nom de plume* of yet another Swedish crime writing duo, and now that Roslund & Hellström are gone (only Anders Roslund still writes), they are one of the most exciting duos for the future: Jerker Eriksson and Håkan Axlander Sundquist are their real names. Eriksson (born in 1974) is a librarian, artist and music producer, and Sundquist (born in 1965) is a musician and artist who has toured internationally with his electro punk band called i love you baby, which Eriksson produced during the 2000s. They originally got to know each other during the 1990s, grew up in the same town (Gävle), and got the idea of writing together on long train journeys through Eastern Europe, on tour with Sundqvist's band.[13]

Their dark and grim crime debut *The Crow Girl*, almost measuring an exhaustive 800 pages, was released in Great Britain and the United States in 2016 and became an instant success. Originally, *The Crow Girl* was intended to be the first novel in a trilogy that was published in Sweden between the years 2010–2012, but the English publisher chose to shoehorn all three novels into one single specially edited version, obviously trying to pick up the relay race after Stieg Larsson—girl-title and all.

The plot starts with the discovery of several mutilated child bodies in different places in Stockholm. The bodies seem to be dried up, conserved, and their genitals removed. Detective Superintendent Jeanette Kihlberg of the Stockholm police starts the hunt for the killer together with her colleague Jens Hurtig. It becomes clear that she is hunting a serial killer as she encounters several other investigations with pedophiles from middle- and upper-class neighborhoods.

Sund's specialty is murder and (more unusually) psychotherapy, and the epicentric character of *The Crow Girl* is the psychotherapist Sofia Zetterlund/ Victoria Bergman, a multiple personality with a dark past consisting of being abused by her father and other men as a child. Thus, the basic question of Sund's entire work is indeed a painful one: "How much can a human being withstand before they break and turn into a monster?"[14] The protagonist Zetterlund/Bergman has already broken into two pieces from the very beginning of the novel. She lives in the same milieu as Stieg Larsson depicts in his

Millennium trilogy, the district of Södermalm in Stockholm. Actually, the nods towards Larsson are frequent as she visits his favorite restaurant and has his books in her bookcase.[15] Nods towards other crime fiction writers and films are also frequent, among others the legendary Maj Sjöwall (of Sjöwall-Wahlöö), who also, in real life, lived in the same blocks as Zetterlund/Bergman at the time.[16] The image of Sund's Stockholm is, perhaps, more somber than ever in Nordic Noir. For example, one chapter begins with the following description:

> Stockholm's implacable winter is hostile and windy; the cold creeps in everywhere and is almost impossible to defend against. During the six months of winter it's dark when the citizens wake up and go to work, and it's dark in the evening when they head home again. For months people live their lives in a dense, suffocating shortage of natural light while they wait for the release of the spring. They shut themselves off, withdrawing into their own private worlds, avoiding unnecessary eye contact with their fellows and shutting out the world around them with the help of iPods, MP3 players and mobile phones. Down in the metro there's scary silence, and every disruptive noise or loud conversation is met with hostile glares or stern comments. For outsiders, Stockholm is a place where not even the sun has enough energy to penetrate the steel-grey sky and, if only for an hour or so, shine down on the godforsaken inhabitants.[17]

In accord with Lisbeth Salander, Larsson's feminist heroine, Zetterlund/Bergman's sexuality is binary, or at least independent of gender norms, which makes her a sexual hero of emancipation in a postmodern society. There is a thoroughly feminist agenda displayed in this novel, represented by the two women protagonists, Zetterlund/Bergman and Jeanette Kihlberg, who initiate a sexual relationship with each other. On one occasion, Zetterlund/Bergman explains the analysis that obviously pervades the entire work of Sund:

> There's a proven link between excess production of male sex hormones and an inclination to commit sexual assaults. You can also regard physical and sexual violence against women and children as a way for a man to construct his masculinity. Through violence the man acquires the power and control that society's traditional gender and power structures suggest are his right.... And there's a connection between social norms and degrees of perversion that, in basic terms, suggests that the more double standards there are in a society, the more likely this sort of boundary transgression is.[18]

In an interview, for the *Washington Independent*, the writers confirm this by stating the seed for the novel:

> Anger. We were cursed with so much crap in the world and felt that we needed to express it. We were simply angry about everything that happened around us and in society (both in Sweden and abroad). Above all, it was frustration at how women are treated. Sexual harassment, fear of being raped, etc.[19]

The Crow Girl was released in Great Britain in the spring of 2016, and in the United States during that summer. Many critics reacted to the gruesome violence and images of molested bodies. One of the most negative ones was the *New York Times* critic Benjamin Percy, who was critical towards several things in the novel, which he called "The last gasp of post–9/11 cynicism." Mainly, his critique concerned the plot as such and one of the main characters, Sofia Zetterlund, whom he thought was constructed "with soap opera clumsiness." Furthermore, regarding the plot, Percy stated, "In the elevated reality of 'Dr. Jekyll and Mr. Hyde,' I can buy into a plot device like this, but here I found it cartoonishly unbelievable, offset by the novel's otherwise grim earnestness. And good lord is it grim." Almost every critic makes parallels to Stieg Larsson, and Percy is no different:

> It's no surprise "The Crow Girl" seems to model itself on the grand daddy of the Swedish crime fiction phenomenon: Stieg Larsson's "The Girl With the Dragon Tattoo." Sund— who is actually a team of two writers, Jerker Eriksson and Håkan Axlander Sundquist— shines a light on pedophilia and human trafficking and child abuse the same way Larsson showcased the victimization of women. There's something incendiary about these novels: They want the reader to feel repelled by the pestilence they're exposing, which merits some applause. But Larsson gives us hope. He successfully transforms Lisbeth Salander from victim to conqueror. We see her suffer, and we empathize with her and root for her revenge. That's why "The Crow Girl" works best in its second half, when the serial killer begins to hunt down a secret ring of pedophiles made up of the Swedish 1 percent.[20]

"There's obviously always darkness in store in thrillers, but *The Crow Girl* feels like it's taken a step further into the night," the critic Alison Flood concluded her review in *The Guardian*.[21] And one of the foremost experts on Swedish and Nordic crime fiction, Barry Forshaw, ties Sund to the existing flora of Nordic Noir giants:

> The narrative slowly and surely exerts an inexorable grip; its multiple time frames do not interrupt the unerring building of tension. And, as with the best Scandinavian crime fiction, from Henning Mankell to Stieg Larsson, there is still room for an acute element of social commentary. Like Mankell and Larsson, the Erik Axl Sund duo are careful to present an unvarnished picture of their society, some distance from the smoothly functioning social democracy that British readers once imagined the country to be (before Swedish crime fiction disabused us of that fragile notion).[22]

In order to analyze Swedish Marxist Noir, I have earlier concluded that the reader could ask some defining questions. One of them concerns who the perpetrator/killer in a plot is. Well, in *The Crow Girl* there are actually several killers. One of them is the dispossessed daughter of Zetterlund/ Bergman, who visits the men and women that have raped her during her youth and kills them in the bloody, spectacular and brutal manner familiar in the genre. These crimes are explained with the criminal-as-victim formula that we are very familiar with by now, as initiated by Sjöwall-Wahlöö in the 1960s—the killer as an avenger, in the line of Lisbeth Salander. Actually, the plot in *The Crow Girl*, in this sense, is very reminiscent of Salander's impetus for revenge in the Millennium trilogy: crimes committed against a defenseless child by the pillars of community, the police, the businessmen, the district attorneys, the lawyers, the parents, etc. This pattern we do understand, and are quite familiar with by now. The image of the pedophile, going from Sjöwall-Wahlöö's outcast loner Ingemund Fransson in *The Man on the Balcony* in 1967, to the horrific collective of powerful, predatory men molesting children in the 2000s, says something about the ruthlessness built into our time where exploitation is a natural part of the capitalist practice, and Sund is deliberately using this familiar image at its very best in *The Crow Girl*.

The other serial killer, however, is more complex, as he belongs to the psychological American thriller tradition. He (or she) is not an ordinary avenger, but a frighteningly lurid creature—a predator—we can't control, understand, or even explain.

This is the place where post-Marxist issues such as gender, queer, and posthuman theory become an interesting part of the conclusion of the plot. Similar to Buffalo Bill in Thomas Harris's *The Silence of the Lambs*, and Åke Larstam in Henning Mankell's *One Step Behind* (or Norman Bates in Hitchcock's *Psycho*, for that matter), the serial killer in *The Crow Girl* is a gender transgressor, perhaps a transsexual, going from being a girl as a child, to becoming a fully predatory male, the exclusive lawyer Viggo Dürer, as an old man. As a woman his/her name is Gilah Berkowitz, and those who know their serial killer history may think of the infamous American murderer David Berkowitz, a conscious nod from the authors for certain. As a child, during the Nazi occupation of Ukraine, Berkowitz had to dress herself as a boy in order to survive, and eventually he/she took the name of a killed Danish soldier, Viggo Dürer, and finally moved to Sweden to start his killing spree. According to the quote above, and it does seem to be a thesis of the writers themselves, a person has to become *a man* to evolve into the predator the police are chasing in *The Crow Girl*. The conclusion seems to be that physically, psychologically, and culturally, modern society has paved the way for this kind of creature. But then, we meet the strange underworld of Viggo Dürer. We follow the police down into his cellar filled with body parts, a scene recalling the terrifying basement of Buffalo Bill in *The Silence of the Lambs*. Only, Dürer does not want to stitch female skins together in order to become a woman—he is already a woman, owning wardrobes filled with neatly hung dresses and blouses.[23] Knight has, in his analysis of the serial killer Buffalo Bill in *The Silence of the Lambs*, emphasized that "the real horror of his crimes is the idea, not the reality … the concept of re-identification of the self through violence.… As a motive for murder, the idea of posthuman metamorphosis is imposed on the simplistic concept of aberrant gayness."[24] A similar perspective could easily be applied to Viggo Dürer.

By the end of the novel, Zetterlund/Bergman studies the Russian serial killer/cannibal Andrei Chikatilo to create an understanding of the murders and finally encounters the truth, without becoming aware of the gender transgressional theme of serial killers:

> One central part of Ed Gein's complex case was his desire to have a sex change and transform himself into his own mother. He tried to make a costume from the skin of women's corpses that he dug up, so he could wear it and become a woman. The article refers to an interrogation where the ritual was described as transsexual, and in the margin Victoria had noted with a red pen:
> THE REPTILE CHANGES ITS SKIN.
> MAN BECOMES WOMAN, WOMAN BECOMES MAN.
> BLURRED GENDER IDENTITY/SEXUAL BELONGING.
> EAT—SLEEP—FUCK.[25]

Dürer/Berkowitz seems to be an unexplainable artist of body parts as he/she has created an extreme, gruesome creature out of several humans that he/she has killed through the years. And this is where Sund differs from other Swedish crime authors, in the conclusion, when Dürer turns into Gilah Berkowitz and reflects upon her deeds:

> She thinks of the art she has created, and she has neither an explanation of what she has done nor any answer as to why she has done it. Art creates itself, because it is inexplicable and primitive. It is Gnosis, child's play, liberated from express intentions.... Becoming an adult is a crime against your own childhood and simultaneously a denial of Gnosis. A child has no gender and being genderless is closer to the primitive, the original. Discovering your gender is a criminal act against the original creator.... I am an insect, she thinks, as she listens to the steps behind her. They slow down and stop. I am a centipede, a myriapod, and I cannot be explained. Anyone who understood me would have to be as sick as I am. There is no analysis.[26]

There is no analysis, and ultimately no explanation for an entire life filled with murder, mayhem, and saved body parts. Finally, the man/woman becomes a mystery of his/her own, lost in his/her own psyche. We don't even know the killer's true identity. Are they really a man, or a woman? Is that distinction important at all? What are the reasons for the killings? Are there strange psychological reasons that the authors do not wish to explain? Or is it plain *evil*? A third possibility is that Sund explores the posthuman theory of Julia Kristeva as proclaimed in her work *Powers of Horror* (1982). To that end, Knight posits that "in contemporary society and the age of the holocaust people are reduced to the level of … the 'abject,' a human entity, rather than a person, who is powerless, connectionless, in both thought and action, a terrible threat to others, and so a natural topic for crime fiction, equally a vision of modern violence and postmodern doubt."[27]

Of course, there are social ingredients in this, such as the suppression of the mind in early childhood, the Nazi takeover in Ukraine during World War II, a domineering father, and so on. But the original question, "How much can a human being withstand before they break and turn into a monster?" doesn't really get answered, does it? Probably since nobody knows the answer. It's just a rhetorical question from the writers intended to invoke pain and reflection in the reader.

One thing is for certain, though—with writers such as Erik Axl Sund waiting in the wings to smash international book readers and give them enough nightmares for a lifetime, there is no reason to be concerned, since there is always a strain of hope for the further development of Swedish Marxist Noir.

Chapter Notes

Introduction

1. Therborn, Göran. *From Marxism to Post-Marxism*. London: Verso, 2008, p. 17.
2. Therborn, *From Marxism*, p. 17.
3. Therborn, *From Marxism*, p. 94.
4. The literary scholar Andrew Pepper has presented a much longer historical lineage of radical political crime fiction in his book *Unwilling Executioner*, stretching over three hundred years, where he argues that the emergence of crime fiction is linked to consolidation of the modern state (p. viii; 4).
5. Berntson, Lennart, and Svante Nordin. *After the Revolution: The Left in Swedish Cultural Debate Since 1968* [Efter Revolutionen. Vänstern i svensk kulturdebatt sedan 1968]. Stockholm: Natur & Kultur, 2017, p. 23.
6. Östberg, Kjell. "Sweden and the Long '1968': Break or Continuity?" *Scandinavian Journal of History*, vol. 33, no. 4, Dec. 2008, pp. 339–40.
7. Bergman, Kerstin. *Swedish Crime Fiction: The Making of Nordic Noir*. Mimesis International, 2014, p. 121–2.
8. Pepper, Andrew. *Unwilling Executioner: Crime Fiction and the State*. Oxford: Oxford University Press, 2016, p. 249.
9. For example, the term Nordic Noir is not used in Nestingen & Arva's very comprehensive and often cited anthology *Scandinavian Crime Fiction* (2011). The first encounter with the term I have found in any book title is Steven Peacock's (ed.) anthology *Stieg Larsson's Millennium Trilogy: Interdisciplinary Approaches to Nordic Noir* (2012). This suggests that Nordic Noir is a more recent, and perhaps more commercial, concept. Although, in the autumn of 2017 the University of Umeå, in northern Sweden, gave a university course on the subject "Nordic Noir as Global Literary Phenomenon." (https://www.umu.se/en/education/courses/nordic-noir-as-global-literary-phenomenon/. Accessed December 31, 2017.
10. Stephen Knight has a short and informative exposition on the term "Noir crime fiction" in general in his book *Crime Fiction Since 1800*, where he mentions Chandler's *The Big Sleep* and Hammett's *The Maltese Falcon* as the great classic noir-works (p. 229).
11. Forshaw, Barry. *Nordic Noir: The Pocket Essential Guide to Scandinavian Crime Fiction, Film & TV*. Harpenden: Pocket Essentials, 2013, p. 10.
12. Forshaw, *Nordic Noir*, p. 9–10.
13. Forshaw, *Nordic Noir*, passim. Although Forshaw's book is named *Nordic Noir*, he never elaborates on the concept itself. This suggests that the term was not in common use at the time, which is probably around 2012, when Forshaw wrote his book.
14. Forshaw, *Nordic Noir*, p. 140–1.
15. Arvas, Paula. "Next to the Final Frontier: Russians in Contemporary Finnish and Scandinavian Crime Fiction." In Nestingen & Arvas, *Scandinavian Crime Fiction*, p. 115.
16. Forshaw, *Nordic Noir*, p. 100–6.
17. A further exposition on these film and television adaptations can be found in Tapper, *Swedish Cops*, pp. 106–17 (Sjöwall-Wahlöö), pp. 182–201 (Mankell), pp. 259–64 (Larsson).
18. Mandel, Ernest. *Delightful Murder* [*Förtjusande mord. Kriminalromanens sociala historia*]. Translated by Sven Erik Täckmark. Stockholm: Alfabeta, 1985, p. 52.
19. Knight, Stephen. *Form and Ideology in Detective Fiction*. London: Macmillan, 1980, p. 4.
20. Berglund, Karl. *Death and Everyday Life: A Quantitative Analysis of Swedish Crime Fiction From the Early 21st Century* [Död och dagishämtningar. En kvantitativ analys av det tidiga 2000-talets svenska kriminallitteratur].

Uppsala: Department of Literature Sociology, 2017, p. 49. The field of research on social critical crime fiction is an ever growing one and some examples ought to be mentioned: Porter, Dennis. *The Pursuit of Crime: Art and Ideology in Detective Fiction*. New Haven, CT: Yale University Press, 1981; Messent, Peter. *The Crime Fiction Handbook*. Chichester: John Wiley & Sons, 2013; Knight, Stephen. *Crime Fiction Since 1800: Detection, Death, Diversity*. Basingstoke: Palgrave Macmillan, 2010; Pepper, Andrew. *The Contemporary American Crime Novel: Race, Ethnicity, Gender, Class*. Edinburgh: Edinburgh University Press, 2000; Horsley, Lee. *Twentieth-Century Crime Fiction*. Oxford: Oxford University Press, 2005; and Rzepka, Charles J. *Detective Fiction*. Cambridge: Polity, 2005.

21. Pepper, *Unwilling Executioner*, p. 80. Pepper mentions scholars such as Franco Moretti, Dennis Porter and Ernest Mandel as belonging to this critical tradition.

22. For example, Stephen Knight has another view on crime fiction in his later work, during the 2000s, where he elaborates on "the modern celebration of Diversity." See Knight, *Crime Fiction Since 1800*, p. 135–219.

23. Hoffman, Josef. *Philosophies of Crime Fiction*. Translated by Carolyn Kelly, Nadia Majid, and Johanna Da Rocha Abreu. Harpenden: No Exit Press, 2013, p. 100.

24. Pepper, *Unwilling Executioner*, p. viii.

25. Berglund, *Death and Everyday Life*, p. 23–4; 132–3.

26. Sales figures are notoriously unreliable, and mostly they originate from the publishing industry itself. Basically, there is no way to control these figures. These numbers are from an article in the Swedish newspaper *Dagens Nyheter*: Söderberg, Noa. "The Fifth Millennium Book Passes the Million Barrier" [Femte Millenniumboken går över miljonstrecket]. Dagens Nyheter, October 11, 2017. https://www.dn.se/kultur-noje/femte-millenniumboken-gar-over-miljonstrecket/. Accessed January 8, 2018.

27. Another one is: King, Donna, and Carrie Lee Smith, eds. *Men Who Hate Women Who Kick Their Asses: Stieg Larsson's Millennium Trilogy in Feminist Perspective*. Nashville: Vanderbilt University Press, 2012.

28. Gregersdotter, Katarina. "The Body, Hopelessness, and Nostalgia: Representations of Rape and the Welfare State in Swedish Crime Fiction." In Åström, Berit et al., ed. *Rape in Stieg Larsson's Millennium Trilogy and Beyond: Contemporary Scandinavian and Anglophone Crime Fiction*. Basingstoke: Palgrave Macmillan, 2013, pp. 88–9.

29. Åström, Berit et al. "Introduction." In *Rape in Stieg Larsson's Millennium Trilogy*, p. 2.

30. Åström, "Introduction," p. 3. Still, as I have already pointed out, this position has traditionally been an area for constant dispute. For example, Marxist scholars such as Stephen Knight and Ernest Mandel have pointed out that crime fiction is a conservative genre where traditional ideologies are upheld and reaffirmed. A recent Swedish study by Karl Berglund (2017) shows a similar perspective, pointing out that Swedish crime novels of the 2000s are not as socially critical as they seem to be. Berglund, *Death and Everyday Life*, p. 122. The feminist scholars focusing on Larsson and Anglophone crime fiction obviously have another perspective.

31. Holmberg, John-Henri, ed. *A Darker Shade of Sweden*. Translated by Holmberg. New York: The Mysterious Press, 2014, p. 10; Tapper, Michael. *The Cop in the Twilight Land: Swedish Police Narratives in Novels and Film 1965–2010* [Snuten i skymningslandet. Svenska polisberättelser i roman och film 1965–2010]. Lund: Nordic Academic Press, 2011, p 207; Hellgren, Per. *Per Wahlöö: Paving the Way for Swedish Crime Fiction* [Nu rasar diktaturerna. Per Wahlöö och vägen till den nya kriminalromanen]. Malmö: Universus Academic Press, 2015, p. 14.

32. Jameson, Fredric. *Raymond Chandler: Detections of Totality*. London: Verso, 2016, p. 6.

33. Marx, Karl. *Capital: A Critique of Political Economy. Vol. 1*. Translated by Ben Fowkes. London: Penguin, 1990, p. 92.

34. Two of the most important works for future Marxism and Soviet communism (likewise, the most misunderstood works blamed for making orthodoxy of the Marxist heritage) were Engels' *Anti-Düring* (1877) and *The Dialectics of Nature* (printed for the first time in 1925). Liedman, *Karl Marx*, pp. 519; 546.

35. Therborn, *From Marxism*, p. 165.

36. Freedman, Carl. "Marxist Theory, Radical Pedagogy, and the Reification of Thought." *College English*, vol. 49, no. 1, Jan. 1987, pp. 70–2.

37. Therborn, *From Marxism*, p. 82.

38. Freedman, Carl. *Critical Theory and Science Fiction*. Middletown, Connecticut: Wesleyan University Press, 2000, p. 10.

39. Freedman, Carl. *The Incomplete Projects. Marxism, Modernity, and the Politics of Culture*. Middletown, Connecticut: Wesleyan University Press, 2002, pp. 14–15; Therborn, *From Marxism*, p. 85.

40. https://en.wikipedia.org/wiki/G%C3%B6ran_Therborn. Accessed December 30, 2017.

41. Therborn, Göran. E-mail to the Author, May 11, 2017.

42. Pepper, *Unwilling Executioner*, p. 6.

43. Nilsson, Roddy. *Foucault: An Introduction*. Malmö: Egalité, 2008.

44. Freedman, *Critical Theory*, p. xv.

45. Freedman, *The Incomplete Projects*, p. 4.
46. Wald, Alan. "Marxism in Noir. The Culture Politics of Race and Class Struggle of the 1940s." *International Socialist Review*, no. 101, July 2016, p. 137.
47. This decline deserves a further exposition. Sean McCann has, in his book *Gumshoe America* (2000), shown how crime fiction authors from the 1930s onward have mirrored the New Deal era and its obvious horrors for the future. During the interwar years, when a whole generation of intellectuals and politicians joined FDR in the effort to adjust liberalism to the special demands of an industrialized economy and an urbanized nation, there was a strong vision of a new liberal democratic community, mainly resulting in an enormous infusion of federal dollars into public works. The dams, aqueducts, bridges, and highways were built during the 1930s, and the military industry was created in the 1940s, and all "became a mythic image of the success of the decentralist New Deal—physical emblems of the partnership of federal financing, local planning, and private enterprise" (p. 143–4). By the 1950s this image had been altered, when giant corporations rose to achieve an alliance between big business and big government during the Eisenhower era, resulting in the military-industrial complex, and a concentration of economic power never seen before (p. 144). Crime fiction from authors such as Hammett, Cain, and Chandler showed the complexity of an industrial and urbanized world, and the problems lying at the heart of the New Deal: racism, greed, corruption, and crime.
48. Freedman, *Critical Theory*, p. xvii.
49. Wald, Alan. E-mail to the Author, June 18, 2017.
50. Wald, "Marxism in Noir," pp. 138–9.
51. Wald, "Marxism in Noir," p. 139.
52. Wald, "Marxism in Noir," p. 152.
53. This section, called "Concerning Ideology," was originally published as part of a longer article of mine with the title "'Gone to Earth' 1975: Sexuality and Ideology in the Last Words of Per Wahlöö" in *Ideas in History. Journal of the Nordic Society for the History of Ideas*. Vol.9. No.1–2. 2015, pp.121–145.
54. Althusser, Louis. "Ideology and Ideological State Apparatuses (Notes Towards an Investigation)." Translated by Ben Brewster. *Marxists Internet Archive*.
55. Ekelund, Alexander. "The Struggle on Science: The Advance of Althusserianism and the Scientific Theoretical Debate of the Swedish 1968-Left" [Kampen om vetenskapen. Althusserianismens frammarsch och den svenska 1968-vänsterns vetenskapsteoretiska debatt]. In Burman and Lennerhed, *Together*, pp. 202f.

56. Therborn, Göran. 1966. "Society as Corporation—Towards a One-Dimensional Society" [Samhället som aktiebolag—Mot ett endimensionellt samhälle]. *Zenit*, no. 2–3, 1966, pp. 4–7.
57. Ekelund, "The Struggle on Science," p. 196.
58. Žižek, Slavoj. *The Sublime Object of Ideology* [Ideologins sublima objekt]. Translated by Lars Nylander. Göteborg: Glänta, 2001, p. 9.
59. Therborn, Göran. *The Ideology of Power and the Power of Ideology* [Maktens ideologi och ideologins makt]. Lund: Zenit, 1981, p. 11.
60. Therborn, *The Ideology of Power*, p. 18.
61. Ekelund, "The Struggle on Science," pp. 222f.
62. Nordin, Svante. *The Philosophers: The Western Thinking Since Year 1900* [Filosoferna. Det västerländska tänkandet sedan år 1900]. Stockholm: Atlantis, 2011, pp. 547f; Ekelund, "The Struggle on Science," p. 197.
63. Ekelund, "The Struggle on Science," pp. 199f.
64. Althusser, "Ideology and Ideological."
65. Althusser, "Ideology and Ideological."
66. Ekelund, "The Struggle on Science," p. 222.
67. Nordin, *The Philosophers*, p. 546.
68. Held, *Introduction to Critical Theory*, pp. 359–60.
69. Kärrholm, Sara. *The Art of Doing a Jigsaw Puzzle: The Detective Novel and the Conjuring up of Evil in the Swedish Welfare State* [Konsten att lägga pussel. Deckaren och besvärjandet av ondskan i folkhemmet]. Stockholm: Symposion, 2005, pp.7–8.
70. Hagberg, Mattias. "Raymond Chandler and the Moral Darkness of Nordic Noir" [Raymond Chandler och den nordiska noir-genrens moraliska mörker]. *Sveriges Radio P1*, September 9, 2014.
71. Jordanova, Ludmilla. *History in Practice*. New York: Bloomsbury Academic, 2010, p. 4.
72. Scaggs, John. *Crime Fiction*. London: Routledge, 2005, p. 91.
73. Nestingen, Andrew. "Unnecessary Officers: Realism, Melodrama and Scandinavian Crime Fiction in Transition," in *Scandinavian Crime Fiction*, ed. by Andrew Nestingen and Paula Arvas. Cardiff: University of Wales Press, 2011, p. 171.
74. McCann, Sean. *Gumshoe America: Hard-Boiled Crime Fiction and the Rise and Fall of New Deal Liberalism*. Durham: Duke University Press, 2000, p. 5.
75. McCann, *Gumshoe America*, p. 11.
76. Wald, "Marxism in Noir," p. 144.
77. Davis, Mike. *City of Quartz: Excavating the Future in Los Angeles*. London: Verso, 2006, p. 40.

78. However, Knight identifies several elements in Ellroy's works that could represent a leftwing critique, for example a less than rigorous critique against a culture that treats women as objects in *The Black Dahlia* (1987) and *L.A. Confidential* (1990), where "patriarchy appropriates and deforms women (as prostitutes are made by plastic surgery to look like film stars) and also developing more fully the processes of corruption and real crime among the police." Knight, *Crime Fiction Since 1800*, p. 211.
79. Zumoff, J.A. "Politics and the 1920s Writings of Dashiell Hammett." *American Studies*, vol. 52, no. 1, 2012, p. 78.
80. Leivo, Janne Osmo Henrik. 2016. *Reflections on Swedish Society in Beck Television Detective Series in the Early 2000s*. Master's Thesis. University of Helsinki, Faculty of Social Studies, p. 19.
81. Chandler, Raymond. "Twelve Notes on the Mystery Novel." In Chandler, *Later Novels*, p. 1005.

Chapter 1

1. McCann, *Gumshoe America*, p. 145.
2. Derrida, Jacques. *Writing and Difference*. Translated by Alan Bass. Chicago: University of Chicago Press, 1978, p. 279.
3. Pynchon, Thomas. *The Crying of Lot 49*. New York: Bantam, 1972, p. 12. Knight describes this novel as "a non-rational and unresolved detective quest and it seems a major stimulus for the detecting without any outcomes beyond the positive power of uncertainty." Knight, *Crime Fiction Since 1800*, p. 206.
4. MacShane, Frank. *The Life of Raymond Chandler*. London: Jonathan Cape Ltd, 1976, p. 50.
5. Freedman, *Critical Theory*, p. 194–5.
6. Fine, David. *Imagining Los Angeles: A City In Fiction*. Las Vegas: University of Nevada Press, 2004, p. x.
7. Asplund, Johan. *Regarding Raymond Chandler [Angående Raymond Chandler]*. Göteborg: Korpen, 2004, p. 22.
8. Jameson, *Raymond Chandler*, p. 6.
9. MacShane, *The Life of*, p. 64.
10. MacShane, *The Life of*, p. 65.
11. MacShane, *The Life of*, p. 66.
12. Davis, *City of Quartz*, p. 17.
13. Cawelti, John G. *Adventure, Mystery, and Romance*. Chicago: University of Chicago Press, 1976, pp. 154–5.
14. McCann, *Gumshoe America*, p. 163.
15. McCann, *Gumshoe America*, pp. 167–8.
16. McCann, *Gumshoe America*, p. 152.
17. Davis, *City of Quartz*, p. 18.
18. Davis, *City of Quartz*, p. 20.
19. Fine, *Imagining Los Angeles*, p. 54.
20. Fine, *Imagining Los Angeles*, pp. 81–2.
21. Fine, *Imagining Los Angeles*, p. 89.
22. Zumoff, "Politics and the 1920s," p. 93.
23. Zumoff, "Politics and the 1920s," p. 93.
24. Scaggs, *Crime Fiction*, p. 74.
25. Zumoff, "Politics and the 1920s," pp. 93; 78.
26. Zumoff, "Politics and the 1920s," p. 85.
27. Freedman, *The Incomplete Projects*, pp. 8–9.
28. Mandel, Ernest. *Delightful Murder [Förtjusande mord. Kriminalromanens sociala historia]*. Translated by Sven Erik Täckmark. Stockholm: Alfabeta, 1985, p. 57.
29. Mandel, *Delightful Murder*, p. 14.
30. Zumoff, "Politics and the 1920s," p. 87.
31. Chandler, Raymond. *Selected Letters of Raymond Chandler*. Ed. Frank MacShane. London: Macmilan, 1983, p. 165.
32. Chandler, *Selected Letters*, p. 295.
33. McCann, *Gumshoe America*, p. 167.
34. Hiney, Tom. *Raymond Chandler: A Biography*. London: Chatto & Windus, 1997, pp. 181–2.
35. Chandler, *Selected Letters*, p. 193. The story of the Hollywood intelligentsia and its passion for communism during the 1940s and 50s has been told in the fictional wild tales of James Ellroy, especially in his novels *The Big Nowhere* (1988) and *Perfidia* (2014).
36. Chandler, *Selected Letters*, pp. 107–8. In the film *Hail, Caesar!* (2015) by the Coen Brothers, the plot circles around a group of communist screenwriters that, along with Herbert Marcuse, kidnap a huge studio star (George Clooney) in 1950s Hollywood. This funny film parody turns the relationship between communists and the Hollywood studio system into a typical *noir* story, which also shows the tight bonds between movies, communists and crime fiction.
37. Chandler, *Selected Letters*, p. 269.
38. Chandler, *Selected Letters*, p. 141.
39. Jameson, *Raymond Chandler*, pp. 6–7.
40. Fine, *Imagining Los Angeles*, p. 120.
41. Asplund, *Regarding Raymond Chandler*, p. 34.
42. Span, Guy. "Paving the Way for Buses—The Great GM Streetcar Conspiracy. Part II—The Plot Clots." *Bay Crossings*, May 2003.
43. Span, "Paving the Way for Buses."
44. Davis, *City of Quartz*, p. 23.
45. Banham, Reyner. *Los Angeles. The Architecture of Four Ecologies*. Berkeley: University of California Press, 2009, pp. 195–6.
46. Banham, *Los Angeles*, p. 199.
47. Banham, *Los Angeles*, p. 202.

48. Marcuse, Herbert. "Some Social Implications of Modern Technology." In Arato and Gebhardt, *Essential Frankfurt School Reader*, p. 143.
49. Quoted in Banham, *Los Angeles*, p. 204.
50. Marcuse, "Some Social Implications," p. 144.
51. Hagberg, "Raymond Chandler."
52. Chandler. "The Simple Art of Murder." In Chandler, Raymond. *Later Novels and Other Writings*. Edited by Frank MacShane. New York: Library of America, 1995, p. 991.
53. Chandler, "Simple Art," p. 985.
54. Richter, David H. "Background Action and Ideology: Grey Men and Dope Doctors in Raymond Chandler." *Narrative*, Vol. 2, No. 1 (January 1994), pp. 35–6.
55. MacShane, *The Life of*, p. 102.
56. Davis, City of Quartz, p. 20f.
57. Nordin, Svante. *The History of Philosophy* [*Filosofins historia*]. Lund: Studentlitteratur, 2009, p. 303.
58. Zumoff, "Politics and the 1920s," p. 88.
59. Hobbes, Thomas. *Leviathan*. McMaster University Archive, p. 79.
60. Paulsen, Roland. *The Labor Society: How Labor Survived Technology* [*Arbetssamhället. Hur arbetet överlevde teknologin*]. Malmö: Gleerups, 2010, p. 32.
61. Hobbes, *Leviathan*, p. 78.
62. Mandel, *Delightful Murder*, p. 40.
63. Chandler, Raymond. *The Long Goodbye*. In Chandler, *Later Novels*, p. 711: ch. 48. Page references in the text to Chandler's novels collected in the Library of America editions, two volumes (New York: Literary Classics of the United States, Inc.) are annotated with chapter numbers after each page number for convenience.
64. Chandler, *The Long Goodbye*, p. 712: ch. 48.
65. Stephen Knight mentions *The Grapes of Wrath* as a saga "of human suffering under contemporary capitalism ... [about] people crunched in the industrial mechanics of the American dream." Knight, *Crime Fiction Since 1800*, p. 126.
66. Actually, the 1930s drought was four distinct events, which occurred in 1930–31, 1934, 1936, and 1939–40. It covered virtually the entire Plains and many crops were damaged by deficient rainfall, high winds, and high temperatures. This, in turn, contributed to the economic decline of the Depression, which sent economic and social ripples throughout the country. http://drought.unl.edu/DroughtBasics/DustBowl/DroughtintheDustBowlYears.aspx. Accessed February 13, 2018.
67. Steinbeck, John. *The Grapes of Wrath*. New York: Penguin, 1978, p. 40.
68. Therborn, *From Marxism*, p. 61.
69. Lenin, V.I. *Imperialism: The Highest Stage of Capitalism* [*Imperialismen som kapitalismens högsta stadium*]. Translated by Alice Wallenius. Lund: Zenit/Cavefors, 1969, p. 86–7; 99.
70. Fine, *Imagining Los Angeles*, p. 95.
71. Hedges, Chris. *Empire of Illusion: The End of Literacy and the Triumph of Spectacle*. New York: Nation Books, 2010, p. 184.
72. Polanyi, Karl. *The Great Transformation: The Political and Economic Origins of Our Time*. Boston: Beacon Press, 2001, p. 242.
73. Polanyi, *The Great Transformation*, p. 244.
74. Polanyi, *The Great Transformation*, p. 238.
75. Wald, "Marxism in Noir," pp. 146–7.
76. Hedges, *Empire of Illusion*, p. 177.
77. MacShane, *The Life of*, p. 71.
78. Chandler, *The Long Goodbye*, pp. 611–12: ch. 32.
79. Chandler, *The Long Goodbye*, p. 436: ch. 4.
80. Davis, *City of Quartz*, pp. 52–3.
81. Barnfield, Graham. "The Urban Landscape of Marxist Noir." *Crime Time*, June 26, 2002.
82. Wald, "Marxism in Noir," p. 137.

Chapter 2

1. Sjögren, Henrik. "Studies In Dictatorship" [*Studier i diktatur*]. *Kvällsposten*, June 30, 1962, p. 4. Author's translation.
2. Pepper, *Unwilling Executioner*, p. 168. Pepper groups Sjöwall-Wahlöö together with other radical Marxist crime authors such as Friedrich Dürrenmatt, Leonardo Sciascia, Jean-Patrick Manchette, and Chester Himes, who got their ideas from all hues and incarnations of Marxism, Situationism, Black Power, and Surrealism (p. 169).
3. Pepper, *Unwilling Executioner*, p. 176.
4. Some of the most extensive studies of this remarkable novel have been carried out by Swedish scholars. For example: Tapper, *The Cop in the Twilight Land*, pp. 161–75; Tapper, *Swedish Cops*, pp. 76–81; and Hellgren, *Per Wahlöö*, pp. 223–269.
5. Sjöwall, Maj, and Per Wahlöö. *The Laughing Policeman*. Translated by Alan Blair. London: Fourth Estate, 2011, p. i.
6. Swedish writer Anders Jonason (1925–1993) is said to have been an even earlier author of hardboiled novels, inspired by forerunners such as Hammett and Chandler. For example, he wrote the novels *Murder, et cetera* (*Mord med mera* [1953]) and *The Grete Case* (*Fallet Grete* [1963]). None of them have yet been translated into English. His detectives are journalists in Stockholm, and Jonason is probably

the first Swedish writer ever to attempt to write in the hardboiled tradition. Bergman, *Swedish Crime Fiction*, p. 20.

7. For Wahlöö's early American releases, see for example the following articles in contemporary Swedish papers: "Meet mr Wahlöö!." *Expressen*, February 11, 1965 (on the release in the U.S. of *The Assignment*); Fagerberg, Sven. "Our Contemporary" [Våra samtida]. *Dagens Nyheter*, April 25, 1966 (on the bad reviews during the U.S. coverage of that novel); and "Swedish Future Thriller Praised by U.S. reviewer" [Svensk framtidsthriller prisad av USA-recensent]. *Svenska Dagbladet*, February 14, 1967 (on the good reviews of *Murder on the Thirty-First Floor*).

8. Beekman, E.M. "Raymond Chandler & An American Genre." *The Massachusetts Review*, Vol. 14. No. 1. (Winter 1973), p. 159.

9. Wahlöö, Per. *The Assignment*. Translated by Joan Tate. New York: Vintage, p. 3.

10. Wahlöö, Per. *Murder on the Thirty-First Floor*. Translated by Sarah Death. New York: Vintage, p. 1.

11. Holmberg, John-Henri, ed. *A Darker Shade of Sweden*. Translated by Holmberg. New York: The Mysterious Press, 2014, p. 10.

12. Holmberg, *A Darker Shade*, p. 11.

13. Wahlöö, Per. "An Ordinary Swedish Boy" [En vanlig svensk grabb]. *Göteborgs Handels och Sjöfartstidning*, May 13, 1954, p. 4. Author's translation.

14. Wahlöö, Per. "Propaganda for the Right of the Fist" [Propaganda för nävrätt]. *Östersunds-Posten*, October 28, 1957, p. 4. Author's translation.

15. Mandel, *Delightful Murder*, pp. 103–4.

16. France, Louise. "The Queen of Crime." *The Observer*, November 22, 2009.

17. Marcuse, Herbert. *One-Dimensional Man*. London: Routledge, 2002, p. 14.

18. Therborn, *From Marxism*, p. 81.

19. Davis, *City of Quartz*, p. 48.

20. Davis, *City of Quartz*, p. 48.

21. Danius, Sara. "Goethe in Hollywood." In Danius. *Death of the Housewife and Other Writings* [*Husmoderns död och andra texter*]. Stockholm: Bonniers, 2014, p. 178.

22. Danius, "Goethe in Hollywood," p. 184.

23. In 1941, when Adorno moved to Los Angeles, Chandler was living at 857 Iliff Street in Pacific Palisades, while Adorno lived not far from there in the nearby Brentwood, at 316 South Kenter Avenue.

24. Held, David. *Introduction to Critical Theory: Horkheimer to Habermas*. Oxford: Polity Press, 2004, p. 91.

25. The connection between Wahlöö, Sjöwall-Wahlöö and Marcuse has been made before. See for example: Tapper, *Swedish Cops*, p. 87, 95; Pepper, *Unwilling Executioners*, p. 187; and Hellgren, "Last Words, 1975," p. 121–6.

26. Wahlöö, *Murder*, p. 118.

27. Marcuse, *One-Dimensional Man*, p. 9.

28. Hellgren, Per. *Per Wahlöö: Paving the Way for Swedish Crime Fiction* [*Nu rasar diktaturerna. Per Wahlöö och vägen till den nya kriminalromanen*]. Malmö: Universus Academic Press, 2015, p. 278.

29. Marcuse, *One-Dimensional Man*, p. 22.

30. Marcuse, *One-Dimensional Man*, pp. 40–1.

31. Marcuse, *One-Dimensional Man*, p. 70.

32. Freedman, *Critical Theory*, p. 22.

33. Wiklund, Martin. *In the Landscape of Modernity* [*I det modernas landskap. Historisk orientering och kritiska berättelser om det moderna Sverige mellan 1960 och 1990*]. Stockholm/Stehag: Symposion, 2006, pp. 220; 428.

34. Borglund, Tore. "The Crime Exposes Society" [Brottet avslöjar samhället]. *Metallarbetaren*, no. 2–3, 1973, p. 39. Author's translation.

35. Pepper, *Unwilling Executioner*, p. 196.

36. Cawelti, *Adventure, Mystery, and Romance*, p. 154f.

37. Blomkvist, Per. "Transferring Technology—Shaping Ideology. American Traffic Engineering and Commercial Interests in the Establishment of a Swedish Car Society 1945–1965." *Comparative Technology Transfer and Society*, vol. 2, no. 3, September 2004, p. 274.

38. Blomkvist, "Transferring Technology," p. 274f.

39. Danius, "Goethe in Hollywood," p. 177.

40. Jameson, *Raymond Chandler*, p. 11.

41. Chandler, *The Long Goodbye*, p. 663: ch. 42.

42. Chandler, *The Long Goodbye*, p. 615: ch. 33.

43. Wahlöö, Per. *The Steel Spring*. Translated by Sarah Death. London: Vintage, 2011, p. 14.

44. The notion of Sweden as a nation with a high suicide rate was established in the 1950s by mostly American and British journalists such as Graham Greene, Taylor Caldwell, and Dorothy Thompson (see Hellgren, *Per Wahlöö*, pp. 253–4). Another example would be the American psychiatrist Herbert Hendin, who wrote an entire book on this subject: *Suicide in Scandinavia: A Psychoanalytic Study of Culture and Character*. New York: Grune & Stratton, Inc., 1964.

45. Wahlöö, *Murder*, pp. 155–6.

46. Blomkvist, "Transferring Technology," pp. 279–80.

47. Blomkvist, "Transferring Technology," p. 291.

48. Wahlöö, *Murder*, pp. 179–80.

49. Blomkvist, "Transferring Technology," p. 283.
50. Blomkvist, "Transferring Technology," p. 291.
51. Marcuse, "Some Social Implications," p. 138f.
52. Hellgren, *Per Wahlöö*, p. 254.
53. Wahlöö, *The Steel Spring*, p. 199.
54. Cawelti, *Adventure, Mystery, and Romance*, pp. 148-9.
55. Therborn, *From Marxism*, p. 170.
56. Mandel, *Delightful Murder*, p. 85.
57. Other studies of *The Steel Spring* have been made before. See for example: Tapper, *The Cop in the Twilight Land*, pp. 166-75; and Hellgren, *Per Wahlöö*, pp. 269-89.
58. Søholm, Ejgil. *Novel of a Crime: Sjöwall-Wahlöö's Work and Reality* [*Roman om en forbrydelse. Sjöwall/Wahlöö's værk og virkelighed*]. Copenhagen: Spektrum, 1976, p. 293.
59. Wahlöö, *The Steel Spring*, pp. 115-6.
60. Freedman, Carl. *The Age of Nixon: A Study In Cultural Power*. Winchester, UK: Zero Books, 2012, p. 56.
61. Wahlöö, *The Steel Spring*, p. 117.
62. Wahlöö, *The Steel Spring*, p. 117.
63. Wahlöö, *The Steel Spring*, p. 118.
64. Ferreter, Luke. *Louis Althusser*. London: Routledge, 2006, p. 34.
65. Sloterdijk, Peter. *Critique of Cynical Reason*. Minneapolis & London: University of Minnesota Press, 1987, p. 371. It should be noted here that Sloterdijk rejects the Marxian, or Marxist, form of dialectics, instead he promotes a "rational (analytic) reconstruction of dialectics in the form of *Universal Polemics*" (pp. 371-9).
66. Held, *Introduction to Critical Theory*, p. 177.
67. At the Soviet writers congress in 1934, Zhdanov delivered a speech in which he consolidated the doctrine of Social Realism as the prevailing norm for all art in the Soviet Union. According to this norm, the writers should not describe reality as it is, but as it *should be*. The head credo of this congress was the famous words of Lenin: "The writer is the engineer of the human soul."
68. Jay, Martin. *The Dialectical Imagination: A History of the Frankfurt School and the Institute of Social Research, 1923-1950*. Berkeley: University of California Press, 1996, p. 173.
69. Wahlöö, *The Steel Spring*, p. 160.
70. Lenin, V.I. "May Day Action by the Revolutionary Proletariat." Translated by George Hanna. *Marxists Internet Archive*.
71. Lenin, "May Day Action."
72. Liedman, Sven-Eric. *Karl Marx: A Biography* [*Karl Marx. En biografi*]. Stockholm: Bonniers, 2016, pp. 253-4.
73. Petrov, Kristian. *Back to the Future: Modernity, Postmodernity, and Generational Identity in Gorbachev's Glasnost and Perestroika* [*Tillbaka till framtiden. Modernitet, postmodernitet och generationsidentitet i Gorbacevs glasnost och perestrojka*]. Huddinge: Södertörn University, 2006, p. 181.
74. Marx, Karl, and Friedrich Engels. *The Communist Manifesto*. Translated by Samuel Moore. London: Penguin, 2015, p. 19.
75. Liedman, *Karl Marx*, p. 650.
76. Wahlöö, *The Steel Spring*, p. 200.
77. This section, called "The Sexual Revolution," was originally published as one of the main sections in two of my earlier articles: "'Gone to Earth' 1975: Sexuality and Ideology in the Last Words of Per Wahlöö" in *Ideas in History: Journal of the Nordic Society for the History of Ideas*. Vol. 9. No. 1-2. 2015, pp. 121-145. And it was published in a shorter version under the headline "Sex and Politics" in "Last Words 1975: Per Wahlöö and the Book That Went Up in Smoke" in *Clues: A Journal of Detection*. Vol. 33. No. 2. 2015, pp. 118-127.
78. Lennerhed, Lena. *The Pursuit of Pleasure: The Sex-Debate in Sweden during the 1960s* [*Frihet att njuta. Sexualdebatten i Sverige på 1960-talet*]. Stockholm: Norstedts, 1994, pp. 9-10; Östberg, "Sweden and the Long '1968,'" pp. 341f.
79. Hellgren, *Per Wahlöö*, p.167.
80. Wahlöö, Per. *A Necessary Action*. Translated by Joan Tate. New York: Vintage, 2013, p. 46.
81. Wahlöö, *A Necessary Action*, p. 61.
82. Wahlöö, *The Assignment*, p. 83.
83. Wahlöö, *The Assignment*, p. 86.
84. Hellgren, *Per Wahlöö*, pp. 192-4.
85. Wahlöö, *Murder*, p. 146.
86. Wahlöö, *The Steel Spring*, p. 23.
87. Wahlöö, *The Steel Spring*, p. 23.
88. Tapper, Michael. *Swedish Cops: From Sjöwall & Wahlöö to Stieg Larsson*. Chicago: Intellect, 2014, p. 91.
89. Tapper, *Swedish Cops*, p. 92.
90. Lennerhed, *The Pursuit of Pleasure*, p. 313.
91. Ferreter, *Louis Althusser*, pp. 40-1.
92. Keetley, Dawn. "Unruly Bodies: The Politics of Sex in Maj Sjöwall and Per Wahlöö's Martin Beck Series." *Clues: A Journal of Detection*, vol. 30, no. 1, 2012, p. 62.
93. Keetley, "Unruly Bodies," p. 55.
94. Tapper, *Swedish Cops*, pp. 84-5.
95. Tapper, *Swedish Cops*, pp. 86-7; 91.
96. Keetley, "Unruly Bodies," p. 60.
97. Lennerhed, *The Pursuit of Pleasure*, p. 312.
98. Lennerhed, *The Pursuit of Pleasure*, p. 307.

99. Lennerhed, *The Pursuit of Pleasure*, p. 308.
100. Held, *Introduction to Critical Theory*, p. 125.
101. Held, *Introduction to Critical Theory*, p. 242.
102. Keetley, "Unruly Bodies," p. 56.
103. Marcuse, *One-Dimensional Man*, p. 28.
104. Van Dover, J. Kenneth. *Polemical Pulps: The Martin Beck Novels of Maj Sjöwall and Per Wahlöö*. San Bernadino, CA: Brownstone Books, 1993, p. 47.
105. Chandler, Raymond. *The Big Sleep*. In Chandler, *Stories & Early Novels*, pp. 589; 592: ch. 1.
106. Sjöwall, Maj, and Per Wahlöö. *Murder at the Savoy*. Translated by Amy and Ken Koespel. New York: Vintage, 2009, p. 47.
107. Van Dover, *Polemical Pulps*, p. 47.
108. Eklund, Stefan. "Detective Lady" [Deckardam]. *Svenska Dagbladet*, June 19, 2010, pp. 6–7. Author's translation. Sjöwall-Wahlöö's homage passage can be found on pp. 76–84 in Sjöwall-Wahlöö, *The Abominable Man*, New York: Vintage, 2009. Chandler's passage can be found in chapter 29 of *The Little Sister*, pp. 382–383 in Chandler. *Later Novels & Other Writings*, New York: Library of America, 1995.
109. Sjöwall, Maj, and Per Wahlöö. "Renewal of the Crime Novel" [Kriminalromanens förnyelse]. *Jury*, vol. 1, no. 1, 1972, p. 9; Stertman, Hans. "The Hardworking Couple" [Det strävsamma paret]. *Jury*, no. 2, 1972, p. 39.
110. Sjöwall, Maj, and Per Wahlöö. *The Fire Engine That Disappeared*. Translated by Joan Tate. New York: Vintage, 1977, p. 34.
111. Hirsch, Paul, ed. *The Law Enforcers*. New York: Pyramid Books, 1969, back cover.
112. Van Dover, *Polemical Pulps*, p. 40.
113. Van Dover, *Polemical Pulps*, p. 19.
114. For example, Sjöwall-Wahlöö self-consciously writes the following in one of their most political achievements, *The Abominable Man*: "Police work is built on realism, routine, stubbornness, and system ... And experience and industry play a larger role there than brilliant inspiration. A good memory and ordinary common sense are more valuable qualities than intellectual brilliance. Intuition has no place in practical police work. Intuition is not even a quality, any more than astrology and phrenology are sciences" (p. 31).
115. Mandel, *Delightful Murder*, p. 80.
116. Held, *Introduction to Critical Theory*, p. 230.
117. Held, *Introduction to Critical Theory*, p. 238.
118. Sjöwall-Wahlöö, *Murder at the Savoy*, p. 204.
119. Sjöwall-Wahlöö, *Murder at the Savoy*, p. 209.
120. Von Mueller quoted in Pepper, *Unwilling Executioner*, p. 176.
121. Søholm, *Novel of a Crime*, p. 298.
122. Søholm, *Novel of a Crime*, p. 299.
123. Søholm, *Novel of a Crime*, p. 300.
124. Pepper, *Unwilling Executioner*, p. 176.
125. Van Dover, *Polemical Pulps*, p. 87.
126. See for example Bergman, *Swedish Crime Fiction*, p. 33.
127. Therborn, *From Marxism*, p. 125.
128. Sjöwall-Wahlöö, "Renewal of the Crime Novel," p. 10. Author's translation.
129. See for example, Marcuse, *One-Dimensional Man*, p. 9.
130. Held, *Introduction to Critical Theory*, p. 76.

Chapter 3

1. Mankell, Henning. *The Man Who Smiled*. Translated by Laurie Thompson. London: Vintage, 2012, p. 1.
2. Mankell, Henning. *The Hand* [Handen]. Stockholm: Leopard, 2013, p. 134.
3. Tapper has discussed the TV series, where Linda Wallander plays an important part, in his book *Swedish Cops*, p. 188–98.
4. Tirén, Sverker, and Eva-Lena Neiman. "I Want to be a Cheerful Reptile" [Jag vill vara en gladlynt reptil]. *Bonniers Litterära Magasin*, vol. 47, no. 1, 1978, pp. 32–3.
5. www.henningmankell.com/author/. Accessed August 22, 2017.
6. Berntson and Nordin, *After the Revolution*, p. 39.
7. Tirén and Neiman, "I Want to be a Cheerful Reptile," p. 36.
8. Tirén and Neiman, "I Want to be a Cheerful Reptile," p. 32. Author's translation.
9. Tirén and Neiman, "I Want to be a Cheerful Reptile," p. 34. Author's translation.
10. Pettersson, Jan-Erik. *Stieg: From Activist to Author* [*Stieg Larsson. Journalisten, författaren, idealisten*]. Stockholm: Telegram bokförlag, 2010, p. 203.
11. Žižek, Slavoj. "Henning Mankell, the Artist of the Parallax View." Lacan.com, 2005.
12. Mankell, *The Man Who Smiled*, cover sheet.
13. Nordin, *History of Philosophy*, pp. 128–9.
14. Tapper, *Swedish Cops*, p. 172.
15. Held, *Introduction to Critical Theory*, p. 22.
16. Tapper, *Swedish Cops*, p. 172.
17. Mankell, Henning. *Before the Frost*. Translated by Ebba Segerberg. London: Vintage, 2005, p. 46.

18. Forshaw, Barry. *The Man Who Left Too Soon: The Life and Works of Stieg Larsson*. London: John Blake Publishing, 2011, p. 260.
19. Jacobsen, Kirsten. *Mankell*. Translated by Inge Knutsson. Stockholm: Leopard, 2012, p. 48.
20. Tapper, Michael. *The Cop in the Twilight Land: Swedish Police Narratives in Novels and Film 1965–2010* [*Snuten i skymningslandet. Svenska polisberättelser i roman och film 1965–2010*]. Lund: Nordic Academic Press, 2011, p. 442.
21. Mankell, *The Man Who Smiled*, p. 414.
22. Mankell, *The Man Who Smiled*, p. 417.
23. McCorristine, Shane. "The Place of Pessimism in Henning Mankell's Kurt Wallander Series." In Nestingen and Arvas, *Scandinavian*, p. 79.
24. Mankell, *The Man Who Smiled*, pp. 416-7.
25. Tirén and Neiman, "I Want to be a Cheerful Reptile," p. 35. Author's translation.
26. Tirén and Neiman, "I Want to be a Cheerful Reptile," p. 36. Author's translation.
27. Mankell, *The Man Who Smiled*, p. 419.
28. McCorristine, "The Place of Pessimism," p. 81.
29. Kaveh, Shamal. "Together Towards the Promised Land of Entrepreneurship: Foucault on Neoliberalism" [Tillsammans mot entreprenörskapets förlovade land. Foucault om nyliberalism]. In Burman and Lennerhed, *Together*, p. 592.
30. Cawelti, *Adventure, Mystery, and Romance*, p. 147.
31. Mankell, *The Man Who Smiled*, p. 228.
32. Mankell, *The Man Who Smiled*, p. 229.
33. Mandel, *Delightful Murder*, p. 119.
34. Kaveh, "Together Towards," pp. 612-3.
35. Kaveh, "Together Towards," p. 609.
36. Mankell, *The Man Who Smiled*, p. 183.
37. Mankell, *The Man Who Smiled*, p. 188.
38. Zaremba, Maciej. *The Price of the Patient: A Report on the Swedish Healthcare and the Market* [*Patientens pris. Ett reportage om den svenska sjukvården och marknaden*.]. Stockholm: Weyler, 2013, p. 16.
39. As an interesting and illuminating contrast to Sweden, the neoliberal change in Great Britain during the Thatcher years in the 1980s, miners' strike, and all up to civil war levels, did not go quietly into that gentle night. Pepper has elaborated on this subject, and he suggests that the neoliberal logic and its reforms in our current epoch are not the triumph of commonsense thinking or a natural order of any kind. Instead, neoliberalism has its own dark history, depicted in the crime fiction works of David Peace and Eoin McNamee, that show how the privatization of public assets and institutions, the ruthless privileging of free trade and individual freedom over collective rights and welfare reforms "had to be brought into the world using extra-legal violence and via the politicized state's eagerness to contract out its work to paramilitary and parapolitical bodies." Pepper, *Unwilling Executioner*, p. 216.
40. Zaremba, *The Price of the Patient*, p. 26.
41. Zaremba, *The Price of the Patient*, p. 78.
42. Zaremba, *The Price of the Patient*, p. 96.
43. Ahlbäck Öberg, Shirin, and Sten Widmalm. "NPM in Swedish" [NPM på Svenska]. In Zaremba, *The Price of the Patient*, p. 124.
44. Polanyi, *The Great Transformation*, p. 239.
45. Mankell, *The Man Who Smiled*, p. 391.
46. Mankell, *The Man Who Smiled*, p. 391.
47. Although, expanding big cities such as Malmö in Sweden and Copenhagen in Denmark are important parts of the playground in Wallander's immediate vicinity.
48. Sjöholm, Carina. "Scania: The Landscape Between Fact and Fiction" [Skåne. Landskapet mellan fakta och fiktion. Henning Mankell]. In Bergman, Kerstin, ed. *The Swedish Landscape of Crime Fiction*, p. 13. Author's translation.
49. Sjöholm, "Scania," p. 13.
50. Sjöholm, "Scania," p. 20.
51. Davis, *City of Quartz*, p. 41.
52. Bergman, *Swedish Crime Fiction*, p. 23.
53. Pettersson, *Stieg*, p. 202.
54. Mankell, Henning. *The Dogs of Riga* [*Hundarna i Riga*]. Stockholm: Ordfront, p. 334.
55. Žižek, "Henning Mankell."
56. Bergman, *Swedish Crime Fiction*, p. 51.
57. Stephen Knight elaborates on the postmodern crime novel in the line of Umberto Eco and describes this sub-genre as something that "by being less determinate in its puzzles and less simply resolved in its processes and outcomes, become[s] a medium to question certainties about the self, the mind and the ambient world." Knight, *Crime Fiction Since 1800*, p. 205.

Chapter 4

1. Maher, John. "Knopf Announces Fifth Book in Larsson's Millennium Series." *Publishers Weekly*, April 11, 2017. https://www.publishersweekly.com/pw/by-topic/industry-news/book-deals/article/73306-knopf-to-publish-fifth-book-in-millennium-series.html. Accessed February 3, 2018. The figures are, as pointed out before, unreliable since they originate from the publisher, with "85 million sold copies" referring to the entire Millennium series, including the fourth book, the Lagercrantz sequel.

2. It is highly likely that the title *The Girl Who Kicked the Hornet's Nest*—named *Luftslottet som sprängdes* (The Castle in the Air that Blew Up) in Sweden—alludes to Patricia Cornwell's crime novel *Hornet's Nest* (1997), since Larsson constantly read feminist crime writers. Speaking of Lisbeth Salander: Knight has pointed out that Cornwell's heroine Kay Scarpetta has a lesbian niece who is an IT-expert, "more wedded to machines than to a woman and her gender choice seems almost insignificant." Knight, *Crime Fiction Since 1800*, p. 216.
3. Pettersson, *Stieg*, p. 220.
4. Holmberg, *A Darker Shade*, p. 2.
5. Holmberg, John-Henri. "Lisbeth Salander Brought to Life on Stage." In Burstein et al. *Secrets*, p. 225.
6. Holmberg, *A Darker Shade*, p. 4. See also, Bergman, *Swedish Crime Fiction*, p. 27.
7. Burstein, Dan. "The Moral Geography of Stieg Larsson." In Burstein et al. *Secrets*, p. 321.
8. Holmberg, John-Henri. "The Man Who Inhaled Crime Fiction." In Burstein et al. *Secrets*, p. 102.
9. Scaggs, *Crime Fiction*, p. 74.
10. Tapper, *Swedish Cops*, p. 248.
11. Pettersson, *Stieg*, pp. 35–6.
12. Referring to Robert Brenner's famous article "Uneven Development and the Long Downturn: The Advanced Capitalist Economies from Boom to Stagnation 1950–1998," originally published in *New Left Review*. Issue 229 (May/June 1998).
13. Jay, *The Dialectical Imagination*, p. xvi.
14. Pettersson, *Stieg*, p. 199.
15. Freedman, *The Incomplete Projects*, pp. 34–6.
16. Brolin, David. *Reconsiderations: Swedish Leftwing Intellectuals in the Change from 70s to 80s* [*Omprövningar. Svenska vänsterintellektuella i skiftet från 70-tal till 80-tal*]. Lund: Celanders, 2015, p. 250.
17. Brolin, *Reconsiderations*, p. 253.
18. Brolin, *Reconsiderations*, p. 61.
19. Berntson and Nordin, *After the Revolution*, p. 62.
20. The situation in Indochina was increasingly complex in the late 1970s and signaled a breakdown of Marxist role models in world politics. The American withdrawal from Vietnam in 1975 did not seem to invoke enough hope among leftist activists, and consequently the political positions on the left were thoroughly confused during these years. In December 1978, Vietnam invaded Cambodia, and in early 1979 the communist regime of Pol Pot was defeated. Pol Pot, in his turn, was allied to China who, in return, attacked Vietnam in February 1979, and Vietnam was allied to the Soviet Union. These matters, concerning conflicts between communist nations, raised several questions among the left throughout the world, especially since wars and imperialistic aggressions, according to left wingers, were something that could only be initiated by capitalist states. Berntson and Nordin, *After the Revolution*, p. 77–8.
21. Gabrielsson, Eva, with Marie-Françoise Colombani. *Stieg & Me: Memories of My Life with Stieg Larsson* [*Millennium, Stieg & Jag*]. Translated by Eva Gabrielsson. Stockholm: Natur & Kultur, 2011, p. 30.
22. Pettersson, *Stieg*, p. 36.
23. Freedman, *Critical Theory*, p. 9.
24. Larsson, Stieg (Severin). "The Nightingale That Sang the Death Song of Capitalism" [Näktergalen som fick sjunga kapitalismens dödssång]. *Internationalen*, nr 42, October 15, 1980, pp. 8–9.
25. Blomqvist, Håkan. "Stieg Larsson: The Excavating Socialist [Stieg Larsson. Den grävande socialisten]. *Internationalen*, no. 17, April 29, 2011.
26. Larsson, Stieg, Stig Eriksson, and Martin Fahlgren. "A Welcome Sobering Up" [Välkommen tillnyktring]. *Internationalen*, no. 48, 1983, p. 5.
27. Larsson et al., "A Welcome Sobering Up," p. 4.
28. Forshaw, *The Man Who Left Too Soon*, p. 3.
29. Holmberg, "The Stieg Larsson Story." In Burstein et al., *Secrets*, p. 255.
30. Blomqvist, "Stieg Larsson."
31. Blomqvist, "Stieg Larsson."
32. Wald, Alan M. *Writing from the Left: New Essays on Radical Culture and Politics*. London: Verso, 1994, pp. 127–8.
33. Trotsky, Leon. *Literature and Revolution*. Translated by Magnus Hedlund and Lars Lindvall. Mölndal: Partisan, 1969, p. 11.
34. Trotsky, *Literature and Revolution*, p. 13.
35. Trotsky, *Literature and Revolution*, p. 294.
36. Trotsky, Leon. "The Social Roots and the Social Function of Literature." *Marxists Internet Archive*.
37. Trotsky, "The Social Roots."
38. Wald, *Writing from the Left*, p. 126.
39. Nordin, *History of Philosophy*, p. 533.
40. Tapper, *Swedish Cops*, p. 255.
41. Knight, *Crime Fiction Since 1800*, p. 207. Tapper, too, makes this connection, although referring to the film adaptation in 1993, not the novel. Tapper, *Swedish Cops*, p. 251.
42. Nordin, *History of Philosophy*, p. 536; Östlund, David. 2014. "Back to the Future? Technology, Communication, and Reason in the Age of Television" [Tillbaka till framtiden?

Teknik, kommunikation och förnuft i tevealdern]. In Burman and Lennerhed, *Together*, p. 306.

43. Ellis, Bret Easton. *American Psycho*. London: Picador, 1991, p. 3. Italics in original.

44. Tapper, *The Cop in the Twilight Land*, p. 622.

45. Larsson, Stieg. *The Girl with the Dragon Tattoo*. Translated by Reg Keeland. London: Quercus, 2008, pp. 7: ch. 113.

46. Forshaw, *The Man Who Left Too Soon*, p. 125.

47. Gemzöe, Lena. *Feminism*. Stockholm: Bilda förlag, 2010, p. 47.

48. Campbell, Beatrix. "A Feminist Sexual Politics: Now You See It. Now You Don't." *Feminist Review*, no. 5, 1980, p. 2.

49. Baksi, Kurdo. *Stieg Larsson, My Friend* [*Min vän Stieg Larsson*]. Stockholm: Norstedts, 2010, p. 111.

50. Baksi, *Stieg Larsson*, p. 114.

51. See Larsson, Stieg. "Swedish and Un-Swedish Violence Towards Women." In Larsson, *The Expo Files*, pp. 129–156.

52. Fister, Barbara. "The Millennium Trilogy and the American Serial Killer Narrative: Investigating Protagonists of Men Who Write Women." In Åström et al., *Rape in Stieg Larsson's Millennium Trilogy*, p. 40. Another scholar emphasizing this aspect is Walton, Priscilla. "'The Girl Who Pays Our Salaries': Rape and the Bestselling Millennium Trilogy," in *Rape in Stieg Larsson's Millennium Trilogy*, pp. 22–4.

53. Baksi, *Stieg Larsson*, p. 149.

54. Richter, David H. "Background Action and Ideology: Grey Men and Dope Doctors in Raymond Chandler." *Narrative*, vol. 2, no. 1, Jan. 1994, p. 36.

55. Jensen, Carsten. "Lisbeth Salander and Our Yearning for Revenge" [Lisbeth Salander och vår längtan efter hämnd]. *Dagens Nyheter*, Sthlm edition, December 20, 2009, p. 13.

56. Gabrielsson with Colombani, *Stieg & Me*, pp. 79–80.

57. Marcuse, *One-Dimensional Man*, p. 128.

58. Marcuse, "Some Social Implications," p. 139.

59. Held, *Introduction to Critical Theory*, pp. 264–5.

60. Bergman, *Swedish Crime Fiction*, p. 88.

61. Bergman, *Swedish Crime Fiction*, p. 96.

62. Tapper, *The Cop in the Twilight Land*, p. 623.

63. Holmberg, *A Darker Shade*, p. 174.

64. Larsson, Stieg. "Brain Power." Translated by John-Henri Holmberg. In Holmberg, *A Dark Shade of Sweden*, p. 179.

65. Larsson, "Brain Power," p. 188.

66. Gabrielsson with Colombani, *Stieg & Me*, p. 37.

67. Gabrielsson with Colombani, *Stieg & Me*, p. 37.

68. Larsson, Stieg. *The Girl Who Kicked the Hornet's Nest*. Translated by Reg Keeland. London: Quercus, 2010, pp. 96–7.

69. Larsson, *Hornet's Nest*, p. 106.

70. Larsson, *Hornet's Nest*, p. 107.

71. Larsson, *Hornet's Nest*, p. 110.

72. Larsson, *Hornet's Nest*, pp. 114; 116.

73. Larsson, *Hornet's Nest*, p. 178.

74. Larsson, *Hornet's Nest*, p. 563.

75. Larsson, *Hornet's Nest*, p. 677.

76. Trotsky, Leon. *The Age of Permanent Revolution* [*Den permanenta revolutionens epok*]. Edited by Isaac Deutscher. Translated by Kenth-Åke Andersson, Martin Peterson, Magnus Hedlund and Lars Lindvall. Mölndal: Partisan, 1969, p. 8.

77. Trotsky, *The Age*, pp. 12–14.

78. Freedman, *Critical Theory*, p. 188.

79. Mandel, *Delightful Murder*, p. 138.

80. Jensen, "Lisbeth Salander and Our Yearning for Revenge," p. 13.

81. Wald, "Marxism in Noir," p. 152.

82. Mandel, *Delightful Murder*, p. 140.

83. Mandel, *Delightful Murder*, p. 141.

84. Barnfield, "The Urban Landscape of Marxist Noir."

85. Greider, Göran. "The Socialist Stieg Larsson Has Been Erased" [Socialisten Stieg Larsson har raderats]. *Expressen*, August 27, 2015.

86. Larsson, *Dragon Tattoo*, p. 42.

87. Parks, Tim. "The Moralist." *The New York Review of Books*, June 9, 2011.

88. Katarina Gregersdotter explains some of these contradictions, for example the breast augmentation, as a way for Salander "to claim control over her body" that has been controlled by others during her entire life. Gregersdotter, "The Body, Hopelessness, and Nostalgia," p. 85–6.

89. Mandel, *Delightful Murder*, p. 27.

90. Freedman, *Critical Theory*, p. 182.

91. Larsson, *Dragon Tattoo*, p. 203.

92. Mandel, *Delightful Murder*, pp. 133, 137.

93. Björk, Nina. "The Dream of Control" [Drömmen om kontroll]. Review of *The Millennium Trilogy* by Stieg Larsson. *Dagens Nyheter*, April 19, 2008, p. 7. Author's translation.

94. Björk, "The Dream of Control," p. 7.

95. Burstein et al., *Secrets*, p. 295.

96. The Frankfurt School theorists, perhaps especially Adorno, got the concept of "false consciousness" from Engels and Hegel and describe this consciousness (invoked by the Culture Industry, the ideology, etc.) as "tailored scientifically to fit the society" and "socially conditioned." Held, *Introduction to Critical Theory*, p. 106.

97. Burstein et al., *Secrets*, pp. 295, 316.

98. Björk, "The Dream of Control," p. 6.
99. Forshaw, *The Man Who Left Too Soon*, p. 63.
100. Forshaw, *The Man Who Left Too Soon*, pp. 62–3.
101. Larsson, *Dragon Tattoo*, p. 46.
102. Greider, "Stieg Larsson the Socialist."
103. Lagercrantz, David. *The Girl in the Spider's Web*. Translated by George Goulding. New York: Random House Large Print, 2015, front cover.
104. Norberg, Johan. "David Lagercrantz: 'All hysterical!'" [David Lagercrantz: "Helt hysteriskt!"]. *Tidningen Vi*, no. 9, 2015, p. 19.
105. Norberg, "David Lagercrantz," p. 20.
106. www.norstedts.se/forfattare/119997-david-lagercrantz. Accessed February 10, 2017.
107. Svedjedal, Johan. "New Millennium Is Skillful and Respectful" [Nya Millennium är skicklig och respektfull]. Review of *The Girl in the Spider's Web*, by David Lagercrantz, *Dagens Nyheter*, August 29, 2015, pp. 4–5.
108. Child, Lee. Review of *The Girl in the Spider's Web*, *New York Times* (Sunday Book Review), September 1, 2015.
109. Lagercrantz, David. "I Was Grabbed by an Obsession" [Jag greps av en tvångstanke]. *Dagens Nyheter*. August 2, 2015, p. 9.
110. Lagercrantz, *Spider's Web*, p. 5.
111. Lagercrantz, *Spider's Web*, pp. 415–6.
112. Lagercrantz, *Spider's Web*, p. 434.
113. Lagercrantz, *Spider's Web*, p. 82.
114. Held, *Introduction to Critical Theory*, p. 265.
115. Nestingen, "Unnecessary Officers," p. 180.
116. Nestingen, "Unnecessary Officers," p. 181.
117. Scaggs, *Crime Fiction*, pp. 86–7.
118. Held, *Introduction to Critical Theory*, p. 209.

Chapter 5

1. Burstein, De Keijzer, and Holmberg. "What You're Afraid of Has Already Happened." In Burstein et al. *Secrets*, p. 124.
2. Klemetz, Elin. "When Fiction Exceeds Reality" [När dikten överträffar verkligheten]. *Filter*, no. 50, June/July 2016, p. 138.
3. In the United Kingdom this book was released as *The Vault* in 2008, and in the United States the novel kept its Swedish title *Box 21*.
4. Unknown author. "Interview with Roslund & Hellström." CrimeHouse.com. April 27, 2011.
5. Taylor, Kate. "Meet the Swedish Crime Writers Not Named Larsson." *The Globe and Mail*, February 25, 2011.
6. Taylor, "Meet the Swedish Crime Writers."
7. Unknown author, "Interview with Roslund & Hellström."
8. Irhede, Ann-Charlotte. "We Had Fallen Out as Hell" [Vi var så in i helvete osams]. *Corren*, October 31, 2016.
9. Anderson, Patrick. Review of *Box 21*, by Roslund & Hellström. *Washington Post*, October 19, 2009.
10. Maslin, Janet. "Stoking the Fire Larsson Ignited." Review of *Three Seconds*, by Roslund & Hellström, *New York Times*, January 5, 2011.
11. Maslin, "Stoking the Fire."
12. Maslin, "Stoking the Fire."
13. Woods, Paula L. "Book review 'Three Seconds.'" Review of *Three Seconds*, by Roslund & Hellström. Special to *Los Angeles Times*, January 30, 2011.
14. Memmott, Carol. "Duo's 'Three Seconds' does Stieg Larsson one better." Review of *Three Seconds*, by Roslund & Hellström, *USA Today*, March 1, 2011.
15. Forshaw, Barry. Review of *Three Seconds*, by Roslund & Hellström. *The Independent*, November 2, 2010.
16. Forshaw, Barry. Review of *Two Soldiers*, by Roslund & Hellström. *The Independent*, July 1, 2013.
17. Schwartz, Nils. Review of *Two Soldiers*, by Roslund & Hellström, *Expressen*, May 18, 2012.
18. Planhammar, Per. "Sharply on a Tsunami of Violence" [Skarpt om tsunami av våld]. Review of *Two Soldiers* by Roslund & Hellström, *Göteborgs-Posten*, June 3, 2012, p. 85.
19. Burstein et al., "What You're Afraid of," p. 126.
20. Tapper, *Swedish Cops*, p. 241.
21. Roslund, Anders, and Börge Hellström. "Preface." In Sjöwall and Wahlöö, *The Man Who Went Up*, p. 9.
22. Roslund, Anders, and Börge Hellström. *Box 21*. Stockholm: Piratförlaget, 2005, pp. 35, 38.
23. Burstein, "What You're Afraid of," p. 127.
24. Roslund, Anders, and Börge Hellström. *Two Soldiers*. Translated by Kari Dickson. London: Quercus, 2014, p. 659. In the English translation by Kari Dickson, Grens has been working twenty-seven years on the force, but in the Swedish original he has an even more impressive thirty-seven years on the job—a mistake I blame the translator for, therefore I have corrected this important figure in my quotation. In the Swedish edition, this quote can be found on page 673.
25. McCann, *Gumshoe America*, p. 18.
26. Lukács, Georg. *Victory of Realism* [*Realismens seger*]. Translated by Lars Bjurman

and Carl Henning Wijkmark. Lund: Arkiv, 1983, p. 111.
27. Held, *Introduction to Critical Theory*, p. 190.
28. Roslund and Hellström, *Two Soldiers*, p. 648.
29. Freedman, *Critical Theory*, p. 9.
30. Pepper, *Unwilling Executioner*, p. 210. Pepper mentions novelists such as Lauren Beukes, James Sallis, and Massimo Carlotto who, in contrast with the radical crime fiction novelists of the 1960s (think, Chester Himes and Sjöwall-Wahlöö), "demonstrate no faith in the idea that capitalism can be directly confronted and overturned. Rather their opposition takes the form of narratives that hyperbolically show the worst excesses and depravities of capitalism" (p. 229).
31. Roslund, Anders, and Börge Hellström. *The Girl Below the Street* [*Flickan under gatan*]. Stockholm: Piratförlaget, 2007, p. 272.
32. Roslund & Hellström, *The Girl Below*, pp. 272-3.
33. Gregersdotter, "The Body, Hopelessness, and Nostalgia," p. 87. The novels referred to in her study are Roslund & Hellström's *Box 21* (i.e., *The Vault*) and Larsson's Millennium trilogy. Marx's concept of commodification is being used in this context and Gregersdotter describes it as "when something which was previously not considered sellable is now ascribed exchange value, and this can include, for example, both gender and bodies." (p. 88). Furthermore, she sees the trafficked slaves as symbols of the "destructive bodily effects of capitalism." (p. 88).
34. Gregersdotter, "The Body, Hopelessness, and Nostalgia," p. 94.
35. Davis, *City of Quartz*, p. 226.
36. Roslund and Hellström, *Two Soldiers*, p. 62.
37. Roslund and Hellström, *Two Soldiers*, p. 41.
38. Wahlöö, *Murder*, p. 113.
39. Roslund and Hellström, *Two Soldiers*, pp. 506-7.
40. Roslund and Hellström, *Two Soldiers*, p. 507.
41. Davis, *City of Quartz*, p. 293.
42. Davis, *City of Quartz*, p. 299.
43. Klemetz, "When Fiction Exceeds Reality," pp. 139-40.
44. Davis, *City of Quartz*, p. 300.
45. Roslund, Anders, and Börge Hellström. *Two Soldiers* [*Två soldater*]. Stockholm: Piratförlaget, 2012, p. 684. This is information obtained from the postscript in the Swedish edition of *Two Soldiers*. In the English Quercus edition, the publisher has unfortunately chosen not to print this info.

46. Davis, *City of Quartz*, p. 274.
47. Roslund and Hellström, *Two Soldiers*, p. 595.
48. Roslund and Hellström, *Two Soldiers*, p. 625.
49. Tapper, *Swedish Cops*, p. 124.
50. Roslund and Hellström, *Two Soldiers*, p. 5.
51. Marcuse, Herbert. *An Essay n Liberation* [*Människans befrielse*]. Translated by Göran Fredriksson. Stockholm: Aldus, 1969, p. 25.
52. Marcuse, *An Essay*, p. 11.
53. Roslund and Hellström, *Two Soldiers*, pp. 481-2.
54. Roslund and Hellström, *Two Soldiers*, p. 465.
55. Roslund and Hellström, *Two Soldiers*, p. 471.
56. Burstein et al., "What You're Afraid of," p. 127.
57. Tapper, *Swedish Cops*, p. 238.
58. Roslund and Hellström, *Two Soldiers*, p. 628.
59. Tapper, *Swedish Cops*, p. 245.
60. Klemetz, "When Fiction Exceeds Reality," p. 136.
61. Klemetz, "When Fiction Exceeds Reality," p. 140.
62. Klemetz, "When Fiction Exceeds Reality," p. 140.
63. Irhede, "We Had Fallen Out."
64. Roslund, Anders, and Börge Hellström. *Three Minutes* [*Tre minuter*]. Stockholm: Piratförlaget, 2016, p. 116-7.
65. Roslund and Hellström, *Three Minutes*, p. 183.
66. Roslund and Hellström, *Three Minutes*, p. 291.
67. Roslund and Hellström, *Three Minutes*, p. 565. Author's translation.
68. Mandel, *Delightful Murder*, p. 121.
69. Mandel, *Delightful Murder*, pp. 123-4.
70. Palmqvist, Mats. "Roslund & Hellström Become Nagging" [Roslund & Hellström blir tjatiga]. Review of *Three Minutes*, by Roslund & Hellström, *Smålandsposten*. June 2, 2016, p. 24; Stenberg, Björn G. "It's Infernally Exciting" [Det är infernaliskt spännande]. Review of *Three Minutes*, by Roslund & Hellström, *Uppsala Nya Tidning*. June 4, 2016.
71. Roslund, Anders, and Börge Hellström. *Three Seconds*. Translated by Kari Dickson. London: Quercus, 2011, p. 23.
72. Klemetz, "When Fiction Exceeds Reality," p. 139.

Chapter 6

1. Tapper, Michael. "With the Cop Under the Magnifying Glass" [Med snuten under

förstoringsglaset]. *Gaudeamus*, November 14, 2011.
2. Lapidus, Jens. "Introduction." In Sjöwall, Maj, and Per Wahlöö. *The Abominable Man*. New York: Vintage, 2009, pp. vii–x.
3. Fauvellered, Louise. "I Would Rather Work with People than Money" [Jag jobbar hellre med människor än pengar]. *Jusektidningen Karriär*, no. 9, Dec. 2015, p. 38.
4. Stenberg, Jens. "Final Word: Jens Lapidus" [Sista ordet: Jens Lapidus]. *Café*, June 2014, p. 170; Leonardz, Jenny. "Lawyer Tracked the Cocaine" [Jurist kom kokainet på spåren]. *Svenska Dagbladet*, July 26, 2006, p. 56.
5. Lapidus, Jens. *Easy Money (XL)* [*Snabba Cash (XL)*]. Stockholm: Wahlström & Widstrand, 2016, p. 9. Ellroy's Underworld USA trilogy consists of *American Tabloid* (1995), *The Cold Six Thousand* (2001), and *Blood's a Rover* (2008).
6. Tapper, Michael. "Stockholm Noir: Neoliberalism as Gangsterism in *Easy Money*." In Gustafsson and Kääpä. *Nordic Genre Film*, p. 111.
7. Forshaw, Barry. Review of *Easy Money*, by Jens Lapidus. *The Independent*. February 29, 2012.
8. See for example Declan Hughes's review of *Easy Money* by Lapidus in *Irish Times* on January 7, 2012, with its telling headline, "Nice plot, shame about the pronouns, verbs, articles."
9. Hansson, Beata. "Curious in a Cone" [Nyfiken i en strut]. *Arbetaren*, no. 26, June/July 2014, p. 16. Author's translation.
10. Geherin, David. *Scene of the Crime: The Importance of Place in Crime and Mystery Fiction*. Jefferson, NC: McFarland, 2008, p. 161.
11. Tapper, Michael. "Stockholm Noir: Neoliberalism as Gangsterism in *Easy Money*." In Gustafsson and Kääpä. *Nordic Genre Film*, p. 108.
12. Freedman, Carl. *Versions of Hollywood Crime Cinema: Studies in Ford, Wilder, Coppola, Scorsese, and Others*. Bristol: Intellect, 2013, p. 26.
13. Liedman, *Karl Marx*, p. 467.
14. Mandel, *Delightful Murder*, p. 110.
15. Freedman, *Versions*, pp. 15–6.
16. Marx, Karl. *Capital: A Critique of Political Economy. Vol. 1*. Translated by Ben Fowkes. London: Penguin, 1990, p. 873.
17. Marx, *Capital*, p. 915.
18. Tapper, "Stockholm Noir," pp. 104–5.
19. Freedman, *The Age of Nixon*, p. 67.
20. Freedman, Carl, and Christopher Kendrick. "Labor and Politics in Dashiell Hammett's *Red Harvest*." In Freedman, *Incomplete Projects*, p. 134.
21. Bergman, *Swedish Crime Fiction*, p. 101.
22. Freedman, *Versions*, p. 27.
23. Hansson, "Curious in a Cone," p. 17.
24. Therborn, *From Marxism*, p. 140.
25. Hansson, "Curious in a Cone," p. 17. Author's translation.
26. Broady, Donald, ed. *Fields of Culture: An Anthology* [*Kulturens fält. En antologi*]. Göteborg: Daidalos, 1998, pp. 13–4.
27. Another interesting character from the hardboiled American tradition that ought to be mentioned, along with Ellroy's anti-heroes, is James Sallis's Driver from his novel *Drive* (2005), a brilliant idea for a character not assimilated to any system and who exists a step or two to one side of the common world, "someone whose violence against the established order, in whatever form, assumes political significance in the context of the larger structures of oppression," as Pepper argues. Certainly, Teddy Maksumic could be a Swedish evocation of the same idea. Pepper, *Unwilling Executioner*, p. 233.
28. MacShane, *The Life of*, p. 52.
29. Lapidus, Jens. *The VIP-Room* [*VIP-rummet*]. Stockholm: Wahlström & Widstrand, 2014, p. 345; Lapidus, Jens. *Sthlm Delete*. Stockholm: Wahlström & Widstrand, 2015, p. 138.
30. McCann, *Gumshoe America*, p. 111–2.
31. Nestingen, "Unnecessary Officers," p. 174.
32. Lapidus, *VIP-Room*, p. 21.
33. Lapidus, *VIP-Room*, p. 92.
34. Lapidus, *VIP-Room*, p. 234.
35. Lapidus, *Sthlm Delete*, p. 113. Author's translation.
36. Lapidus, *Sthlm Delete*, p. 148.
37. Lapidus, *Sthlm Delete*, p. 168.
38. Lapidus, *Sthlm Delete*, p. 206.
39. Lapidus, *Sthlm Delete*, p. 305.
40. Bourdieu, Pierre. *Counterfire: Texts Against the Spreading of Neoliberalism* [*Moteld. Texter mot nyliberalismens utbredning*]. Stockholm: Symposion, 1999, p. 127. Author's translation.
41. The concept of "electronic slum" shows up in the Swedish Beck films (1997-) written by Rolf Börjlind. See Tapper, *Swedish Cops*, p. 228.
42. Bergman, Kerstin. "The Well-Adjusted Cops of the New Millennium: Neo-Romantic Tendencies in the Swedish Police Procedural." In Nestingen and Arvas, *Scandinavian Crime Fiction*, p. 35.
43. Bergman, "The Well-Adjusted Cops," p. 43.

Chapter 7

1. In the following, I will address him as Arne Dahl, not Jan Arnald, since his crime fiction novels, as Dahl, and not his original persona, Arnald, is of interest in this study.

2. Wesslén, Gunnar. "Arne Dahl Was Born From Political Rage" [Arne Dahl föddes ur politisk vrede]. *Dagens ETC*, May 23, 2016, p. 20. Author's translation.
3. Pepper, *Unwilling Executioner*, p. 235.
4. Bergman, *Swedish Crime Fiction*, p. 148-9.
5. Bergman, *Swedish Crime Fiction*, p. 137.
6. Bergman, *Swedish Crime Fiction*, p. 64.
7. www.salomonssonagency.se/arne-dahl. Accessed February 3, 2018.
8. Hagström. Johanna. "This is My Masterpiece" [Det här är mitt storverk]. *Göteborgs-Posten*, July 5, 2014, p. 46.
9. Torén Björling, Sanna. "Sanna Torén Björling Meets Jan Arnald" [Sanna Torén Björling möter Jan Arnald]. *Dagens Nyheter*, June 12, 2011, p. 6.
10. Johnson, Mats. "Terrorism Reaches Sweden" [Terrorismen når Sverige]. Review of *Afterquake*, by Arne Dahl. *Göteborgs-Posten*, September 13, 2006, p. 90.
11. Bergman, *Swedish Crime Fiction*, p. 139.
12. Dahl, Arne. "Introduction." In Sjöwall and Wahlöö, *Murder at the Savoy*, p. xii.
13. Torén Björling, "Meeting Jan Arnald," p. 6.
14. Dahl, "Introduction," pp. xii–xiii.
15. Schwartz, Nils. "Dahl's Great Swedish Dystopia" [Dahls stora svenska dystopi]. Review of *Last Couple Out*, by Arne Dahl, *Dagens Nyheter*, June 16, 2014, p. 6. Author's translation.
16. Marx, Karl. *Early Writings*. Translated by Rodney Livingstone and Gregor Benton. London: Penguin, 1992. p. 423.
17. Dahl, "Introduction," p. xii.
18. Jay, *The Dialectical Imagination*, p. 4.
19. Freedman, Carl. "The Strongest Link: SF as Social Register." *Science Fiction Studies*, vol. 30, no. 2, July 2003, p. 178.
20. Freedman, Carl. "Science Fiction and Critical Theory." *Science Fiction Studies*, vol. 14, no. 2, July 1987, p. 181.
21. As we have seen earlier, Freedman's concept of critical theory does not only concern Marxist theory, but also a broader theoretical framework from Kant to Freud, Sartre and even a post-Marxist such as Foucault.
22. Freedman, "Science Fiction and Critical Theory," p. 187.
23. Freedman, *Critical Theory*, p. 56.
24. Freedman, "Science Fiction and Critical Theory," p.197.
25. Freedman, "Science Fiction and Critical Theory," p. 187.
26. *The Steel Spring* is neither only a sci-fi novel nor a crime fiction novel, but *both*. There is actually a police investigator trying to solve a problem at the same time as the story is set in a vaguely recognizable near future. Hence, Darko Suvin's famous definition of science fiction is applicable to this novel: "the literature of cognitive estrangement." Freedman, *Critical Theory*, p. xvi.
27. Marcuse, Herbert. *Protest, Demonstration, Revolt* [*Das Ende der Utopie*]. Translated by Maj and Paul Frisch. Stockholm: Aldus Bonniers, 1968, p. 13.
28. Freedman, *Critical Theory*, p. 6.
29. Therborn, Göran. *The Killing Fields of Inequality* [*Ojämlikhet dödar*]. Translated by Henrik Gundenäs. Lund: Arkiv, 2016. pp. 10, 36.
30. Davis, Mike. *Planet of Slums* [*Slum. Världens storstäder*]. Translated by Gunnar Sandin. Lund: Arkiv, 2007, p. 226.
31. See for example, Crouch, Colin. *Post-Democracy* [*Postdemokrati*]. Translated by Henrik Gundenäs. Göteborg: Daidalos, 2011; and Mouffe, Chantal. *On the Political* [*Om det politiska*]. Translated by Oskar Söderlind. Hägersten: Tankekraft, 2008.
32. Pepper mentions, in his impressive book *Unwilling Executioner*, an interesting paradoxical movement, a complicated passage back and forth between sovereignty and neoliberalism, in contemporary society: "the simultaneous waning and intensification of [state] sovereignty" (p. 208). For example he mentions the anti-leftist maneuverings or drug prohibition initiatives from the 1970s onwards into the post-9/11 security boom by state agencies as a strengthening of state power. Yet, there is another contemporary movement that suggests that the modern state is "being eroded by the flow of capital, people, information, goods and economic power that crisscross and undermine territorial borders" (p. 208).
33. Dahl, Arne. *Chinese Whispers* [*Viskleken*]. Stockholm: Bonniers, 2011, p. 13.
34. Dahl, *Chinese Whispers*, p. 111.
35. Dahl, *Chinese Whispers*, p. 127.
36. Dahl, *Chinese Whispers*, p. 299. Author's translation.
37. Dahl, *Chinese Whispers*, p. 299. Author's translation.
38. Dahl, *Chinese Whispers*, pp. 460–1.
39. Werth, Nicolas. *Cannibal Island: Death in a Siberian Gulag*. Princeton, NJ: Princeton University Press, 2007, pp. 162–3.
40. Dahl, Arne. *Musical Chairs* [*Hela havet stormar*]. Stockholm: Bonniers, 2012, p. 22. Author's translation.
41. Dahl, *Chinese Whispers*, p. 38.
42. Dahl, Arne. *Last Couple Out* [*Sista paret ut*]. Stockholm: Bonniers, 2014, p. 230. Author's translation.
43. Dahl, *Musical Chairs*, p. 244.
44. Dahl, *Musical Chairs*, pp. 247–8. Author's translation.

45. Dahl, *Musical Chairs*, pp. 469–70. Author's translation.
46. Jay, *The Dialectical Imagination*, p. 46.
47. Crouch, *Post-Democracy*, p. 47.
48. Crouch, *Post-Democracy*, p. 50.
49. Risen, James, and Mark Mazzetti. "30 False Fronts Won Contracts for Blackwater." *New York Times*, September 3, 2010.
50. Dahl, Arne. *Blind Man's Bluff* [*Blindbock*]. Stockholm: Bonniers, 2013, p. 435.
51. Dahl, *Blind Man's Bluff*, p. 43.
52. Mouffe, *On the Political*, p. 17–19.
53. Mouffe, *On the Political*, p. 124.
54. Dahl, *Blind Man's Bluff*, p. 373.
55. Dahl, *Blind Man's Bluff*, p. 474.
56. Crouch, *Post-Democracy*, p. 20.
57. Crouch, Colin. "Markets, power and politics: Is there a liberalism beyond social democracy?" *Policy Network*, May 5, 2011, p. 22.
58. Crouch, *Post-Democracy*, p. 36.
59. Crouch, *Post-Democracy*, p. 110.
60. Dahl, *Blind Man's Bluff*, p. 44.
61. Dahl, *Blind Man's Bluff*, p. 45. Author's translation.
62. Dahl, *Blind Man's Bluff*, p. 458. Author's translation.
63. This number of pages refers, of course, to the Swedish editions.
64. Dahl, *Last Couple Out*, p. 127.
65. Dahl, *Last Couple Out*, pp. 212; 213.
66. Freedman, *Incomplete Projects*, p. 148.
67. Marx, *Capital*, p. 125.
68. Therborn, *From Marxism*, p. 13.
69. Marx, *Capital*, p. 175.
70. Marx, *Capital*, pp. 165, 209.
71. Dahl, *Last Couple Out*, pp. 433–5.
72. Marx, *Capital*, p. 928.
73. Sjöwall, Maj, and Per Wahlöö. *The Terrorists*. Translated by Joan Tate. New York: Vintage, 2013, pp. 279–80.
74. Tapper, *Swedish Cops*, p. 102.
75. Dahl, *Last Couple Out*, p. 559. Author's translation.

Chapter 8

1. Cullberg, Jonas. "The Ahndoril Couple is Lars Kepler" [Paret Ahndoril är Lars Kepler]. *Svenska Dagbladet*, August 12, 2009, p. 4.
2. Schuessler, Jennifer. "Inside the List." Review of *The Hypnotist*, by Lars Kepler, *New York Times*, July 8, 2011.
3. Cullberg, "The Ahndoril Couple," p. 4. Author's translation.
4. Åkesson, Johan. "We Live the Best Lives in the World" [Vi lever världens bästa liv]. *Dagens Nyheter*, November 28, 2011, p. 12.
5. The French term *peripétie* supposes a radical change in the course of events in the story.
6. Boda, Lisa. "Social Criticism—An Obvious Part in the Writing" [Samhällskritik—en självklar del i skrivandet]. *Nya Ludvika Tidning*, November 25, 2011, p. 19. Author's translation.
7. Svensson, Julia. "Writing Is Like Resurrecting the Dead" [Att skriva är som att återuppväcka de döda]. *Sydsvenskan*, August 22, 2009, pp. 6–7. Author's translation.
8. Karlsson, Johanna. "Sweden's Most Wanted Author Speaks Out" [Sveriges mest eftersökta författare talar ut]. *Helsingborgs Dagblad*, August 22, 2009. Author's translation.
9. Åkesson, "We Live the Best Lives," p. 17. Author's translation.
10. www.salomonssonagency.se/larskepler. Accessed January 9, 2017.
11. www.larskepler.com. Accessed May 5, 2017.
12. Andersson, Carl Erland. "A Sure Success" [En säker framgång]. Review of *The Hypnotist*, by Lars Kepler, *Göteborgs-Posten*, July 24, 2009, p. 54. Author's translation.
13. Anderson, Patrick. "Lars Kepler's The Hypnotist: Thriller Is A Disturbing Meditation On Evil." Review of *The Hypnotist* by Lars Kepler, *Washington Post*, July 17, 2011.
14. Wilson, Laura. "Crime Roundup—Reviews." Review of *The Hypnotist*, by Lars Kepler, *The Guardian*, May 28, 2011.
15. Farabee, Mindy. "Swedish Thriller Skews Sexy." Review of *The Hypnotist*, by Lars Kepler, *Los Angeles Times*, July 14, 2011.
16. Grossman, Lev. "Grand Larssony." *Time Magazine*, June 27, 2011.
17. Persson, Magnus. "Skillfully Made Entertainment Violence" [Skickligt utfört underhållningsvåld]. Review of *The Hypnotist*, by Lars Kepler, *Svenska Dagbladet*, July 29, 2009, p. 6.
18. Caffrey, Andrew. Review of *The Nightmare*, by Lars Kepler, *Boston Globe*, July 11, 2012.
19. Tapper, *Swedish Cops*, pp. 36–7.
20. Fister, "The Millennium Trilogy," p. 43.
21. Fister, "The Millennium Trilogy," p. 43.
22. Knight, *Crime Fiction Since 1800*, p. 212.
23. Knight, *Crime Fiction Since 1800*, p. 213.
24. Barbara Fister's history of the serial killer narrative puts *The Silence of the Lambs* in the center of this genre during the 1980s and 90s. See Fister, "The Millennium Trilogy," pp. 43–47.
25. Stephen Knight has another definition of *American Psycho* as "a crime novel recounting the experiences—or the fantasies—of a Wall Street yuppie in both his obsessive quest for the perfect lifestyle and his increasingly violent attacks on women." Knight, *Crime Fiction Since 1800*, p. 218.

26. The Red Riding quartet consists of the novels *Nineteen Seventy-Four* (1999), *Nineteen Seventy-Seven* (2000), *Nineteen Eighty* (2001), *Nineteen Eighty-Three* (2002). Vaguely connected to the Red Riding novels, and a continuation of the hardboiled historical narrative, is Peace's next novel, *GB84* (2004), about the great U.K. miners' strike in 1984 and the battle against Margaret Thatcher.

27. Sund is the pen name for the writing duo Jerker Eriksson and Håkan Axlander Sundquist. *The Crow Girl*, released in English in 2016, was originally a novel trilogy published between the years 2010–2012 in Sweden. When it was published by Harvill Secker in Great Britain and Knopf in the U.S. in 2016, the trilogy had been shoehorned into one brick-thick volume measuring almost 800 pages, although the English edited version excludes quite a bit from the Swedish editions.

28. Scaggs, *Crime Fiction*, pp. 116–7.

29. Liedman, Sven-Eric. *Between the Trivial and the Inexpressible* [*Mellan det triviala och det outsägliga*]. Göteborg: Daidalos, 1998, pp. 118–9.

30. Tapper, *Swedish Cops*, p. 36.

31. Tapper, *Swedish Cops*, p. 37.

32. Knight, *Crime Fiction Since 1800*, p. 218.

33. Knight, *Crime Fiction Since 1800*, p. 218–9. Knight refers to *American Psycho* and Val McDermid's *The Mermaids Singing* in the quote.

34. Mandel, *Delightful Murder*, p. 50.

35. Scaggs, *Crime Fiction*, pp. 99–100.

36. Andersson, "A Sure Success," p. 54.

37. Kepler, Lars. *The Rabbit Hunter* [*Kaninjägaren*]. Stockholm: Bonniers, 2016, p. 281. Author's translation.

38. Forshaw, *Nordic Noir*, p. 38.

39. Åkesson, "We Live the Best Lives," p. 15; Domellöf-Wik, Maria, and Martin Erlandsson. "Writing Together Became A New Love" [Att skriva ihop blev en ny förälskelse]. *Göteborgs-Posten*, November 12, 2016, p. 54.

40. Åkesson, "We Live the Best Lives," p. 15.

41. Jameson, *Raymond Chandler*, p. 58.

Conclusion

1. Chandler, "A Simple Art of Murder," p. 988.

2. Wald, *Writing from the Left*, p. 132.

3. Wald, "Marxism in Noir," pp. 139–40.

4. Hagberg, "Raymond Chandler and the Moral Darkness."

5. Fine, *Imagining Los Angeles*, p. 136.

6. Jay, *The Dialectical Imagination*, pp. 193–4.

7. Ekman, Kajsa Ekis. *The Being and the Commodity* [*Varat och varan: Prostitution, surrogatmödraskap och den delade människan*]. Stockholm: Leopard, 2010, p. 120.

8. Freedman, *Critical Theory*, pp. 12–3. *Tel Quel* was a French avant-garde literary and philosophical journal published in Paris between 1960 and 1982. It became the platform for influential French philosophers such as Roland Barthes, Jacques Derrida, Michel Foucault, Umberto Eco, Bernard-Henri Lévy, and Julia Kristeva. For a time, the journal cooperated with the French Communist Party, and in the 1970s it was influenced by Maoism. In the late 1970s it eventually distanced itself from Maoism.

9. Therborn, *From Marxism*, pp. 61–2.

10. Wald, "Marxism in Noir," p. 144.

11. The Tom Stilton series consists of *Spring Tide* (2012), *The Third Voice* (2013), *Black Dawn* (2014) and *Sleep Little Willow* (2016).

12. Marx, *Capital*, p. 92.

13. Wennberg, Anders "Detail-Jerker and Synopsis-Håkan" [Detalj-Jerker och Synopsis-Håkan]. *Gefle Dagblad*, May 23, 2011, p. 19.

14. Sund, Erik Axl. *The Crow Girl*. London: Vintage, 2017, p. 81.

15. Sund, *The Crow Girl*, pp. 616, 231.

16. Sund, *The Crow Girl*, p. 629.

17. Sund, *The Crow Girl*, p. 458.

18. Sund, *The Crow Girl*, p. 455.

19. Clark, Susan Storer. "An Interview with Erik Axl Sund." *Washington Independent*, July 12, 2016.

20. Percy, Benjamin. "A Serial Killer Stalks Stockholm in This Creepy Nordic Noir." Review of *The Crow Girl*, by Erik Axl Sund, *New York Times*, July 27, 2016.

21. Flood, Alison. "The Crow Girl by Erik Axl Sund Review—Relentlessly Disturbing." *The Guardian*, April 26, 2016.

22. Forshaw, Barry. Review of *The Crow Girl*, by Erik Axl Sund, *Financial Times*, April 29, 2016.

23. Sund, *The Crow Girl*, p. 702.

24. Knight, *Crime Fiction Since 1800*, p. 213.

25. Sund, *The Crow Girl*, pp. 652–3.

26. Sund, *The Crow Girl*, p. 757.

27. Knight, *Crime Fiction Since 1800*, p. 219.

Works Cited

Books

Arato, Andrew, and Eike Gebhardt, eds. *The Essential Frankfurt School Reader*. New York: Continuum, 1985.

Asplund, Johan. *Regarding Raymond Chandler* [*Angående Raymond Chandler*]. Göteborg: Korpen, 2004.

Baksi, Kurdo. *Stieg Larsson, My Friend* [*Min vän Stieg Larsson*]. Stockholm: Norstedts, 2010.

Banham, Reyner. *Los Angeles: The Architecture of Four Ecologies*. Berkeley: University of California Press, 2009.

Berglund, Karl. *Death and Everyday Life: A Quantitative Analysis of Swedish Crime Fiction from the Early 21st Century* [*Död och dagishämtningar. En kvantitativ analys av det tidiga 2000-talets svenska kriminallitteratur*]. Uppsala: Department of Literature Sociology, 2017.

Bergman, Kerstin. *Swedish Crime Fiction: The Making of Nordic Noir*. Mimesis International, 2014.

———, ed. *The Swedish Landscape of Crime Fiction: From Scania to Lappland* [*Deckarens svenska landskap. Från Skåne till Lappland*]. Göteborg and Stockholm: Makadam, 2014.

Berntson, Lennart, and Svante Nordin. *After the Revolution: The Left in Swedish Cultural Debate Since 1968* [*Efter Revolutionen. Vänstern i svensk kulturdebatt sedan 1968*]. Stockholm: Natur & Kultur, 2017.

Bourdieu, Pierre. *Counterfire: Texts Against the Spreading of Neoliberalism* [*Moteld. Texter mot nyliberalismens utbredning*]. Stockholm: Symposion, 1999.

Broady, Donald, ed. *Fields of Culture: An Anthology* [*Kulturens fält. En antologi*]. Göteborg: Daidalos, 1998.

Brolin, David. *Reconsiderations: Swedish Left-wing Intellectuals in the Change from 70s to 80s* [*Omprövningar. Svenska vänsterintellektuella i skiftet från 70-tal till 80-tal*]. Lund: Celanders, 2015.

Bronson, Eric, ed. *The Girl with the Dragon Tattoo and Philosophy: Everything Is Fire*. Hoboken, New Jersey: John Wiley & Sons, Inc., 2012.

Burman, Anders, and Lena Lennerhed, eds. *Together: Politics, Philosophy, and Aesthetics in the 1960s and 1970s* [*Tillsammans. Politik, filosofi och estetik på 1960- och 1970-talen*]. Stockholm: Atlas, 2014.

Burstein, Dan, Arne De Keijzer, and John-Henri Holmberg, eds. *Secrets of the Tattooed Girl: The Unauthorised Guide to the Stieg Larsson Trilogy*. London: Phoenix, 2011.

Cawelti, John G. *Adventure, Mystery, and Romance*. Chicago: University of Chicago Press, 1976.

Chandler, Raymond. *The Big Sleep*. In Chandler, *Stories & Early Novels*, pp. 587–764.

———. *Later Novels & Other Writings*. Ed. Frank MacShane. New York: Library of America, 1995.

———. *The Long Goodbye*. In Chandler, *Later Novels*, pp. 417–734.

———. *Selected Letters of Raymond Chandler*. Ed. Frank MacShane. London: Macmillan, 1983.

———. *Stories & Early Novels*. Ed. Frank MacShane. New York: Library of America, 1995.

Crouch, Colin. *Post-Democracy* [*Postdemokrati*], trans. Henrik Gundenäs. Göteborg: Daidalos, 2011.

Dahl, Arne. *Blind Man's Bluff* [*Blindbock*]. Stockholm: Bonniers, 2013.

———. *Chinese Whispers* [*Viskleken*]. Stockholm: Bonniers, 2011.

———. *Last Couple Out* [*Sista paret ut*]. Stockholm: Bonniers, 2014.

———. *Musical Chairs* [*Hela havet stormar*]. Stockholm: Bonniers, 2012.
Danius, Sara. *Death of the Housewife and Other Writings* [*Husmoderns död och andra texter*]. Stockholm: Bonniers, 2014.
Davis, Mike. *City of Quartz: Excavating the Future in Los Angeles*. New York: Verso, 2006.
———. *Planet of Slums* [*Slum. Världens storstäder*]. Translated by Gunnar Sandin. Lund: Arkiv, 2007.
Derrida, Jacques. *Writing and Difference*. Translated by Alan Bass. Chicago: University of Chicago Press, 1978.
Ekman, Kajsa Ekis. *The Being and the Commodity* [*Varat och varan: Prostitution, surrogatmödraskap och den delade människan*]. Stockholm: Leopard, 2010.
Ellis, Bret Easton. *American Psycho*. London: Picador, 1991.
Ferretter, Luke. *Louis Althusser*. London: Routledge, 2006.
Fine, David. *Imagining Los Angeles: A City in Fiction*. Las Vegas: University of Nevada Press, 2004.
Forshaw, Barry. *The Man Who Left Too Soon: The Life and Works of Stieg Larsson*. London: John Blake Publishing, 2011.
———. *Nordic Noir: The Pocket Essential Guide to Scandinavian Crime Fiction, Film & TV*. Harpenden: Pocket Essentials, 2013.
Fowles, Anthony. *Raymond Chandler*. London: Greenwich Exchange, 2014.
Freedman, Carl. *The Age of Nixon: A Study in Cultural Power*. Winchester, UK: Zero Books, 2012.
———. *Critical Theory and Science Fiction*. Middletown, CN: Wesleyan University Press, 2000.
———. *The Incomplete Projects: Marxism, Modernity, and the Politics of Culture*. Middletown, CN: Wesleyan University Press, 2002.
———. *Versions of Hollywood Crime Cinema: Studies in Ford, Wilder, Coppola, Scorsese, and Others*. Bristol: Intellect, 2013.
Gabrielsson, Eva, with Marie-Françoise Colombani. *Stieg & Me: Memories of My Life with Stieg Larsson* [*Millennium, Stieg & Jag*]. Translated by Eva Gabrielsson. Stockholm: Natur & Kultur, 2011.
Geherin, David. *Scene of the Crime: The Importance of Place in Crime and Mystery Fiction*. Jefferson, NC: McFarland, 2008.
Gemzöe, Lena. *Feminism*. Stockholm: Bilda förlag, 2010.
Gustafsson, Tommy, and Pietari Kääpä, eds. *Nordic Genre Film*. Edinburgh: Edinburgh University Press, 2015.
Hedges, Chris. *Empire of Illusion: The End of Literacy and the Triumph of Spectacle*. New York: Nation Books, 2010.
Held, David. *Introduction to Critical Theory: Horkheimer to Habermas*. Oxford: Polity Press, 2004.
Hellgren, Per. *Per Wahlöö: Paving the Way for Swedish Crime Fiction* [*Nu rasar diktaturerna. Per Wahlöö och vägen till den nya kriminalromanen*]. Malmö: Universus Academic Press, 2015.
Hiney, Tom. *Raymond Chandler. A Biography*. London: Chatto & Windus, 1997.
Hirsch, Paul, ed. *The Law Enforcers*. New York: Pyramid Books, 1969.
Hobbes, Thomas. *Leviathan*. McMaster University Archive. https://socserv2.socsci.mcmaster.ca/econ/ugcm/3ll3/hobbes/Leviathan.pdf. Accessed February 23, 2015.
Hoffman, Josef. *Philosophies of Crime Fiction*. Translated by Carolyn Kelly, Nadia Majid, and Johanna Da Rocha Abreu. Harpenden: No Exit Press, 2013.
Holmberg, John-Henri, ed. *A Darker Shade of Sweden*. Translated by Holmberg. New York: The Mysterious Press, 2014.
Horsley, Lee. *Twentieth-Century Crime Fiction*. Oxford: Oxford University Press, 2005.
Jacobsen, Kirsten. *Mankell*. Translated by Inge Knutsson. Stockholm: Leopard, 2012.
Jameson, Fredric. *Raymond Chandler: The Detections of Totality*. London and New York: Verso, 2016.
Jay, Martin. *The Dialectical Imagination: A History of the Frankfurt School and the Institute of Social Research, 1923–1950*. Berkeley, Los Angeles and London: University of California Press, 1996.
Jordanova, Ludmilla. *History in Practice*. New York: Bloomsbury Academic, 2010.
Kärrholm, Sara. *The Art of Doing a Jig-saw Puzzle: The Detective Novel and the Conjuring up of Evil in the Swedish Welfare State* [*Konsten att lägga pussel. Deckaren och besvärjandet av ondskan i folkhemmet*]. Stockholm: Symposion, 2005.
Kepler, Lars. *The Rabbit Hunter* [*Kaninjägaren*]. Stockholm: Bonniers, 2016.
King, Donna, and Carrie Lee Smith, eds. *Men Who Hate Women Who Kick Their Asses: Stieg Larsson's Millennium Trilogy in Feminist Perspective*. Nashville: Vanderbilt University Press, 2012.
Knight, Stephen. *Form and Ideology in Detective Fiction*. London: Macmillan, 1980.
Knight, Stephen. *Crime Fiction Since 1800: Detection, Death, Diversity*. Second Edition. Basingstoke: Palgrave Macmillan, 2010.
Lagercrantz, David. *The Girl in the Spider's Web*. Translated by George Goulding. New York: Random House Large Print, 2015.
Lapidus, Jens. *Sthlm Delete*. Stockholm: Wahlström & Widstrand, 2015.

_____. *The VIP-Room* [*VIP-rummet*]. Stockholm: Wahlström & Widstrand, 2014.
Larsson, Stieg. *The Expo Files*. Translated by Laurie Tompson. London: Maclehose/Quercus, 2013.
_____. *The Girl Who Kicked the Hornet's Nest*. Translated by Reg Keeland. London: Quercus, 2010.
_____. *The Girl with the Dragon Tattoo*. Translated by Reg Keeland. London: Quercus, 2008.
Lenin, V.I. *Imperialism: The Highest Stage of Capitalism* [*Imperialismen som kapitalismens högsta stadium*]. Translated by Alice Wallenius. Lund: Zenit/Cavefors, 1969.
Lennerhed, Lena. *The Pursuit of Pleasure. The Sex-Debate in Sweden During the 1960s* [*Frihet att njuta. Sexualdebatten i Sverige på 1960-talet*]. Stockholm: Norstedts, 1994.
Liedman, Sven-Eric. *Between the Trivial and the Inexpressible* [*Mellan det triviala och det outsägliga*]. Göteborg: Daidalos, 1998.
_____. *Karl Marx: A Biography* [*Karl Marx. En biografi*]. Stockholm: Bonniers, 2016.
Lukács, Georg. *Victory of Realism* [*Realismens seger*]. Translated by Lars Bjurman and Carl Henning Wijkmark. Lund: Arkiv, 1983.
MacShane, Frank. *The Life of Raymond Chandler*. London: Jonathan Cape Ltd., 1976.
Mandel, Ernest. *Delightful Murder* [*Förtjusande mord. Kriminalromanens sociala historia*]. Translated by Sven Erik Täckmark. Stockholm: Alfabeta, 1985.
Mankell, Henning. *Before the Frost*. Translated by Ebba Segerberg. London: Vintage, 2005.
_____. *The Dogs of Riga* [*Hundarna i Riga*]. Stockholm: Ordfront, 1992.
_____. *The Hand* [*Handen*]. Stockholm: Leopard, 2013.
_____. *The Man Who Smiled*. Translated by Laurie Thompson. London: Vintage, 2012.
Marcuse, Herbert. *An Essay On Liberation* [*Människans befrielse*]. Translated by Göran Fredriksson. Stockholm: Aldus, 1969.
_____. *One-Dimensional Man*. London: Routledge, 2002.
_____. *Protest, Demonstration, Revolt* [*Das Ende der Utopie*]. Translated by Maj and Paul Frisch. Stockholm: Aldus Bonniers, 1968.
Marx, Karl. *Capital: A Critique of Political Economy. Vol. 1.* Translated by Ben Fowkes. London: Penguin, 1990.
_____. *Early Writings*. Translated by Rodney Livingstone and Gregor Benton. London: Penguin, 1992.
Marx, Karl, and Friedrich Engels. *The Communist Manifesto*. Translated by Samuel Moore. London: Penguin, 2015.
McCann, Sean. *Gumshoe America: Hard-Boiled Crime Fiction and the Rise and Fall of New Deal Liberalism*. Durham: Duke University Press, 2000.
Messent, Peter. *The Crime Fiction Handbook*. Chichester: John Wiley & Sons, 2013.
Mouffe, Chantal. *On the Political* [*Om det politiska*]. Translated by Oskar Söderlind. Hägersten: Tankekraft, 2008.
Nestingen, Andrew, and Paula Arvas, eds. *Scandinavian Crime Fiction*. Cardiff: University of Wales Press, 2011.
Nilsson, Roddy. *Foucault: An Introduction*. Malmö: Egalité, 2008.
Nordin, Svante. *The History of Philosophy* [*Filosofins historia*]. Lund: Studentlitteratur, 2009.
_____. *The Philosophers: The Western Thinking Since Year 1900* [*Filosoferna. Det västerländska tänkandet sedan år 1900*]. Stockholm: Atlantis, 2011.
Paulsen, Roland. *The Labor Society: How Labor Survived Technology* [*Arbetssamhället. Hur arbetet överlevde teknologin*]. Malmö: Gleerups, 2010.
Peacock, Steven, ed. *Stieg Larsson's Millennium Trilogy: Interdisciplinary Approaches to Nordic Noir on Page and Screen*. New York: Palgrave Macmillan, 2013.
Pepper, Andrew. *The Contemporary American Crime Novel: Race, Ethnicity, Gender, Class*. Edinburgh: Edinburgh University Press, 2000.
_____. *Unwilling Executioner: Crime Fiction and the State*. Oxford: Oxford University Press, 2016.
Petrov, Kristian. *Back to the Future: Modernity, Postmodernity, and Generational Identity in Gorbachev's Glasnost and Perestroika* [*Tillbaka till framtiden. Modernitet, postmodernitet och generationsidentitet i Gorbacevs glasnost och perestrojka*]. Huddinge: Södertörn University, 2006.
Pettersson, Jan-Erik. *Stieg. From Activist to Author* [*Stieg Larsson. Journalisten, författaren, idealisten*]. Stockholm: Telegram bokförlag, 2010.
Polanyi, Karl. *The Great Transformation: The Political and Economic Origins of Our Time*. Boston: Beacon Press, 2001.
Porter, Dennis. *The Pursuit of Crime: Art and Ideology in Detective Fiction*. New Haven, CT: Yale University Press, 1981.
Pynchon, Thomas. *The Crying of Lot 49*. New York: Bantam, 1972.
Roslund, Anders, and Börge Hellström. *Box 21*. Stockholm: Piratförlaget, 2005.
_____. *The Girl Below the Street* [*Flickan under gatan*]. Stockholm: Piratförlaget, 2007.
_____. *Three Minutes* [*Tre minuter*]. Stockholm: Piratförlaget, 2016.
_____. *Three Seconds*. Translated by Kari Dickson. London: Quercus, 2011.

———. *Two Soldiers* [*Två soldater*]. Stockholm: Piratförlaget, 2012.
———. *Two Soldiers*. Translated by Kari Dickson. London: Quercus, 2014.
Rzepka, Charles J. *Detective Fiction*. Cambridge: Polity, 2005.
Scaggs, John. *Crime Fiction*. London: Routledge, 2005.
Sjöwall, Maj, and Per Wahlöö. *The Abominable Man*. Translated by Thomas Teal. New York: Vintage, 2009.
———. *The Fire Engine That Disappeared*. Translated by Joan Tate. New York: Vintage, 1977.
———. *The Man Who Went Up in Smoke* [*Mannen som gick upp i rök*]. Stockholm: Piratförlaget, 2012.
———. *Murder at the Savoy*. Translated by Amy and Ken Koespel. New York: Vintage, 2009.
———. *The Terrorists*. Translated by Joan Tate. New York: Vintage, 2013.
Sloterdijk, Peter. *Critique of Cynical Reason*. Minneapolis: University of Minnesota Press, 1987.
Søholm, Ejgil. *Novel of a Crime: Sjöwall-Wahlöö's Work and Reality* [*Roman om en forbrydelse. Sjöwall/Wahlöö's værk og virkelighed*]. Copenhagen: Spektrum, 1976.
Steinbeck, John. *The Grapes of Wrath*. New York: Penguin, 1978.
Sund, Erik Axl. *The Crow Girl*. London: Vintage, 2017.
Tapper, Michael. *The Cop in the Twilight Land: Swedish Police Narratives in Novels and Film 1965–2010* [*Snuten i skymningslandet. Svenska polisberättelser i roman och film 1965–2010*]. Lund: Nordic Academic Press, 2011.
———. *Swedish Cops: From Sjöwall & Wahlöö to Stieg Larsson*. Chicago: Intellect, 2014.
Therborn, Göran. *From Marxism to Post-Marxism*. London: Verso, 2008.
———. *The Ideology of Power and the Power of Ideology* [*Maktens ideologi och ideologins makt*]. Lund: Zenit, 1981.
———. *The Killing Fields of Inequality* [*Ojämlikhet dödar*]. Translated by Henrik Gundenäs. Lund: Arkiv, 2016.
Trotsky, Leon. *The Age of Permanent Revolution* [*Den permanenta revolutionens epok*]. Edited by Isaac Deutscher. Translated by Kenth-Åke Andersson, Martin Peterson, Magnus Hedlund, and Lars Lindvall. Mölndal: Partisan, 1969.
———. *Literature and Revolution*. Translated by Magnus Hedlund and Lars Lindvall. Mölndal: Partisan, 1969.
Van Dover, J. Kenneth. *Polemical Pulps: The Martin Beck Novels of Maj Sjöwall and Per Wahlöö*. San Bernadino, CA: Brownstone Books, 1993.

Wahlöö, Per. *The Assignment*. Translated by Joan Tate. New York: Vintage, 2013.
———. *Murder on the Thirty-First Floor*. Translated by Sarah Death. New York: Vintage, 2013.
———. *A Necessary Action*. Translated by Joan Tate. New York: Vintage, 2013.
———. *The Steel Spring*. Translated by Sarah Death. London: Vintage, 2011.
Wald, Alan M. *Writing from the Left: New Essays on Radical Culture and Politics*. London: Verso, 1994.
Werth, Nicolas. *Cannibal Island: Death in a Siberian Gulag*. Princeton, NJ: Princeton University Press, 2007.
Wiklund, Martin. *In the Landscape of Modernity* [*I det modernas landskap. Historisk orientering och kritiska berättelser om det moderna Sverige mellan 1960 och 1990*]. Stockholm: Symposion, 2006.
Williams, Tom. *A Mysterious Something in the Light: The Life of Raymond Chandler*. Chicago: Chicago Review Press, 2012.
Zaremba, Maciej. *The Price of the Patient: A Report on the Swedish Healthcare and the Market* [*Patientens pris. Ett reportage om den svenska sjukvården och marknaden.*]. Stockholm: Weyler, 2013.
Žižek, Slavoj. *The Sublime Object of Ideology* [*Ideologins sublima objekt*]. Translated by Lars Nylander. Göteborg: Glänta, 2001.
Åström, Berit, Katarina Gregersdotter, and Tanya Horeck, eds. *Rape in Stieg Larsson's Millennium Trilogy and Beyond: Contemporary Scandinavian and Anglophone Crime Fiction*. Basingstoke: Palgrave Macmillan, 2012.

Articles and Essays

Ahlbäck Öberg, Shirin, and Sten Widmalm. "NPM in Swedish" [NPM på Svenska]. In Zaremba, *The Price of the Patient*, pp. 122–153.
Åkesson, Johan. "We Live the Best Lives in the World" [Vi lever världens bästa liv]. *Dagens Nyheter*, November 27, 2011, pp. 10–17.
Althusser, Louis. "Ideology and Ideological State Apparatuses (Notes Towards an Investigation)." Translated by Ben Brewster. *Marxists Internet Archive*. www.marxists.org/reference/archive/althusser/1970/ideology.htm. Accessed June 29, 2015.
Anderson, Patrick. "Lars Kepler's The Hypnotist: Thriller Is a Disturbing Meditation on Evil." Review of *The Hypnotist* by Lars Kepler. *Washington Post*, July 17, 2011. www.washingtonpost.com/entertainment/books/lars-keplers-the-hypnotist-thriller-is-a-disturbing-meditation-on-evil/2011/07/05/

gIQAOeIdKI_story.html?utm_term=.017bafc88934. Accessed July 20, 2017.

———. Review of *Box 21*, by Roslund & Hellström. *Washington Post*, October 19, 2009. www.washingtonpost.com/wp-dyn/content/article/2009/10/18/AR2009101801843.html. Accessed February 13, 2017.

Andersson, Carl Erland. "A Sure Success" [En säker framgång]. Review of *The Hypnotist*, by Lars Kepler, *Göteborgs-Posten*, July 24, 2009, p. 54.

Arvas, Paula. "Next to the Final Frontier: Russians in Contemporary Finnish and Scandinavian Crime Fiction." In Nestingen & Arvas, *Scandinavian Crime Fiction*, pp. 115–127.

Barnfield, Graham. "The Urban Landscape of Marxist Noir." *Crime Time*, June 26, 2002. www.crimetime.co.uk/features/marxistnoir.html. Accessed January 13, 2017.

Beekman, E.M. "Raymond Chandler & an American Genre." *The Massachusetts Review*, vol. 14, no. 1, Winter 1973, pp. 149–173. *JSTOR*: www.jstor.org/stable/25088327. Accessed July 8, 2013.

Bergman, Kerstin. "The Well-Adjusted Cops of the New Millennium: Neo-Romantic Tendencies in the Swedish Police Procedural." In Nestingen & Arvas, *Scandinavian Crime Fiction*, pp. 34–45.

Björk, Nina. "The Dream of Control" [Drömmen om kontroll]. Review of *The Millennium Trilogy* by Stieg Larsson. *Dagens Nyheter*, April 19, 2008, pp. 6–7.

Blomkvist, Per. "Transferring Technology—Shaping Ideology. American Traffic Engineering and Commercial Interests in the Establishment of a Swedish Car Society 1945–1965." *Comparative Technology Transfer and Society*, vol. 2, no. 3, September 2004, pp. 273–302. Project Muse, doi:10.1353/ctt.2005.0001. Accessed November 20, 2012.

Blomqvist, Håkan. 2011. "Stieg Larsson. The Excavating Socialist" [Stieg Larsson. Den grävande socialisten]. *Internationalen*, no. 17, April 29, 2011. www.internationalen.se/2011/05/stieg-larsson-den-gravande-socialisten/. Accessed January 5, 2017.

Boda, Lisa. "Social Criticism—An Obvious Part in the Writing" [Samhällskritik—en självklar del i skrivandet]. *Nya Ludvika Tidning*, November 25, 2011, p. 19.

Borglund, Tore. "The Crime Exposes Society" [Brottet avslöjar samhället]. *Metallarbetaren*, no. 2–3, 1973, pp. 38–39.

Burstein, Dan. "The Moral Geography of Stieg Larsson." In Burstein et al. *Secrets*, pp. 321–329.

Burstein, De Keijzer, Holmberg. "What You're Afraid of Has Already Happened." In Burstein et al. *Secrets*, pp. 123–128.

Caffrey, Andrew. Review of *The Nightmare*, by Lars Kepler, *Boston Globe*, July 11, 2012. www.bostonglobe.com/arts/books/2012/07/11/the-nightmare-lars-kepler/457wtd2u2F6Owz04A3PW1J/story.html. Accessed April 4, 2017.

Campbell, Beatrix. "A Feminist Sexual Politics: Now You See It. Now You Don't." *Feminist Review*, no. 5, 1980, pp. 1–18. *JSTOR*: www.jstor.org/stable/1394695. Accessed March 30, 2016.

Chandler, Raymond. "The Simple Art of Murder." In Chandler, *Later Novels*, pp. 977–992.

———. "Twelve Notes on the Mystery Novel." In Chandler, *Later Novels*, pp. 1004–1011.

Child, Lee. Review of *The Girl in the Spider's Web*, by David Lagercrantz, *New York Times* (Sunday Book Review), September 1, 2015. www.nytimes.com/2015/09/06/books/review/the-girl-in-the-spiders-web-by-david-lagercrantz.html. Accessed January 19, 2017.

Clark, Susan Storer. "An Interview with Erik Axl Sund." *Washington Independent*, July 12, 2016. www.washingtonindependentreviewofbooks.com/features/an-interview-with-erik-axl-sund. Accessed June 23, 2017.

Crouch, Colin. "Markets, power and politics: Is there a liberalism beyond social democracy?" *Policy Network*, May 5, 2011, pp. 19–24. www.policy-network.net/pno_detail.aspx?ID=3997&title=Is+there+a+liberalism+beyond+social+democracy%3f. Accessed July 20, 2017.

Cullberg, Jonas. "The Ahndoril Couple is Lars Kepler" [Paret Ahndoril är Lars Kepler]. *Svenska Dagbladet*, August 12, 2009, p. 4.

Dahl, Arne. "Introduction." In Sjöwall and Wahlöö, *Murder at the Savoy*, pp. ix–xiii.

Danius, Sara. "Goethe in Hollywood." In Danius, *Death of the Housewife*, pp. 165–184.

Domellöf-Wik, Maria, and Martin Erlandsson. "Writing Together Became a New Love" [Att skriva ihop blev en ny förälskelse]. *Göteborgs-Posten*, November 12, 2016, pp. 54–55.

Ekelund, Alexander. "The Struggle on Science: The Advance of Althusserianism and the Scientific Theoretical Debate of the Swedish 1968-Left" [Kampen om vetenskapen. Althusserianismens frammarsch och den svenska 1968-vänsterns vetenskapsteoretiska debatt]. In Burman & Lennerhed, *Together*, pp. 191–229.

Eklund, Stefan. "Detective Lady" [Deckardam]. *Svenska Dagbladet*, June 19, 2010, pp. 6–7.

Farabee, Mindy. "Swedish Thriller Skews Sexy." Review of *The Hypnotist*, by Lars Kepler, *Los Angeles Times*, July 14, 2011. http://articles.latimes.com/2011/jul/14/entertainment/la-et-book-20110714. Accessed July 20, 2017.

Fauvellered, Louise. "I Would Rather Work with People than Money" [Jag jobbar hellre med människor än pengar]. *Jusektidningen Karriär*, no. 9, Dec. 2015, p. 38.

Fister, Barbara. "The Millennium Trilogy and the American Serial Killer Narrative: Investigating Protagonists of Men Who Write Women." In Åström et al., *Rape in Stieg Larsson's Millennium Trilogy*, pp. 34–50.

Flood, Alison. "The Crow Girl by Erik Axl Sund Review—Relentlessly Disturbing." *The Guardian*, April 26, 2016. www.theguardian.com/books/2016/apr/26/the-crow-girl-erik-axl-sund-review. Accessed July 5, 2017.

Forshaw, Barry. Review of *Easy Money*, by Jens Lapidus. *The Independent*. February 29, 2012. www.independent.co.uk/arts-entertainment/books/reviews/easy-money-by-jens-lapidus-7462465.html. Accessed July 20, 2017.

———. Review of *The Crow Girl*, by Erik Axl Sund, *Financial Times*, April 29, 2016. www.ft.com/content/ec71c72a-0b99-11e6-b0f1-61f222853ff3?mhq5j=e1. Accessed July 5, 2017.

———. Review of *Three Seconds*, by Roslund & Hellström, *The Independent*, November 2, 2010. www.independent.co.uk/arts-entertainment/books/reviews/three-seconds-by-roslund-and-hellstr-m-2122519.html. Accessed February 13, 2017.

———. Review of *Two Soldiers*, by Roslund & Hellström. *The Independent*, July 1, 2013. www.independent.co.uk/arts-entertainment/books/reviews/review-two-soldiers-by-roslund-hellstr-m-quercus-1699-8682019.html. Accessed February 13, 2017.

France, Louise. "The Queen of Crime." *The Observer*, November 22, 2009. www.theguardian.com/books/2009/nov/22/crime-thriller-maj-sjowall-sweden. Accessed May 23, 2014.

Freedman, Carl, and Christopher Kendrick. "Labor and Politics in Dashiell Hammett's *Red Harvest*." In Freedman, *Incomplete Projects*, pp. 127–146.

Freedman, Carl. "Marxist Theory, Radical Pedagogy, and the Reification of Thought." *College English*, vol. 49, no. 1, Jan. 1987, pp. 70–82. JSTOR: www.jstor.org/stable/377790. Accessed February 1, 2013.

———. "Science Fiction and Critical Theory." *Science Fiction Studies*, vol. 14, no. 2, July 1987, pp. 180–200. JSTOR: www.jstor.org/stable/4239815. Accessed February 1, 2013.

———. "The Strongest Link: SF as Social Register." *Science Fiction Studies*, vol. 30, no. 2, July 2003, pp. 176–178. JSTOR: www.jstor.org/stable/4241166. Accessed February 1, 2013.

Gregersdotter, Katarina. "The Body, Hopelessness, and Nostalgia: Representations of Rape and the Welfare State in Swedish Crime Fiction." In Åström, Berit et al., ed. *Rape in Stieg Larsson's Millennium Trilogy*, pp. 81–96.

Greider, Göran. "The Socialist Stieg Larsson Has Been Erased" [Socialisten Stieg Larsson har raderats]. *Expressen*, August 27, 2015. www.expressen.se/debatt/socialisten-stieg-larsson-har-raderats/. Accessed February 23, 2017.

Grossman, Lev. "Grand Larssony." *Time Magazine*. June 27, 2011. http://content.time.com/time/magazine/article/0,9171,2078113,00.html. Accessed April 6, 2017.

Hagberg, Mattias. "Raymond Chandler and the Moral Darkness of Nordic Noir" [Raymond Chandler och den nordiska noir-genrens moraliska mörker]. *Sveriges Radio P1*, September 9, 2014. http://sverigesradio.se/sida/artikel.aspx?programid=503&artikel=5959419. Accessed July 18, 2017.

Hagström, Johanna. "This is My Masterpiece" [Det här är mitt storverk]. *Göteborgs-Posten*, July 5, 2014, pp. 46–47.

Hansson, Beata. "Curious in a Cone" [Nyfiken i en strut]. *Arbetaren*, no. 26, June/July 2014, pp. 16–18.

Hellgren, Per. "'Gone to Earth' 1975: Sexuality and Ideology in the Last Words of Per Wahlöö." *Ideas in History: Journal of the Nordic Society for the History of Ideas*, vol. 9, no. 1–2, 2015, pp. 121–145.

———. "Last Words 1975: Per Wahlöö and the Book That Went Up in Smoke." *Clues: A Journal of Detection*, vol. 33, no. 2, 2015, pp. 118–127.

Holmberg, John-Henri. "The Man Who Inhaled Crime Fiction." In Burstein et al. *Secrets*, pp. 99–105.

———. "The Stieg Larsson Story." In Burstein et al. *Secrets*, pp. 237–293.

Hughes, Declan. "Nice Plot, Shame About the Pronouns, Verbs, Articles." Review of *Easy Money*, by Jens Lapidus. Irish Times, January 7, 2012. www.irishtimes.com/culture/books/nice-plot-shame-about-the-pronouns-verbs-articles-1.441133. Accessed July 27, 2017.

Irhede, Ann-Charlotte. "We Had Fallen Out as Hell" [Vi var så in i helvete osams]. *Corren*, October 31, 2016. www.corren.se/kultur-noje/vi-var-sa-in-i-helvete-osams-om4361027.aspx. Accessed February 13, 2017.

Jensen, Carsten. "Lisbeth Salander and Our Yearning for Revenge" [Lisbeth Salander och vår längtan efter hämnd]. *Dagens Nyheter*, Sthlm edition, December 20, 2009, pp. 12–13.

Johnson, Mats. "Terrorism Reaches Sweden" [Terrorismen når Sverige]. Review of *Afterquake*, by Arne Dahl. *Göteborgs-Posten*, September 13, 2006, p. 90.

Karlsson, Johanna. "Sweden's Most Wanted Author Speaks Out" [Sveriges mest eftersökta författare talar ut]. *Helsingborgs Dagblad*, August 22, 2009. www.hd.se/2009-08-22/sveriges-mest-eftersokta-forfattare-talar-ut. Accessed April 21, 2017.

Kaveh, Shamal. "Together Towards the Promised Land of Entrepreneurship: Foucault on Neoliberalism" [Tillsammans mot entreprenörskapets förlovade land. Foucault om ny liberalismen]. In Burman & Lennerhed, *Together*, pp. 591–624.

Keetley, Dawn. "Unruly Bodies: The Politics of Sex in Maj Sjöwall and Per Wahlöö's Martin Beck Series." *Clues: A Journal of Detection*, vol. 30, no. 1, 2012, pp. 54–64.

Klemetz, Elin. "When Fiction Exceeds Reality" [När dikten överträffar verkligheten]. *Filter*, no. 50, June/July 2016, pp. 134–142.

Lagercrantz, David. "I Was Grabbed by an Obsession" [Jag greps av en tvångstanke]. *Dagens Nyheter*. August 2, 2015, pp. 4–9.

Lapidus, Jens. "Introduction." In Sjöwall & Wahlöö, *The Abominable Man*, pp. vii–x.

Larsson, Stieg, Stig Eriksson, and Martin Fahlgren. "A Welcome Sobering Up" [Välkommen tillnyktring]. *Internationalen*, no. 48, 1983, pp. 4–5. www.marxistarkiv.se/skribenter/stieg_larsson/stieg_larsson.pdf. Accessed February 2, 2017.

Larsson, Stieg (Severin). "The Nightingale Who Sang the Death Song of Capitalism" [Näktergalen som fick sjunga kapitalismens dödssång]. *Internationalen*, no. 42, October 15, 1980, pp. 8–9.

Larsson, Stieg. "Swedish and Un-Swedish Violence Towards Women." In Larsson, *The Expo Files*, pp. 129–156.

Lenin, V.I. "May Day Action by the Revolutionary Proletariat." Translated by George Hanna. *Marxists Internet Archive*. www.marxists.org/archive/lenin/works/1913/jun/15.htm. Accessed July 12, 2014.

Leonardz, Jenny. "Lawyer Tracked the Cocaine" [Jurist kom kokainet på spåren]. *Svenska Dagbladet*, July 26, 2006, p. 56.

Maher, John. "Knopf Announces Fifth Book in Larsson's Millennium Series." *Publishers Weekly*, April 11, 2017. https://www.publishersweekly.com/pw/by-topic/industry-news/book-deals/article/73306-knopf-to-publish-fifth-book-in-millennium-series.html. Accessed February 3, 2018.

Marcuse, Herbert. "Some Social Implications of Modern Technology." In Arato and Gebhardt, *Essential Frankfurt School Reader*, pp. 138–162.

Maslin, Janet. "Stoking the Fire Larsson Ignited." Review of *Three Seconds*, by Roslund & Hellström, *New York Times*, January 5, 2011. www.nytimes.com/2011/01/06/books/06book.html. Accessed February 13, 2017.

McCorristine, Shane. "The Place of Pessimism in Henning Mankell's Kurt Wallander Series." In Nestingen & Arvas, *Scandinavian*, pp. 77–88.

Memmott, Carol. "Duo's 'Three Seconds' does Stieg Larsson one better." Review of *Three Seconds*, by Roslund & Hellström, *USA Today*, March 1, 2011. http://books.usatoday.com/book/roslund—hellstrom-three-seconds/r145257. Accessed February 17, 2017.

Nestingen, Andrew. "Unnecessary Officers: Realism, Melodrama and Scandinavian Crime Fiction in Transition." In Nestingen & Arvas, *Scandinavian*, pp. 171–183.

Norberg, Johan. "David Lagercrantz: 'All hysterical!'" [David Lagercrantz: "Helt hysteriskt!"]. *Tidningen Vi*, no. 9, 2015, pp. 14–23.

Östberg, Kjell. "Sweden and the Long '1968': Break or Continuity?" *Scandinavian Journal of History*, vol. 33, no. 4, Dec. 2008, pp. 339–352.

Östlund, David. 2014. "Back to the Future? Technology, Communication, and Reason in the Age of Television" [Tillbaka till framtiden? Teknik, kommunikation och förnuft i teveåldern]. In Burman & Lennerhed, *Together*, pp. 263–314.

Palmqvist, Mats. "Roslund & Hellström Become Nagging" [Roslund & Hellström blir tjatiga]. Review of *Three Minutes*, by Roslund & Hellström, *Smålandsposten*. June 2, 2016, p. 24.

Parks, Tim. "The Moralist." Review of *The Millennium Trilogy*, by Stieg Larsson. *The New York Review of Books*, June 9, 2011. www.nybooks.com/articles/2011/06/09/moralist-stieg-larsson/?printpage=true. Accessed July 24, 2017.

Percy, Benjamin. "A Serial Killer Stalks Stockholm in This Creepy Nordic Noir." Review of *The Crow Girl*, by Erik Axl Sund, *New York Times*, July 27, 2016. www.nytimes.com/2016/07/31/books/review/erik-axl-sund-crow-girl.html?_r=0. Accessed July 5, 2017.

Persson, Magnus. "Skillfully Made Entertainment Violence" [Skickligt utfört underhållningsvåld]. Review of *The Hypnotist*, by Lars Kepler, *Svenska Dagbladet*, July 29, 2009, p. 6.

Planhammar, Per. "Sharply on a Tsunami of Violence" [Skarpt om tsunami av våld]. Review of *Two Soldiers* by Roslund & Hellström, *Göteborgs-Posten*, June 3, 2012, p. 85.

Richter, David H. "Background Action and Ideology: Grey Men and Dope Doctors in Raymond Chandler." *Narrative*, vol. 2, no. 1, Jan. 1994, pp. 29–40. *JSTOR*: www.jstor.org/stable/20107022. Accessed July 8, 2013.

Risen, James, and Mark Mazzetti. "30 False Fronts Won Contracts for Blackwater." *New York Times*, September 3, 2010. www.nytimes.

com/2010/09/04/world/middleeast/04 blackwater.html. Accessed May 8, 2017.

Roslund, Anders, and Börge Hellström. "Preface." In Sjöwall & Wahlöö, *The Man Who Went Up*, pp. 5–10.

Schuessler, Jennifer. "Inside the List." Review of *The Hypnotist*, by Lars Kepler, *New York Times*, July 8, 2011. www.nytimes.com/2011/07/17/books/review/inside-the-list.html. Accessed April 12, 2017.

Schwartz, Nils. "Dahl's Great Swedish Dystopia" [Dahls stora svenska dystopi]. Review of *Last Couple Out*, by Arne Dahl, *Dagens Nyheter*, June 16, 2014, p. 6.

Schwartz, Nils. Review of *Two Soldiers*, by Roslund & Hellström, *Expressen*, May 18, 2012. www.expressen.se/kultur/roslundhellstromtva-soldater/. Accessed February 13, 2017.

Sjögren, Henrik. "Studies in Dictatorship" [Studier i diktatur]. *Kvällsposten*, June 30, 1962, p. 4.

Sjöholm, Carina. "Scania: The Landscape Between Fact and Fiction" [Skåne. Landskapet mellan fakta och fiktion. Henning Mankell]. In Bergman, Kerstin, ed. *The Swedish Landscape of Crime Fiction*, pp. 13–21.

Sjöwall, Maj, and Per Wahlöö. "Renewal of the Crime Novel" [Kriminalromanens förnyelse]. *Jury*, vol. 1, no. 1, 1972, pp. 9–11.

Span, Guy. "Paving the Way for Buses—The Great GM Streetcar Conspiracy. Part II—The Plot Clots." *Bay Crossings*, May 2003. www.baycrossings.com/Archives/2003/04_May/paving_the_way_for_buses_the_great_gm_streetcar_conspiracy.htm. Accessed January 5, 2015.

Stenberg, Björn G. "It's Infernally Exciting" [Det är infernaliskt spännande]. Review of *Three Minutes*, by Roslund & Hellström, *Uppsala Nya Tidning*, June 4, 2016. http://www.unt.se/kultur-noje/litteratur/det-ar-infernaliskt-spannande-4244770.aspx. Accessed July 27, 2017.

Stenberg, Jens. "Final Word: Jens Lapidus" [Sista ordet: Jens Lapidus]. *Café*, June 2014, p. 170.

Stertman, Hans. "The Hardworking Couple" [Det strävsamma paret]. *Jury*, no. 2, 1972, pp. 37–39.

Svedjedal, Johan. "New Millennium is Skillful and Respectful" [Nya Millennium är skicklig och respektfull]. Review of *The Girl in the Spider's Web*, by David Lagercrantz, *Dagens Nyheter*, August 29, 2015, pp. 4–5.

Svensson, Julia. "Writing is Like Resurrecting the Dead" [Att skriva är som att återuppväcka de döda]. *Sydsvenskan*, August 22, 2009, pp. 6–7.

Söderberg, Noa. "The Fifth Millennium Book Passes the Million Barrier" [Femte Millenniumboken går över miljonstrecket]. *Dagens Nyheter*, October 11, 2017.https://www.dn.se/kultur-noje/femte-millenniumboken-garover-miljonstrecket/. Accessed January 8, 2018.

Tapper, Michael. "Stockholm Noir: Neoliberalism as Gangsterism in *Easy Money*." In Gustafsson and Kääpä. *Nordic Genre Film*, pp. 104–118.

———. "With the Cop Under the Magnifying Glass" [Med snuten under förstoringsglaset]. *Gaudeamus*, November 14, 2011. www.gaudeamus.se/2011/11/med-snuten-underforstoringsglaset/. Accessed July 18, 2017.

Taylor, Kate. "Meet the Swedish Crime Writers Not Named Larsson." *The Globe and Mail*, February 25, 2011. www.theglobeandmail.com/arts/books-and-media/meet-theswedish-crime-writers-not-named-larsson/article568187/. Accessed February 13, 2017.

Therborn, Göran. 1966. "Society as Corporation—Towards a One-Dimensional Society" [Samhället som aktiebolag—Mot ett endimensionellt samhälle]. *Zenit*, no. 2–3, 1966, pp. 4–7.

Tirén, Sverker, and Eva-Lena Neiman. "I Want to be a Cheerful Reptile" [Jag vill vara en gladlynt reptil]. *Bonniers Litterära Magasin*, vol. 47, no. 1, 1978, pp. 32–37.

Torén Björling, Sanna. "Sanna Torén Björling Meets Jan Arnald" [Sanna Torén Björling möter Jan Arnald]. *Dagens Nyheter*, June 12, 2011, p. 6.

Trotsky, Leon. "The Social Roots and the Social Function of Literature." *Marxists Internet Archive*. www.marxists.org/archive/trotsky/1923/art/tia23b.htm. Accessed July 18, 2017.

Unknown author. "Interview with Roslund & Hellström." CrimeHouse.com. April 27, 2011. www.thecrimehouse.com/interview-withroslund-hellstrom/. Accessed July 18, 2017.

Wahlöö, Per. "An Ordinary Swedish Boy" [En vanlig svensk grabb]. *Göteborgs Handels och Sjöfartstidning*, May 13, 1954, p. 4.

———. "Propaganda for the Right of the Fist" [Propaganda för nävrätt]. *Östersunds-Posten*, October 28, 1957, p. 4.

Wald, Alan. "Marxism in Noir: The Culture Politics of Race and Class Struggle of the 1940s." *International Socialist Review*, no. 101, July 2016, pp. 137–152.

Wennberg, Anders. "Detail-Jerker and Synopsis-Håkan" [Detalj-Jerker och Synopsis-Håkan]. *Gefle Dagblad*, May 23, 2011, p. 19.

Wesslén, Gunnar. "Arne Dahl Was Born Out of Political Rage" [Arne Dahl föddes ur politisk vrede]. *Dagens ETC*, May 23, 2016, p. 20–21.

Wilson, Laura. "Crime Roundup—Reviews." Review of *The Hypnotist*, by Lars Kepler, *The*

Guardian, May 28, 2011. www.theguardian.com/books/2011/may/28/crime-review-roundup-laura-wilson. Accessed April 5, 2017.

Woods, Paula L. "Book review 'Three Seconds.'" Review of *Three Seconds*, by Roslund & Hellström. Special to *Los Angeles Times*, January 30, 2011. http://articles.latimes.com/2011/jan/30/entertainment/la-ca-anders-roslund-20110130. Accessed February 13, 2017.

Žižek, Slavoj. "Henning Mankell, the Artist of the Parallax View." Lacan.com, 2005. www.lacan.com/zizekmankell.htm. Accessed July 18, 2017.

Zumoff, J.A. "Politics and the 1920s Writings of Dashiell Hammett." *American Studies*, vol. 52, no. 1, 2012, pp. 77–98. *Project Muse*: doi: 10.1353/ams.2012.0012.

Theses

Leivo, Janne Osmo Henrik. *Reflections on Swedish Society in Beck Television Detective Series in the Early 2000s*. Master's Thesis. University of Helsinki, Faculty of Social Studies, 2016. https://helda.helsinki.fi/bitstream/handle/10138/167180/Leivo_mediaandglobalcommunication.pdf?sequence=1. Accessed July 12, 2017.

Short Stories

Larsson, Stieg. "Brain Power." Translated by John-Henri Holmberg. In Holmberg, *A Darker Shade of Sweden*, pp. 173–191.

Correspondence

Wald, Alan. E-mail to the author, June 18, 2017.
Therborn, Göran. E-mail to the author, May 11, 2017.

Internet

www.drought.unl.edu
www.henningmankell.com
www.larskepler.com
www.norstedts.se/millennium
www.salomonssonagency.se
https://en.wikipedia.org/wiki/G%C3%B6ran_Therborn
www.umu.se

Index

Adler-Olsen, Jussi 9
Adorno, Theodor W. 10, 14, 16–18, 20, 23, 26, 44, 45, 52–53, 58, 73, 82, 119, 127, 208, 226n23, 231n96; *see also* Frankfurt School
Ahl, Kennet 150
Ahlbäck Öberg, Shirin 88
Ahndoril, Alexander 190, 192, 193, 204, 205; *The Diplomat* (novel) 192, 193; *The Director* (novel) 193–194; *see also* Kepler, Lars
Ajvide Lindqvist, John 190
Alfredsson, Karin 150
Algren, Nelson 71
alienation 19, 20, 22, 23, 50, 57, 59, 60, 68, 73, 74, 75–77, 83, 96–97, 141, 143, 152, 212, 213
Althusser, Louis 16, 17, 61, 77, 78, 105, 208, 212; on ideology 21–23
Alvtegen, Karin 95, 212
American Pyscho (novel) *see* Ellis, Bret Easton
Amiel, Jon 198
Anderson, Patrick 132, 195
Anderson, Perry 17
Andersson, Carl Erland 195, 200
Angleton, James Jesus 113, 173
anticolonialism 42, 73, 78, 90, 153
anti-Vietnam War Movement 81, 98, 112
Aristophanes 125
Aristotle 53, 169
Arnald, Jan 164, 190, 234n1; *see also* Dahl, Arne
Arvidsson, Tomas 150
Asimov, Isaac 125, 169
Asplund, Johan 31
Assange, Julian 123
Attenborough, Richard 72
Ausonius, John 99, 129
Autopia 36–38; Swedish Autopia 55–58, 119
Axlander Sundquist, Håkan 150, 215, 217, 237n27; *see also* Sund, Erik Axl

Baader-Meinhof gang 101, 175
Bakhtin, Mikhail 18

Baksi, Kurdo 12, 107
Baldacci, David 194
Balibar, Étienne 17
Ballard, J.G. 169
Ballinger, Bill S. 70
Balzac, Honoré de 30, 31, 34, 47, 128, 137, 155, 169
Banham, Reyner 37–38
Banville, John 123
Barthes, Roland 17, 237n8
Baudrillard, Jean 105, 109
Bauman, Zygmunt 17
Baumgarten, Bernice 35
Beekman, E.M. 48
behaviorism 199
Benjamin, Walter 10, 17
Berglund, Karl 10, 12
Bergman, Ingmar 92, 193
Bergman, Kerstin 12, 15, 91, 92, 109, 154, 162, 165
Bergström, Lasse 96
Berkeley, George E. 71
Berkowitz, David 218
Berry, John 26
Beukes, Lauren 233n30
Bezzerides, A.I. 45
Bildt, Carl 113
Birkegaard, Mikkel 9
Björk, Nina 118–120
Black Mask (magazine) 33
Blackwater (company) 88, 173, 179
Blaedel, Sara 9
Blix, Hans 193
Bloch, Ernst 10, 17, 18
Blomkvist, Per 57–58
Bodström, Thomas 150
The Boston Strangler (book) *see* Frank, Gerold
The Boston Strangler (film) 197
Boström, Severin 102, 103
Bourdieu, Pierre 17, 155, 161

247

bourgeois crime writers (Swedish) 8, 162, 211–212
The Bourne Identity: film 191; novel 119
Bradbury, Ray 111
Brahe, Tycho 193
Bratt, Peter 98
Brecht, Bertholt 52; estrangement-effect 54
Brenner, Robert 230*n*12
The Bridge (TV series) 9, 15
Bronson, Eric 13
Brown, Dan 96
Bryson, Valerie 17
Bundy, Ted 198, 199
Burstein, Dan 97
Bush Administration 100, 173
Butler, Octavia 169
Börjlind, Cilla 144, 150, 212, 214, 234*n*41, 237*n*11
Börjlind, Rolf 144, 150, 212, 214, 234*n*41, 237*n*11

Caffrey, Andrew 196
Cain, James M. 14, 26, 32, 42, 45, 136, 223*n*47
Calvin, John 40
Camp, William 71
Campbell, Beatrix 17, 107
Camus, Albert 11
capital-labor conflict 42; *see also* class issues; Marxism
Capone, Al 40, 56, 86
Capote, Truman 71, 72
Car Society 36–38, 55–58, 119
Carlotto, Massimo 233*n*30
Carlsson, Christoffer 150
Carlsson, Ingvar 113
Carpenter, John 197
Carson, Rachel 25
Castells, Manuel 17
Cawelti, John G. 31, 55, 86
Ceder, Camilla 150
Chandler, Florence Dart Thornton 29
Chandler, Maurice Benjamin 29
Chandler, Raymond 29–33; *The Big Sleep* (novel) 15, 32, 36, 44, 49, 56, 68, 69, 91, 221*n*10; on communism 14, 33–36; *The High Window* (novel) 49, 91; *The Lady in the Lake* (novel) 39, 49, 71, 110; *The Little Sister* (novel) 49, 70, 228*n*108; *The Long Goodbye* (novel) 32, 41, 44, 49, 56, 86, 91, 97, 152; "The Simple Art of Murder" (essay) 38–39, 152, 206
Chase, James Hadley 26, 50
Chikatilo, Andrei 219
Child, Lee 123–124, 203
Chomsky, Noam 144
Christie, Agatha 39, 48, 135, 204, 206
Clancy, Tom 146, 148
class issues 18, 29, 30, 31, 44, 59, 61, 63–65, 68, 69, 73–74, 81, 91, 103, 128, 137–139, 142, 145, 155, 160–161, 182, 192, 201, 202, 207, 209, 213; *see also* Marxism
Clooney, George 224*n*36
Cody, Liza 107
Coelho Ahndoril, Alexandra 190, 192, 193; *see also* Kepler, Lars
Coen Brothers 224*n*36
Cold War 4, 25, 35, 185
Colletti, Lucio 17
colonialism 5, 42, 43, 59–60, 77, 153, 171
commodification 13, 57, 69, 75, 83, 139, 148, 186, 233*n*33; *see also* Marxism
commodity fetishism 160, 185–187; *see also Capital* (book); Marx, Karl; Marxism
Communist Workers Union 103
Connelly, Michael 106, 198
Connolly, James 61
conspiracy movies 111–112
Cook, William 72
Cornwell, Patricia 107, 198, 230*n*2
The Count of Monte Cristo (novel) *see* Dumas, Alexandre
Craig, Daniel 9
Craven, Wes 197
Creasy, John 70
Cressey, Donald R. 71
crisis of Marxism 6, 19, 20, 98, 100–101
critical theory 6, 16, 20, 23, 26, 44–45, 58, 115, 231*n*96, 235*n*21; and crime fiction 50–55, 73, 169–170
Crouch, Colin 179, 181–183, 185; phantom corporations 179, 185
cultural studies 6
culture industry 10, 50, 52, 53, 73, 157, 231*n*96; *see also* Adorno, Theodor W.; Frankfurt School; Horkheimer, Max
Culture Revolution 54, 178
Curtiz, Michael 25
Curtois, Stéphane 176

Dabney, Joseph, B. 36, 39, 44
da Costa, Catrine 99, 110
Dahl, Arne 165–168; *Blind Man's Bluff* (novel) 24, 167, 180–184, 209; and *Capital* (book) 185–188; *Chinese Whispers* (novel) 24, 167, 173–175, 188; commodification theory 186–187; *Last Couple Out* (novel) 24, 167, 177, 184–189, 209; *Musical Chairs* (novel) 24, 167, 175–180, 185; on Utopia 168, 170–171; *Watching You* (novel) 168; *see also* Arnald, Jan
Dahmer, Jeffrey 198, 199
Damon, Matt 191
Dassin, Jules 26
Davidsen, Leif 9
Davis, Angela 17
Davis, Mike 14, 25–26, 32, 37, 39, 45, 52, 91, 139, 141, 172
Deaver, Jeffery 106, 198
Debray, Régis 17

de la Motte, Anders 150
Delany, Samuel R. 112
DeLillo, Don 167
Della Volpe, Galvano 17
Demaris, Ovid 71
Demme, Jonathan 198
Democratic Alliance 113
d'Encausse, Hélène Carrère 176
De Palma, Brian 151
Derrida, Jacques 16, 30, 209, 237n8
de Tocqueville, Alexis 82, 86, 89
de Tracy, Destutt 22
The Dialectic of Enlightenment (book) *see* Frankfurt School; Horkheimer, Max; Adorno, Theodor W.
dialectical materialism 62, 189
dialectics 1, 15, 18, 23, 53, 61–63, 204, 206–209, 227n65; *see also* Marxism
Dick, Philip K. 18, 112, 169
Dickens, Charles 30, 31, 44, 110, 138, 155, 169
Dieterle, William 25
Dillinger, John 40
The Director (novel) *see* Ahndoril, Alexander
discourse 6, 14, 15, 18, 19, 20, 53, 73, 102, 155, 187, 210
Dmytryk, Edward 26
Dostoevsky, Fiodor 110, 200
Dumas, Alexandre 175; *The Count of Monte Cristo* (novel) 175-178
Dust Bowl drought 41, 225n66
Dystopia 38, 64, 111, 112, 115, 159

Eagleton, Terry 17
Easy Money (novel) *see* Lapidus, Jens
Ebervall, Lena 150
Eco, Umberto 229n57, 237n8
eco-humanism 6
Edwardson, Åke 9, 199
Ekman, Kajsa Ekis 208; *see also* post-dialectical theory
Ekman, Kerstin 95
Ellis, Bret Easton 105–106, 152, 198, 200; *American Psycho* (novel) 106, 200, 236n25, 237n9
Ellroy, James 26, 106, 151, 152, 156, 163, 166, 234n27; *The Big Nowhere* (novel) 224n35; *The Black Dahlia* (novel) 99, 198, 224n78; *L.A. quartet* (book series) 106, 151; *Perfidia* (novel) 224n35; *Underworld USA* trilogy (book series) 234n5
Engels, Friedrich 6, 16, 62, 63, 64, 222n34, 231n96; *see also* Marxism
Enger, Thomas 9
Eriksson, Jerker 150, 215, 217, 237n27; *see also* Sund, Erik Axl
Eriksson, Kjell 212
European Turn 92, 163, 165
exchange-value 20, 155
excursus 20, 111, 156, 172, 201, 203

false consciousness 20, 22, 51, 92, 119–120, 231n96
false dialectics 208–210, 214
Farabee, Mindy 196
Fearing, Kenneth 21
Feenberg, Andrew 108
feminism 6, 13, 17, 79, 95, 99, 100, 103–104, 105, 106–109, 114, 121, 123, 124, 149, 200, 209, 213, 216, 222n30, 230n2
La Femme Nikita (film; TV series) 120
film noir 21
financial capital 42, 159, 172, 176, 185, 188
Fincher, David 165, 198
Fine, David 14, 30, 32, 42, 208
Firestone, Shulamith 17
Fister, Barbara 107, 197
Fleischer, Richard 72, 197
Fleming, Ian 165
Flood, Alison 217
Foreman, Carl 26
Forshaw, Barry 8, 12, 84, 107, 133, 151, 217, 221n13
Forsyth, Frederick 111
Fossum, Karin 9, 196
Foucault, Michel 16, 18, 105, 119, 209, 237n8; on neoliberalism 86–87; as post–Marxist 17, 235n21
Fowles, Anthony 14
Franco, Francisco 59, 183
Frank, Gerold 72
Frankfurt School 16, 23, 26, 51–52, 175, 231n96; *see also* Adorno, Theodor W.; Horkheimer, Max; Marcuse, Herbert
Fraser, Nancy 17
Freedman, Carl 18, 19, 20, 30, 100, 102, 115, 118, 138, 152–153, 154, 170, 171, 209; on commodity fetishism 186; on critical theory 16, 169, 235n21
Freud, Sigmund 16, 23, 30, 67, 68, 199, 209, 235n21
Friedkin, William 198
Friedman, Milton 82, 98
Friis, Agnete 9
Frimansson, Inger 95

Gabrielsson, Eva 12, 108, 112
Gacy, John Wayne 198
Gedin, Eva 120
Geijer Affair 94–95, 110
Gein, Ed 198, 199, 219
George, Elizabeth 107
Gerhardsen, Carin 150
The Girl in the Spider's Web (novel) 122–125; *see also* Lagercrantz, David
The Godfather (novel) 152–153
Goldmann, Lucien 17
Gothenburg Riots 100
Grafton, Sue 107
Gramsci, Antonio 17
Gray, Martin 192

Great Depression 15, 20, 25, 33, 36–37, 40, 42–45, 77, 90, 206, 225n66
Great Recession (2008) 20
Grebe, Camilla 8
Gregersdotter, Katarina 13, 139, 231n88, 233n33
Greider, Göran 117, 121
Grisham, John 106, 124
Grossman, Lev 196
Guillou, Jan 94, 95, 98, 116, 142, 148, 150
Gustafsson, Lars 100–101
Gyllander, Varg 150

Habermas, Jürgen 16, 17, 18; on technology 109, 125
Hagberg, Mattias 15, 24, 38, 208
Halliburton (company) 88, 173
Hammett, Dashiell 5, 11, 14, 26, 40, 44, 46, 49–50, 59, 90, 92, 206, 221n10, 223n47, 225n6; as communist 33–34, 45; *Red Harvest* (novel) 33, 97, 137, 154
Harris, Thomas 106, 124, 194, 197, 198, 199; *The Silence of the Lambs* (novel) 165, 195, 198, 200, 218, 236n24
Hedges, Chris 42
Hedström, Ingrid 150, 212
Hegel, G.W.F. 16, 51, 62, 73, 82, 231n96
Heimer, Gun 106
Heinlein, Robert A. 112, 169
Held, David 62
Hellström, Börge 24, 129, 131, 145, 149, 150, 214
Hemingway, Ernest 21, 31, 46, 48, 97, 108, 128
Hendin, Herbert 58, 226n44
Hepburn, Audrey 120
Highsmith, Patricia 70
Himes, Chester 14, 45, 46, 225n2, 233n30
Hiney, Tom 14, 34
Hirsch, Paul 71
Hitchcock, Alfred 197, 218
Hitler, Adolf 52, 58
Hjorth, Michael 150
Hobbes, Thomas 40, 83, 95, 152
Hoffman, Josef 10–11
Hollywood 9, 20, 25, 29, 35, 40, 45, 52–53, 54, 96, 132, 202, 224n35, 224n36
Holmberg, John-Henri 48, 96–97, 103
Holmén, Martin 150
Holmér, Hans 150
Holt, Anne 9, 150
Homicide: Life on the Street (TV series) 165
Honneth, Axel 17
Hooper, Tobe 197
Hoover, J. Edgar 34
Horkheimer, Max 10, 17, 23, 26, 45, 58, 82–83, 178; *The Dialectic of Enlightenment* (book) 14, 20, 52–53; see also Frankfurt School
Hosseini, Khaled 96

House Un-American Activities Committee (U.S.) 35
Huntford, Roland 78
Huxley, Aldous 51
hyper-realism 136–137, 162
The Hypnotist (novel) see Kepler, Lars
Hyppolite, Jean 17

IB Affair 98, 110, 113
Ibrahimovic, Zlatan 122
ideology 10, 21–23, 45, 52, 57, 59, 77, 85, 86–87, 89, 108, 114, 117–118, 157, 167, 182, 200; see also Althusser, Louis; Marcuse, Herbert
Indriðason, Arnaldur 9
Ingemarsson, Kajsa 190
Ingenito, Ernie 72
instrumental reason 20, 109, 125
Intercrime series see Dahl, Arne
involution 171–172, 182
Irish, William 50

Jaggar, Alison 17
James, E.L. 96
Jameson, Fredric 10, 14, 16, 17, 31, 36, 56, 205
Jansson, Anna 9, 95
Jay, Martin 52–53, 62, 169
Jeffreys, Sheila 107
Jensen, Carsten 108, 116
Joensuu, Matti 9
Johnson, Mats 166
Johnson, Paul 176
Jokinen, Seppo 9
Jonason, Anders 225n6
Jónasson, Ragnar 9
Jordanova, Ludmilla 24
Joyce, James 30, 168

Kaaberbøl, Lene 9
Kafka, Franz 166
Kakutani, Michiko 120
Kalliokoski, Anne-Marie 106
Kant, Immanuel 16, 51, 235n21
Kärrholm, Sara 24, 136
Kautsky, Karl 6, 63
Keetley, Dawn 67–69
Kelly, Wynton 166
Kemper, Ed 198
Kendrick, Christopher 154
Kennedy, Ludovic: and *Ten Rillington Place* (book) 72
Kepler, Johannes 193
Kepler, Lars 190–193; and class 192, 201, 202, 204; *The Hypnotist* (novel) 190, 191, 194, 195, 196, 200, 201; *The Rabbit Hunter* (novel) 24, 195, 201–205; and serial killers 195, 196, 197–200, 201, 202–203; see also Ahndoril, Alexander
Khmer Rouge 101
Khrushchev, Nikita 5, 22
The Killing (TV series) 9, 15

Index

Kinnaman, Joel 132
Kinsey, Alfred 68
Kirchheimer, Otto 26
Knight, Stephen 10, 105, 197, 200, 218, 219, 221n10, 222n22, 222n30, 224n3, 224n78, 225n65, 229n57, 230n2, 236n25
Knopf, Alfred A. 46, 48
Korsch, Karl: and *Marxism and Philosophy* (book) 17
Kracauer, Siegfried 10
Krafft-Ebing, Richard 71
Kristeva, Julia 200, 237n8; *Powers of Horror* (book) 219
Ku Klux Klan 33
Kubrick, Stanley 103
Kurt Wallander (character) 79–80, 83–84, 86–88, 90–91, 92–93, 109, 116, 165, 203, 208, 229n47; *see also* Mankell, Henning

Lacan, Jacques 209
Läckberg, Camilla 8, 150, 162, 211
Laclau, Ernesto 17
Lagercrantz, David 13, 122–125, 127, 214, 229n1; *The Girl Who Takes an Eye for an Eye* (novel) 125, 214; *see also The Girl in the Spider's Web* (novel)
Lagercrantz, Olof 122
Lang, Fritz 25, 197
Lang, Maria 95, 150
Lapidus, Jens 151–152; and Bourdieu 155, 161; *Easy Money* (novel) 151–152, 156; and Ellroy 151–152, 156, 163; *Sthlm Delete* (novel) 24, 156, 157, 159–162; *The VIP-Room* (novel) 24, 156–159, 160
Lardner, Ring, Jr. 26
Larsson, Stieg 95–97; and "Brain Power" (short story) 111–112, 115; computer technology 108–109, 125, 127; and feminism 99, 100, 103, 105, 106–108, 114, 121; *The Girl Who Kicked the Hornet's Nest* (novel) 24, 95, 98, 105, 111–115, 230n2; *The Girl with the Dragon Tattoo* (novel) 13, 95, 96, 106, 110, 115–122, 132, 133, 191, 194, 197, 199, 217; as postmodernist 103, 105, 107, 109, 110–111, 115, 117, 118–119, 123, 126, 127; and Trotsky 96, 97, 101–105, 108, 114–115; *see also* Lisbeth Salander (character)
Larssonists 189, 203, 210, 214, 215; *see also* Rozovsky, Peter
Lasch, Christopher 159
Le Carré, John 148, 165, 166
Lefebvre, Henri 17
Le Guin, Ursula 18, 169
Lehane, Dennis 123, 131, 151, 152, 163, 198
Lehtolainen, Leena 9
Lem, Stanislaw 18
Lenin, V.I. 6, 16, 18, 22, 23, 54, 104, 115, 179; *Imperialism: The Highest Stage of Capitalism* (book) 42, 102; on literature 62, 227n67; on revolutionary situation 63; revolutionary theory 61, 64, 78, 81, 114, 144; transition theory 63; *What Is to Be Done?* (book) 64
Leninism 62, 73, 177; *see also* Marxist-Leninism
Leninist turn 73
Lennerhed, Lena 68
Leone, Sergio 103
LeRoy, Mervyn 151
Lévy, Bernard-Henri 237n8
Lewis, C.S. 139
Lidman, Sara 82
Lindqvist, Sven 82
Lisbeth Salander (character) 97, 100, 105, 107–109, 112, 113, 114, 115–121, 122, 124, 125, 127, 133, 159, 196, 203, 210, 214, 216–217, 230n2, 231n88; *see also* Larsson, Stieg
Little Caesar (film) 151
Ljunghill, Pontus 150
Ljungstedt, Mari 8, 162
Locke, John 40
London, Jack 30
Losey, Joseph 26
Lowenthal, Leo 26
Lubitsch, Ernst 25
Ludlum, Robert 123, 165; *The Bourne Identity* (novel) 119, 191; *The Road to Gandolfo* (novel) 115
Lukács, Georg 16, 137, 169; *The Historical Novel* (book) 18, 169; *History and Class Consciousness* (book) 17, 83, 187
Lundgren, Eva 106
Lundkvist, Artur 164
Luxemburg, Rosa 16, 104; *The Accumulation of Capital* (book) 102, 153
Lyotard, Jean-Francois 105

Macdonald, Ross (Kenneth Millar) 30, 70, 92, 185, 208
Macherey, Pierre 17
Machiavelli, Niccolo 85
MacShane, Frank 13–14, 31, 39, 156
Maddow, Ben 21, 26, 45
Made in Sweden (book series) 130; *see also* Roslund, Anders
Mafia-capitalism 42–44, 58, 86, 153, 154, 157, 162
Mainwaring, Daniel 45
Malmkvist, Siw 137–138
Maltz, Albert 45
Mammon (TV series) 9
Mandel, Ernest 16, 18, 40, 50, 59, 87, 104, 115, 116, 117, 118, 119, 138, 147, 200, 222n21, 222n30; *Delightful Murder* (book) 10, 18; *Late Capitalism* (book) 16, 34
Manhunter (film) 198, 199
Mankell, Henning 79–80; *Before the Frost* (novel) 79–80, 83, 94; *The Dogs of Riga* (novel) 79, 92, 179; *Faceless Killers* (novel) 81, 85, 89, 100, 166; *The Man Who Smiled* (novel) 24, 79–80, 82, 83, 84–89, 91, 94,

100, 158, 187; and Maoism 80–82, 97; and New Left 44, 80–83; *One Step Behind* (novel) 79, 164, 199, 218; *The Troubled Man* (novel) 80, 92, 165
Mann, Michael 198, 199
Mann, Thomas 52
Mao Zedong 6, 80, 101, 102, 154, 178, 188; Maoism 73, 80–81, 101–102, 103, 237n8
Maoism *see* Mankell, Henning; Mao Zedong
Mara, Rooney 9
Marcuse, Herbert 16, 17, 18, 26, 37, 44, 45, 54, 77, 109, 114, 119, 224n36, 226n25; alienation, *An Essay on Liberation* (book) 143; and Autopia 58; *Das Ende der Utopie* (book) 170; *Eros and Civilization* (book) 68–69; and ideology 22–23; *One-Dimensional Man* (book) 51–52, 53, 108, 149; and repressive desublimation 66, 67; revolutionary subject 73, 78, 84; "Some Social Implications of Modern Technology" (essay) 38, 58; and Utopia 53–54, 170–171; *see also* Frankfurt School; Horkheimer, Max
Marklund, Liza 9, 95, 150, 212
Martin Beck (character) 47, 60, 66, 70, 74, 84, 92, 109, 110, 126, 134, 137, 188, 203
Marx, Karl 13, 15, 18, 20, 152; and alienation 19, 20, 22, 23, 60, 75; *Capital* (book) 15, 16, 20, 34, 102, 152–153, 185–188; *The Communist Manifesto* (book) 16, 64; *Economic and Philosophical Manuscripts* (book) 83; historical materialism 137; and praxis 168–170, 175, 177–179, 209; and primitive accumulation 152–154, 155, 160; "Theses on Feuerbach" 168–169
Marxism 4–5, 6; and crime fiction 10–12, 18, 45, 138, 154–155, 187, 225n2; crisis of 20, 98, 100–101; definition 15–17; and feminism 107, 139, 233n33; Marxist Noir 21; *see also* dialectics
Marxism-Leninism 4, 103, 106
Maslin, Janet 132
materialism 168
Matthau, Walter 47
Mayo, Morrow 31
McBain, Ed (Evan Hunter) 70, 72, 92
McCann, Sean 14, 25, 26, 29–30, 31, 32, 34, 157, 223n47
McCarthy, Joseph 20, 33
McCorristine, Shane 85, 86
McCoy, Horace 32
McDermid, Val 106, 107, 198, 237n9
McNamee, Eoin 229n39
McNaughton, John 198
Meinhof, Ulrike 175; *see also* Baader-Meinhof gang
Meins, Holger 175
Melin, Martin 150
Memmott, Carol 132–133
Meyer, Stephanie 96
Miéville, China 169

Millar, Kenneth 97; *see also* Macdonald, Ross
Millennium trilogy (novels) 9, 12–13, 15, 94, 95–96, 106, 109, 111, 112, 117, 119, 125–127, 133, 136, 159, 162, 194, 203, 216, 218; *see also* Larsson, Stieg
Millett, Kate 107
modernism 30, 52, 53, 55, 57, 58, 205
Monk, Thelonius 166
monopoly-capitalism 54
Monster (TV series) 9
Moorcock, Michael 169
Moretti, Franco 222n21
Motley, Willard 45
Mouffe, Chantal 16, 17, 18; and post-politics 181–182, 183; *see also* post-democracy
Mussolini, Benito 85
Myrdal, Jan 82

Nazi-Germany 43, 81, 89
Nazino Affair 175–176; *see also* Werth, Nicolas
Nazis 25, 43, 44, 89, 99, 103, 108, 109–110, 112, 113, 144, 149, 166, 183, 213, 218, 219
Nelson, Earle 72
neoliberalism 12, 25, 79, 82, 83, 86–89, 98, 100, 101, 125–126, 138–139, 141, 143, 156–159, 161, 171–175, 176–177, 179, 181, 183, 207, 209, 229n39, 235n32
Nesbø, Jo 9, 26, 133, 196, 203
Nesser, Håkan 9, 94, 95, 123, 144, 150, 199, 212
Nestingen, Andrew 25, 125–126, 158, 221n9
New Deal 14, 20, 25, 31, 43, 89, 223n47
New Public Management 86–89, 213
Nielsen, Niels Mors 60
Nietzsche, Friedrich 85, 185, 188
Nilsonne, Åsa 95, 150
9/11 21, 80, 100, 152, 170, 171, 173, 176, 188, 201, 217, 235n32
1968 3, 4, 5, 6, 56, 80, 81, 101, 167, 207–208, 214–215
Nixon, Richard M. 112; the Nixon era 111–112
Norberg, Liam 150
Nordell, Melissa 107
Nordin, Svante 101
Noyce, Philip 198

Oates, Joyce Carol 30
October Revolution (1917) 17, 63, 99, 114, 172
O'Donnell, Peter 116
Offe, Claus 17
Opcop quartet (book series) 167; *see also* Dahl, Arne
Orwell, George 51, 66, 111
Östberg, Kjell 6
Ovid 166

Pacino, Al 151
Palm, August 192
Palm, Göran 82

Index 253

Palme, Olof *see* Palme murder
Palme murder 94, 99, 110, 113, 131
Paretsky, Sara 97, 106, 107
Parks, Tim 117
Patterson, James 106, 194, 197, 198, 200
Peace, David 198, 229n39, 237n26; *see also* Red Riding quartet
Peacock, Steven 13, 221n9
Peckinpah, Sam 103
Pentagon Papers 112
Pepper, Andrew 7, 10, 11, 15, 17, 46, 55, 74, 75, 138, 164–165, 221n4, 222n21, 225n2, 229n39, 233n30, 234n27, 235n32
Percy, Benjamin 217
permanent revolution *see* Trotsky, Leon
Persson, Leif GW 9, 94–95, 142, 150, 162, 211
Persson, Magnus 196
Persson Giolito, Malin 150
Pessoa, Fernando 193
Peterson, Magnus 119
Pettersson, Jan-Erik 12, 81, 82, 92, 99
Pipes, Richard 177
Planhammar, Per 133
Polanski, Roman 103
Polanyi, Karl 18, 44, 59, 82, 83, 86, 153, 162, 174; *The Great Transformation* (book) 43, 89
Pollock, Friedrich 26
post-democracy 181–183; *see also* Crouch, Colin; Mouffe, Chantal
post-dialectical theory 209
posthuman theory 200, 201, 218–219; *see also* Kristeva, Julia
post-industrialism 3, 18, 105, 155
Post-Marxism 15, 105–106, 127, 155, 181, 184, 189, 209, 218, 235n21; definition 16–18
Post-Marxist Noir 21, 180–184, 208, 209–210, 212; definition 212–213
postmodernism 16, 20, 30, 85, 86, 91, 110, 117, 167, 179, 189, 198, 208, 216, 219; and crime fiction 30, 105, 111, 118, 119, 126, 198, 202, 224n3, 229n57; critique against 208–209, 210, 214; definition 98, 101, 105–106, 115; and feminism 107; and Stieg Larsson 99, 103; *see also* posthuman theory
post-politics 4, 18, 86, 181, 185, 189; *see also* Crouch, Colin; Mouffe, Chantal
Powell, Michael 197
Pravda (newspaper) 104
praxis *see* Marx, Karl
Preminger, Otto 25
Prendergast, William 71
primitive accumulation *see Capital* (book); Luxemburg, Rosa; Marx, Karl
Prince, Eric 173
Proust, Marcel 30
Psycho (film) *see* Hitchcock, Alfred
psychoanalysis 199, 213
Puzo, Mario 153
Pynchon, Thomas 30, 45, 103, 167

racism 3, 25, 77, 79, 85, 90, 99, 111, 182, 183, 209, 210, 213, 223n47
radical democracy 18; *see also* Mouffe, Chantal
radical feminism 213; *see also* feminism
Rankin, Ian 86
Ray, Nicholas 25
Reagan, Ronald 82, 98
realism 12, 18, 25, 32, 48, 62, 76, 102, 125, 137, 162, 169, 201–202, 227n67, 228n114; *see also* hyper-realism; Lukács, Georg; Roslund & Hellström
Red Army Fraction 101
Red Brigades 101
Red Riding quartet (book series) 198, 237n26; *see also* Peace, David
Reed, Evelyn 17
Rees, Melvin Davis 72
Reid, Ed 71
reification 19, 75, 82–83, 85, 212; and crime fiction 187–188; definition 77, 88, 186–187; *see also Capital* (book); Lukács, Georg
Reinfeldt, Fredrik 149
Ressler, Robert 199
revolution 5, 18, 20, 54, 66, 75, 81, 103, 143, 169, 172, 189, 208, 209
revolutionary theory 6, 60–64, 78, 104, 114; *see also* Lenin, V.I.; Marcuse, Herbert; Trotsky, Leon
Richter, David H. 39, 108
Robinson, Edward G. 151
Robinson, Kim Stanley 169
Roosevelt, Franklin D. 43–44, 86, 90
Rosenberg, Göran 100
Rosenberg, Stuart 47
Rosenfeldt, Hans 150
Roslund, Anders 24, 129–130, 131, 134, 141, 144, 145, 149, 150, 215
Roslund & Hellström 1, 13, 24, 32, 109, 128–129, 130–132; *The Girl Below the Street* (novel) 138–140; and Marxism 137, 138–139, 143, 147–148, 149; and realism 134–137; *Three Minutes* (novel) 24, 130, 145–148; *Three Seconds* (novel) 130, 132, 133, 145, 146, 148; *Two Soldiers* (novel) 24, 130, 133, 135, 137, 139–145, 148, 149, 232n24, 233n45
Roslund & Thunberg *see Made in Sweden* (book series)
Roth, Philip 151
Rowbotham, Sheila 17
Rowling, J.K. 96
Rozovsky, Peter 203
Rubin, Gayle 17
Rudberg, Denise 162, 211

Sahindal, Fadime 107
Sallis, James 233n30, 234n27
Samuelsson, Per E. 150
Sandoe, James 35
Saroyan, William 32

Index

Sartre, Jean-Paul 17, 235n21
Sayers, Dorothy 39, 107, 123, 206
Scaggs, John 25, 33, 97, 126, 199, 200
Scarface (film) 151
Schoenberg, Arnold 52
Schultz, Dutch 40
Schwartz, Nils 133, 168
Sena, Dominic 198
serial killer films 197–198, 199
serial killer novels 74, 105–106, 113, 116, 175–177, 195, 197–201, 202–203, 215, 217–219, 236n24
the sexual revolution 65–69, 107
Signal Hill strike 32
Sigurdardóttir, Yrsa 9
Silbersky, Leif 150
The Silence of the Lambs (film) 165, 198; novel 194, 195, 198, 199, 200, 218, 236n24; *see also* Harris, Thomas
Sinclair, Upton 32, 33, 90
Sjöholm, Carina 91
Sjöwall, Maj 13, 24, 26, 46, 47, 51, 58, 70, 95, 214, 216
Sjöwall-Wahlöö 47–48, 69–75; *The Abominable Man* (novel) 70, 72, 73, 202, 228n114; *Cop Killer* (novel) 67, 71, 73, 110; *The Fire Engine That Disappeared* (novel) 70, 71, 72, 74, 87, 147; *The Laughing Policeman* (novel) 47, 66–67, 71, 72, 74; *The Locked Room* (novel) 73; *The Man on the Balcony* (novel) 68, 71, 74, 199, 218; *Murder at the Savoy* (novel) 69–70, 72–74, 87, 166–167, 202; *Roseanna* (novel) 47, 48, 67–68, 71, 72, 74, 199; on sexuality *see* the sexual revolution; *The Terrorists* (novel) 67, 73, 188; view on crime fiction 77–78
Skinner, B.F. 199
Sloterdijk, Peter 62, 227n65
The Snowman (film) 9; novel 96
social crime writers (Swedish) 211–212
The Socialist Party of Sweden 102–103
Söderberg, Hjalmar 142
Søholm, Ejgil 13, 74
Solanas, Valerie 107
Solis, Magdalena 72
Solzhenitsyn, Alexandr 101
Speck, Richard 72
Spiderman (comic book character) 108
Spillane, Mickey 26, 49, 50
Stalin, J. V. 5, 6, 22, 58, 61, 101, 102, 104, 115, 176
Stalinism 22, 43, 62, 97, 102, 103, 104, 175
Starkweather, Charles 72
Steiger, Brad 72
Steinbeck, John 32, 45, 51, 83, 86, 90, 97, 153; *The Grapes of Wrath* (novel) 41–42, 43, 44, 225n65
Sterling, Bruce 108
Stone, Oliver 198
Storm, Hans Otto 32
Stroheim, Erich von 25

structuralism 6, 209
Sund, Erik Axl 24, 150, 212; *The Crow Girl* (novel) 199, 215–220, 237n27; and postmodernism 216, 219
Superman (comic book character) 108, 124, 203
surplus-value 20, 155; *see also* Marxism
Suvin, Darko 235n26
Svedelid, Olov 162
Svedjedal, Johan 123
Swedish Autopia 55–58, 119; Autopia 36–38
Swedish New Left 5, 22, 44, 54, 67, 73, 80–81, 89–90, 102, 113, 170
Symons, Julian 70
Tapper, Michael 11–12, 13, 15, 18, 66, 67, 68, 83, 84, 97, 105, 106, 134, 144, 145, 148, 150, 152, 154, 159, 189, 197, 200, 230n41

Tarantino, Quentin 108
Teapot Dome scandal 32
technocracy 20, 109
Tel Quel (journal) 209, 237n8
Ten Rillington Place (film) *see* Fleischer, Richard
Thatcher, Margaret 82, 98, 229n39, 237n26
Therborn, Göran ix–x, 3–4, 51, 75–76, 155, 172, 186; and ideology 22; and post-Marxism 16–17, 213
Thorarinsson, Arni 9
Thorwald, Jürgen 71–72
Three Seconds (novel) *see* Roslund & Hellström
Three Seconds (aka *The Informer*; film) 132
Thunberg, Stefan 130
Thurman, Uma 108
Till, Eric 198
Towne, Robert 32, 45, 103
Trenter, Stieg 95
Trenter, Ulla 95
Trosell, Aino 95
Trotsky, Leon (Lev Davidovich Bronstein) 6, 16, 18, 102; on culture 206–207; *History of the Russian Revolution* (book) 17; *Literature and Revolution* (book) 104–105; permanent revolution 108, 114–115, 149; Trotskyism 97, 101–102, 103, 106–107
Trumbo, Dalton 26
Trump, Donald J. 21, 86, 99, 100
Turing, Alan 122
Tursten, Helen 95, 212
Twain, Mark 30

Unruh, Howard 72
urban apartheid 139–140, 145; *see also* Roslund & Hellström
Utopia 5, 53–54, 75, 101, 161, 168, 170–171, 179, 204; *see also* Marcuse, Herbert

Van Dover, J. Kenneth 13, 69–70, 72, 75
Vasa, Gustav 83

Vietnam War 5, 20, 54, 59, 60, 64, 65, 67, 68, 77, 81, 98, 101, 112, 113, 141, 230n20
VPK of Sweden (party) 101, 121, 192
Vuorio, Hannu 9

Wahlberg, Karin 150
Wahlöö, Per 7, 13, 16, 26–27, 47, 116, 127, 183, 206, 212, 214, 226n7, 226n25; *The Assignment* (novel) 48, 65–66, 67, 226n7; and Chandler 24, 32; and communism 54; criticism against Chandler & Hammett 49–50; *Murder on the Thirty-First Floor* (novel) 24, 26–27, 46, 48, 51, 53–54, 56–57, 66, 75, 115, 140, 207, 226n7; *A Necessary Action* (novel) 46, 47, 59, 65, 67, 108; and sexuality 65–69; *The Steel Spring* (novel) 24, 56–57, 59, 60–65, 66, 67, 89, 110, 162, 170, 188, 207–208, 235n26; *see also* Sjöwall-Wahlöö
Wahlöö, Sylvia ix
Wald, Alan M. ix, 25, 43, 45, 214; and Marxist Noir 19–21, 63, 116, 207; on Trotsky 104–105, 206–207
Walker, Andrew Kevin 165
Walsh, Jill Paton 123
Walters, Minette 107
Wambaugh, Joseph 45

War on Terror 20, 21, 100, 167, 207
Warren, Robert Penn 46
Watergate scandal 98, 112
Waugh, Hillary 70
Weber, Max 23
Wennstam, Katarina 150, 212
Werth, Nicolas 175, 177
West, Nathanael 32
Westerstrand, Jenny 106
Whitman, Charles 72
Wild West 31, 40
Williams, Tom 14
Wilson, Laura 195
The Wire (TV series) 165
Wittgenstein, Ludwig 11
Woods, Paula L. 132
World War I 42, 152
World War II 34, 37, 52, 89, 103, 110, 112, 125, 131, 166, 179, 192, 213, 219
Wright, Richard 21, 45

Zahavi, Helen 105
Zaremba, Maciej 88
Zhdanov, Andrei 227n67
Zizek, Slavoj 10, 59, 82, 92
Zumoff, J.A. 33–34, 40